Sasquatch in the Psyche

Death Anxiety, Deep Memory and an Enduring Enigma

DAVID SALISBURY BROWN MITCHELL

Foreword by Joshua Cutchin

McFarland & Company, Inc., Publishers
Jefferson, North Carolina

Library of Congress Cataloging-in-Publication Data

Names: Mitchell, David S. B. author
Title: Sasquatch in the psyche : death anxiety, deep memory and an enduring enigma / David Salisbury Brown Mitchell.
Description: Jefferson, North Carolina : McFarland & Company, Inc., Publishers, 2026 | Includes bibliographical references and index.
Identifiers: LCCN 2025053362 | ISBN 9781476699714 paperback ♾
ISBN 9798368600130 ebook
Subjects: LCSH: Sasquatch—Psychological aspects | Cryptozoology—Psychological aspects | BISAC: PSYCHOLOGY / Psychopathology / Anxieties & Phobias
Classification: LCC QL89.2.S2 M58 2026
LC record available at https://lccn.loc.gov/2025053362

ISBN (print) 978-1-4766-9971-4
ISBN (ebook) 979-8-3686-0013-0

Printed in the United States of America

McFarland & Company, Inc., Publishers
Box 611, Jefferson, North Carolina 28640
www.mcfarlandpub.com

To the memory keepers and seekers of truth—past, present,
and future—who move with respect and restraint, may we
ever remember your wisdom, insight, and courage.

Sasquatch in the Psyche

Acknowledgments

First and foremost, I wish to thank the nonlocal creative force that pervades All that Is for filtering these words through me. Much of what I have written here felt like it flowed through me and was not a creation of my own mind.

I thank my wife and son for their unrelenting support as I have spent much too long much too often hammering away at the keyboard, arranging and rearranging this work in digital space.

I thank my parents, my sister, and my extended family for being either generally okay with or effusively supportive of my interest in this subject.

I thank Jake Glazier for asking me to pen the chapter for *Paranormal Ruptures* that eventually led to this book, and for believing in my vision and position on the subject of Sasquatch.

I thank Joshua Cutchin for his faith, support, and excitement in what I have penned herein, for being a champion of this work, and for penning the wonderfully kind foreword to this volume.

I thank my friends Julia Mossbridge, Alex Anne Tyler, Kim Burkland-Ward, Afiya Mbilishaka, and Mitchell Reid for their support and feedback as well. Additionally, I offer my gratitude to everyone who has been willing to review earlier drafts of this text or the chapter that it is grounded in, including Gareth Patterson, Phillip Cash-Cash (Cayuse and Nez Perce), Harvey Pratt (Cheyenne and Arapaho), Greg Eghigian, Brea Rock, Sebastienne Grant, Jonathan Erickson, Cindy Shearer, Shederick McClendon, and my wonderful fall 2023 Advanced Topics doctoral students.

Last but certainly not least, I thank the larger community of scholars, field investigators, content creators, and curators of wisdom inside and outside of the Bigfooting community who have contributed directly or indirectly to what this book has become. In no particular order, that list is comprised of colleagues, friends, and acquaintances near and far, including but not limited to: Fred Roehl (Curyung Tribal Member), Lisa Semmler, Brett Eichenberger, Jill Remensnyder, John Baranchok, Brian McCormack, and Kim Burkland-Ward.

I thank you all deeply.

Table of Contents

Foreword

by Joshua Cutchin

In May 2023, I had the honor of attending the Archives of the Impossible conference at Rice University in Houston, Texas, hosted by Dr. Jeffrey Kripal. The weekend was transformative for me. Each scholar's presentation held me in rapt fascination, covering everything from UAP to psi phenomena to spirit interactions and more—all my favorite topics—in a sensitive, thoughtful manner.

Well ... *most* of my favorite topics.

Sometime over the course of the weekend, I realized the absence of my dearly beloved cryptids. With the exception of a passing mention or two, they were nowhere to be found. Here we were, discussing a host of fringe topics in an academic setting ... yet little to no mention of the undiscovered animals of cryptozoology.

Throughout my time at Rice, I toyed with the idea of broaching the topic with Dr. Kripal. Surely, we could bring topics like lake monsters, Mothman, and large, hairy hominids like Bigfoot into the discussion in a mature way.

But as I played out that conversation in my head, it always ended in the same question: Who, if anyone, would I suggest at a future event to discuss cryptids in a context consistent with the goals of the archives? After all, cryptozoology is obsessed with a simple binary question—"Real or Not?"—and the tenor of scholarship at Rice was *light-years* beyond that tired discussion.

Suffice it to say, I hadn't yet read Dr. David S.B. Mitchell's *Sasquatch in the Psyche.* If I had, the answer would have been obvious.

Interpretations of Bigfoot—perhaps appropriately, given how they appear in footage and photographs—invite *low-resolution* interpretations of the phenomenon. David Mitchell's work dials in the focus, bringing a level of clarity and relief to the issue as stark as switching from an old tube television to a plasma screen. *Sasquatch in the Psyche* represents a similar leap forward in how we tackle the subject.

A book like this is long overdue. The truth of the matter is that the academy rarely engages seriously with Bigfoot and other relict hominids (or *homins*). When it does, it primarily focuses on first principles: "Are they real?"

Doing so, the academy marches lockstep with the physicalist doctrine of Materialism. The phenomenon's loftier implications, the ones that span the psychosocial and transpersonal dimensions, potentially offering insight about humanity as a whole, go undiscussed.

On the rare occasions that these facets *are* addressed, they come from scholars firmly asserting that Bigfoot and other homins are nothing more than a modern legend. They reflect human nature with the kind of mirror only held up by deep-seated mythological impulses, rather than any *real* phenomena.

Contrast this with the current discussion around something like UAP—unidentified aerial phenomena, the UFOs of yesteryear. Scholarship in recent decades has not only embraced the topic's ontology—"UFOs are *somehow* real"—but also nested the phenomenon within all sorts of "fancy" academic concepts: dual aspect monism, the search for *prisca theologia*, quantum physics, social and religious movements.

The UFO presents obvious confrontations to the status quo in scientific, sociological, and spiritual domains. Homins? *Bigfoot?* Not so much. Perish the thought.

What this represented all along was yet another reductionist trap. I've even stumbled into it from time to time myself. Now, in 2024, here comes David Mitchell, crowbar in hand, to free us from that trap.

What I'm trying to articulate is that the academy has painted itself into a corner. Either homins don't exist but have a lot to say about us psychosocially or *they are real* but just animals, posing no more implications to the human condition than squirrels, kangaroos, bears, or chimpanzees. Few, if any (to my knowledge), have dared to entertain both positions.

Scholars have done so at their own peril. Transpersonal studies, psychology, social dynamics—these are the waters in which David Mitchell swims. To be fair, a handful of more adventurous academics have flirted with the ideas that he addresses vis-à-vis homins, but none come anywhere close to engaging the topic with the same sensitivity, nuance, and scope he exhibits—*especially* not while simultaneously adopting the position that these things might possess an objective ontology.

Reading *Sasquatch in the Psyche* for the first time, I experienced a profound realization, one that only happens once in a lifetime, or once every few decades: *I am holding a game-changer in my hands.* Having devoured David Mitchell's book in just a few days, I am even more convinced of that likelihood. This book has the potential to reshape cryptozoology, to change the conversation, if properly embraced and integrated. To bring cryptozoology into the humanities and social sciences, where it can rightfully stand alongside other fringe topics enjoying newfound legitimacy: spirits, psi, UAP, and all the rest.

There's a bit of irony here. I've long criticized cryptozoology for abandoning these ideas in favor of a late-19th-century "bag-it-and-tag-it" imperialist mentality. The motivation is clear: cryptozoologists want to sit at The Cool Kids' Table, i.e., among the biologists and zoologists. They want to be taken seriously. *Sasquatch in the Psyche* is exactly the invitation for which they yearn. It's just that The Cool Kids inviting them are a different crowd—the humanities and social sciences departments—sitting in a different part of the cafeteria.

At the same time, this criticism of mine has always personally rung a bit hollow, even hypocritical. Because *I* sure haven't been able to figure out what homins say about the human condition.

My most Bigfoot-centric work to date, 2020's *Where the Footprints End*, co-authored with Timothy Renner, has a certain "carny" aesthetic. I love those books, but it's true. I remember speaking with Patrick Harpur, who was kind enough to offer an endorsement of the book, and having no answer when he asked, "What's your thesis?" The best I could muster: "Bigfoot's weird."

If *Where the Footprints End* simply highlighted the more peculiar aspects of homin encounters and brought them to the fore, *Sasquatch in the Psyche* goes a step further. David Mitchell peels them apart and provides a possible framework for *why* these experiences are so confronting, and what they might tell us about our interactions as a species from a macro-perspective—or, as David's own grandfather would so wisely say, "viewed from the bridge." The anomalous aspects observed by witnesses aren't solely garnish on an otherwise outlandish tale. They are crucial to understanding their significance.

Sasquatch in the Psyche is many things. Compelling stories fill its pages. It offers a primer on how to engage with these topics in a critical, thoughtful way—directly and clearly, free of the usual obfuscation that too often characterizes similar approaches when discussing anomalies from a psychosocial angle.

Above all, it's the most important book on Bigfoot and other homins in *decades.* I do not say that lightly. Yes, other publications have more tables and graphs, discussing dermal ridges and piloerection and midtarsal breaks and all sorts of persuasive evidence. But David Mitchell accomplishes the extraordinary: he says something about homins that is both *new* and *insightful.*

To that end, *Sasquatch in the Psyche* is also what I would characterize as a *reckoning*, if not for cryptozoology as a whole, then at the very least for the study of Bigfoot and other mystery homins. Amidst all the plaster casts and hair samples, the wood knocks and the thermal footage, cryptozoologists have swept heaps of deeper issues under the proverbial rug. Issues of liminality, of mortality, of time, of Othering, of survival, and, most importantly, issues of race.

David brings it all together in an elegant fashion, the so-called relict complex immensely powerful in its explication and comprehensive utility. Why, he asks, do we simultaneously wish to kill, love, possess, and *be* these creatures (or, perhaps more accurately, these *people*)? David has discovered something more elusive than any mysterious specimen lurking in the woods: our perceptions of homins are inextricably tied up in our perceptions of *ourselves.* This is the insightful line of inquiry he provides, one of many that I sincerely believe will blossom in the wake of this book's publication.

It's nothing short of a paradigm-changer in how we engage with homins at the level above their basic existence. Because, in many ways, that might be the *least* interesting aspect of the phenomenon. David moves beyond whether or not these things are "real," instead choosing to focus on what *kind of* "real" they are.

As David deftly illustrates, there is an *abundance* of fertile ground within cryptozoology *begging* for cultivation across the psychosocial dimension. Homins deserve just as much attention and admiration as our most "highbrow" mysteries. It's just that no one has stepped forward to demonstrate that.

Sasquatch in the Psyche brings with it a fundamental change for cryptozoology. Where do the footprints end? Perhaps back where they started. At ourselves.

Joshua Cutchin has appeared on hundreds of paranormal programs, including Coast to Coast AM, *and is regularly invited to speak at paranormal conferences about his work. In 2022, he released his two-part masterwork:* Ecology of Souls: A New Mythology of Death & the Paranormal. *His latest book on the paranormal is 2025's* Fourth Wall Phantoms: Reflections on the Paranormal, Narrative, and Fictions Becoming Fact. *Joshua has also contributed numerous forewords and essays to various collections. He has appeared on the hit History Channel television series* Ancient Aliens *and was featured in 2024's breakout UFO documentary,* Cosmosis. *He is a regular guest on the* Where Did the Road Go? *podcast and maintains an online presence at JoshuaCutchin.com.*

Preface

Some of my earliest memories are of having a deep sense, an intuitive knowing, that there are beings and creatures that exist in our woods, lakes, oceans, and rivers who may often go unseen, but are nonetheless real. As I got older and began to read, I came to realize that those beings occupied the spaces of mythology, folklore, and legend, and at times leaked out into the pages of cryptozoology, ufology, and Fortean studies. I was fortunate to have been raised in an immediate and extended family where my pursuit of information about these subjects was encouraged if not embraced. I recall many happy afternoons and evenings spent engulfed in these books: either at my aunt and uncle's house in their den or in the backyard tree house, with me and my cousins voraciously poring through the books there, particularly focusing on those thin, black, hardbound volumes from the Time-Life book series; or perhaps lounging in the "play room" or dining room in my childhood home, enamored by Jacques Cousteau's *The Ocean World*, David Peters's *Giants of Land, Sea, & Air: Past and Present*, or Tom McGowen's *Encyclopedia of Legendary Creatures*, the latter of which I checked out quite often from my elementary school library. Ghouls, goblins, ghosts, sea serpents, lake monsters, Yeti, Sasquatch, aliens, and more all existed in that fertile space, somewhere between my two ears, those wonderfully illustrated and written pages, and the conversations that some of my family members and friends held with me in den rooms and in tree houses.

My soul sang.

For most of my childhood, I wanted to be a naturalist, a marine biologist, or even a veterinarian. In that order. I wanted to explore the mysteries of the natural world and all that lies within it, and to help conserve and cultivate it all for present and future generations. However, for some reason that I still cannot fully fathom, by my middle school years I had begun to convince myself that these deep and ever-beguiling mysteries were no longer there, that scientists and explorers had figured everything out about the wondrous creatures and beings that exist on this wide, blue planet. But my soul still hungered for mystery, and over the coming years—including encouragement from wonderful science, anatomy, biology, and cognitive science teachers in middle school, high school, and college—I shifted my focus from the external natural world to examining the inner psychological world of the human brain and mind, what was for me another frontier of human understanding.

That shift led me to pursue an interdisciplinary undergraduate degree in human development at the University of California at San Diego and immediately thereafter to enter graduate school at Howard University to study psychology. All the while, my interest in the deep mysteries that lie beyond the human mind were still there and persuaded me to seek out communion with some of my classmates as we pondered questions regarding human evolution, the wisdom held within Indigenous and traditional cultures, the nature of human suffering, and the non-human intelligences that most certainly exist beyond this wide, blue planet. Despite my engaging in-class education, these moments of communally cultivated connection with my classmates were what really helped to make my soul sing more fully again. We would watch documentaries such as *Zeitgeist* and *The Secret Life of Plants* and discuss them over sumptuous sandwiches and smoothies purchased from Sankofa Café & Bookstore, a cherished staple of the community and a veritable storehouse of pan–African wisdom that was located directly across the street from Howard University. We pondered the transpersonal, ontological, and metaphysical questions that bind our humanity together and which, when left unfulfilled, threaten to tear it apart.

Again, my soul sang.

Now it was time for me to put into practice elsewhere what I had been learning, engaging with, and experiencing with my colleagues and classmates.

As I was finishing my PhD, I applied for and was offered a limited-term instructor position in the psychology department at the University of West Georgia (UWG). I accepted and soon found my soul spiraling upward and outward into an expansive place that felt more fully integrated. I met wonderful new colleagues and students and further cultivated a community that resonated with some of the passions that I had begun to unearth during my time at Howard University. I eventually joined the tenure-track faculty and began to teach classes that helped me to further engage my interests in transpersonal, parapsychological, memorial, and other resonant phenomena and methods in their application to the understanding and flourishing of humans and other beings on this planet. I also began to more regularly listen to the works of content curators and creators, video essayists, podcasters, and more, who cultivated and curated information that soundly resonated with my early years reading the Time-Life books and with my renewed interest in myth and oral history.

While I deeply appreciated the community and content that I was able to engage with at UWG, I eventually felt called elsewhere. I now teach in the Research Psychology doctoral program within the School of Consciousness and Transformation at the California Institute of Integral Studies (CIIS), which is another resonant space that allows me to further cultivate dialogue around some of my interests. Some of my current and recent scholarly work involves publications and curricula that revolve around mythological and encounter narratives about *liminal entities* such as Sasquatch and hungry ghosts and what they might teach us about the suffering, the flourishing, and the meaning of being human. Even so, one might find it odd that someone in my position would find it necessary to pen a book on the present subject, but to that I would simply reply that these liminal entities have direct relevance to understanding, if not contemplating, fuller and more transpersonal identity, both for individuals and for the collective. Therefore, I see no contradiction in these endeavors.

In some of my efforts to extend my service beyond the classroom, I am a member of the leadership team for the Exceptional Experiences Empowerment Alliance (a multi-tiered project dedicated to supporting exceptional experiencers and those professionals and coaches who work with them), the general body of the Society for Scientific Exploration (i.e., the only professional academic organization that I know of that supports research and theory-building on the subject of Sasquatch), and the general body of Project ZooBook (i.e., a curated, virtual community of scholars, researchers, and academics as well as experiencers and enthusiasts who share an interest in Sasquatch; Maher, 2022, September 21).

In all, this book is a tribute to my deep passion, cultivated by my natal personality and by my family, to understand and support those people, beings, and phenomena placed at the margins of the scientific and academic world.

To be in such service, my soul sings.

Broadly speaking, the following work is just such a work of soul service, an endeavor to intertwine, elaborate, and enumerate upon heterodox phenomena, theories, and concepts, and also to introduce and expand upon several of my own, in an effort to provide some semblance of coherence around what I perceive to be a most important and prescient matter. I find myself re-bidden, or perhaps re-bitten, by the toothy grins of Sasquatch and their kin, those at once foreboding and formidable visages that find purchase in the fruits of my inquiring mind. Drawing from fields and approaches including critical and depth psychology, ethology, anthropology, transpersonal psychology, parapsychology and Forteana, in addition to cryptozoology and hominology, I reflect on Western culture's deep and abiding reticence to approach the subject of Sasquatch and related "undiscovered" bipedal beings elsewhere around the world. The establishment of mainstream Western scientific culture and the collective psyche from which it emerges is invited once again into what Dmitri Bayanov (2012) has termed a "re-discovery" of hairy hominoids inhabiting "the forests of the mind" (p. 40); and what I propose is, relatedly and quite significantly, a re-discovery of that collective psyche itself.

Introduction

Approach, Audience, and Anecdote

Broadly speaking, this volume is a consideration of ways in which we understand ourselves and the ways in which we understand Sasquatch: how do we differ, and how do we converge? Broadly, what makes us human? Specifically, what are the parameters around which the Western collective psyche (i.e., culture) answers this question? Conversely, what makes someone or something inhuman or perhaps more succinctly, human-denying? Such questions span numerous academic disciplines from cosmology to religious studies, from sociology to psychology, and from anthropology to biology and more, but they are still questions that are not particularly well understood within the frameworks and perspectives of Western science and academia. These are questions that are at the heart of the present book: specifically, the potential reasons as to why humans who have been enculturated into Western culture have denied and disparaged the subject of Sasquatch and other hairy humanoids.

First, I must state that, although I draw from various theories and present references where I can, this work represents a speculative as well as intuitive inquiry into the potential reasons for mainstream Western culture's deep reticence to consider fringed or minoritized subjects of study: in this case, Sasquatch and their kin. My hope is that at least some of the material herein will resonate with you at some level: somatic, emotional, cognitive, and/or conative. Perhaps there may be resonance at even deeper levels.

Perspective and Population

Second, it may be helpful for us to consider who the target audiences are for this bipartite endeavor. In this volume, unlike many other works involving the homin phenomenon, I largely sidestep the ontological question surrounding mainstream Western scientific discovery of Sasquatch and other similar entities around the world. Instead, I focus on epistemology and phenomenology of those who either approach or deny that these beings exist in some form or fashion. As such, I take seriously the claim that focusing on the human side of the homin phenomenon is key, and I present various streams of inquiry involving the potential existential threats that homins may pose to the human psyche. Herein, I also propose that different ontological camps inside and outside of the Bigfooting community should listen to each other's perspectives more fully and integrate with other historically marginalized or non-mainstream fields of study within the Western world including transpersonal psychology, parapsychology, consciousness studies, and contemplative studies.

Similar to what others (e.g., Baranchok, 2021; Bindernagel, 2010; Pruitt, 2023; Short, 2024) have stated previously, my position is that it is not enough to determine whether such and such a being exists *out there*, but that the aspiring and inquiring mind must also consider the psychological and cultural milieu within which these entities are either recognized or pushed aside. Thus, while I offer a summary of what I believe are some of the most compelling evidentiary sources regarding the subject of Sasquatch and other homins, my primary focus of inquiry which I have outlined elsewhere (Mitchell, 2023) is not to convince anyone of their existence but instead to speculate on potential psychological reasons for the deep and pervasive reticence in general (and within Western culture in particular) toward considering these beings and related phenomena as worthy of valid inquiry. Indeed, as Baranchok (2021) has aptly stated, due to the ability for psychological science to grasp concepts and phenomena that are literally unseen or elusive (e.g., intelligence), it is appropriate for those trained in the discipline to comment on another elusive phenomenon (i.e., that of the mystery of Sasquatch).

For these reasons, I hold space for those narrative truths and thematic patterns from oral and written literature regarding Sasquatch and their kin, drawing from spaces (e.g., subject area content creation, citizen scientists, experiencers, etc.) that have largely been marginalized within Western mainstream institutions and even, at times, within the Bigfooting community itself. Further, I have chosen to include a variety of these narratives for several reasons that I believe hold practical value: (a) given the relative overabundance of social media that focus on narratives from folkloric, mythological, historical, and eyewitness accounts, I would be bypassing a vast treasure trove of data that contain narrative, if not also historical, truth if I did not seriously consider these media herein; (b) despite variation in the extent to which sources are vetted, those social media that focus on Sasquatch and related phenomena are often much more relevant to experiencers and are more up-to-date than are traditionally published sources; (c) those citizen scientists, weekend warriors, and others who create content focused on the Sasquatch mystery are the ones with their boots on the ground and eyes to the hills in a way that vastly outnumbers the quantity of academics who are publicly involved with the phenomenon (cf. Hill, 2017 for discussion of citizen scientists and amateur research and investigation groups); (d) some of the most astute handful of academics who are publicly involved in Sasquatch as a subject of study collaborate with citizen scientists who produce social media, allowing for a confluence of expertise; and (e) in alignment with my first point, these same media can perform a therapeutic if not more generally ameliorative function by providing a space for experiencers to communicate with one another and to share firsthand and secondhand encounter narratives. As such, it is these various social media that provide a crucial role for the Bigfooting community and which can serve as a potent source of information for scientists and scholars alike.

In general, I suspect that the content herein will appeal to readers who find substance in the potential intersections of psychology, hominology, and cryptozoology and who feel drawn to engage in critical consideration of the potential foundations for the treatment of the subject of Sasquatch in mainstream Western culture. The entry point will appeal to individuals who have an interest in anomalous topics and the potential depth and breadth of their psychological significance. Further, you will be asked to go on something of a hero's journey, deeply considering material regarding the psyche and its relation to the bogeymen and bogeywomen of the world who have been with us in various forms since time immemorial. Not all of the material herein will be equally appealing, and some may be disquieting, unappetizing, or may even offend some of your sensibilities, but if you are able to consider the whole of what is being said and not lose the forest for the trees, then I strongly suspect that you will be led beyond the normal ken, traveling into the deep strata of the unconscious that can bind our humanity together as well as break us apart.

Fundamentally, this text is interdisciplinary in scope, and transdisciplinary in its intention, which is one of its core strengths. Thus, beyond the avid lay reader who is curious about the Sasquatch phenomenon, there are several particular target audiences for whom this text is intended:

- Academics: One target group consists of academics who stand at the vanguard of entertaining the Sasquatch phenomenon seriously. That is, this book is for those who are willing to critically examine the psychocultural paradigms that pervade the academy and to apply true skepticism to those anomalous and exceptional experiences that are often cast out of said academy. These individuals include edge scientists, doctoral students, and others. In essence, this segment of the population are true skeptics rather than pseudo-skeptics, denialists, debunkers, or cynics.
- Open-minded experiencers, investigators, and enthusiasts: This book foregrounds the experiences and narratives of those who encounter Sasquatch and Sasquatch-like beings, as well as those of the field investigators and citizen scientists who have often been marginalized by mainstream Western scientific and academic institutions. Therefore, another target group consists of the experiencer, avid field investigator, or citizen scientist who has intuited deeper meaning behind the Sasquatch mystery and how it is received by such institutions.
- Mental health professionals serving entity experiencers: The deeper cultural and psychological significance of the Sasquatch phenomenon is discussed herein, including consideration of the unconscious, death anxiety, and ontological shock. In general, a central consideration herein is to understand the depth and breadth of how and why this phenomenon might manifest in the lives of experiencers. As such, material from this text will appeal to mental health professionals who work with and counsel individuals who have had experiences that fall outside of what is expected or thought of as normal in this society—and particularly those who have had Sasquatch encounters.

Regardless of what population(s) you find yourself in, this book has found its way to you. If you accept the call to continue through this book, as you make your way through it, I simply ask that you "view it from the bridge," as my paternal grandfather used to say. This remark, with its imagery based on the captain bridge on a ship, was advice to take a broader or grander perspective of a thing, particularly when such a thing can present a problem or challenge. For me, the realization that the bridge has been a resounding and resonant image from all of the branches of my family makes such an axiom all the more profound. As metaphor and symbol, bridge structures—both those on ships and those that join landmasses—provide one with an elevated and/or cohesive perspective on challenges or inquiries that we might have.

Some Terms and Context

Next, I must note some context and terminology. Regarding Western culture, I have chosen this particular collective target psyche due to its outsized influence on the paradigms that pervade the current consensus reality. In particular, the European collective has had a profound impact on mainstream scientific and academic institutions and holds a salient position in relation to our subject as the only major culture on this planet that I am aware of that does not consider the homin phenomenon to be genuine. That psyche, forged in what the late, imminent anthropologist Michael Bradley (1973) has referred to as the ice and fire of archaic Europe, has achieved a peculiar state, arguably holding a space of ambivalence, being both immense powerful and privilege and yet also conveying intense fears and hatreds against self and other. In this volume, I therefore strive to critically probe this collective psyche in ways that both expand on and deepen what others such as Bindernagel (2010) and Machovec (2022) have advanced previously.

With that said, it is a reasonable estimate that the majority of those individuals who are publicly involved in the pursuit of Sasquatch tend to be males of European descent. Or, as Regal (2011) and Hill (2017, p. 62) offer, a questionnaire initiated by Regal has indicated that the Bigfooting community tends to consist of 30- to 40-year-old working class Caucasian men. Still, if my reasons for providing this broader context and focusing on Western culture in particular are not abundantly apparent yet, I will attempt to elaborate further.

Given the powerful influence that mainstream Western culture has on both non-mainstream Western and non–Western cultures, it is particularly important to take note of how the ways in which people think about the Sasquatch mystery is influenced by that power.

To be sure, despite the fact that the term Sasquatch is itself derived from First Nations terminology and conceptual understanding, the very language that is used to describe, define, and understand the phenomenon under study in these pages is largely terms that are used to refer to hairy humanlike beings are framed within a Western, Anglo-Saxon point of view. Let us now consider in summary what some of the important terms are to further contextualize things.

An understanding of how Sasquatch and other hairy humanlike beings have been situated for most of their modern history (i.e., since about 1924 or thereabouts) within the North American Bigfooting and scientific communities, we must consider how these entities have been thought of (and therefore, languaged) for much of that history. For example, commenting on the discovery of fossils of *H. floresiensis* in Indonesia, cultural anthropologist Gregory Forth (2022, p. 20, emphasis in original) states:

> Before the discovery of the fossil hominin, "*Homo*" applied mostly to humans like us, Neanderthals, and the now-upgraded "ape-men" (formerly named *Pithecanthropus*) *Homo erectus*. By paleontological and zoological convention, "anthropus," though Greek for "human," has always been applied to hominins that, in terms of their physical form and geological age, are intermediate between *Homo* (including ourselves) and both the great apes and more humanlike apes, such as the several species of Australopithecines.

Further, Britannica states:

> Hominidae has been a subject of much debate among taxonomists. Formerly, humans alone (with their extinct forebears) were placed in Hominidae, and the great apes were placed in a different family, Pongidae. However, morphological and molecular studies now indicate that humans are closely related to chimpanzees, while gorillas are more distant and orangutans more distant still. Since classification schemes aim to depict relationships, it is logical to consider humans and great apes as hominids—that is, members of the same zoological family, Hominidae [Britannica, n.d., para. 2].

Thus, the genealogical and conventional taxonomic waters are rather muddy, as the names alone that are used to label these various genera (i.e., plural of genus), species, and so forth, do not necessarily conform to their etymological roots. Furthermore, a number of (at times) overlapping terms are used to describe beings that are human or related to humans: (a) *hominoids* (Hominidae), literally meaning "humanlike," is the most general term, referring to all beings in the primate superfamily, from great apes to monkeys, that are not human but resemble us (e.g., Forth, 2022, pp. 4–5); (b) *hominids* are those beings that include the human line and the great apes; (c) and lastly, *hominins* are those beings that are directly in the human line, including humans and are most recent evolutionary ancestors, the Australopithecines.

Numerous appellations have been proposed to label the hairy, humanlike beings that are said to inhabit this planet—beings that occupy an archetypally and physically liminal space, and there is no small share of discussion about how to refer to the beings commonly known as Bigfoot or Sasquatch (Shiel, 2011). Abominable Snowmen (ABSMs, Sanderson, 2008), *wildman/wildwoman* (e.g., Breedlove, 2019b; Forth, 2007), *Hairy Man* (e.g., Roehl, 2023, March 3; Strain, 2012), and many, many more terms have been used to describe them. Terminology regarding human and humanlike beings is important because it helps to clarify—or, in some cases, obfuscate—relationship between "us" and "them," or to clarify characteristics or patterns with one or the other group. In short, it indicates identity, or at least, is an attempt at doing so. Zoologist, cryptozoologist, and founder of the term "cryptozoology," Ivan T. Sanderson (1911–1973) referred to all scientifically unclassified specimens collectively as the *abominable snowmen*, or *ABSMs* (Sanderson, 2008, p. 12). Others such as Meldrum (2006) have advocated for the term *relict hominoid*. However, according to Dmitri Bayanov, "simultaneous use" of terms such as relict hominoid, hominin, and relict hominid "is caused by our lack of exact knowledge regarding the taxonomic level of the 'uncatalogued' primates in question, as well as by changes of taxonomy in primatology itself" (2019, p. 25).

As we can see, the matter of nomenclature is a rather tricky one, largely due to matters of perceived lack of clarity on the ontology of these beings among the largely European American Bigfooting community. If, as in the case of Sasquatch and other upright bipedal beings of the same kind, their nature is not known, and if a given name often presumes some ontological structure, we find ourselves at a bit of an impasse. Coleman and Huyghe (2006) describe what they refer to as the *lumping problem*:

> The concept of Bigfoot ... hides a larger truth, lumps considerable differences and just plain confuses the picture. In our global natural history culture, "Bigfoot" throws into a blender any notion of the many differences in behavior, footprints, hair color, height, physique, family units, diet, living arrangements, daily cycle, and other unique overall patterns that exist from one group of these beings to another [Coleman & Huyghe, 2006, p. 6].

In my estimation, the lumping problem is an important epistemological (i.e., the study of how we know about our reality) as well as ontological (i.e., the study of the nature of reality itself) concern that I try to deal with respectfully in these pages. For these reasons as well as others, I tend to shy away from using the term "Bigfoot" to refer to any of the various hairy, bipedal beings of North America. For those of us who are genuinely interested in probing the Sasquatch mystery, it would do us well to consider how the words that we use to describe the subjects of our inquiry affect our ability to grasp it.

I have considered utilizing the term *non-human intelligence* (NHI), often used in ufology, to refer to Sasquatch and their kin, but I find doing so to be rather presumptive and rather unclear, since many Indigenous narratives state that Sasquatch are, in fact, a people (e.g., Fusch, 1992), thereby indicating that they are more human than not. Terms like relict hominoids or hominins at least uplift the status of Sasquatch to that of people but also limit their ontological structure to being purely biological in nature and conforming to some version of the phylogenetic tree, a matter which we will return to in time herein. For now, just note that the prevailing or master narrative that has permeated the European American Bigfooting community since the advent of the modern phenomenon in 1958 has been to favor the *flesh-and-blood (ontological) hypothesis* (cf. Morehead, 2024),[1] which simply states that Sasquatch is a being that lives, breathes, eats, procreates, and dies, in more or less the same manner that all sexual, endothermic (i.e., warm-blooded) organisms tend to do on this planet (e.g., Jones, 2021). Other terms from the ufological literature (e.g., *Visitors*; Strieber, 2016) and hominological/ufological literature (e.g., *the Locals*; Powell, 2018) are useful due to their focus on behavior and relationality as well as due to the lack of a priori ontological presumption, but they can also be so general as to not be able to clearly differentiate between presumed types of entities.

Notwithstanding these considerations, for the purpose of this writing, I have chosen to use Bayanov's (2014, p. 112) term *homin*. Taking an even more parsimonious approach than those outlined above, Bayanov advanced the name "as a substitute for hominoid, hominid, wild bipedal primate, wild man, yeti, *almasty*,[2] sasquatch, and the rest of [the] ethnic names for the creatures under study" (2014, pp. 12–13). He further delineates the nomenclature as follows:

> A homin is a living (non-fossil) non-sapien hominid (hominin). How closely are [homins] related to *Homo sapiens*? As closely as wolves to coyotes or as wolves to domestic dogs, judging by fertile interbreeding between humans and homins. A homin is a human being, but seemingly not a sapiens human being, and that is why we need a special name for him [*sic*]. Accordingly, there is humankind and hominkind. What's the difference? Not in appearance, not in morphology, but in mentality, in ecology, that is existentially? The crucial difference seems to be in the relation with the environment, i.e., with nature. *Homo sapiens* have built civilization by "conquering" and "enslaving" nature, while Homin-the-Wild Man has existed sort of melting into nature. No sapiens aborigines have such close and intimate links with nature as homins do. So the best qualifier for them is nature. They are a nature people, and each of them is a nature person. Like it or not, in terms of "otherness," each of us [humans] is either a "tech person" or "hi-tech person" [Bayanov, 2014, pp. 12–13].

Per the origins of hominology, this portrait of homins that Bayanov paints falls in line with folkloric, historical, as well as modern eyewitness accounts of these beings which are reported across time and space. Further, while Bayanov is clearly aware of the at times vast physical differences in size, strength, and the like, between hominkind and humankind, he chooses to focus instead on a behavioral approach rather than a biological one. Quite poignantly, the distinction that Bayanov (2014) makes is not one that is centered on anatomy or appearance—factors which are exceedingly important in Western naturalistic science—but is instead one that is essentially focused upon psychology, sociology, and culture. Herein lies the rub: what separates *Homo sapiens* from hominkind is the presence of what in humankind is a conspicuous and durable material culture that at times is very much at odds with the environment—a matter that some enthusiasts and investigators into Sasquatch phenomena have been quick to note (e.g., Meldrum, 2006). Of course, it is just such a material culture that has led many scholars to dub our present planetary age as the *Anthropocene*, utterly defined by the presence of human material projects, products, and plastics. However, hominkind, broadly speaking, seems to be possessed of no general compunction to bend the environment to their will—or at least, to create the kinds of elaborate physical structures that are supportive of workways, lifeways, and the like in the manner that we humankind tend to do (e.g., Bradley, 1973).

Further, my intentional shift to utilizing the term homin to describe our hairier kith and kin bears a more subtle and simple goal: that is, to situate their closeness rather than difference from humans, their continuity rather than discontinuity from us, in all of our shared complexity. Thus, bearing in mind the distinct ways in which language contextualizes as well as formalizes associations between one thing and another, especially in a psychoanalytic sense (Webley & Zackariasson, 2023), I choose Bayanov's (2014) term to draw out similarity or treatment in kind in order to cultivate a reflective, if not transpersonal, mode of awareness.

Fundamentally, Bayanov's (2014) mention of *otherness* is at the heart of our considerations in this text: that otherness, often termed alterity in academic circles, is defined by *ambivalence*, by physical as well as psychological borders (i.e., liminal spaces), and by inner-outer as well as large-small distinctions (Doubková, 2024). The persistent inability for people to recognize and healthily accept otherness within or otherness without is arguably one of the most challenging issues that humanity faces and, I strongly sense is also part and parcel of the anxiety that tends to come along with encountering homins.

Such encounters tend to be studied within the fields of *cryptozoology* and *hominology*: two disciplines that exist on the margins of Western science, yet which bridge a crucial space that tends to be pushed aside by this very same culture. Bernard Heuvelmans (1916–2001), now known as the father of the discipline (e.g., Furek, 2024, p. 182), defined cryptozoology as the study of "truly singular, unexpected, paradoxical, striking, or emotionally upsetting" creatures (Heuvelmans, 1983, p. 5). Those creatures under study came to be known and categorized as *cryptids*. However, taking up a call to focus more upon the manner in which data about such creatures is collected, senior editor and specialist in UFO and psychic phenomena George Eberhart (2005, p. 104) provides the following revision:

> Cryptozoology is "the examination and evaluation of ethnographic, testimonial, and physical evidence to determine the probable identity of an animal species or variety that is either undescribed by science or that exists at a time or in a locality not recognized by a majority of experts."

With the above proposed revisions to the definition of the field, Eberhart focuses more on the liminal nature of cryptozoology as well as the methodology utilized by those who may consider themselves to be cryptozoologists. Further, professor of English and specialist in folklore Peter Dendle suggests the following as he looks at comparisons and dissimilarities between medieval cryptozoology and contemporary cryptozoology:

> The cultural significance of contemporary cryptozoology bears many similarities to, as well as some differences from, the cryptozoology of the pre-modern world. In a sense, it can be argued that the term "cryptozoology" is itself an anachronism when applied to pre-modern cultures. By the study of "hidden animals," cryptozoologists expressly mean animals unconfirmed by contemporary science (that is, not appearing in standard textbooks), and such a distinction might seem to make less sense in the periods before the central organization of scientific knowledge. Yet, no age has been without its share of hidden creatures, and confirmation of purported species has been a vital and consciously debated issue among the collectors of human knowledge for thousands of years. Furthermore, it is not the vast myriad of undiscovered mites or new varieties of zooplankton that cryptozoologists are really interested in; it is the large, sensational creatures that fill us with a fresh sense of wonder and surprise that dominate the discussions [Dendle, 2006, p. 192].

To be sure, it is those larger organisms and entities that have yet to be accepted by mainstream orthodox science in the Western world that are so alluring for those who find themselves drawn to cryptozoology. A recent yet brief summary of the history of the field of study can be found in the work of Foxon (2024b).

Eyewitness Report and Anecdote

On that note, it goes without saying that the manner in which cryptozoologists and hominologists tend to first find out about their subjects of study is via witness self-report. And according to Paul LeBlond, translator of the English edition of Heuvelmans's *Neanderthal: The Strange Saga of the Minnesota Iceman*, it was Boris

Porshnev, founder of hominology, who stated: "Never would the study of a specimen, dead or alive, provide as much scientific information as the accumulation of eyewitness reports" (Heuvelmans, Coleman, & LeBlond, 2016, para. 5 of Translator's Introduction).[3] Or, as archaeological scientist and lecturer Myra Shackley has posited in the epilogue to her influential text *Still Living?: Yeti, Sasquatch and the Neanderthal Enigma*, we learn the following:

> If both apelike and manlike wildmen do exist, it seems that the strongest evidence comes from recent or near recent sightings and descriptions. To turn the discussion on its head for one moment, it is easy to see that the assumption that they do *not* exist rests on the belief that our world is so thoroughly explored, so well charted that no unclassified creatures will ever be discovered. It is equally easy to demonstrate how ill-founded this assumption is. There are still vast areas of the world whose Natural History is almost completely unknown… [Shackley, 1983, p. 166].

The position that both Porshnev and Shackley take here is essentially diametrically opposed to the master narrative that has typified the cryptozoological field as well as mainstream Western sciences for decades: that is the position that typically places firsthand encounters at the very bottom of the list of potentially valid or reliable evidence. Yet, holding to Porshnev and Shackley's accounts, the late, eminent professor, anatomist, and anthropologist Don Jeffrey Meldrum (1958–2025) often shares an insightful comment dealing with a dialogue between himself and a colleague: that a colleague once told him that accounts of Sasquatch were "just stories," to which the former replied, "Stories that apparently leave tracks, shed hair, void scat, vocalize, are observed and described by reliable experienced witnesses. Hardly just stories" (Cutchin, 2025, p. 247).

As a further case in point, let us consider the matter of the anecdote. Former police officer, experiencer, and content curator Brian King-Sharp (2024) has asserted:

> Anecdotal accounts also contribute to the body of evidence supporting the existence of Sasquatch. Witnesses from diverse backgrounds and locations have reported encounters with this elusive creature. These accounts often share common details, describing a towering, hairy creature with humanlike features [King-Sharp, 2024, p. 237].

Arguably, *anecdotes*—what professional cynic of fringed phenomena and author Michael Shermer states are "stories recounted in support of a claim" (2002, p. 48)—are a proxy for eyewitness testimony, eyewitness testimony is a proxy for memory, and memory is a proxy for identity, trust, and confidence in anything that can be marginally considered to be subjective. However, from one perspective, the difference between anecdote and formal qualitative data is simply a matter of how the information is collected (i.e., of method). Indeed, as renowned edge biologist, theorist, and author Rupert Sheldrake (2003, p. 26) reminds us, the Greek etymology of anecdote (i.e., from *an* + *ekdotos*) simply means an unpublished story, and such stories have been utilized in disciplines such as medicine and law to great effect, forming the basis of case histories and more once they move from being unpublished to being disseminated in print. At such a point, such stories provide the foundation of potential future research. Or as aforementioned Gregory Forth quite poignantly states, in line with Jeffrey J. Kripal's (2019) correct assertion that anecdotes are evidence, "the plural of anecdote is data" (Barackman & Fay, 2024, November 30, 1:09:10). Such a perspective on the anecdote is, in my opinion, a pragmatic one. As posited by members of the North American Wood Ape Conservancy (NAWAC)—formerly the Texas Bigfoot Research Center, or TBRC, is one of the more natural science-forward organizations investigating Sasquatch—"an oft-repeated misnomer regarding anecdotes is that they have no or very little value in the world of science. To the contrary, observation is the beginning of science" (Colyer et al., 2015, p. 185). Such a contention is spot on. Therefore, an anecdote can emerge as a significant data point, particularly when it is compared with and contrasted against other known data points. And though I may be accused of being too obsequious with my commentary on the matter, Greg Bishop has rightly noted that the very phenomena that we are considering are known for being "repeatable, but not on demand" (e.g., Cutchin, 2025, p. 243).

Fortunately, the approach that eyewitness memory and report are nigh useless has been challenged by a growing cadre of researchers, and a burgeoning set of data suggests not just that eyewitness memory is not as fallible as other researchers have led the public to believe (e.g., Bauer, 2020; Mickes et al., 2025). For example, Wixted and colleagues (2018) share the following:

> When investigators probe eyewitness memory, either via identification procedures (recognition tests) or interviews (recall tests), the information they receive is likely to be very reliable if the following conditions are met: (a) Witnesses were not previously exposed to distorting or contaminating information, (b) the witness's memory is being probed for the first time, (c) witnesses are not "tricked" into providing desired information (e.g., through the use of biased lineups or suggestive interview questions), (d) the witness's metacognitive monitoring guides his or her responding (either by withholding a response if uncertain or explicitly reporting his or her level of confidence), and (e) the investigator is sensitive to the witness's level of confidence (i.e., relying on high confidence responses while attaching less weight to low-confidence responses) [Wixted et al., 2018, pp. 332–333].

Furthermore, Wixted, Mickes, and their colleague Brent Wilson double down on these assertions in a more recent paper that summarizes literature on eyewitness memory: in a 2025 paper published in *Trends in Cognitive Sciences*, they state unequivocally: "The new message is that eyewitness memory is much more reliable on the first test of uncontaminated memory than was previously believed" (p. 9). In general, then, such findings suggest that absent undue or extreme influence such as persistent leading questions, eyewitness memory is not demonstrably unreliable. Additionally, research suggests that the memory distortions evoked by experimental manipulation are not quite as robust or as reliable as many have been led to believe (e.g., Brewin & Andrews, 2014, 2017), and that only testing eyewitnesses once rather than multiple times allows for more accurate and reliable recall (e.g., Mickes et al., 2025). Moreover, contrary to the BFRO's stated position that qualitative data (or specifically, anecdotes) are not testable, it should be noted that entire branches of scientific research are dedicated to collecting, analyzing, and interpreting such data; to be sure, matters of validity and reliability most definitely apply to qualitative research methods as well, albeit using different terminology. Indeed, so-called anecdotal information can lead to insights such as development of patterns and themes that emerge from larger datasets—insights that have formed the basis for the subject at hand in our present inquiry.

Further, let us briefly consider the matter of flashbulb memories, which is particularly relevant to exceptional experiences. In their article on source memory and *flashbulb memory*, Davidson and colleagues (2005) provide us with a succinct definition of the latter, stating that "a flashbulb memory (FM) is a vivid, enduring memory for how one learned about a surprising, shocking event. It thus involves memory for the source of event information, as opposed to memory for the event itself" (p. 1). Events which produce such memories tend to pervade popular culture and are therefore experienced by many people. In North America, examples from recent decades include events such as 9/11, or those surrounding the lives and deaths of figures such as Princess Diana, Aaliyah, Prince, David Bowie, and Michael Jackson.

Interestingly, Davidson and colleagues (2005) emphasize that the content and context of a memory are two separate concerns which can each be studied on their own, although research on the latter is fewer and farther between than research on the former. One implication of this process is that one may retain an accurate memory of an event, but not retain an accurate memory as to where or how they learned about that event. While flashbulb memories are not immune from distortion over time, Davidson and colleagues (2005) point to past literature (e.g., Christianson, 1989; Davidson & Glisky, 2002; Neisser & Harsch, 1992; Schmolck, Buffalo, & Squire, 2000) which suggests that these memories tend to be more accurate and reliable than are memories of other events that occur around the same time, as the latter are less strongly emotionally valenced than their flashbulb-inducing counterparts.

Further complicating the matter is when one considers the role that trauma might play in memory formation. For example, clinical psychologist Michael Adamse comments:

> So, if we see an event that is possibly even traumatic ... what we're likely to do is take a still frame and a moving shot of that experience. And we're going to archive that in our brains. And it gets seared in the sense that ... it is permanent. It's a permanent image. Because it's so profound for us and it's so out-of-the-box for us. So, we put it in our minds, we park it there, and we will keep that, seared if you will, for the rest of our lives [Eichenberger, 2022].

Adamse's commentary encapsulates what can occur with a flashbulb memory; however, what is further implicated by his comments is the fact that traumatic memories may be even more likely to persist than just flashbulb memories alone. Traumatic events such as those that may occur during a homin encounter can have a profound impact on experiencers, and so much so that some members of the Bigfooting community have strongly encouraged eyewitnesses to seek support from experienced and caring professionals, and to not be afraid to vet those professionals beforehand to ensure that proper help (rather than mocking, denial, etc.) will be received (e.g., Carpenter, 2022). We will further consider the matter of trauma in Section II of this text.

Exceptional Human Experience and Homin Entity Encounters

Other considerations regarding the deep weird can be categorized with terms offered up by critical parapsychologist and feminist Rhea White. She proffered the term *exceptional human experiences* (or simply *EHEs*) has a slightly different denotation from exceptional experiences. There were *five types of EHEs* (i.e., mystic/unitive, psychic, encounter, unusual death-related, normally occurring). As a category of experiences, by some estimates, EHEs are reported within as low as 30 percent and as high as 91 percent of the adult population (Sagher et al., 2019). For the purposes of our present discussion, the *encounter-type experiences* (aka *entity encounters*) are most relevant, as they are defined as consisting of the following examples (Palmer & Braud, 2002, p. 60):

- Ancestors encounter
- Angel encounter
- Apparition (of the living)
- Apparition (of the dead)
- Demonic encounter
- Divine encounter
- Folk entity encounter
- ET encounter
- Ghost encounter
- Guardian angel encounter
- Helper encounter
- Haunt encounter
- Imaginary playmate encounter
- Incubus/succubus encounter
- Interspecies encounter
- Mediumistic materialization encounter
- Multiple personality encounter
- Night terrors encounter
- Poltergeist encounter
- Possession encounter
- Sense of presence encounter
- UFO encounter
- UFO abduction encounter

Notably, terminology denoting an encounter with a hairy humanlike entity is missing from the above list, despite the fact that other humanoids are included. As such, I suggest that the term *homin entity encounters*—a reference to the totality of ways in which beings such as Sasquatch, yeti, yowie, and more around the world interface with human physical, psychological, psychic, or other sensory or perceptual capacity and meaning-making (e.g., Vallee & Davis, 2005)—fall under the general rubric of *exceptional experiences* and within entity encounters in particular. Exceptional experiences are also known as *anomalous experiences* (Cardeña, 2017; Cardeña et al., 2014) and *exceptional human experiences* (e.g., Palmer & Hastings, 2013; White, 1994), and are those categories of events that defy Western paradigmatic assumptions about the nature and boundaries of human potential or reality, and may include a whole spectrum of spontaneously or intentionally generated experiences and entities.[4]

Further, homin entity encounters share several features in common with many of the entity types noted by Palmer and Braud (2000), including but not limited to the following: soundless motion across substrates; telepathy; perceived distortion of shape; the *Oz factor* (time dilation, silent environment, mists or fogs, etc.; Randles, 2001). The Oz factor, coined by noted paranormal investigator and author Jenny Randles, includes "ambient sounds that just seem to disappear; an eerie stillness and silence; the flow of time stopping inexplicably and leaving a numbing timelessness" (Randles, 2001, p. 4). To be sure, this perceived ambient strangeness has been associated with homin as well as other entity encounters.[5]

Moreover, while the term "entity" may evoke various connotations, I use it here in the broadest of ways, to denote something or someone with an existence and, potentially, with volition, capable of being perceived and/or interacting with others.

Using the term "entity" can also potentially sidestep some of the typical ontological claims about the nature or provenance of beings from Sasquatch[6] to other non-human intelligences.

Specifically, adding Bayanov's (2014) nomenclature, I posit that the term *homin entity encounters* offers a breadth and depth of connotations while denoting the potential for paranormality. Despite implying that at least some of the narratives tied to these beings are evidence of a flesh-and-blood nature from our relatives within the hominin line, the term denotes commonality or relationship to the human condition, thereby looping back to us.

Per White's (Palmer & Braud, 2002) above listing, I suggest that homin entity encounters are most in alignment with what have been termed *folk entity encounters*, though other encounters mentioned above arguably coincide with homin entity encounters at least to at least some degree. Specifically, as I hope to demonstrate throughout this book, experiencers who encounter hairy, humanlike beings throughout the world have a variety of experiences, some of which are quite terrifying (e.g., akin to demonic, poltergeist, or haunt encounters), but others of which are sublime (e.g., akin to angel, divine, or imaginary playmate encounters).[7] Interestingly, due to the at times volatile nature of the encounter (and also due to potential social or other human-generated blowback after sharing an encounter), it is generally thought that the number of people who actually choose to report their entity encounters is but a fraction of the actual population of experiencers.

Part of the matter here is that for scholars such as Rhea White, it was more important to focus on the personally transformative potential of the events rather than on their ontology, per se: a focus that was a significant departure from what was at the time conventional experimental parapsychology, and that also departs from the dominant Western approaches to scientific endeavors. Further, while she identified five categories of encounters, White's EHEs also refer to those events that can invoke positive and integrative psychological response, including awe, inspiration, and wonder, and which can potentially cultivate wholeness (rather than dispersion or fragmentation) of human identity. When introducing the term, White poignantly comments that "a major problem with Western civilization in the last half of the 20th century is that we have an impoverished view of human being in general, which in turn diminishes our sense of the worth of individuals, including ourselves" (1994, para. 4). Her position that Western culture itself has created a problematic setting for human potential is one that we will return to throughout the course of this text.

It is precisely the matter of attempting to understand the labyrinthine behaviors and impetuses among the great apes that has led Wrangham and Peterson (1996) to consider that it is extremely difficult—but also entirely necessary—to not lose the forest for the trees when it comes to great ape intelligence. As they reflect upon the multifarious narratives that have emerged from field research and interactions with great (and even lesser) apes across time and space, they simply conclude that, "with apes, too many intriguing stories suggest that there are minds in the forest" (p. 256). In the case of the homins who also populate countless narratives across time and space, many who have had brief or even prolonged encounters with them have come to the very same conclusion: that there is a mind, perhaps even a human—if not humanlike—mind behind those eyes. And if there are indeed minds such as ours and theirs in the forest, then perhaps respecting those minds and preserving the space that supports them may be in everyone's best interest.

With that said, it should be noted that a recent re-emergence of a broader range of descriptive nomenclature (e.g., *cryptoterrestrials*, or intelligent, humanlike beings who have remained on earth, hidden from human eyes) bodes well for the development of more overarching theorizing about the ontological status or hidden reality that underlie these various entity experiences. Despite the fact that the authors of a speculative article on the potential cryptoterrestrial origin of UAP assert that they believe their hypothesis is likely false (Lomas et al., 2024), the fact that they have published such work and that it essentially went viral in early June 2024 is a positive sign for the easing of stigma with regards to such fringed subjects. Regarding the encounters themselves, the person or persons witnessing the event may be the recipient of information in the form of visions, telepathic messages, or other sensations.

While the above information helps to paint a general description of Sasquatch, it mostly comes from individuals who had fleeting, single-time encounters (i.e., *onetime* or *spontaneous experiencers*). Importantly, more detailed information can come to light from *extended experiencers*. Extended or long-term experiencers are individuals who have continued encounters with entities across longer spans of time (e.g., from months to years), at least some of which can include intentional rather than spontaneous interaction on the part of the experiencers themselves. They can be distinguished from those individuals who have brief, spontaneous or chance encounters. Referring specifically to Sasquatch encounters, experiencer and field investigator Autumn Williams uses the terms "long-term experiencer" rather than "extended experiencer," as well as the term "incidental witness" to refer to spontaneous experiencers (Williams, 2010, Locations 93–104).

Fringed Disciplines and The Other

Wildlife biologist John Bindernagel's (1941–2018) entire seminal 2010 book was dedicated to the matter of scientific discovery of these beings, to critical thinking, and the entrenched reticence within the academic establishment toward pursuing the subject of study. Indeed, the impetus for the present book also lies within the realm of human acceptance, awareness, and consciousness of these Othered beings,[8] and what might be done about the state of affairs that the Western psyche imposes upon them.

Landing upon a potential evolutionary target for the impetus of such reticence, Heuvelmans (1959) suggested in his opus *On the Track of Unknown Animals* that early conflicts between anatomically modern humans and homins may have been quite conflictual, resulting in one side very nearly exterminating the other. Quite poignantly, he reflected, "whether they are 'sub-men' or 'super-beasts,' we should learn much if we could meet creatures which showed, even if distantly, what we had once been, or were descendants of our rivals which were once near to exterminating us and which we may hardly have exterminated" (Heuvelmans, 1959, p. 87). This sentiment is something that forms the focus of much of what we are considering in this volume. However, despite claims to the contrary, science as an institution does not necessarily tend to seek theories, evidence, or subjects of study outside of what is currently accepted as fact or founded. Thus, Heuvelmans's call to "learn much" about our past, and therefore our present and even future, has tended to fall on deaf ears within the scientific establishment relative to the homin phenomenon: a state of affairs that Meldrum has notably referred to as a "relative void of passivity" within the academy (2006, p. 44) and Pruitt has aptly stated is a mainstream media which is "near-totally devoid of informative content" (2023, p. 246).

In this way, I suggest that particularly within this Western milieu, both homins and those who pursue them as viable subjects of study are cast as the *liminal Othered*—objects and entities that are ascribed an ontological limbo wherein their nature is perpetually in question. They are liminal in that they are placed at risk (Boykin, 1986) for being marginalized, pre-situated so as to not be fully visible or valid. Arguably, such a position is ascribed due to the perceived and/or actual *anti-structural* status of these subjects or personages, thereby denoting lack of conformity to an accepted and expected nature of reality. Of anti-structure, Hansen (2001, p. 59) poses that it "evokes the idea of disruption, of the border between chaos and order, of being anti-establishment..." (p. 59), thereby indicating an object that runs counter to mainstream, paradigmatic, or hegemonic assumptions. In essence then, Hansen proposes that any such phenomenon is fundamentally marginal, liminal, and trickster at its core, thereby *unbounded* and not defined by spatial, temporal, or social dictates. Some such unbounded phenomena include Sasquatch sightings, cattle mutilations, and UFO flaps (Hansen, 2001, p. 210).

The study of subjects such as these is constrained and confined into *fringed disciplines* (Mitchell, 2023) both inside and outside of the academy—that is, to areas of study that are defined relatively due to the amount of power they hold that either confirms or denies their epistemologically, ontologically, and/or methodologically valid status. Fringed disciplines necessarily tend to be placed in what Sagan (1979) has referred to as the borderlines of the academy. As such, to be fringed—or perhaps more specifically, "placed in the fringe" or "currently fringed" might do as well—refers to the amount of actual or perceived power held within these fields of study relative to the amount of power held within more socially accepted, established disciplines; however, these two poles exist in a state of constant dynamic (or more specifically, dialectic) tension, and in due time, those formerly fringed fields of study, subjects of study, and individuals who pursue such study, may rise into the Weltbild of the ivory tower.

I intentionally use the term as a transitive verb (i.e., as in "to fringe") rather than as an adjective (i.e., as in "fringe"), as with the more accepted, albeit oft-pejorative, term *fringe science*. I posit that the latter term connotes an inflexible power structure wherein those areas of study that are stratified below and to the margins of the mainstream academy are forever imprisoned there, incapable of broader acceptance. However, as scholars such as Bauer (Fall 2022) and Thomas Kuhn (2012) have stated, the history of science is littered with fluidity of movement. It follows that, instead of being doomed or destined to remain forever at the margins of the academy, scholars and citizen scientists within fringed disciplines exert a relative degree of agency to the extent that, eventually, they may move into more mainstream acceptance (e.g., the post–2017 movement that is presently occurring within ufology).

As such, this book is in part an exercise in asserting some modicum of that agency—what consummate scholar of Black, educational, and cognitive psychology, A.W. Boykin refers to as *the power to define*—in the service of those fringed disciplines which are (or could be) engaged in the homin phenomenon. Therefore, the intent behind the term fringed discipline is similar to the thrust of Boykin's (1986) phrasing of the term "placed at risk" (as opposed to simply "at risk") to define power dynamics more accurately within educational and other societal structures which probabilistically rather than deterministically impact what is deemed to be an acceptable subject of study. To be sure, the fields of cryptozoology and hominology have been asserting their own relative power since their inception.

Additionally, to be fringed, one might consider a similar term—frayed—wherein there is damage to the borders of some substrate or material, causing it to lack coherence and structure around its perimeter, becoming in a sense discontinuous with the rest of the substrate. It is within this liminal zone of incoherence that fringed disciplines tend to exist or even proliferate. In their Othered state, these disciplines are at the same time objects of revulsion, disbelief, and horror within this particular collective psyche, while also being palettes onto which awe, reverence, and enchantment with nature are painted. These are precisely the phenomena and academic pursuits that are labeled as *pseudoscientific* (e.g., Sagan, 1995),[9] as the derogatory and demeaning popular term "*woo*," or as misguided, illogical, irrational, and unworthy of study. To quote my colleague, critical parapsychologist Jacob Glazier—to whom I am ever grateful for inviting me to write on the homin phenomenon in the *Paranormal Ruptures* anthology—"it's okay not to be sure ... that's okay. And it's also okay to ... research these things and not dismiss them. And it's okay to ... bring them into the fold of what's considered academic discourse, right? They should be a part of the conversation" (Sinclair, 2024, March 1). Or, as Tobe Johnson—extended experiencer, *Strange Bräu Radio* host and content curator, author of *The Owl Moon Lab: A Paranormal Experiment* and co-producer of the *A Flash of Beauty* documentary series—poignantly states of the phenomenon, "This is not a story for those seeking answers to questions they think they already know. This is a story about questions that ask harder questions. For me, it started in the forest and ends in the forest" (Location 239 of 372, 2023). While Tobe's comment refers specifically to his book and the events that comprise the studies that he and colleagues such as Darrell Adams undertook at the Owl Moon Lab, the "story" to which he refers is also the homin phenomenon writ large and related phenomena. Arguably, the closer one operates to the center of mainstream institutions, the more courage is required to step foot into that forest.

As a whole, of course, the homin phenomenon tends to find itself engaged with infringed disciplines. Specifically, those accounts have tended to be studied within cryptozoological and hominological pursuits, though they may also overlap significantly with humanities (e.g., folklore, mythology, comparative religion, etc.) and other disciplines that study or take into consideration the *paranormal* (i.e., the range of subjects and phenomena that fall outside of the range of what are historically and culturally considered to be normative; Block, 2020).

As we bring this introduction to a close, I invite you in these pages to consider the conventional as well as unconventional sides of the homin phenomenon and to reflect upon what material herein resonates most with you or is most insightful. I wish you a fruitful journey.

View It from the Bridge

This introduction has outlined some of the terminology that is central to understanding the breadth of the phenomenon, including Dmitri Bayanov's nomenclature of "homin" to describe relict hominoids who are phylogenetically closely related to humans, the field hominology that studies homins, and the field of cryptozoology to which Sasquatch and other homins have been regulated for most of the history of their study in the West. Further, the focus has aimed at Western culture and its implementation of mainstream science that has placed anti-structural, anomalous phenomena in the margins of the academy (i.e., in fringed disciplines, which tend to have less power relative to mainstream disciplines). Those fringed disciplines tend to contain subjects of study that are Othered and that may involve exceptional human experiences (White, 1994).

Lastly, before moving on, there are several opportunities for reflection that I ask you to consider as you finish each chapter:

a. *cognitive*: How does the material that you just read align with or counter your beliefs, thoughts, or opinions about the homin phenomenon? Have your thoughts and/or beliefs shifted as a result of reading it?

b. *emotional*: What images or feelings have come up for you regarding the material from this chapter? Have your feelings about the subject of the homin phenomenon shifted at all? What information was most compelling or resonant for you?

c. *somatic*: What sensations, if any, have you noticed with your body as a result of reading this material? Have you had to pause, move, or re-orient/re-position yourself (e.g., in relation to your immediate or larger environment) while reading it?

d. *conative*: What do you hope or expect to do, if anything, with the material that you just read? How do you intend to utilize or investigate the information further in terms of your thinking, behavior, etc.? How might the material herein be of benefit to particular segments of the population (i.e., experiencers, investigators, scholars, etc.)?

Section I

Entry Points and Evidence

To the naïve observer who is unfamiliar with the subject of Sasquatch or homins in general, it might seem odd to hear that there is a plethora of evidence in support of the existence of these entities. For example, Cutchin and Renner (2020a, p. IX) have stated that other fringed phenomena of study suffer from "bigfoot envy" due to the overwhelming evidence in support of the latter beings. Further, episode 5 of season 1 of *Chasing Bigfoot: The Quest for Truth* suggests that "compared to any other cryptozoological creature, Bigfoot has more potential evidence in support of its existence than any other cryptid" (Meyer-Evans, 2020, March 15). In this section, we examine some of the best evidence that is presently available.

1

Death, (Re)Discovery, and Deep Memory

In general, we might consider that for those uninitiated in the homin phenomenon, the evidence in favor of the existence of these entities can be overwhelming in at least two ways: not only is it remarkable in its sheer quantity, but it is also potentially psychologically startling, capable of overpowering one's sense of rationality or stability in one's worldview. However, even if all of the evidence that we will consider in this volume was actually due to hoax, misidentification, or some kind of mass hallucination, the homin phenomenon still leaves very real traces in the minds of those whom it touches—traces that are often challenging to deal with and that carry the residue of trauma.

But before we delve into these matters, I would first like to make several statements as a matter of ethics. My purpose in writing this text is not to contribute to fearmongering of non-human entities, nor is it to incite violence, disgust, or angst against them, and many if not most reports of human-homin contact result in the homin doing no harm at all. As J. Robert Alley states, for example, "It appears that sasquatches are as difficult to anger as the gentlest of the great apes, the gorilla, and just as in that species, sasquatches indulge in threat displays simply to bluff any animal threatening them, thereby avoiding conflict" (pp. 47–48). In many narratives, restraint exhibited by homins appears to be a key component of the encounter: they could aggress but refrain from doing so. However, given their apparent strength as well as size, speed, and often *uncanny* reported similarity to humans, they seem to incite discomfort, anxiety, and fear in the human psyche in even the most benign of encounters (e.g., Hanks et al., 2025, April 13, 53:00–53:33).

That said, narratives of their behavior indicates that their character is as widely distributed as ours is, wherein many homins seem to be curious about us, some seem to enjoy our presence, others tend to observe from afar, while still others seem to aggressively defend their territory or actively assault humans. If at least some of the encounter narratives are due to contact with actual beings—entities who are often described as being quite human in appearance—then it would not be beyond the realm of healthy speculation to consider that overall homin behavior would also mirror ours in some form or fashion, including the good, the bad, and the ugly.

On that premise, in this volume we consider the manner in which homins may be encoded and perceived within the human psyche broadly speaking, and within Western culture specifically, as objects of suspicion, awesome power, and horror.

Death Anxiety

Despite the many benign or neutral accounts of contact, death and anxiety show up in several important ways in homin entity encounter narratives. The first is physical death, while the second is psychological or even cultural death. Both can be quite threatening when perceived either subtly or saliently by the human psyche. We provide a theoretical foundation here and will delve more deeply into these threats in Section II.

Single Species and Persistent Multiple Species Hypotheses

Regarding the matter of death anxiety, we first turn to the matter that Heuvelmans (1959) posited: that humans and homins may have been, at least at one point in our archaic past, quite near to one obliterating the other. This point cannot be overstated, particularly when we consider how dangers to physical survival are a primary driving force among organisms to secure adaptive advantage and to persist on this planet.

Despite the fact that it does not conform to existing data very well, the *Single Species Hypothesis* is a paradigm that has dominated anthropological and archaeological disciplines for decades (Meldrum 2016, 2017); however, Meldrum (2016, 2017) has stated that the *Persistent Multiple Species Hypothesis*, which suggests that more than one species can propagate in a given niche, is not only a more accurate portrayal of the available data, but it suggests that the *Principle of Competitive Exclusion* is not the only or even preferred manner in which life interacts on this planet. Speaking about these matters, Meldrum states the following at the opening to Darcy Weir's insightful documentary *Sasquatch Among Wildmen*:

> Back in the '60s and '70s, there was a notion—a paradigm—that … was central to anthropology … the idea that there could be only one hominin species occupying an exclusive hominin niche … the ecological principle that no two species could occupy the same niche was incorporated into the fabric of anthropology and influenced the way … the fossil record was viewed. And so … human evolution was seen as this single file march, this very singular procession of one species giving rise to another, and being succeeded by it, and so on down the pike. We now know, however, that rather than this single file march, there was this *bushy tree* … this diversity of hominins that existed across the landscape at any given slice of time in the past, and that many of those branches on this bushy tree have persisted alongside … our own lineage until much more recently than … had ever been acknowledged [Weir, 2020, 2:02–3:16].

Due to the fact that the Multiple Species Hypothesis is the rule rather than the exception across the breadth of hominin evolution (e.g., Meldrum, 2017), and the fact that genetic introgression between us and other species within the genus *Homo* such as *H. neanderthalensis*,[1] it is not a stretch of the imagination in the least to consider frequent clashes between homins and those of us who have become *H. sapiens*.

Meldrum also makes this assertion elsewhere (e.g., Meldrum, 2017), and it falls in line well with the available archaeological, anthropological, and forensic evidence—at least, when one is willing to step outside of the box and view the data as they are.

Regarding stepping outside of the box, I would argue that few phenomena ask mainstream Western culture to do so more than myth does. Those cosmological and cosmogonical narratives may defy clear linearity and yet they situate humanity within the broader web of existence and with each other. Traditionally, myth has served as the overarching set of narratives that define a group's reality or worldview, thereby positioning that group in relation to the broader cosmos or to the creative flux of existence.[2] For example, reflecting upon the work of businessman Eli Sagan as he reflects on violence in contemporary American society and its counterpart in ancient Greece, Marimba Ani states that "myths allow people to imagine what they cannot do" (2007, p. 378). Or, as founder of archetypal psychology James Hillman (1926–2011) states, the Western myth of a random and violent cosmos leaves the observer "in dread and senseless incomprehensibility" (2017, p. 60), thereby vastly limiting what is possible for the soul thus enculturated. Herein we might find a potent insight about the lack of an effective and pervasive myth about homins in European American mainstream culture. One might consider myth to be so much more than the term's desiccated modern usage (i.e., one that is diametrically opposed to the word's original intent); instead, myth and mythology is more congruent with a spiritually cultivated narrative by and for a people that is a treatise which is about truth, cosmologically, ontologically, epistemologically, and axiologically speaking. In creating and sustaining a myth about homins, the collective psyche of a community must admit what it can and cannot do, realizing limits and envisioning means of surpassing them, when and where necessary. Cosmologically speaking, there is a particular set of laws, such as All is Random, All is Mind, or All is Love (bounded by axiology) that is manifested in the universe. It is up to ontology to manifest those laws, and it is up to epistemology to make those laws known to the people.

"Homin Teems" and Neanderthal Predation Theory

To speculate on the above questions and build upon my previous work regarding this matter (Mitchell, 2023), I propose that the Western psyche and the culture that is mutually constituted from/of it are in fact not naïve to the existence of homins, as I initially assumed. In fact, Western culture—a culture that has consumed or cannibalized so many other cultures the world over—is anything but unaware of the existence of homins. I posit that instead of people wandering unawares through clearings, hunting in woods, or coming across a sudden flash of a hairy arm or leg while driving down a darkened road, caught totally unaware of a presence *unknown*, these experiences represent encounters with entities that have remained largely *unremembered*.

Drawing on critical, transpersonal, and comparative approaches and theories, including but not limited to transpersonal psychology, hominology, cryptozoology, mythology, folklore, theoretical biology, anthropology, and Black studies, I attempt to establish a transdisciplinary position that considers factors that may have influenced the psychological and cultural development of early humans, and which has likely persisted into the present. Like some of my academic and citizen scientist forebears, I credit early human interactions and competition with other humanlike beings as creating an intolerance for ambiguity and a deep desire for control over one's circumstances within the collective western welt build. Indeed, as others (e.g., longtime field investigator and experiencer Tim "Coonbo" Baker; Eichenberger, 2025, January 24, 19:00–19:48) have done, I posit that at least some of our hairy kith and kin very much resemble Vendramini's (2009) proposed revised rendition of what Neanderthals likely look(ed) like.

Additionally, I speculate on ways in which the deep memory of competition and collaboration with homins in general (rather than just competition with Neanderthals, as posited by theoretical biologist Danny Vendramini) across early and recent human history may have led to specific manifestations of psychological and culturally bound action, including but not limited to racially motivated violence, xenophobia,[3] and internecine discrimination. Moreover, another difference between our proposals is that Vendramini (2009) seems to suggest that reports around the world of hairy humanlike beings are due only to the survival and activation of a genetic memory of archaic battles with Neanderthals; while I am of the opinion that a subset of reports may be due to such *teems*,[4] I take the position that at least some reports of homins from around the world may be due to extant groups having persisted into modern times. Vendramini asserts that teems are patterns encoded in noncoding genetic material that preserve emotional memories across generations. Vendramini provides the following definition of a teem, which I include in its entirety from the text wherein he introduced the term:

> This trauma encoded mutational sequence is here called a "teem." Once encoded, the teem is inherited by offspring, and when expressed in limbic system cells, may be retrieved and experienced as an "emotional memory" of a single specific event or circumstance, albeit, with no associated semantic or declarative memory, and no physical consequences (injury, etc.) of the event. Only the emotions of the stressor event are inherited. The term, "teem" is in fact, derived from "Trauma Encoded Emotional Memory." To the extent that teems convey experiential information (in the form of emotions) from one generation to the next without recourse to learning or cultural protocols, teemosis is a functional instructionist process. Significantly though, teems do not contain information about physical traits so have no deleterious Lamarckian consequences [Vendramini, 2005, p. 514].

In general, it is *emotional memory*—a matter which we will return to throughout this text—that allows the organism to retain, prepare for, and respond to the most essential information within the environment (e.g., Levine, 2015, p. 22), and both emotional and procedural memory function as implicit memory, operating at the unconscious rather than conscious level.

In terms of the human experience, these emotional memories, be they positive, negative, or neutral, can be preserved in what Stanislav Grof refers to as systems of condensed experience (COEXes), which he discusses as follows:

> The unconscious material associated with them typically forms multilevel dynamic constellations for which I have coined the term systems of condensed experience or COEX systems (Grof 1975, 2000). A typical COEX system consists of many layers of unconscious material that share similar emotions or physical sensations; the contributions to a COEX system come from different levels of the psyche. More superficial and easier available layers contain memories of emotional or physical traumas from infancy, childhood, and later life. On a deeper level, each COEX system is typically connected to a certain aspect of the memory of birth, a specific BPM;[5] the choice of this matrix depends on the nature of the emotional and physical feelings involved. If the theme of the COEX system is victimization, this would be BPM II, if it is fight against a powerful adversary or sexual abuse, the connection would be with BPM III, for a positive COEX comprising memories of deeply satisfying and fulfilling situation BPM I or IV and so on. The deepest roots of COEX systems underlying emotional and psychosomatic disorders reach into the transpersonal domain of the psyche. They have the form of ancestral, racial, collective, and phylogenetic memories, experiences that seem to be coming from other lifetimes ("past life memories"), and various archetypal motifs.

Further, what he refers to as *teemic emotions* are, in other words, "genetically archived emotional memories of a somatic emotion originally experienced by a lineal forebear." He continues:

> Rather than freshly minted and spontaneously experienced, they are recalled, regurgitated, expressed, or in the language of teem theory, "triggered" by something in the organism's present environment, just as events jog a normal memory [Vendramini, 2022, p. 200].

Therefore, the author proposes a general mechanism by which, as Darwin suggested (Vendramini, 2022, p. 193), emotions can be heritable. Such a proposition is quite interesting and insightful, given the potential survival of being able to pass on such information in addition to any cultural artifacts to subsequent generations. Further, the author proposes the following: "As well as containing information about the organisms environment be it a river in flood, a predatory fox, a truffle, or a pinprick emotional memories can also precipitate behaviours that potentially increase survival rates and contribute to reproductive success" (pp. 85–86). Importantly, Vendramini points out that at the level of individual psychology, emotional memories tend to be stored implicitly or in a *non-declarative* fashion (i.e., in a manner wherein they tend to be stored and retrieved without conscious intent), rather than in an explicit or *declarative* manner (i.e., with conscious intent). A great deal of information can be encoded through non-declarative processes. Indeed, the process tends to be most amenable to emotionally salient information, and stimuli that are most relevant to one's survival would definitely fit the bill. If the stimulus is strong enough, then information about it can be preserved quite readily. Over time and across larger and larger numbers of individuals, if the stimulus is strong enough (e.g., a catastrophic or survival-threatening situation), then information about it will tend to be perpetuated within a teemic emotion.

Having stated that, as Vendramini (2009) has asserted in his work on the Neanderthal predation theory, there was distinct convergence of early humans (i.e., specifically, the Skhul-Qafzeh populations from Mount Carmel) with the *Eurasian Neanderthals* (distinguished from the population of classic Neanderthals from higher latitudes in Europe) in the area now known as the Levant. Importantly, Vendramini also proposes that this cohabitation and, apparently significant competition, occurred for a period of about 50,000 years, from 100,000 to 50,000 years ago.

The argument presented here is that the rather robust and aggressive Neanderthals viewed early humans as a food source and viewed the women as exhibiting sexual potential. Relevant to our present discussion, he also suggests that, barring the specific conditions that made our own brand of species so unique (e.g., being relatively hairless), Neanderthals would have likely continued the same trends toward hairiness and physical robustness that have predominated within our evolutionary line. Important for our present considerations, we might consider why humans have tended to be relatively denuded in relation to the great apes, especially when hairiness can present so many advantages—particularly in extreme climates. Vendramini (2009, pp. 130–131) suggests that in the presence of selective pressures which favored quickly distinguishing early humans from hairy, predatory Neanderthals, our own evolutionary line would have tended toward less hair. Furthermore, he states that hairy humans would have been selected out from sexual competition in such a decisive way that they would have been "in danger of being socially ostracized and even murdered" (p. 131). I suggest that both dark-colored hair and dark-colored skin have been largely unconscious triggers for not just Vendramini's Neanderthal teems, but for more generic teems—that is, *homin teems*—related to our past (and present) contact with other hairy bipeds as well.

In general, my position that homins have at least at times predated upon humans, leading to a persistent death anxiety among the latter, overlaps with Vendramini's (2009) Neanderthal predation theory, which he grounds in his *teem theory*. Essentially, the theory rests on the idea that early humans were hunted by large, hairy, bipedal beings (i.e., Neanderthals) who pushed humanity not just to the brink of extinction but into our present physical, cultural, and psychological form of the fully modern human. His teem theory, on the other hand, suggests the following:

> While the "Mendelian Inheritance System" (MIS) exclusively moderates the inheritance of physical traits, it is suggested the second, nonMendelian system (here called "Teemosis") exclusively moderates the inheritance of non-physical, environmentally acquired quantums of adaptive information configured as emotion, which is the basis of all emotions, innate behaviour and instincts. That is to say, while coding genes moderate physical evolution, ncDNA [non-coding DNA] moderates emotional and behavioural evolution [Vendramini, 2004, p. 513].

In other words, he suggests that there are two systems for passing on traits to subsequent generations: (a) that which operates through the typical coding DNA (i.e., in a Mendelian system, named for the famed geneticist Gregor Mendel who worked with pea plants to better understand the mechanisms of genetic inheritance); (b) and another parallel process, operating through non-coding DNA, formerly known as junk DNA (i.e., in a non–Mendelian system). The former system is what most students of biology learn about in textbooks, however it is the noncoding process that Vendramini posits is responsible for retaining and passing on sensorial triggers to environmental stimuli that elicit extreme emotions—stimuli (i.e., that are stress-inducing) which can potentially be threats to the survival of a species. Importantly, the author states that the adaptive value of these teems is that they can be generated and passed on, thereby enhancing the fitness of the organism and potentially its progeny. It follows then that those survival-oriented behaviors that operate at an unconscious and literally irrational (i.e., via non-rational means) level could be propagated trans-generationally through Vendramini's teemosis. This is an important claim for the purposes of our topic at hand.

Even though Vendramini (2009) does not think that homins such as Sasquatch exist in any ontologically real way, the depiction of Neanderthals that he and digital artist Arturo Balseiro have come up with is notably similar in a variety of ways to contemporary reports of hairy bipeds that have been reported around the world, as both depictions feature hair-covered bodies, dark-colored hair and/or skin, lack of visible neck, robust musculature, barrel chest, large and sunken eyes, heavy brow ridge, relatively flat face, and lack of protruding ears. I would be remiss if I did not note that the only real difference between Vendramini's scenario and what oral and written history of encounters with homins exhibit is time and place. That is, his theory posits archaic contact with Neanderthals in the Levant and Europe, while the homin literature proposes similar contact with bipedal humanlike beings since archaic times all around the world. For example, around the Caucasus region of central Eurasia, Myra Shackley (1982) reported the following from her investigations:

> In many cases, Almas are known to have voluntarily associated themselves with modern man. A lama at the monastery of Lamyn-Hegen is one of several supposed cross-breeds between Mongolian men and Almas women.... Another story tells of an Almas woman who was found breast-feeding a human infant, which could be claimed to be proof of genetic compatibility, and [Boris] Porchnev[6] himself exhumed the body of the daughter of a female Almas from the Caucuses and found that it had "pronounced Neanderthal features" [Shackley, 1982, p. 39].

It cannot be overstated that this particular region of the world that extends from Russia and Mongolia in the north to Türkiye in the south is of special importance due to its connection to the origination, promulgation, or reification of what has become European culture, and to the archaic history of humanity as a whole. Moreover, this region overlaps with what would have been the theorized home of the Eurasian Neanderthal discussed in Vendramini's work. Notwithstanding that, the fact that hominologists in Europe, Asia, and North America have contributed so much to documenting the existence of human-homin contact such as sexual relations and genetic introgression in the northern hemisphere is also quite significant.

It is important to note that the limbic system is associated with recognition and response to relational, social, and physical information in the environment so that the individual can navigate that environment with greatest ease and fluency. As such, the limbic system is tied to identifying and recording emotional stimuli, which are processed and preserved in the amygdala and hippocampus, respectively. When environmental stimuli that are presented to an individual or group are extreme enough, those stimuli can provoke a traumatic response. If that trauma is sufficient enough, the information about the precipitating event or stimulus can become embedded within a teem that can be preserved in one's genetic lineage and activated or triggered at a later date. Vendramini provides a helpful example to illustrate the process:

> Emotional perception is a crucial component of the teemosis process. It allows a turkey that survives a traumatic predatory attack by a hawk to encode a hawk teem that includes the

> emotions of terror and the transduced emotional precept of the hawk's wing shape and flight characteristics. When inherited by progeny, the shape of a hawk's wing and its flight characteristics are transduced by the new born turkey chick. This triggers the ancestral hawk teem, recalling its emotions of terror, which inevitably initiates an escape response.
>
> This hypothesis argues that all instincts and innate behaviour in animals (with the exception of reflex actions, kineses and tropisms) are encoded, genetically archived and inherited as quantums of emotion. When a teem is triggered, it releases emotions, some of which predispose the organism to specific behaviours [Vendramini, 2005, pp. 514–515].

However, while his position is that early humans encountered the perilous threat of Neanderthals in specific regions of the Levant and Eurasia, I suggest that humans have encountered homins in various (i.e., bedeviling as well as beneficent) forms from our archaic past into the present, and have developed different psychological and cultural strategies to adapt to their presence.

In my opinion, despite the fact that neither author makes direct reference to each other, both Levine (2015) and Vendramini (2009) are saying more or less the same thing about memory and the passage of information from one successive generation to another, but are using different reference points. Both scholars focus on the impact of the persistence of memory on the human form across generations, but the former focuses on transgenerational transmission cases over a relatively short period (e.g., hundreds of years) in the modern day to argue for body-based procedural memory being passed on, while the latter focuses primarily on transmission across a relatively long time period (e.g., tens of thousands of years) in the archaic past to argue for gene-based emotional memory being passed on to successive generations. But ultimately, both authors converge on the importance of trauma being passed on vertically from one generation to the next, and on the potential adaptive value of being able to retain such information for individual and group survival. Thus, the theses of both authors can support my central argument that death anxiety is the primary driver for the mythic and denialist (e.g., Western) approaches toward the homin phenomenon.

In all, Western culture has historically enacted behaviors that indicate a sense of particular physical and psychosexual vulnerability (e.g., Bradley, 1991; Welsing, 2004), and also continues to do so (e.g., Kaye, 2021). For example, as Kaye (2021) postulates, extreme examples of European male heteronormativity and androcentrism such as toxic masculinity and a particular strain of involuntary celibacy (i.e., incel) are evidence of deeper cultural, sociological, and psychological matters at hand. And some scholars such as Wrangham and Peterson have asserted that it is male primates at large, from chimpanzees to humans, who tend to play out violent and aggressive behavior that is "demonic at unconscious and irrational levels" (1996, p. 199). Such an assertion falls in line with the thesis focusing on uncovering the unconscious foundation behind the problematic behaviors of males in general.

But to be clear, we turn to one account that speaks to the general manner in which I believe these beings have been encoded in the global collective psyche: as generally unassuming and non-aggressive, but at times displaying a very real threat, threat enough to develop significant measures to cope with their presence. In episode 365 of the *Bigfoot Society* podcast, a man known simply as Old Bear talks about a harrowing encounter that he had while deer hunting in West Virginia when he was

16, as well as the aftermath of the incident. During the encounter, he was run out of the woods by a male Sasquatch who appeared to be chasing several does before becoming aware of Old Bear. After running back to meet up with his dad and telling what happened, his father instructed him to not tell his mother or grandmother, who would surely prevent any of the men in the family from hunting ever again. It also came out years later that Old Bear's father and uncle had heard what were most likely Sasquatch yelling in the woods themselves before his own encounter. Old Bear says of his investigations of Sasquatch in the southeastern United States:

> With these creatures, I found that most of 'em don't want nothing to do with us. They don't want to interact with us. They don't want to be bothered with us humans because we're dangerous. Most of [the] times when ... somebody sees one, they've got a gun or they've got some type of weapon in their hand typically when they run into humans, whether it's spring, summer, or fall, or winter. And they don't want anything to do with us. They've been shot at for hundreds of years here in the U.S. alone and across the world, and they're afraid of us. Most of 'em are.
>
> But I've also found that there're some of 'em out there, Bigfoot out there, that kinda want to turn us into dinner. And I've had ... a few experiences with those types, and it's always been a struggle to survive. And, because they're so big and powerful, and they're so aggressive, and the way they do things—it's always like they're a military unit, and that's how they act. Even the ones who don't want anything to do with us, they act more like there is a general (which, I found out over the years is a big male Alpha), and what he says goes and the Clan does what he says.... It can be dangerous if you get too close to 'em, they let you know. They may show themselves, or they may make screams or howls, or whatever, and they throw rocks [Byron, 2023, December 18].

Later in the interview, Old Bear continues by talking about a gentleman by the name of Robert Henderson who had mentored him into field investigating and who had had a benign encounter with a Sasquatch previously. The event occurred during a field investigation involving some relatively aggressive Sasquatch (or, yahoo, as they are sometimes called in the region) one winter in the mid-nineties on Summersville Lake in West Virginia. Mr. Henderson ended up going missing and never being found. Old Bear states that he thinks that a yahoo took his friend, saying of Henderson: "I found his hat three weeks later at the entrance to a cave with a rock stuck on top of it, and that's all that I ever found" (Byron, 2023, December 18). I am staunchly of the position that respect for homins the world over—or at least respect for the idea that they may actually exist—needs to inform anything that humans do with regards to them.[7]

Given the circumstances, I suggest that over the course of human history, it has not taken many accounts such as the disappearance of Robert Henderson or becoming dinner for a Sasquatch for the potential danger of Hairy Man to become readily suffused in the deep memory of our species, leading to explicit myths and lore in many cases, and to outright denial in others.

And lastly for now, I wish to state that despite the terms that I use in this text (e.g., Sasquatch, homins, etc.) to refer to reports and narratives of large (and sometimes small) hairy humanlike beings, I make no ontological claim as to who they are, save favoring the diverse and deep non-European and European Indigenous perspectives around that world that predate those colonizing Western epistemological frames, upholding postmodern conceptualizations of these ancient narratives such as *co-creation* (e.g., Bishop, 2016; Cutchin, 2022), and holding space for the likelihood that narratives which are encapsulated as referring to Sasquatch or homins in general may flow from multiple underlying causes. That is to say that I favor a true skepticism that simply allows the data to speak for itself. As the founder of Cryptovania TV, Jason Trost, illustrates this philosophy about 43 minutes into the documentary *Mountain Devil 2: The Search for Jan Klement*:

> With people coming out with ... these ideas that are against the mainstream, a lot of times, you're hesitant to come out with your sightings, and your ideas, and your experiences. And really, how can you have accurate data if people are afraid to come forward? Um, and so ... if you want accuracy, you've got to accept ... all of the phenomenon. Um, you can't just restrict it ... if you only accept things that can be proven right here, right now, you're gonna limit yourself. You're gonna limit the data that you have for crunching [Cavalline, 2020].

Thus, the epistemological and methodological constraints that are placed on what is known about reality (i.e., ontology) can prematurely limit potential quality data that can help to expand or push understanding forward. Indeed, the variety of evidence (e.g., Cutchin & Renner, 2020a) that we consider here in Section I presses the boundaries of what members of the Bigfooting community as well as mainstream science consider to be admissible data. Whether they are flesh and blood remnants of the past, ghosts of beings that no longer exist, archetypes projected into the wilderness, spirits that assume the form of bipedal beings, some combination of the above, or something entirely different, people are encountering—and have been encountering for millennia—hairy, humanlike figures in the forests, plains, and mountains of this world, and to deny that there is something very real behind these sightings and encounters is to deny oneself something truly vital about human history and human existence.

Regarding my own *positionality* (i.e., one's own relation to the subject at hand, including my biases, beliefs, and background, and the context that these create in interaction with said subject), I have an abiding interest in effectively perceiving the nature of the problem: that is, the matter of why the deep denial and reticence surrounding the subject of Sasquatch and other relict homins has persisted as it has within Western culture. My earliest consciously recollected memories are of having a kind of noetic sense, absent any real learning or enculturation, that there are entities on this earth and beyond that go bump in the night, from ghosts to hairy humanlike beings and beyond. Following this trajectory and the plethora of evidence in support of these entities, I have often found the Bigfooting community faced with the question of what counts as evidence and what to do with said evidence. Importantly, the community is just as impacted by the values and vices of Western culture as is the most epistemologically conservative mainstream academic, at times adhering even more stringently to those perceived dictums and dictates than professional scholars do. In other words, to an extent, everyone swims in the mainstream realm of culture (e.g., Boykin, 1986), albeit to varying degrees.

Accordingly, the potential beneficial nature of having an object to fight against is reflected in Hansen's (2001) commentary on an insightful narrative that reflects the deeper psychological dimensions of the treatment of these phenomena:

> Bigfoot can be partly understood in terms of projection and paranoia. Anthropologist Henry Sharp, in his book *The Transformation of Bigfoot* (1988), tells of a small Chipewyan society in which tensions between two brothers threatened the group's existence. A hunt for Bigfoot brought them together in a common purpose even though neither had a firm belief in the creature. The hostility within the group was projected outward onto a common enemy, and that strengthened the social bonds. Each brother realized that he needed the other as an ally. The fear of Bigfoot was therapeutic and adaptive [Hansen, 2001, p. 608].

In the chapter upon which this book is based (Mitchell, 2023), I reflect upon the significance that the above narrative may hold for established mainstream Western science and culture. Herein, it matters not whether Sasquatch represents a real or imagined threat: what matters is its significance for group cohesion in the face of fear of death. The problem that arises is that the "strengthened … social bonds" are tenuous at best, and capricious at worst. It is not enough to unite a group against a common enemy, real or imagined. Ideally, the unity of a group should be formed by common values related to a greater ethical good rather than simply repelling a perceived threat. Consequently, the Chipewyan narrative is instructive and insightful in that it points directly to this matter: without the consistent coherence of the relationship between members of the group, the whole community is threatened. The lynchpin, therefore, is that Sasquatch (or Sasquatch-as-gatekeeper, or Sasquatch-as-cannibal-spirit) establishes a taboo: the people must not turn from each other, for therein lies ruin.

Further, we might consider that from within the European psyche seems to emerge at times a deep and seething rage at being denied. That is to say that what other groups may consider to be cultural taboo or transgressions, the Western mind generally accepts as being normal, acceptable, or even necessary for its own salvation. Therefore, in a process akin to Yurugu's own impetuous and impertinent ethic (Ani, 2007), the imperative for the Western collective as a whole is arguably to prove its own worth by identifying and then forcing all perceived boundaries and threats into submission. Those boundaries may be the taboos of other cultural groups or even taboos housed within the confines of the European psyche itself. Note that before Europeans began warring with other people, they were warring with themselves (e.g., Menakem, 2021), though if we look deeper into archaic prehistory as Bradley (1991), Welsing (1994), Vendramini (2009), Diop (e.g., Wobogo, 1976), and others propose, the picture becomes a bit more complex, converging on at times violent archaic contact with other humanlike beings and/or struggle to eke out survival within the confines of unforgiving terrain. However, those boundaries may be perfectly natural limits placed on the human body and being, the most salient of which being mortality itself and the processes of aging and decay that come along with it. Indeed, toward the end of her full interview for the *A Flash of Beauty* documentary, Sonya Zohar comments:

> One of the frailties of mankind is that mankind and science seems to think that it's okay to invade any environment … we think if we can get to the moon, then we should go. And we think if we can get to Mars, then we should go. And we think if we should dive to that deepest part of the ocean, then we should go. But we actually don't ever estimate the subtle layers of the fabric of all things that are all connected when we do these things [Eichenberger, 2024, January 1].

Those subtle layers to which Sonya refers tend to be most apparent in those fringed and marginalized spaces and people that European culture has aimed to suppress and/or repress. The ripples that are sent out from the impetuousness and the insecurity (of Yurugu) eventually return back to their source, having disturbed the fabric of all levels of reality: physical, psychological, subtle, spiritual, and everywhere in-between. Some sense of realization might arise at the deep rifts and ruptures that have been perpetuated in the name of progressivism, positivism, and the like, but by then the damage has been done. Ultimately, the cannibal spirit is left to survey the cannibalized shell of its host, with nothing else to consume.

Following this train of thought through what Welsing (2004) refers to as the European brain-computer (i.e., a culturally derived collective psyche), to be denied a thing becomes associated with a very threat to one's survival. Or, if we take Ani's (2007) approach, Yurugu's fear is of being impotent: therefore, of being unable to perpetuate his own likeness in the world. For both Welsing and Ani, the European collective psyche is predicated on an extreme propensity to perpetuate itself by identifying, confronting, and stamping out anyone and anything perceived as a threat to that perpetuation.

Further, *to deny that which denies* can be elevated to a moral principle, an axiom worthy of greatest expression and manifestation. Indeed, that which denies may be the earth beneath our feet, the waterways of this planet, nature itself, the cultures of other non–European peoples, or the non-conforming aspects of the collective European psyche.

As Red Grossinger, Sasquatch field investigator and author, states, "I found a lot of time the White folks are not quite as open to deal with-, with the Sasquatch. For them, it-, you know, it takes a while to understand it more" (Shiver, 2021, November 30). Red's comment came immediately after he remarked about a witness of German descent who had taken two years to tell his daughter of his own sighting of a Sasquatch walking on the side of a road. There does indeed seem to be a pattern of eyewitnesses—the large majority of those who end up being interviewed or in the literature on the subject being of European descent—who have such entity encounters are quite reticent to tell anyone, including their loved ones.

Scholars such as Vendramini (2009) have gone so far as to elevate high emotion to the level of being impressed upon one's genes, able to be transmitted trans-generationally. Specifically, following upon papers that he has published previously, he summarizes the potential mechanism as follows:

> High intensity emotions (typically caused by predatory attacks, accidents and other traumatic misadventures) can be imprinted into an area of an animal's DNA called *nonprotein-coding DNA* (ncDNA). This is the area of DNA that was often dismissed as "junk DNA."
>
> For example, if a turkey survives a hawk attack, its emotional response (terror, anguish etc.) can be encoded into its ncDNA and, under certain circumstances, these traumatic emotions can be inherited by its offspring.
>
> When this molecular encoding occurs, it is inherited by progeny as a nebulous *emotional memory*. It is this emotional memory that future generations of turkey chicks used to identify dive-bombing hawks. Importantly though, the episodic memory of the experience is not inherited, nor are any physical consequences. If a boy is mauled by a dog, his lacerated

> wounds are not inherited, nor is the intellectual memory of the attack. Only the traumatic emotions are inherited [Vendramini, 2009, p. 182].

As stated early on, he calls this process of passing on such emotional memories teemosis and uses it as a lynchpin in his theory that predatory contact between Neanderthals and early humans in the Levant created an environment of such high stress that adaptive mechanisms needed to be inherited in order to assist the survival of the species. Some of these mechanisms would have been derived in subsequent generations as psychological tendencies and processes that remained within the fabric of human culture.

Vendramini (2009) has suggested that it is entirely plausible that such a form of memory is preserved in ncDNA via epigenetic effects. Those effects may include environmental stressors like predation, natural disasters, and other potentially trauma-inducing factors that would lead to strains on a population's ability to survive. Incidentally, it is also these types of traumatic events that can become encoded in mythological narratives, some of which we will consider herein. The author speaks further of the potential biological mechanisms for such long-term changes in genetic and behavioral disposition in other writings (e.g., Vendramini, 2005). These mechanisms may indeed overlap with clinically relevant or theoretically derived constructs, such as those *legacy burdens* that are discussed in Internal Family Systems (Falconer & Schwartz, 2023).

It is interesting to note that, despite Vendramini's far-reaching and well-researched assertions, he also seems to propose that sightings of Sasquatch, yeti, *barmanu*, and other hairy homins are simply the result of the persistence of archaic teems and are therefore essentially psychogenic (i.e., created by the mind):

> While no rock-solid scientific evidence has emerged to prove any of these bipedal, forest-dwelling cryptids actually exist (although cryptozoologists remain hopeful that proof will someday emerge) their sheer ubiquity across disparate cultures on different continents and separated by thousands of years has long puzzled ethnographers and anthropologists [Vendramini, 2009, p. 301].

I posit that the body of available written and oral history and trace evidence in its totality presents just such "rock-solid evidence." Indeed, he suggests that Neanderthals were wiped out by *Cro-Magnons*[8] who invaded Europe on a warpath to exterminate their former adversaries, with that deeply meaningful if not traumatic emotional memory being encoded in our lineage even into the present moment in various and sundry ways, including in the works of content creators from artists to science-fiction writers and more (p. 301). These emotional memories that are preserved through non-coding DNA may be triggered by essentially any environmental stimuli that generate or afford a strong enough response in the percipient. Such stimuli can include portrayals of bogeymen-like beings in horror films; dark and ambiguous human-shaped figures; faces with large, glowing eyes; heads covered with hoods and/or shrouded eyes; hunched backs or slouched posture; humans with hirsutism; and darkly clad humans.

Vendramini is cognizant, as he states earlier in his book, that he is rather heavy-handed in his all-in approach to generate a unified field theory for the development of fully modern humans by using Neanderthals as a one-stop scapegoat for all manner of psychological and physical developments in what has become our particular stock of hominin: anatomically modern humans.

Still, the idea that his proposed teems have persisted into the present can still be coterminous (e.g., not mutually exclusive) with my proposition that pervasive aversion toward the subject of Sasquatch in mainstream Western culture is due to unconscious death anxiety of hairy bipeds, potentially both Neanderthal and otherwise (e.g., Sasquatch, etc.). As such, the presence of teems—not just for Neanderthal, but for any and all dark-haired, dark-skinned bipedal beings that could have posed a threat to our survival—seems to be one means of discussing the development and persistence of unconscious memories from humanity's evolutionary past. As mentioned, I suggest that a more generic teem than a Neanderthal teem (i.e., a homin teem) may account for the varied and persistent human behaviors that result in approach and avoidance of large, hairy, humanlike beings—whether that behavior is done within the mind, in the environment, or both. Following the available cryptozoological and hominological literature (e.g., Bayanov, 2014; Sanderson, 2008), it is not just Neanderthals but other homins throughout the world who have competed with us humans for resources, at times potentially using as food sources or as mates. Thus, I would suggest a more general homin teem that would include emotional memories of contact with any and all homins that have lived alongside us, from the archaic past to the present. This homin teem would function in largely the same way that Vendramini's teem does but would potentially be even more robust because it would include homins who humanity has encountered outside of the Levant and Europe—where mainstream science states that early humans came into contact with and eventually exterminated Neanderthals.

Still, I leave it to my colleagues in other disciplines to consider whether the homin teem hypothesis utilized here is either *too* parsimonious or should be replaced with another one to better understand humanity's general reactions to these entities. Consequently, my general sense is that a transdisciplinary appraisal of the psychological, biological, cultural, mythological, and spiritual means by which unconscious memories—and particularly those that have significant meaning for humanity—is necessary for a more robust understanding of where humanity has been and where we might be headed. Moreover, as I reflect on convergences and divergences between my proposal and that of Vendramini (2009), the continued existence of homins may present a continued or persistent threat that the collective Western psyche in particular (i.e., absent a functional master narrative to explain any genuine existence of these beings) is unable to deal with consciously at present as a whole, leaving those enthusiasts and investigators to deal directly and intentionally pursue and prepare the collective for re-discovery of and encounter with the subject. That is, for a kind of re-disclosure, if I may, borrowing on Bayanov's (2014) contention that *re-discovery* of homins is more or less imminent.

Following this course of thought, the *Bigfoot curse* is a phenomenon that shows up in numerous ways in Indigenous and European American lore, and according to Cutchin and Renner (2020a), has become something of a meme within the community of researchers and enthusiasts of the subject. As Renner states (2020a, p. 247), "a number of Native American cultures regard Bigfoot as an omen of impending death." For example, host of *Subarctic Alaska Sasquatch* and extended experiencer, Fred Roehl of the Curyung Tribal Council, and co-author Stevi Falukos (2024) reflect on the deep superstition that is often tied to even speaking about Hairy Man within Indigenous American communities. That approach is also taken elsewhere within Indigenous American communities such as among the Lakota (Boulier, 2017, p. 420), Kwakwaka'wakw Nation (Germer, 2018, September 8), and the Northern Cheyenne of Idaho (Smyth, 2023, June 27). Moreover, the infamous *Ruby Creek incident* involving the death of the members of the Chapman family demonstrates how the curse may unfold, even if it does not manifest immediately (Sanderson, 2008, pp. 45–47). If there is some kind of ontological reality behind the curse, then what befell the Chapman family should stand as a keen warning to keep one's distance from the Hidden People and to not go seeking them out.[9] Another encounter involving the potential curse occurred on June 15, 2018, and is related by Bigfoot Michigan Rob, as it may have involved the death of his girlfriend Cindy—on June 15, 2018, while the two were on Lake Cadillac in Michigan (Karnafel, 2023, December 15).

While the most potent manifestations of the curse of Bigfoot seem to produce physical, psychological, or spiritual ruptures in our relationship with ourselves or with others, it may manifest by bedeviling people in less lethal ways (e.g., Noël, 2023, p. 291). Such manifestations overlap significantly with poltergeist phenomena and odd electromagnetic effects (e.g., Edgar, 2023; Mayes, 2022) that are reported in haunted houses and with UFO/UAP activity (cf. Vaughn, 2024, pp. 146–148 for a brief summary of this overlap via the work of paranormal investigator Chuck Zukowski). The idea that the presence, intent, or some other aspect of a homin may impact physical matter (e.g., electrical equipment; Kelleher & Knapp, 2005, p. 47; King-Sharp, 2024, May 5) in the surrounding area, and particularly in ways that cause dysfunction or malfunction of electric or battery-operated devices, is at the least an adjacent phenomenon to the curse of Bigfoot, as both manifestations deal with negative or evidence-suppressive effects[10] of encountering Sasquatch.

Ambivalence

In all, following the works of Vendramini (2009) and others, I suggest that it is the possibility of encountering death at the hands of homins that has persisted in the collective human psyche since time immemorial. However you, the reader, respond internally to the content in this text, I suggest that it is not just a function of your own individual psychology and physiology, but of the culture and deep memory that are interwoven with them as well. I proffer that there is a deep sense of ambivalence present within the human psyche, and particularly within the Western collective, with regards to the dark-colored liminal entities who are at the center of our speculation. Due to the great mystery as well as death anxiety that I suggest these homins can engender in humans, I find it reasonable that a general approach-avoidance attitude is developed, albeit typically unconsciously, within the collective psyche.

As Baranchok (2021) explains ambivalence, "One option we want, desire or love (approach) and the other we find repulsive, distasteful, unpleasant, or anxiety-producing (avoidance)" (p. 70). Renowned somatic psychologist Peter A. Levine states that these attraction-repulsion mechanisms (aka hedonic valences) are essentially hard-wired into all living organisms, providing impulses to help guide us through our environment (2015, p. 26). As such, both potentials exist simultaneously within the psyche, representing a kind of superposition of possibilities for how to treat homin entity encounters—a state of affairs that has been noted by others as well (e.g., Bader et al., 2010; Hill, 2017, p. 36). Or, as a centerpiece to the chapter upon which this current work is built, we turn to the words of professor emerita and interdisciplinary scholar Donna Haraway, who illumines: "To be human is to be on the opposite side of the Great Divide from all the others and so to be afraid of—and in bloody love with—what goes bump in the night" (Haraway, 2008, p. 11). To me, homins are what go bump in the night as well as within those shadowy spaces of the *collective* (i.e., universal) and *social unconscious* (i.e., comprised of group-based images such as "the church," "civilization," etc., that form one's basis for group-based thinking, bias, feeling, and the like; Burrow, 1924, p. 231).

With that said, it should be noted that if homins are indeed conscious beings themselves, such ambivalence towards us may well be at play. As Noël (2022) notes, Sasquatch may exhibit both avoidance (e.g., as potentially evinced in hiding, walking away, etc.) *and* approach (e.g., peeking from behind trees, looking at us through windows, etc.) behaviors towards us. And while Baranchok (2021) has rightfully argued that it is unclear as to whether fear or vigilance best describes their observed behavior, there seems to be a general sense within the Bigfooting community that homins exhibit this kind of approach-avoidance character. Or as experiencer, expert outdoorsman, and media personality Les Stroud comments, "one of the most accurate descriptive terms I've heard that may apply to Sasquatch, if they do indeed exist, is 'curiously afraid'" (Stroud, 2020, December 19, 34:20).

But to return to the human side of this divide, we might recall Bayanov's (2012, p. 38) simple yet poignant remark: "The history of man's relations with homins is full of ambivalence." To illustrate, in an interview that seems to no longer be available, Brittany—wife of experiencer Chad Granger—succinctly illustrates such dissonance. After her husband's encounter, she reflects on whether or not she would like to see a Sasquatch personally and states the following: "I want to see them in person, but I'm scared for that day. So, I … hope I do see them, but I hope I don't, 'cause I don't know what I'd do if I ran into a Bigfoot myself" (Eichenberger, 2024, January 7). As odd as her response may sound to some, I believe she has brilliantly illustrated the persistent tension present within the approach-avoidance response—a behavior that I have personally experienced on many occasions. With the knowledge of entities such as Sasquatch, as well as any potential *vicarious trauma* that she experienced after Chad and Austin's encounter, such a response is quite understandable; furthermore, if the propositions such as those that Heuvelmans (1959), Vendramini (2009), and I propose about violent, if not simply contentious, archaic contact with hairy bipedal beings in the remote past hold any historical truth to them, and if there is a persisting and accessible (albeit unconscious) deep or genetic memory of said contact, then it would be reasonable to consider that such ambivalence would be even more pronounced within the individual psyche of the non-experiencer. Moreover, the looming threat of the numinous, both awesome and terrifying, is arguably ever-present when it comes to the possibility of encountering such entities.

In the case of transgenerational trauma and its extreme archaic form (i.e., what we might consider to be *paleotraumas*, a subject that we will return to in Section II), a kind of preconscious anxiety and hypervigilance may be amassed within the populace, though I suspect that this scenario too can lead to hyperreactivity and depletion of energy. A kind of interaction between these traumas (e.g., sustained by emotional memories of varying intensities via teems) could potentially lead to an additive or multiplicative effect within the individual body and/or collective psyche/longbody, persisting in deep memory. The *longbody* is, generally speaking, the lasting past, present, and future communal and spiritual bonds between the people and the flora, fauna, and land with which they are connected (Aanstoos, Fall/Winter 1986; Roll, 1987; Vaughn, 2024, pp. 259–260).

That context leads us to the matters of *narrative truth* (i.e., the perceived subjective meaning associated with a phenomenon or event) and *historical truth* (i.e., the perceived objective accuracy of a phenomenon or event), terms coined by Donald Spence, each of which are steeped in the history and practice of psychology (namely, psychoanalysis) and have broader implications for the philosophy of science. Reflecting on the place that these two truths hold in psychoanalysis à la Spence, Sass and Woolfolk (1988) summarize that narrative truth deals with coherence (i.e., the formation of meaningful patterns that can be constructed from within the recalled experience) and correspondence (i.e., association to factual, objective worldly events).

I thereby posit that focusing on the potentially meaningful patterns of themes with regards to the phenomena discussed herein is crucial, as they help to establish the means and manners by which people perceive their reality, rather than just focusing on the so-called objective nature of that reality itself. According to Thomsen and Brinkmann (2009, p. 297), "Of course, in some contexts, historical truth is important, not least because many individuals will be interested in a truthful understanding of their own lives.... In other contexts, it is simply the interviewee's current self-interpretation that is of interest." As eminent scholars such as Jerome Bruner (1990) have proffered, uncovering meaning is absolutely central to the study of the psyche. With that said, I find explicit discussion of meaning and narrative truth to be missing from much of the present naturalistic cryptozoological discourse, even though such truth is a wonderful bridge between cryptozoology, other fringed disciplines, and psychological science. As Linda S. Godfrey (2016), the late author of Fortean phenomena, has stated, examining patterns in eyewitness accounts is essential.

Collective Memories

Some researchers have attempted to determine the amount of time that certain cultural artifacts (e.g., music, current events, etc.) tend to remain in our awareness as a society and have differentiated or disentangled the types of memory that are involved in such a process. Candia et al. (2019), for example, define *communicative memory* as our conscious awareness and daily musings that we have with each other, and *cultural memory* as composed of such tangible repositories as physical recordings that we create to retain and store information that we deem to be of collective importance (see Ann Rigney, 2015 for a review of the evolution of the concept). Examining various digital and archival sources, one finding from their research suggests that music decays from our communicative memory more quickly than other artifacts such as biographies. These examples offer important data for the influencers, content curators, and content creators of the Bigfooting community, as academia alone cannot be relied upon in its present incarnation for the preservation of scientifically relevant or historical information regarding the subject of Sasquatch. Therefore, sources of knowledge production and retention such as social media, those often independently published books on the subject, as well as mapping projects, museums, and conferences, are the curated sites within which information and data are preserved for posterity.

Other scholars have provided further conceptual clarity as to what comprises some of these forms of memory. Assmann and Czaplicka (1995) share that communicative memory has a degree of informal, adaptive fluidity as it manifests in our everyday interactions with each other. In collaboration with fellow Egyptologist, memory studies scholar, and spouse, Aleida Assmann, the three offer:

> For us the concept of "communicative memory" includes those varieties of collective memory that are based exclusively on everyday communications. These varieties, which M. Halbwachs gathered and analyzed under the concept of collective memory, constitute the field of oral history [Assmann & Assman, p. 126].

Thus, the functionality of communicative memory can occur through structures as diverse as family units and entire nations. The vehicles or containers for this type of memory include everyday conversations, gossip, and jokes which are all constrained by the situations and places within which they take place. Assmann and Czaplicka suggest that communicative memory is bound to a duration of time of no more than 80 to 100 years (i.e., three or four generations), and that collective memory is of a longer duration, requiring stronger cultural underpinnings than communicative memory alone to persist. Clearly, in one way or another, Sasquatch and their kin have been retained within humanity's collective memory, as well as within our communicative memory in certain ways.

In all, what we are asked to strongly consider is that the threats that homins present (which we will consider more thoroughly in Section II) can be summarized as the resurgence and/or recognition of a deep and persistent trauma that has been passed on trans-generationally from archaic contact into the present. Indeed, while previous research had found that various non-human organisms can encode and vertically transmit traumatic memories and/or epigenetically express behaviors across multiple generations (e.g., Klengel et al., 2016; Klosin et al., 2017), 2025 was the first year that such findings were replicated in a human sample (Mulligan et al., 2025). Researchers found that within a sample of three generations of immigrants to Syria (i.e., 138 individuals across 48 families), exposure to violence resulted in observable changes in up to 14 regions across the genome. Taken as a whole, such studies seem to corroborate Vendramini's (2009) teemosis and potentially provide further support for a mechanism that could encode and transmit Neanderthal (or more generally, homin) teems, the emergence of trauma at the individual level that can manifest in the form of PTSD—a matter that we will also return to in Section II.

As such, while I have not been entirely explicitly about it, *deep memory* lies at the heart of our journey. Broadly conceived, the term refers to the creation and retention of, as well as access to, transpersonal and/or ancient—even archaic—experience or wisdom through a medium that can be utilized by a sentient, or especially a sapient, psyche (e.g., the collective unconscious, DNA, Akashic Records, etc.). Deep memory tends to exist in various implicit (i.e., intuitive, ineffable, pre-verbal, somatic, imaginal, etc.) memorial and consciousness modes and mental as well as bodily states that do not rely on cortical or conscious intent to create, store, or retrieve said information.

Deep memory is alternatively known as *ancestral memory* or *genetic memory*,[11] though these other terms diverge a bit in their meaning. I use deep memory to more specifically refer to the largely unconscious and/or preconscious representation of information that tends to be passed along in emotional, embodied, and otherwise procedural and implicit ways and which can potentially encode the most iconic and meaningful moments and interactions throughout human history, paleohistory, and perhaps beyond into even deeper evolutionary time, spaces which—following older Indigenous traditions—some Western transpersonal theorists such as Grof (2012) have found persist, contained buried within the contemporary human psyche. Of course, oral tradition is the oft-used bridge within traditional cultures to link such pre-conscious and unconscious encoding with conscious recollection of said information. The information retained in Vendramini's (2009) suggested process of teemosis would thereby be categorized as part and parcel of deep memory.

Due to its nature, deep memory is decidedly transpersonal in that it extends well beyond the individual person into the species' deep past and potentially beyond. Further, it is similar to Freud's racial memory or to Jung's collective unconscious, wherein as psychologist Stephen R. Heyman concludes the following:

> For both Freud and Jung … not only can memories be transmitted through the unconscious to succeeding generations, but this is a very important process. These are memories which have occurred repeatedly and are extremely significant in each individual life. For both theorists, these memories may remain dormant, unless triggered by parallel events in an individual's life. For Freud, as for Jung, more than traumatic material can be transmitted: memories capable of maintaining man's cultural advances are available for integration into one's life, to serve as a powerful guide [Heyman, 1977, p. 464].

Thus, if events that are impactful enough to be retained in deep memory can indeed be vertically transmitted to successive generations, then it is those events and emotional inductions that would be most key to humanity's growth, development, and/or demise that would be most likely to be preserved therein. In this way, memory at both the individual and collective level is as influential scholars such as William James (1984) have proposed it to be: an adaptive or functional tool for the survival of the human being. On this point though, I must be clear that my thesis on deep memory and the homin phenomenon overlaps with, but does not entirely agree with, that of anthropologist Dawn Prince-Hughes, who states the following:

> Ape-man experiences are those of a directly experienced, externalized archetype; informed by biological memory and contextualized and made increasingly material in the remembering and retelling of the experiences to receptive and contributing listeners, who are themselves effected by their own memory matrixes. In other words, people out in the woods, going about their business in a natural setting, really do "experience" encounters with the ape-man. They are not hallucinating, they are externalizing—during states of "possessedness"—a set of feelings, ideas, and actions to make sense of a set of internal and external representations [Prince-Hughes, 1997, p. 12].

While I would not be surprised if these externalized archetypes occur in some subset of the experiencer population, I suspect that they do not comprise all contemporary reports of homins throughout the world.

Arguably, deep memory persists even when people attempt to repress or suppress its contents. And while some experiencers are Sasquatch enthusiasts or investigators traversing the outdoors in various ways, many others are self-ascribed non-believers or Sasquatch cynics who have their own seemingly spontaneous encounters. Thus, while I agree with Prince-Hughes's and Vendramini's (2009) assessment that an *archetypal memory* persists of humanity's own evolutionary past with homins, I am not currently of the opinion that such archetypal forms and their cultural-derived continuations are the sole or even primary factor involved in people's encounters. In other words, while there may well be some kind of archetypal basis for people's experiences (cf. Cutchin & Renner, 2020a), it appears to me that some kind of ontological reality to the encounters also exists separate and apart from the human psyche.

I suggest that, coupled with what may be an archetypal memory of our own evolutionary past as (and/or archaic contact alongside) humanlike apes and/or apelike humans, it is the threat to our own survival that these Wholly Other homins pose that is most potent, persisting within deep memory of our species and emerging through us in different ways across time and space.

If the narratives that we have considered herein are any proper measure, then a deep memory of violent and deadly encounters has been etched into humanity's collective consciousness, with each culture that has retained that memory enacting that information differently: either by intentionally maintaining myth and lore about these beings (i.e., through a *mythic mode*), or by encasing any conscious recollection in the thick fog of forgetting (i.e., through a *denialist mode*). It is arguably spaces such as the Bigfooting community that operate at the confluence of these two modes of action toward the homin phenomenon.

It follows that, in part, it is deep memory, as well as its typical mode of preservation via oral history, that I have wished to uphold and honor in this text. According to the Akan tradition of West Africa, we find the aphorism that is oft-stated as simply: *sankofa*. According to sources such as Dr. Quan-Baffour (2012), we find the following derivation for the term: *san* for "return," *ko* for "go," and *fa* for "take," which taken together can therefore mean "go back and reclaim" (pp. 2–3). In Indigenous traditions wherein such a premise is offered, we have an explicit denotation that it takes energy to bring things together (e.g., to bring one's attention to the present moment, to bring one's awareness to attaining to the deeds of one's ancestors, etc.). Like yoga and its ancient Kemetic analogue, *sema tawi* (e.g., Bynum, 2012, pp. 16–17), or unification of the two lands, sankofa is a concept that offers great depth and complexity in terms of its underlying philosophy and embodied practice. Or as Menakem (2021) states with his emphasis on somatic abolitionism, "...it is inside our bodies where ... conflict will need to be resolved" (p. xvii). With these concepts, the movement toward reclamation of a forgotten or unresolved past is the same: at its most basic level, it is that of remembering. Indeed, the individual threads that compose a person, a community, or a system in general might be woven back together across spacetime. In this text, the most basic question that I have posed is simply, "What has the Western psyche attempted to forget with regards to the phenomenon of Sasquatch, and why has it attempted to forget it?"

While some scholars have made the transpersonal significance of deep memory clear elsewhere (e.g., Grof, 2012), it bears repeating that there may well be a reason that people do not tend to have direct and immediate conscious access to the bulk of their own memories, let alone to the memories of any previous states of being that their families, family lines, or species have been through. Given the fact that the *cognitive load* (i.e., the amount of information that we can hold in mind and consider at any given moment) tends to be a limiting factor in our daily lives, and consequences to overloading one's sensorial, cognitive, emotional, or perceptual system may include burnout, fatigue, and depleted resources to respond to the demands of daily living, there is a very real and practical purpose to forgetting things or to at least temporarily displacing information outside of consciousness awareness in order to focus on pertinent matters in the present. Therefore, the denialist mode of deep memory has its place in serving to buffer the psyche against overload.

At the level of the most rudimentary procedural memory (Levine, 2015), consisting of reflexes, habits, and behaviors that are enacted through what has been called muscle memory, we might posit that inborn actions such as grasping, sucking, and the Babinski reflex, which are apparently hardwired in the brain at birth, are somatic representations of deep memory at the broadest level. They are innate, unlearned actions that help the young to survive when they are most vulnerable. Levine discusses three types of procedural memory (i.e., learned motor actions, emergency responses, and approach or avoidance tendencies), and I suggest that each of these types of implicit memory, but particularly the second and third types, may be implicated in this deep memory of human-homin interaction. Key to both my assertions and those of Vendramini (2009), it is not just trauma that can be transmitted from generation to generation, but also information that can aid survival (Levine, 2015, pp. 166–167).

Due to its potential potency, recollection of information from deep memory is at least at times done in *alternative states of consciousness (ASCs)*, such as psychedelic-assisted therapies, or other inducers of ASCs such as holotropic breathwork (Grof, 2012). ASCs are typically comprised of moments wherein one's awareness or attention is not collapsed onto externally oriented behaviors or experience in a typical ego-focused mode. Everyday examples of ASCs include the exceptional human experiences of daydreaming and déjà vu (e.g., White, 1994), though other ASCs can be associated with exceptional experiences. For example, an encounter that Carl Jung and his colleague had in Ravenna, Italy, or the one that he had while riding on a train in Kenya, may be evidence of some deep memory being accessed and projected into the present (Jung, 1989), similar to what Prince-Hughes has proffered as a reason for the homin phenomenon. In these occurrences, some old wellspring of knowledge seems to have briefly sprung to the surface of the mind and to have been reflected there in the outer world.

Deep memory is thereby something that is necessarily irrational and avolitional, at least to an extent, requiring a presence of mind—perhaps a compassionate and courageous approach—that is able to accept what is laid before it, rather than push it away. But deep memory's destructuring nature is precisely the kind of characteristic that makes it potentially problematic to encounter.

In the case of exceptional experiences at the level of the individual, the experient or percipient may find themselves in a state of utter denial, or in what may be considered to be a real-life instantiation of the *refusal of the call* noted in Joseph Campbell's (2008) hero's journey. For example, in an apt parallel to the homin encounter experience, Keith Thompson (1989) posits that UFO encounter experiencers may very well find themselves musing, "If I just keep the memory [of the contact] to myself, maybe it will just go away" (p. 127). We must consider that if numerous individuals are having frightening, or even traumatic, entity encounters across not just years, but millennia, that this attempt to actively suppress the experience may end up displacing it into the unconscious. Thompson's reflection on narratives such as that of Whitley Strieber, who has consciously chosen to accept the call to adventure despite the great terror that it has induced in his life, is key here as he considers that Strieber was "left hanging in the ambiguous margins of being" (p. 127). As an abductee of what he terms the "visitors," Strieber's experience shares themes with other UFO abductees as well as with homin experiencers. One might consider the question: what does one do when their sense of stability and control over who they are is utterly shattered? The sense of liminal Otheredness from oneself is a state that is capable of evoking *spiritual emergency* (Grof & Grof, 1989) in the truest sense. Moreover, it is a state that can be modeled in terms of disparities in one's sense of self and the world, and in terms of agency or lack thereof (Belz & Fach, 2012), and is antithetical to the establishment or continuation of a sense of confidence or stable identity, as the late anthropologist Michael Bradley (1973) might argue.

Importantly, if any large-scale suppression is taking place in a culture wherein there are no generally accepted myths that validate the existence of homins, then the need for displacing the anxiety-producing material would likely be heightened.

However, if there really has been violent human-homin archaic contact, if Cro-Magnons did indeed put an end to the millennia-long reign of terror enforced on early humans by hairy bipeds, and if homin teems have encoded that memory, then David Brewster's following comment for his August 1970 reporting in *Seattle* magazine is quite insightful:

> To some of the Indians in British Columbia, the Sasquatch are the last of a race of giants who have nearly exterminated themselves in warfare. To a Mercer Island [British Columbia] doctor

> who became one of the several Sasquatch scholars in the area, they are the pathetic, last descendants of the Neanderthalers, a race rudely pushed aside during the last Ice Age by Cro-Magnon man (who has always felt guilty about the whole affair) [Brewster, 1970, August, para. 5].

In my estimation, Brewster's words echo those of Heuvelmans (1959) on conflictual archaic contact between humans and homins just as they replicate Vendramini's (2009) assertions about violence between Cro-Magnon and Neanderthal. Moreover, if the guilt that Brewster has described has any bearing on the contemporary collective Western psyche (in particular), then we may understand any reticence toward understanding and re-discovery of homins within this collective in a broader context.

View It from the Bridge

This chapter has covered the threat of death that homins may pose humans, which is argued to be the means through which archaic, at times likely traumatic, encounters between early humans and homins have been preserved into the present. We have seen that Vendramini's Neanderthal predation theory and teem theory posit that early humans were predated upon by Neanderthals—beings whom Vendramini has described whose physical and behavioral features overlap significantly with modern descriptions of homins. Teems are significant emotions encoded in genes that are tied to trauma and other salient stimuli that function as the mechanisms for creating and perpetuating memories of large, dark-colored, hairy bipeds who presented a perceived or actual threat to early humans. Those deep memories are triggered in anatomically modern humans by environmental stimuli, most particularly by the presence of homins who can evoke death anxiety in humans. Oral histories about homins fall in line with the Persistent Multiple Species Hypothesis which posits that many different groups of homins can exist simultaneously in an ecological niche. At the individual level, defense mechanisms operate to protect the ego from consciously dealing with the death anxiety evoked by the presence or potential perception of homins. These concepts and theories that we have considered in this chapter will help to provide the psychological and cultural foundation for the rest of the text. Further, this chapter has dealt with the curse of Bigfoot that has been reported in the written and oral literature. Namely, I have summarized the curse of Bigfoot, which is essentially the totality of negative effects that can occur after people encounter Sasquatch. The curse particularly involves the likelihood of death or misfortune befalling the experiencer or the person's close family or community members. Its most malicious effects (i.e., physical death) are primarily discussed in Indigenous American lore, but other less serious effects are also reported and discussed among European Americans.

This chapter has also covered the concept of deep memory, which is argued to be the means through which archaic, at times likely traumatic, encounters between early humans and homins have been preserved into the present. It has also echoed Vendramini's position about Neanderthal predation theory and teem theory, focusing on the threat of trauma as well as how it has been likely passed down since archaic times. Those deep memories are triggered in anatomically modern humans (i.e., us) by environmental stimuli, most particularly by the presence of homins who can evoke death anxiety in humans. This chapter has also dealt with the matter of approach-avoidance behavior in light of the deep ambivalence that the potential threat that homins can produce within the human psyche.

Before moving on, I would encourage you to pause and consider at least one of the reflective prompts on cognitive, emotional, somatic, or conative matters that I have posed above.

2

Presence, Past and Present

While there may be distinct types of homins around the world (e.g., Coleman & Huyghe, 2006; Sanderson, 2008, p. 13), they are generally said to convey some mixture of traits that are simultaneously similar to anatomically modern humans and yet are also remarkably distinct. Contrary to some Indigenous traditions, homins occupy spaces in the collective Western imagination that are oftentimes separate and apart from the mainstream, the mundane, and the conscious considerations of the populace. To be clear, for the purpose of this text, I use the term "mainstream" to refer to the degree of seriousness with which a subject or person is treated within the context of generally accepted scientific, educational, and media venues. In other words, "mainstream" is not so much about whether an informational unit is recognizable but is more so about how it is received. Therefore, that which is prominent or popular is not necessarily also accepted as valid or true by the masses. Just because of the prevalence of tv shows and films dedicated to paranormal topics does not mean that these same topics are taken seriously by the majority of scientific, academic, or other professional organizations or institutions. Matters such as beliefs and aliefs (i.e., unconscious attitudes) about a subject are therefore important when it comes to mainstream culture.

Moreover, that which is mainstream tends to be hegemonic, and is thereby treated as self-explanatory or as common sense, within a given cultural milieu or sociocultural context. As Boykin et al. (2005) proffer, the European American mainstream is typified by an emphasis on the cognitive elements of the psyche over the affective elements (e.g., by the supremacy of rationality over the irrational), by individual autonomy (e.g., via competitive individualism), by the bifurcated individual (e.g., as in Cartesian dualism, wherein the mind and physical body are viewed as separate and incommensurable elements of the person), and by materialism (i.e., the intellectual acquisition and physical prominence of all things as objects).

As an example, until about December 2017, the subject of ufology was quite familiar—in part through structures such as science fiction media depicting alien invasions and the like—but was associated with ridicule (at times in the guise of skepticism) as opposed to open and honest empiricism.[1] Further, I use the term to refer to the quantity and quality of subjects that originate or are conveyed through those means and modes of communicative memory (Assmann, 2011)—artifacts of culture that allow information to persist in the collective consciousness—and other cultural artifacts that are most prevalent at a given point of time among a group of people. For example, most relevant to the present discussion is the scientific mainstream, which is defined by the conferences, publications, educational institutions, and the like, which are most salient and which have accumulated the greatest power to concretize and delineate the current state of affairs within various scientific disciplines, and also to impact the public's mindset regarding both normative and fringe or borderland subjects of study.

Accordingly, the psychological pull of the various subjects of study under the umbrella of cryptozoology are noted in Brian Regal's poignant commentary. In the introduction to his text, he notes:

> These monsters are apish and disturbingly like us. They have stalked the dark parts of the human psyche, as well as forests, for millennia. If they are real, they are older than we are, yet they leave behind only footprints and questions [Regal, 2011, p. 7].

While, as we have seen, there is much more to indicate homins' presence than "only footprints and questions," the general tone and tenor of Regal's comments are well-stated. We now turn to a more in-depth discussion of the fringed disciplines that have featured Sasquatch and other homins as well as some of the evidence found therein.

The tendency among naturalistic cryptozoology is to propose a hominoid provenance of sightings, thereby suggesting a non-human lineage (e.g., through the great ape hypothesis; Bindernagel, 1998, 2010). Where cryptozoology posits a non-human origin of its subjects of study, hominology focuses specifically upon the study of upright, bipedal beings, tending to propose that they fall directly within the human line and are therefore hominins or, more generally, that evidence of their persistence is to be found throughout religion, mythology, folklore, and eyewitness accounts (e.g., Bayanov, 2014; Bayanov & Murphy, 2017). Of particular import, Bayanov (2012, p. 40) proposes:

> Cryptids are usually hidden in forests, mountains, lakes and oceans. The object of this research is likely hidden in natural forests and mountains, but above all it lurks hidden in the "forests of the mind." If not for these forests, the problem might have been resolved long ago. The task of hominology is to take the creature out of these dark forests and into the light of objectivity.

Bayanov's position is both philosophically and psychologically inclined, as it posits the very real necessity for an effective hominological (as well as cryptozoological) endeavor to address and understand the minds of the people who impact these fields. Consequently, one convergence between both fields was the tendency to take quite seriously the contentions found in folklore, historical archives, eyewitness reports, and the like, of Indigenous and traditional cultures (e.g., Bayanov, 2014; Sanderson, 2008).[2]

Despite their otherwise divergent opinions on the subject of homins, scholars such as Bindernagel (2010) and Naish (2014, September 17, 2016) suggest that the discipline of cryptozoology has tended to be as much about the humans who do—as well as those humans who do not—pursue it as it is about the enigmatic subjects of study themselves. This point is not one to be taken lightly.

Unfortunately for those who wish to continue to deny the existence of homins, the evidence in their favor amounts to veritable mountains rather than molehills. However, such treasure troves of data are treated as what Jack Hunter (2021a) has termed *damned data*, with their evidentiary value consigned, at least for the time being, to the frayed fringes and forgotten forests of the collective Western consciousness.

Homin Appearance

The physical differences apparent between homins and humans would be immediately perceivable in features such as hair and size. With the modern homin phenomenon, the most obviously notable characteristic of these beings has been their large foot size. Some insightful data on this matter emerges from a dataset primarily compiled over four decades by Canadian journalist and Sasquatch researcher John Willison Green (1927–2016). Retired zoologist and hominologist Wolf Henner Fahrenbach analyzed these data, including some of the descriptive statistics (e.g., means (*m*) and standard deviations (sd) from some of Green's population (*N*) datasets): (a) from an *N* of 706, a foot length of *m*=15.6"(sd=3.1");[3] (b) from an *N* of 438, a ball width of *m*=7.2"(sd=1.69"); (c) from an *N* of 123, a heel width of 4.83"(sd=1.17"); from an *N* of 89, a height of *m*=8.1' (sd=15"; Fahrenbach, 1997–1998).[4] Fahrenbach's analyses of these data as well as additional variables such as gait, height, weight, and more indicate that, while purported homin data overlap with those of anatomically modern humans and higher primates, that they diverge enough to indicate a separate and distinct population of beings.

Using the tools of modern forensic anthropology and some well-placed speculation, Vendramini (2009) paints an intriguing picture of what our early competitors on the Levant may have looked like—a picture that is particularly relevant for our present discussion:

> From a distance, an approaching Neanderthal would instantly strike you as alien, resembling a tall, heavily muscled gorilla, rendered even more massive by its thick coat of extra long and thick fur. *You would feel as if you have just come across the abominable snowman or bigfoot* [Vendramini, 2009, p. 83, emphasis added].

Vendramini's rendition is quite interesting given the distinct overlap present in his commentary and the general description of homins the world over. As others have posited, comparing Neanderthals to Sasquatch, the former beings could have posed a significant physical challenge to early humans, with bodies that were built for sprinting more than long distance running, and with arms that could potentially throw spears rather well in a manner similar to the way in which baseball pitchers or football quarterbacks hurl objects (Brown et al., 2024, March 3).

Representing the disagreement about what the *almas* or almasty are (e.g., Coleman & Huyghe, 2006), scholars such as Bradley (1991) have posited that these homins represent a modern holdover of the Neanderthal, and hominologists such as Koffmann (e.g., Koffmann, 2014 as cited in Bayanov, 2014), Bayanov (2014), and Burtsev (e.g., Margaryan et al., 2021) have uncovered folkloric and forensic evidence in support of the continued existence of the almas. Vendramini's (2009) description is an exceptionally apt one. This convergence in theories has occurred despite the fact that he does not subscribe to the position that modern reports of homins are due to the actual existence of any non-human hominids in the present era.

Many of the features that Coleman and Huyghe (2006) associate with Neanderthal, including a heavy brow ridge, bowlegged stance, and stocky and muscular build, overlap with other depictions of Neanderthal, including that which Vendramini and digital sculptor Arturo Balseiro have constructed (Vendramini, 2009).[5] Importantly, that overlap includes Neanderthal being covered with hair, which is an interesting corroboration of modern reports of extant homins around the world. However, there is divergence between these sources on the matter of facial features (and ontology of modern reports), where Vendramini (2009) advocates for a decidedly non-human appearance, including something more akin to a non-human primate. For example, he posits a pug nose (2009, p. 88) while Patrick and Huyghe favor a hooded "large, broad nose," (2006, p. 25).

Further, while homins are variously described along a continuum from ape-like humans to humanlike apes, a significant subset of them fits quite well with Vendramini's (2009) overall description. Where he points to Neanderthals as apex predators in their ecological niche, Pruitt (2023) points to Sasquatch as most likely being ambush predators. Both groups of homins are said to either have cannibalized humans, have cannibalized each other, or both. If large, (potentially) hairy homins have indeed predated upon humans, such a scenario may well have presented significant selective pressures for humans across at least the past 100,000 years or so of our evolutionary history.

Vendramini (2009) proposes that Cro-Magnons, a more evolved form of the earlier Levantine humans who were predated upon by Neanderthals, took on many of the hyper-aggressive, unemotional, and calculating dispositions of their former attackers, hunting them to extinction from the Levant and then across Europe.

As Cindy Hsin-Yee Huang puts it simply and poignantly in *Sapiens*, "What neanderthals looked like has always mattered. More than just accompanying artwork, Neanderthal visualizations represent a touchstone for what it means to be human" (Huang, 2024, February 21, para. 9). This matter of the boundaries that define and describe the outline of humanity is precisely the point that we find ourselves at again and again, and those boundaries are culturally defined, perhaps in part at least through the deep memory that said culture encodes.

Further regarding the general physical appearance of the Sasquatch of North America, we consider a narrative taken down by investigator Bart Nunnelly who interviewed a Cherokee gentleman who simply wanted to be known as "M.F." Relating what the "Old people of the forest" look like after over a decade of continuously observing them in the 1960s while they foraged, M.F.'s description fits the historical and contemporary eyewitness narratives quite well (Nunnelly as cited by Coleman, 2006, December 27):

> They had black skin and an average size of eight to ten feet tall, although he had seen one awhile back that was at least a twelve footer. Their eyes were a dark brown color with no visible whites or irises. They were bearded, had thin lips, a weak chin and a flat, wide nose like individuals of African descent. They had normal looking hands of a large size with pale

> colored palms, but their feet had an opposing toe sticking out at an angle away from the other four toes, like an ape's or chimp's. They had extremely long arms which hung down past their knees and could run quadrupedally 35 to 40 mph. The females also possessed beards, though shorter than the males. They were of more stocky build, had furry breasts[6] and carried their young beneath them clinging to their bellies. He described the males as being covered with short, straight, usually dark hair, with longer areas of about six inches at the beard, backs of the head and genital areas.

While conflation (i.e., unintentionally merging two different experiences from two different sources) or source misattribution (i.e., thinking information was learned from one source when it was actually learned somewhere else) cannot, per se, be discounted in the above narrative, statements such as the note that females had "furry breasts" match well with what is seen or heard of in other narratives and evidence (e.g., Alley, 2018, p. 72). For instance, "Patty," the famous subject from the PGF (i.e., Patterson-Gimlin film) from 1967, stands among those encountered homins who demonstrate such anatomy.

In terms of their hair color, John Green's data reported by Meldrum (2006, p. 213) suggest the following ratios within the population: 50 percent are dark or black color; 25 percent are brown; 15 percent are light in color; and 8 percent are gray.[7] Pyle's (2017) introduction to his text *Where Bigfoot Walks* lists reported colors of the homins as russet, gray, beige, black, and brown. The *Bigfoot Field Research Organization (BFRO)* is currently the largest association that collects reports across North America. The organization supports a three-tier classification system for reports that a number of investigators and field researchers both inside and outside of the BFRO have adopted: (a) *Class C* encounters are defined as those that are from secondhand sources, thirdhand sources, and sources of unknown provenance; (b) *Class B* encounters are defined as firsthand encounters that do not involve a clear and relatively close visual sighting of the subject, and therefore may include other sensory information (e.g., auditory, olfactory, etc.); and (c) *Class A* encounters, the gold standard of eyewitness reports, are defined as those instances wherein clear visual evidence is obtained making the probability of misidentification or hoaxing extremely low (Baranchok, 2023, December 11; BFRO, n.d.).[8] The system can be a helpful guide to categorize the quality of reports for both experiencers and investigators. In cases where it is relevant and reasonable to do so, I use the same system within this book to categorize evidence. And unless otherwise stated, the experiencer narratives that I share are all Class A encounters.

But returning to the matter of physical appearance, the BFRO also states on the Anatomy page of its website that 50 percent of hair—not fur—tends to be:

> black or dark ... through various shades of reddish-brown and gray to white. The body can have varicolored patches of hair. Older animals have increasingly grey hair, though color does not appear to change from childhood to adulthood. Hair is variously glossy clean and shiny, fluffy, or dirty, matted and unkempt ("angora goat dreadlocks" [Fahrenbach, 1997–1998]), probably a function of native curliness, age, or of recent immersion in water or lack thereof. Females have been reported to be cleaner than males.

Other sources concur that paler individuals are likely those who are more advanced in age (e.g., Matthews, 2024, p. 115). Moreover, the findings that Sasquatch hair lack a medulla (e.g., King-Sharp, 2024, April 14) and tend to taper at the end have helped to spur the interest of field investigators looking to assess the anatomy of hair samples retrieved in the field. Further, Matt Pruitt's (2023) coverage of the hair color of these beings across North America largely maps onto the above data. He adds the following, suggesting a potential relationship between hair color and size of the subjects: "juvenile individuals are consistently reported as black or near-black, trending towards dark brown or red in sub adults, brown or cinnamon in adults, and gray in the largest and most massive individuals" (p. 185). Still others have suggested that the color of the hair changes depending on the age of the entity (e.g., Germer, 2024, January 26), the season of the year, or the region in which they are seen (Newkirk & Newkirk, 2024, December 30).

Additionally, the BFRO states the following information about skin color reported on Sasquatch:

> Skin color ranges from the deepest black or charcoal to deep brown, "sunburned" reddish brown, and gray. Some areas, like the nose, appear at times in a shiny, oily black color. The palms are lighter in color, and the soles of the feet quite light, presumably as a result of thick sole pads composed, as in other primates, of fat and connective tissue. A few albinistic sasquatches have been seen, whose skin color was pink.[9]

Several considerations arise with this summary description. Of note, of course, is the fact that according to sources such as journalist John Green's 3,000 or so reports (which have now been incorporated into Scott Tompkins's free and publicly available *Bigfoot Mapping Project* database), at least half of all sightings are of beings with dark-colored (i.e., black or brown) hair, and that reports tend to note dark-colored skin as well. Elsewhere, we find corroborating assertions (e.g., Short, 2024, p. 14).

Or, according to well-known extended experiencer Janice Carter Coy, as she comments on the homins, who are found in her area of eastern Tennessee, "Bigfoot skin is black like old saddle leather." She states,

> Their skin is not oily and they don't have wrinkles or pock marks on them. The skin is also dry looking to me, but I'm not meaning, in any sense of the word, that the skin has any appearance of flakiness. It is a good bit like our skin is and will show highlights in the sun. They don't have a ridge going to their ears. They do have a ridge above the pronounced brow ridge that goes around the skull under the hair on their heads. It doesn't show well because of the hair. It is necessary to clarify that Fox's hair is black and shiny in color and in the sun exhibits some blue highlights around the upper portions of his body [Green & Coy, 2001, p. 131].

Similarly, while Wes Germer's *Sasquatch Chronicles* podcast does not present any statistical mode of analysis regarding data, the media footprint (no pun intended) and sample size of experiencers within the show are worth noting. During one episode (2021, March 5a), an Alabaman experiencer who saw a chocolate brown-colored homin on the side of a road behind a stand of young pine trees asked Germer to comment on his assessment of the general color of these beings. Germer replied with the following statement:[10]

> I've actually had reports of them being brown.... I would say black is probably the most common color, and then the auburn (kind of the reddish color people talk about). and then the gray seems to be the ... next. Most people describe the face being kind of gray looking—kind of that battleship gray color.... But I have heard of it being that chocolate brown ... in between black and like a true brown, kind of a chocolate brown.

In essence then, Germer's position supports the general notion that homins (at least of North America) tend to be darker in color, with the majority ranging from black to brown.

In this brief survey of colors reported of homins, we turn next to consummate Russian-French hominologist Marie-Jeanne Koffmann's (1919–2021) summary of this characteristic reported in sightings of the almasty which are reported to live in and around the Caucasus mountains. She states,

> "Where there is no fur, the skin is black" (Δ 52k). "The skin of the face is black" (♀ 54k) "The skin of the palm of the hands is dark reddish brown.... On the buttocks, the fur is absent, the skin is dark reddish brown" (x 141k).[11]

One Indigenous American extended experiencer by the name of Suzy reports having had years of contact with a family of Sasquatch when she was younger. As a neglected only child growing up with her mother and alcoholic stepfather in Maine in the late 1950s and early 1960s, she spent a lot of time by herself outdoors. The elder Sasquatch and his kind are described as follows:

> Their hair changed with the seasons. In summer, it was a lighter brownish-red, deepening towards a mahogany color in the winter, with fine long hair growing longest between neck and head. The hair of their undercoat is almost fluffy when seen on its own. During the winter, the hair on their faces increases. Their eyes are round—not oval like the human eye tends to be. [Suzy] doesn't recall seeing the whites of their eyes: just darkness under their brows. An interesting quality she mentioned is that their eyes give a red glow at night, allowing her to locate [the elder] even in complete darkness. Their skin is dark and brown, heavily pigmented: very unlike Caucasian skin tone. The heel, sole, and sides of their feet are free of hair. They appear flatfooted with no noticeable arch. Their hands are very large with long fingers. They are tall, but not outlandishly so. She remembers [the elder] and his mate being six-to-seven feet tall.
>
> Their vocalizations vary from a deep roar to conversational or inquiring noises, including the grunts she and [the elder] used to communicate. They move quickly and silently, unless trying to intimidate. They regularly travel distances for important things like food.
>
> She remembers realizing at about 9 or 10 years old: "I was old enough to know that this wasn't an animal. It," I thought, "was more like a human. Only it was a very big human. But it wasn't a human." Because at that age, I knew then that they weren't something that was a normal thing you saw [Hilsmeyer, 2017].

Suzy's description maps onto both Class A and Class B sightings that have been recorded in databases such as that which the BFRO maintains. While there are indeed exceptions to the general rule, the statement that the elder male's skin was not like that of a Caucasian's is telling and describes the tendency for Sasquatch reports to describe them as being relatively darkly melanated in their hair, skin, or both. Suzy's encounters were all the more powerful because of her domestic situation: as stated in the narrative, her mother neglected her and her stepfather was physically and verbally abusive. As such, the relationship that she reflects on having built with the elder Sasquatch and his consort over a number of years was extremely meaningful to her. When her mother abruptly moved her away from that home to get them both away from her stepfather, Suzy was understandably mournful.

As a detailed encounter from whitetail deer hunter Michael Bleuler of Biloxi, Mississippi, provides, he describes the following of his encounter while hunting a powerline on December 16, 2020, about 27 minutes into his interview with Mike Paterson of *Sasquatch Ontario*:

> There was a point where he did, like, a yawn. I don't know if that's something what they do, but when he yawned, that's when I got to see his teeth. His teeth: they were square like ours. Not exactly like ours ... they were like big, square Chiclets ... kind of like horse teeth, but ... even wider and thicker than that. The inside of his mouth—his gums—were like either black or really dark, dark purple. The hair ... on the top of his head was nothing like the hair on his chest or his back ... the hair on top of the head was just spiky. Like a gorilla. It didn't have long hair on the top of the head [Paterson, 2023, March 28].

Further, aside from the estimated size of the being, the following encounter that John Bindernagel (2010, p. 34) discusses is indicative of some of the general anatomical and experiential characteristics that have come to be associated with Sasquatch. It was originally reported in the *Daily Democrat* of Woodland, California, on April 9, 1891:

> Mr. Smith describes the animal as being about six feet high when standing, which it did not do perfectly but bent over, after the manner of a bear. Its head was very much like that of a human being. The trapezie [*sic*] muscles were very thick and aided much in giving the animal its brutal look. The brow was low and contracted, while the eyes were deep set, giving it a wicked look. It was covered with long shaggy hair, except the head, where the hair was black and curly.

The stature, combination of anatomically modern and more archaic traits, color and length of the hair, as well as the imposing frame and countenance of the subject in Mr. Smith's encounter are good matches for the general manner in which Sasquatch has been described. Indeed, the comment that experiencers often make that the subjects look like they have no neck dovetails well with the report of extremely thick trapezius muscles where that tissue obscures visibility of the neck. The tendency toward a clearly visible neck within anatomically modern humans has, in Vendramini's (2009) thinking, contributed to a more readily distinguishable physique between humans and Neanderthals. The same general argument can be made of the distinction between humans and other extant homins, given accounts such as the above narrative that discusses the heavily muscled trapezii and the thickness of the sternocleidomastoids that tends to be reported in firsthand accounts. Sasquatch and other homins have been associated with all of the above physical and/or psychological characteristics, and therefore, according to theories such as Vendramini's (2009; i.e., which posits unconscious triggers from persisting teems), any unconscious and/or conscious association with large, hairy bipedal beings could activate defenses within the human psyche. The more gracile features of modern humans would surely stand in stark contrast to the more robust features of homins, and contact with these homins or with aspects of their features would likely trigger homin teems within the percipient.

It is possible that at least some groups of humans are marginalized or Othered because of an unconscious association with those homins who, at least at times, are said to demonstrate these very same traits. For example, let us consider the matter of Down syndrome. When it comes to reports of facial characteristics that tend to generalize among certain groups, there is at least a small subset of reports wherein eyewitnesses are reminded of some of the facial features that tend to be found in Down syndrome among anatomically modern humans (e.g., Karnafel, 2023, December 15; Byron, 2025, March 7, 41:34–42:33; Byron, 2025, April 22, 33:51–34:10). For example, transpersonal psychotherapist and extended experiencer Brian McCormack describes an encounter with a female homin on Staten Island, of all places, wherein the entity "looked like she had Down Syndrome" (Byron, 2024, July 8, 24:00). Moreover, there have been reports of humans with Down syndrome being tended to by Sasquatch. In one illuminating narrative, the individual submitting the report (simply referring to himself as "Doctor-in-law to the Kooks") was the brother-in-law of someone with Down syndrome, Jamie, the latter of whom had seemed to have established a long-term friendship of sorts with the matriarch of a Sasquatch family (Warren, 2024, March 8). The report refers to a series of events that took place in Ohio in 1982. To paraphrase our doctor-in-law, the group of Sasquatch may have accepted Jamie's presence because they perceived or sensed that he was different.

Regarding autism and autistic savantism, there is some compelling work that Christopher Noël (e.g., 2022) has presented. Those characteristics reported in the homin literature are many, but they include *echolalia*, which is repetition of sounds and noises in one's environment (e.g., LeGro, 2021, July 15; Noël, 2022; Warren, 2023, November 17, 28:00)[12] as well as aversion to change, or as Noël (2022, p. 44) puts it, a focus on imposing or requiring structure, order, and arrangement upon or from the environment (LeGro, 2021, July 15).

Where Vendramini's theory posits a deep and extreme impact on human development as a result of being predated upon by Neanderthals, Noël's Sasquatch Savantism theory posits a different approach: that Sasquatch may be descendants of Denisovans or Neanderthals and may have developed some highly specialized traits that overlap in significant ways with human savantism as a result of living alongside humans that belies a constellation of approach and avoidance behaviors. Moreover, Noël suggests that in our shared or common ancestors, autistic-like traits would have granted a survival advantage or evolutionary fitness. If such traits were indeed advantageous in certain natural and/or built environments, then that may help to explain why such traits have been retained among both humans and homins.

Further, if we modify Vendramini's suggestion that Neanderthals were wiped out and instead posit that they were decimated, and if we also suggest that humans were as impactful on homin evolution as they were on us, then we can paint a more complete picture of how we have impacted each other evolutionarily in this great matrix of life on our shared planet.

In all, Noël's position on the savantism theory seems quite reasonable, demonstrating heuristic value in connecting a number of seemingly disparate elements of Sasquatch behavior. We will return to Noël's work elsewhere in the text as well.

World Lore

As aforementioned, journalist John Green wrote 3,000 reports: reports which are now housed on the *Bigfoot Mapping Project* thanks to significant effort by GIS analyst, project creator, and Sasquatch podcaster Scott Tompkins. Tompkins summarizes the efforts of the Project in an article that he has published with the *Relict Hominoid Inquiry* (Tompkins, 2021) and continues his efforts to collate and disseminate relevant, crowdsourced information to the public regarding Sasquatch encounters and reports. Elsewhere in the Americas, reports of bipedal beings such as the *mapinguari* or *ucumar* are found from the tip of Alaska down through Patagonia in South America (e.g., McGrath, 2022; Newton, 2005). The Caribbean even boasts of its own storied hairy hominoids, including the *yeho* of the Bahamas (Newton, 2005, pp. 499–500). Westward across the Pacific Ocean, the *aikanaka* and *menehune* may be homin-like beings of smaller stature (i.e., standing from two to three feet tall) reported in the lore and contemporary history of the Hawaiian Islands (Coleman & Huyghe, 2006; Dixon, 2004; Prince-Hughes, 1997; Short, 2024), the *maeroero* is said to exist in New Zealand (Prince-Hughes, 1997), and the yowie, *yay-ho*, or yahoo is a towering hairy biped reported in Indigenous and colonial narratives from Australia (Coleman & Huyghe, 2006;[13] Healy & Cropper, 2006, 2023; Newton, 2005; Opit & Byrnes, 2009). In the words of Australian zoologist, cryptozoologist, author (e.g., Opit & Byrnes, 2009), and radio host Gary Opit, who shares the following counterpoint about homins from halfway around the world:

> The ... original Australians ... every single, ah, language group had very detailed ... information and names on ... at least two species of unknown relict hominid in Australia. We generally know the large ... species that ... stand around about two to three metres ... in height. Then there's also very large numbers of reports of a very small species ... that only stands a metre or so high (so around about four feet). And so, there's also a possibility that it's some kind of marsupial ape, which is particularly interesting because some of the early reports described these Australian bigfoot as having a pouch with a young one [Kaldy, 2020, 30:09–31:05].

Elsewhere in Oceania northward into southeast Asia are reports of hairy bipeds, including the *orang pendek* and *lai ho'a* of Indonesia (Forth, 2005), as well as the *hibagon* of Japan (Documentaries–Crash-Course Cryptozoology, 2023, October 9; Newton, 2005). In eastern Eurasian literature and oral history are reports of the almasty, *yeren*, *rusalka*, and barmanu (e.g., Bayanov, 2014; Martinez, 2011/2017; McGrath, 2022). Of course, the yeti or meh-teh, also known as the abominable snowman, is perhaps the most famous cousin of the North American Sasquatch (Porshnev, 2000, p. 31; Sanderson, 2008) found within Eurasia, and the yeren of China is well-known around the world as well (e.g., Meldrum & Guoxing, 2012). While reports from western Eurasia may not be as well known, narratives of beings such as the woodwose of Scandinavia (e.g., Cutchin & Renner, 2020a) and the *basajaun* of the Basque region of Spain are perhaps more familiar to people. (McGrath, 2022). And last but certainly not least, the vast continent of Africa contains its own assortment of homins such as the *otang*, *ogo*, and *agogwe* (e.g., Patterson, 2020), as well as the *muhalu*, *kakundakari*, and *sehite* (Prince-Hughes, 1997). As an insightful example of what homins exist in Africa, Gareth Patterson (1963–2026) turns to the words of the late, esteemed Zulu healer and wisdom keeper, Credo Mutwa, who shares the following in an interview:

> Sir, in the country called Zimbabwe, where I had my encounter in 1959, there is also another creature. This is the most amazing creature, and I saw it once, and so did several other people, some Black and some White, who were with me. This creature is a huge creature, and shaped

> exactly like a gorilla, but it is unlike a gorilla, which often walks on its feet, as well as on its knuckles. The creature I'm talking about, sir, stands about 8 feet or 9 feet high, and is built exactly like a gorilla, but its body is very powerful. Its shoulders are very wide, its neck is very thick. It is covered with thick, rough fur, like no other wild animal in Africa. It is a humanoid creature, with thighs and legs and feet, as well as arms and hands which look exactly like those of a human being, only covered with a heavy mat of dark-brown fur. This creature, sir, is known as Ogo by the people of Zimbabwe. And schools of people have seen this creature, hundreds over the many generations. Some of these creatures have been seen right here in South Africa, in isolated bushy and mountainous places. And these Ogo are, detail for detail, exactly like what the Native American people of the Northwestern United States call a Sasquatch or Bigfoot. In fact, I say it is the same creature and we have it right here in southern Africa. It is also exactly the same creature, but with a totally different skin color, as the one that is seen by the people of Nepal on the slopes of the Himalaya mountains, the creature that is called a Yeti [Martin, 1999, September 30].

Credo Mutwa was not one to mince words, nor was he one to speak hyperbolically or in the abstract. My sense of him is that he spoke with great care to accurately represent what he knew, both from his own experience and from the lineages that he carried in his spirit. Consequently, I have decided to include this particular segment of his interview because he speaks directly to the commonality of homin descriptions that are present in sightings across time and space. Indeed, Jeff Glickman, forensic examiner and information technologist who worked for the North American Science Institute to attempt to disprove evidence of Sasquatch, states the following:

> [Big hairy monster] BHM myths are thought to have existed for as long as humans have had language. Pliny [the Elder] reports an encounter with a BHM in 0 AD. There is no reason for us to expect that a universal myth that transcends cultures and time should disappear from use in modern times [Glickman, 1998, p. 32].

Further complicating matters, in Sanderson's (2008) thinking, the hominoid evolutionary tree was constructed as follows, in descending order from modern man to the sub-hominids: (a) modern man (consisting of Australoids, Mongoloids, Negroids, Caucasoids, etc.); (b) ancient man and proto-pygmies (the latter of which give rise to African and "Oriental" ABSMs including the Agogwe and Teh-lma); (c) sub-men, neo-giants (which give rise to American and Asiatic ABSMs, including Sasquatch, Sisimite, and Tok), and Neanderthals (which give rise to the Western and Eastern *kaptar* and Eastern *almas*, among others); (d) apelike submen (which included the Gigantopithecines and the Pithecanthrioines). Finally, the sub-hominids such as the Australopithecines form another lineage tied to the pongids, among which some ABSMs such as the Meh-Teh are included (e.g., Sanderson, 2008).

It is also worth noting that there have been some attempts to determine general physical characteristics of hairy, bipedal beings. Some agreement across sighting reports and older narratives concerns the typically bipedal mode of locomotion, the body covered predominantly in hair, the relatively long arms compared to the length of the legs, the prominent brow ridge, the generally human-looking hands, the broad feet with in-line toes, the *mid-tarsal break* of the foot,[14] and the typically dark-colored skin. The *sagittal crest*, presenting as a bony protuberance that runs lengthwise (i.e., sagittally) along the midline of the skull is present in some eyewitness reports, and is related to the overall size of the being. The crest is present in great apes such as silverback gorillas. Noting such similarities across some of the extant literature led the late John Bindernagel to create a profile of Sasquatch that is based on some of the most commonly reported features (Bindernagel, 2010).

Field biologist Ranae Holland of *Finding Bigfoot* fame reflects:

> If I look at the whole historical record ... which is the oral traditions of Indigenous people around the world ... the majority of them say it's not a flesh-and-blood animal. It's something beyond science. Call it what you will. My beliefs align much more in that realm than [it being] a biological species [King-Sharp & Barnett, 2024, April 1, 35:17–35:35].

While there may be differences in how Sasquatch is conceived among those who are memorykeepers, experiencers, or pursuers of the subject, there is general consensus around the world that the homin phenomenon is an ancient one indeed. Thus, any implication that the subject of Sasquatch is only an invention of 20th-century Western popular culture (e.g., Buhs, 2009), particularly post 1958, is as unfounded as it is ethnocentric.

Following this discussion, we come to examine luminaries such as cryptozoologist Ivan T. Sanderson (2008) and hominologist Dmitri Bayanov (2014), who have also established that a wealth of data exists within narratives of these beings, that such narratives have served as much of the basis for scientific inquiry into the existence of previously undiscovered organisms the world over, and that simply setting them aside would be—or rather, has been—a catastrophic error that derails the pursuit of legitimate (and revolutionary) science. The marginalization and maligning of such narratives is precisely why the late wildlife biologist John Bindernagel (2010) was able to say that the Sasquatch was still considered an anomaly, "unrecognized as an existing North American mammal species in 2010" (p. 206).

Given the case of the almas of central Eurasia, it is insightful to consider the various names ascribed to other homins in the area. For example, Bradley shares the following:

> Continuing east across Afghanistan, the Uzbek, Tadzhik, Kirghiz and Kazakh S.S.R.'s, and across the Badakshan Autonomous Area, there are literally hundreds of reports of creatures similar to the Caucasus *Kaptar.* Most of these reports were collected by the 1958 Russian expedition. Depending upon the local language, these creatures are called *Gul-Biavan, Dev, Almas.* In general, witnesses say that they are the size of a small man, covered with reddish brown hair or fur, have very broad and heavy feet and seem to have a primitive form of language. Caves are their favourite homes and they have been seen to use simple tools [Bradley, 1991, p. 99].

The above excerpt provides some awareness of the degree of variation that can be seen not just in the names of homins, but in their size and culture. While the matter of relatively large homins is the subject of the present book, the matter of smaller ones known variously by names such as littlefoot (Healy & Cropper, 2006) and other nomenclature, is one that is quite important and interesting, yet extends beyond the remit of this text. Elsewhere around the globe, in addition to the kinds of narratives discussed above by Credo Mutwa, there are other similarities that are found in local and Indigenous folklore as well as world mythology (e.g., Heuvelmans, 2016, p. 261). Aside from homins tending to be more or less hairy, from Enkidu of the ancient *Epic of Gilgamesh* through modern narratives such as the skunk ape to the barmanu, they are also said to have long arms and to interact with humans in some rather specific ways.

Central to his thesis, Vendramini also suggests that these Neanderthals, far from looking like the cavemen that they are often portrayed as, may well have had eyes that glow at night due to the development of a tapetum lucidum, a heavy brow ridge, kyphotic (i.e., stooped) posture, dark fur covering their bodies, *leathery skin* more so resembling that of the great apes, extremely robust musculature, and that given the length of their vocal cords, they were likely to have a deep timbre to their voice, producing guttural growls that would likely not reach the level of articulation that anatomically modern humans have attained. Importantly, it must be noted that each of these features is distinct from attributes that fully modern humans have and yet is coterminous with contemporary reports of homins from around the world. Sasquatch are often said to have glowing eyes of varying colors (e.g., Warren, 2024, April 19), to have pronounced brows, to stand and walk with a forward lean, to sport skin and long hair that tends to be darkly colored, too often look like bodybuilders, and to produce vocalizations that are deep, throaty, and exceptionally loud. Importantly, the author states, "Humans everywhere consider a slouched ape-like walk, typified by hunched shoulders, rigid torso, bow-legged, forward lean and loosely swinging arms as physically unattractive" (p. 135). Indeed, when it comes to impressions that North American homins tend to leave on witnesses (or at least those witnesses of European stock), the perception is often one of monstrosity and abnormality, which are characteristics that tend to be conferred upon liminal entities in general.

Indigenous American Tradition and Lore

Oral tradition, purveyor of much of this damned data throughout the world, can be characterized as the culturally grounded impetus for maintaining history through the spoken word and its various implements. It has been defined as "a preference for oral/aural modes of communication in which both listening and speaking are treated as performances and in which oral virtuosity—the ability to use alliterative, metaphorically colorful, graphic forms of spoken language—is emphasized and cultivated" (Boykin, 1986, p. 61). Accordingly, the communication of the past becomes participatory in nature, co-constructed in the present between audience and speaker.

With its fluidity and depth, however, the oral tradition has operated in orthogonal (i.e., perpendicular, literally at right angles to) opposition in the Western psyche to the maintenance of a clear, stable, and linear epistemology—that is, one that creates, retains, and accesses information and knowledge primarily through a different mode.

As anthropologist Dr. Marimba Ani (2007) might argue, for the collective European psyche, myths represent a dangerous precept of becoming—rather than being—where historical and scientific fact are not cleanly separated from legend, metaphor, and the perceived messiness that oral history can bring with it. In other words, myth viewed in this manner may present a kind of destructuring conundrum: it is not easily defined or confined to basic and reductionist categories held within the dominant European or European American cultural paradigm. As anthropologist Gregory Forth reflects in a commentary on the separation of myth and science relevant to his area of inquiry (i.e., homins in the Indonesian islands), he states that the term myth "can also be understood in the more popular sense of an 'untruth' or "idea without foundation.'" (Forth, 2023, p. 1). Therefore, within the Western cultural milieu, myth is often relegated to the scientific sidelines, to the arena of unsubstantiated flimflam, and to the musings of the uneducated and ignorant—quite the diametric opposite of myth's beginnings. Indeed, by necessity, oral history (e.g., in Homer's epic poetry) and the mythology that it encodes have required quite sophisticated ways of committing information to memory that were not really needed with the later advent of written history (e.g., in Plato's treatises).

One such data point involves the tendency within Indigenous American cultures to speak of homins as people rather than as animals, the latter of which tends to be done within Western culture. For example, anthropologist Ed Fusch (1992, p. 18) states the following of the philosophy on Sasquatch among the Colville Indigenous Americans:

> Among the various tribes comprising the Colville Confederation, Sasquatch was referred to by several different names but a conceptual thread permeates all of their beliefs. He was always considered a human being, members of their own species. Prior to the arrival of the white man, the only people known to the Indians were other Indians and Sasquatch.
>
> The Lake Band of Indians called him "Skanicum" which translates to "Stick Indian." Some Indians referred to him as "Scwe-ney-tum," derived from the original sc'wanay'tex meaning "stick (= woods) Indian."

Thus, according to this interpretation of the Colville account, Sasquatch were similar to (rather than distinct from) humans. Such a narrative runs counter to many of the more prominent suppositions that have dominated in the field of cryptozoology since Sasquatch/Bigfoot came back into popular consciousness in the late 1950s.

Or, in a more sinister turn of their uncanny relationship with humans, Fred Roehl—Curyung Tribal Council member, extended experiencer, and host of the *Subarctic Alaska Sasquatch* channel and website—states:

> I was raised with the knowledge. You know, we were warned as kids. You know, especially my Aunt Lucy. Rest in peace.... She was the main one back ... when we were little when everyone would be off to fish camp and what not, and we were too young. Um, she would watch us at my grandma's house. And she would always warn us, you know, "Watch out for the Hairy Man. The Hairy Man will snatch you." But, you know, as a little kid, you don't realize the reality of it [Karnafel, 2024, November 7, 7:42–8:08].

The varied narratives often speak to the mythological truths or deep memory that is at the core of the human experience of the phenomenon.

Much has been written elsewhere to support the existence of homins (e.g., Meldrum, 2006; Bindernagel, 2010). The deep history of mythological, cosmological, and folkloric narratives of these beings from all over the world offers a wealth of information that is both culturally and regionally specific and is also relatively universal: while there are ethnographic differences in how these beings are reported to look or are said to act, both giant and diminutive hairy humanlike beings are said to exist almost everywhere on the planet outside of the north and south poles. In North America alone, well over 100 distinct Indigenous American names refer to a variety of homin figures, often translated as *Hairy Man* or Elder Brother (e.g., Alley, 2018; Strain, 2008). For example, the late nurse, extended experiencer, and hominologist Bobbie Short (1936–2013) reports in her posthumously published *The De Facto Sasquatch* that for the Dena'ina (from the Chickaloon region of Alaska), the *gilyuk*, "was not a legendary creature."

> [The Dena'ina's] father's grandfathers told them he was a reality and they spoke of the Gilyuk people with all the same realities as the bear and wolf. *Gilyuk*, they said, was a shaggy haired giant who wore a little hat and ate man, woman and children [Short, n.d., p. 160].

While the "little hat" reference is not elaborated upon, there are enough reports of homins having a sagittal crest in Bigfooting lore to reasonably suggest that the inclusion of this feature may illustrate the conical shape produced by said crest that are seen in some homins as well as some particularly large great apes (e.g., silverback gorillas, etc.), and may be an analogue to reports of homins being at first sight to look they are wearing hoodies (e.g., Germer, 2020, September 8, 41:53). Indeed, such a physical feature has been noted in other reports elsewhere around the world, such as one Australian witness who had an encounter in Sherbrooke Forest, Victoria at age 18 in 1970. He says of the entity with a dome-shaped head: "At first I thought it was a very, very huge person wearing a funny, furry, gray hat" (Harrison, 2020, June 16, 6:54). Generally speaking, this dome-shaped appearance is a unique physical feature that anatomically modern humans do not tend to have.[15]

Further, Yakima elder and former forestry worker Mel Skahan states:

> There's a story that the Yakimas have that [Sasquatch are] part of us. That ... there were three groups of people here on the reservation. There were the Big People, there were the Yakimas, and then there were the Little People. And during the European migration in this direction, the Yakimas kind of got curious of ... the new tools and new trinkets coming across. And they moved down into the valleys, while ... the Big People wanted nothing to do with it. Yakimas tried to go back into the High Country and rejoin them, but ... were told that ... if they wanted to continue with ... what they were seeing, then they were not allowed to come back [Squatch Mafia, 2023, June 25, 44:16–45:00].

The narrative that Skahan shares is a warning that the Yakima must not lose their ways due to the influences of the European colonists, and that if the Yakima people were to continue down that path, then they would lose their connection to the Big People. The term "sasquatch" was developed by Canadian John Walter Burns (1888–1962) who was an agent of the Chehalis Indian Reservation and worked extensively to catalogue reports of Sasquatch among Indigenous Canadians (Burns, 1929, April 1; Furek, 2024, p. 179). The now-ubiquitous noun is an Anglicized version of the word *sésquac* (or *sesquac*) from the Halkomelem language of the Coast Salish Nation (Meldrum, 2006, p. 50). Sasquatch means "wild man of the woods" and *qelqelitl* indicates a female *sésquac* (Strain, 2012, p. 276). There are numerous regional and local differences in terms of behavior as well as appearance such as degree of visible hair covering the body (e.g., Breedlove, 2019b). For example, cryptozoologist Loren Coleman states that Sasquatch reports are said to be more violent and aggressive in reports from the northeastern and southeastern United States, where narratives of Sasquatch attacks on dogs are also much more frequent (Breedlove, 2019b).

But the very term "Sasquatch" speaks to the varied and often pained history between Indigenous Americans and European colonizers (e.g., Pruitt, 2023). I use the term precisely because much of the modern lore that exists parallels the term itself: both the word Sasquatch and the way in which the *Bigfooting community*[16] has taken up the subject reveal a European American façade on top of an Indigenous American frame (e.g., Shute, 2024, February 19). It is difficult to think of the way in which the subject has matured in North America without considering both of these cultural influences.

Accordingly, there is lore that goes deep and wide and is tainted by the sordid and suffered history imposed upon non-European minds and bodies by interloping European colonists. About 27 minutes into the 1997 documentary *Drumming for Bigfoot*, the late Tribal liaison, author, extended experiencer, and field investigator Henry Franzoni (1957–2024) shares the following:

> My big claim to fame with, ah, Bigfoot research is that it struck me one day that the Native Americans knew a lot more about Bigfoot or Sasquatch than us White people did. So, I found all the names of Bigfoot that I could find that were Native American names. I found over 100 names. And I plugged them into the US government's Geographic Names Information System and found 2,300 places in America that have been named for these creatures.
>
> Then, assuming that this is also a place (these places were places they wanted to hang out), I found that on a map, these places followed the summit ridges and the summit peaks of all the mountain ranges in America—particularly here in Oregon and in Washington. Over here [walks to map on his wall] on the 3D relief map, I found that the Indian place names and modern sighting reports fall along the summit ridges and peaks of the coast range, the summit ridges and peaks of the Cascade Range, and in particular, the highest density is between these three mountains: Mount Saint Helens, Mount Adams, and Mount Rainier. And the triangle formed within that is the highest density of Indian place names having to do with Bigfoot or Sasquatch [Chesna's Footage Room, 2019].

One of the matters that is perhaps most important when it comes to assessing the quality of available evidence in favor of any phenomenon—homins included—is to cultivate nuanced understanding around it. For example, it is not wise to simply cast all Indigenous American accounts of homins as non-indicative of a non-hominological origin (e.g., Trey the Explainer, 2024, February 8; Ward & Radford, 2024, January 12, 34:00), or as inscrutable, unknowable, or wholly and unalterably Other. Similarly, it is disingenuous to state that any and all depictions of beings that are hairy and/or upright are likely illustrations or narratives of Sasquatch. The reality tends to be more complicated than that, but the legacy of European colonialism has tended to color any discourse around such matters in a pall of nondescript duality.

Further, we learn of the history of mutual support that some Indigenous American communities speak of occurring in the even more recent past. For example, in the words of Derek Webster of the Omaha Nation and member of Rez Squatching Research team, Omaha women whose husbands were conscripted into service during World War II had a particular rapport with *Ci'Tonga*, the Hairy Man, during that time which aided both groups:

> The males were drafted or they were going to war. All these women, you know, had to do pretty much everything on their own because the men were gone, you know, off to war. When the war was finally over, some made it back. Some didn't. And what they told us was that the Ci'Tongas always helped the ones that their husbands never made it back. So I asked them how? How—how did they help them? "Before it got cold," she said, "the would drop them trees along that bluff. When it dried out, they would drag 'em down close to the shack and break it up for firewood before it got cold." In return, the lady would give 'em food, give 'em pies, whatever they were eating. They took it out to the timber and fed them. One thing that stuck out to me was they coexisted with the Ci'Tongas here. All we're doing is reconnecting with the Ci'Tongas in the reservation, in our Tribe [Brost, 2023, 39:23–40:40].

Webster's description jibes with the deep history of Indigenous Americans and the homins who they share the land with—a history that goes back at least 14,000 years. This history tells us that in the face of adversity, these different Tribes of people would come together to support each other. Moreover, much of the tension between Indigenous Americans and those who would become European American has mirrored the denial and marginalized treatment of homins within the Western collective. For this reason, one can understand the tone and tenor of those such as Tom Sewid's approach (e.g., Lynn, 2024, October 4, 14:00) to reclaiming the subject of Sasquatch for and by Indigenous people as opposed to simply allowing European Americans the power to define the phenomenon.

Moreover, in the inaugural episode of Untold Radio Network's *Discover Sasquatch*, Christopher "OG" Reinhardt interviews Todd Gatewood, who poignantly states the following just under 50 minutes into the episode:

> I've been told by elders and wisdom keepers of the Tribes that when the White man was to come to proliferate this country enough that they were told by the tribe of the Sasquatch that they [i.e., the Sasquatch themselves] would go to the High Country and come down during migratory times or salmon runs, and if they [i.e., the Indigenous folk] told the White men where they were, they would come and take their women and children. This is why you're not going to have a lot of … Indigenous help finding them [Reinhardt, 2024, January 8].

Those unconscious wishes and conflicts push out anything that presents as Other, including what is likely to be a deep memory of contact with homins all over the world. For example, as chiropractor and physical scientist J. Robert Alley shares having been told by the late anthropologist Vladimir Markotic[17] decades ago: "Robert, I know you know every country in the world has some form of hominid: not just in mythology, but in a physical existence" (Hajicek & Hajicek, 2024, March 20). Despite the dualistic nature of the comment, discriminating mythological evidence from physical evidence, Markotic's point is well-taken and is a theme that will hopefully become clearer as we proceed through Section I and beyond.

Indeed, to make a general point, one witness from western Montana provided another narrative to Smyth wherein he and his family (his father, an Indigenous American Tribal member, and his mother, a European American resident on the reservation) had maintained pre-birth and autobiographical memories of Sasquatch. About an hour and 23 minutes into an episode of *The Bigfoot Project* that summarized the most popular stories of 2023 (Smyth, 2023, October 18), in a narrative titled "Hairy Man, the Dirty Little Secret," the writer shares the following regarding his own experiences as well as stories that he had received from his father:

> I live on a reservation and the population of Native Americans to Whites is about 50-50. My father is a tribal member, and my mother is not. I am therefore a White descendant and I've grown up experiencing both sides of the culture, so to speak, and have spent time in their rough neighborhoods and at White-owned ranches and farms. Both Whites and Indians have stories that they rarely tell because they're so paranormal in nature. Let me tell you about something that people don't talk about here.
>
> When my father was born he was conscious this is something he would never tell a stranger, but I'm telling you what he told me. He remembers being in a waiting room before birth and surrounded by thousands of babies some were deformed some were sickly, some were Black and Asian and other races, and one of them was covered in hair. It's impossible for me to explain this part better than he could, but basically he saw the Waiting Room for Souls coming to this particular area of the world, and he was one of the few led through.
>
> I'm only sharing this detail because as a child I had dreams about the Hairy Man and his family, before I was ever exposed to the concept of Bigfoot. These dreams were frightening and unexplainable, and only made sense years later when my father related this to me. In my opinion, the Hairy Man is somehow related to this area in a big way, and my ancestors—having been the first to settle this area—have had extensive experiences with the Hairy Man that have been buried under generations of secrecy and tight lips. Sasquatch may be a part of my genetic memory as well as my father's and our grandfather's. Sasquatch, after all, was named after the Tribe who lives here now who had named them *sasq'ets*, or Wild Men of the Mountains.

Here, we begin to get a sense of the potential paranormal nature of the being that is called Hairy Man, as well as the extent to which members of the community have maintained memory of Sasquatch, albeit in a rather closeted manner. It is interesting that both he and his father had dreams or visions of Sasquatch, and that his father reports even having such an awareness from before he was born (i.e., what some scholars have termed an intermission experience that occurs between death and rebirth; Haraldsson & Matlock, 2016). The writer from Montana then goes on to share the following narrative:

> So my father was born with precognition of the Hairy Man. Years later, as a boy who was playing in the living room with many brothers, when one of them burst through the door screaming and crying for my grandmother to come out and make him go away, this was the first time the Hairy Man had reappeared in my father's life. My uncle (also a child at the time) had seen his Sasquatch in a small garden outback, which was next to a small creek. The Sasquatch was stealing vegetables and ran off after being sighted.[18] Nobody spoke of this event afterwards. Sasquatch was taken for granted back then anyways, and my grandmother—raising a full house of young boys by herself—had no desire to encourage them to panic, which they were.
>
> As the years went by, my father reached his early 20s, and stories had been popping up around the reservation about a Wild Man breaking into houses and scaring children at night. Indian Town, as it was called, was the downtown area with government housing, and is a rough neighborhood that I grew up in myself. As a kid, Indian Town was a very tight-lipped place and people didn't speak about these events to anyone but close relatives. At night in Indian Town, someone very large and smelly had been rummaging through garbage and trashing yards. A couple houses had been broken into and completely trashed. Food from the cupboard was taken that a bear or other wild animals wouldn't have been able to access. People couldn't decide whether it was a wild animal, an alcoholic, or a drug addict, or just kids causing trouble. This carried on for some years.
>
> One family in particular started to be visited by Hairy Man. Almost every night they would come home and see the door left open, their food taken, and the animals cowering under the

table. This routine was so familiar that they treated it as a common occurrence. Like a family ghost, as my father put it: something that's there, but the family is afraid to acknowledge. They kept their lips tight, but word of mouth got around. People were getting nervous. Everyone started to lock their doors. At night, dogs were acting cowardly for no apparent reason. The Wild Man was having his way. Free reign. He was getting bold. He started to break into houses during the middle of the day. Children would see him and flip out. Police were called. Meetings were held. The town was becoming more and more shaken up by the presence of this unknown intruder. This was when something incredible happened to the particular family who was favorited by the Hairy Man. They had become so lax and accepting of the Hairy Man's presence, that one night while standing on the porch, the father was yanked off by his feet in full view of the entire family. They screamed and huddled together and cried while whatever it was fought with the dad on the porch. The sounds of fighting and screaming and knowing that your father was powerless against whatever it was—it must have been unspeakably traumatic for the kids. They're now grown up like myself, and I wonder to this day how much this affected their lives.

I have included enough of the story here to give a sense as to where the writer is going, and I would encourage the interested inquirer to listen to the rest of the story on Lynn Smyth's channel. It is the elements of death anxiety, trauma, and dissonance that I wish to point out in the rather poignant narrative above. Regarding death anxiety and trauma, the degree of fear and preoccupation that was present in the Indian Town community seems to have been quite palpable. It should also be noted that, as far as the narrative is presented, there was only one Hairy Man causing all of that havoc. It would be wise to consider what multiple negative encounters with more than one of these beings across many, many generations could do for a group's genetic memory. The residents of Indian Town did not know who the thief was, and a number of potential suspects were suggested. It is interesting to me that even though there was an oral history present of Sasquatch in the community, according to the writer, Sasquatch was not even suspected as a potential culprit.

European American Lore

Additionally, local appellations given to these entities across English-speaking North America include but are not limited to the following: (a) the Minerva Monster of Ohio (Breedlove, 2015); (b) catamounts, which are variously referred to as big cats as well as Sasquatch-like beings (Byron, 2024, April 1; Cutchin & Renner, 2020a; Eichenberger, 2025, January 24, 3:33; Reinhardt, 2024, March 18); (c) Momo, the Missouri Monster (Breedlove, 2019a; Cutchin & Renner, 2020b); (d) the Honey Island Swamp Monster of Louisiana (Cutchin & Renner, 2020b; Petakov, 2024, March 10); (e) the Myakka Skunk Ape of Florida (Newton, 2005; Whitley, 2007), (f) the Mogollon Monster of Arizona (Germer, 2021, March 5b; Gymlan, 2022, October 23); (g) the Ohio Grassman (History, 2021, May 26; Newton, 2005); (h) the Alabama White Thang (e.g., Sprague, 2024, April 4); (i) the Walker County Wildman of Georgia (e.g., Weatherly & Renner, 2021); (j) the Hebbardsville Hillbillies (Coleman, 2006, December 27; Nunnelly, 2006), (k) the Billy Holler Booger of Georgia (Miles, 2000; Weatherly & Cutchin, 2021); (l) the Bardin Booger of Florida (Carlson, 2005, p. 83), (m) the White Witch of Stinchcomb, Oklahoma (Terrell, 2024, May 26), (n) Whistling Jack of Walden Ridge, Tennessee (Lamana, 2024, November 22), and the Beast of Whitehall (e.g., Gosselin & Gosselin, 2018). It should be noted that, while a minority of sightings of homins across time and space involve beings that appear to be all-white in color (e.g., Powell, 2018, pp. 169–170), those encounters tend to be striking enough that they become etched in local memory. Those cases include a local white variant in the state of Georgia (Hudson, 2020, 2:01:21; Vaughn, 2024, p. 305), the Pennsylvania White Bigfoot (e.g., Nick, 2023, January 8), the Alabama White Thang (e.g., Sprague, 2024, April 4), and the White Witch of Stinchcomb, Oklahoma (Terrell, 2024, May 26).

In addition to the specific regional folklore, as stated by an official manuscript published by the NAWAC, there are a large number of historical and eyewitness accounts that pre-date European colonization of North America and which mesh with modern reports of Sasquatch. In a monograph issued by members of the organization, they posit:

> historical accounts indicate an awareness of such an animal—whether based on myth or authentic encounters—that substantially predates any modern media- or hoax-driven phenomenon. The historical accounts also indicate that there was a familiarity with such an animal, or concept of it, in the south-central region of North America that was antecedent to Euro-American settler reports from the Northwest. The region in general has a history to such an extent that there exists a litany of nicknames that supposedly were derived from encounters with wood apes, such as the "wildman," "the Noxie Monster," "the Honka," "Momo," "the Fouke Monster," "Ol' Mossyback," "Monkey Man," and "Rougaru," to name just a sample. Many, if not most, of these names were well-established before the modern media phenomenon, begun in the late 1950s, of "Bigfoot" [Colyer et al., 2015, p. 185].

Therefore, there is much more to the story of Sasquatch than mere misidentification, wild imagination, or fantastical speculation that mysterious bipedal beasts haunt the woods of North America and beyond. Moreover, the Fouke monster noted above was the basis for the famous film *The Legend of Boggy Creek* and its sequel. Documentary productions such as *Mysterious Encounters* and *Small Town Monsters* and more provide poignant examinations of regional and local humanoid figures that are reported across North America.

Among those incidents that have made their way into North American Sasquatch lore, the *Bauman incident* from Teddy Roosevelt (Murphy, 2010, p. 39; Roosevelt, 1893), the Ruby Creek incident (e.g., Green, 2004b; Lyons, 1950; Sanderson, 2008; Short, 2024, pp. 88–89), the *Ape Canyon encounter* of 1924 (Beck, 1967; Breedlove, 2019; Hajicek & Hajicek, 2023, December 20)[19] stand among the most well-known and influential narratives.

Despite some of these similarities, the term Sasquatch should not per se be used to refer to one monolithic group of beings (Coleman & Huyghe, 2006). Indeed, there is a variety of reports about the way these homins look and behave. For example, David Paulides states the following:

> Looking back in Bigfoot research in the 1940s to the 1960s, there is mention of two distinctly different creatures, one has a hairy face and is very large, one doesn't have a hairy face and a smaller. One of the creatures is forceful and sometimes violent, while the other is passive [Paulides, 2017, p. 437].

Thus, in this thinking, there are at least several distinct types of entities who people are seeing and referring to under the same nomenclature.

Additionally, a common pattern that is found in Sasquatch encounter narratives is the aforementioned wood knock. For example, despite the selection bias inherent in the data collection method, a full 26 percent of respondents had experienced *wood knocks*[20]—a matter that we will return to later on—according to Bader and colleagues' survey of attendees at a 2009 conference organized by the North American Wood Ape Conservancy, or NAWAC; Bader et al., 2017, p. 221. These instances are typically perceived to be a mode of communication used to indicate information such as current position. The knocks that are particularly loud and resonant have been called *thunder knocks* (coined by content curator, field investigator, and experiencer Chris "OG" Reinhardt) or *power knocks*.

That said, some of these knocks may be used to warn people to stay out of an area. For example, about nine minutes into an episode of *The Bigfoot Project*, one experiencer and his friend who are hunting at Compass Lake, Florida, hear a roaring vocalization accompanied by a knock, "hit[ting] the trees with a log or something" (Smyth, 2024, March 28). In another encounter that occurs in east Texas, a man was warned of the presence of what was, in his perception, a Sasquatch, as he went to add corn to his hunting game feeder: "As I was about to walk around a bush, all of a sudden, this thing came alive. I mean, the bush was shaking. The big oak tree next to it was shaking. So, I stopped, walked backwards a bit, watching this, thinking that maybe a black bear had come on my property. This thing kept on like crazy. I kept walking backwards thinking, 'Whatever this is, all I have is this .22. I have to aim for the eye. I kept walking backwards. The further away I got, the more this thing would calm down'" (Smyth, 2024, March 28). The Class B encounter was also accompanied very soon by other evidence, including a 17-inch print and chattering in the woods that the witness heard with members of the BFRO who he had invited to his property.

One of the most remarkable extended experiencer accounts that I know of at present concerns interactions that Janice Carter Coy and her family experienced at their farmstead in Madisonville of eastern Tennessee. Janice's grandfather, Robert Carter, Sr., had developed what Janice deems to have been a respectful relationship with a Sasquatch named Fox who visited the farm over a period of about five decades. Robert, Janice, and her sister, Lila, had numerous, regular encounters with Fox and his clan over the course of the sisters' childhood and teen years.

Other individuals within the Bigfooting community have endeavored to set clear protocols for themselves and/or others in order to develop a sense of consistency and trustworthiness in support of establishing human-homin relations. Presumably, similar to ways in which secure attachment is generated, these actions helped to create a sense of consistency and helped to release greater comfort in any entities observing the humans at the sites. Such protocols are precisely the kind of behavior that are used when engaging with individuals who are neurodivergent in a way that trends toward autism, ADHD, and/or OCD. That is, his protocol jibes well with Noël's (2022) insightful contention that Sasquatch behavior overlaps significantly with aspects of autism and autistic savantism in humans.

The impact that these entities can have on humans seem to be at least as meaningful for extended by experiencers as it is for onetime experiencers. Understandably, heightened emotions, including everything from terror to awe, can be part and parcel of the lived experiences of this group. In all, it is the extended experiencers across time and space who offer a unique and varied glimpse into the manners and means by which human and homin interaction can be engaged in a way that is not entirely uncomfortable, violent, or dangerous for either group.

Despite some claims to the contrary (Lomas et al., 2024), other common features of reports include the entities engaging in *peeking* from behind trees as well as into "windows and tents," approaching campfires, and watching people sleeping out in the open in sleeping bags (e.g., Jones, 2023; Warren, 2023, October 31). The infamous, if not iconic, Beast of Boggy Creek (i.e., the Fouke monster) was known for leering into and reaching through windows (Pierce, 1972). Or as another example, Scott Carpenter has provided his recollection of a neighbor telling him a story of a likely juvenile male Sasquatch being a "peeping Tom," looking in a window at a teenage girl (Kruse & Grover, 2019, December 11). Such stealthy behavior is noted throughout Indigenous American as well as European American accounts, both old and new. Typically, it is thought that homins see humans before humans see homins. Momo, the Missouri Monster, was reported by two young women to have been staring at them from some brushes while they were eating their lunch (Breedlove, 2019a). Or as another example, experiencer Jason Miller has stated that the juvenile male Sasquatch who he and his daughter saw was positioned well enough within some foliage beside a hiking trail that he could see them while concealing his own presence (Irwin, 2024, April 20). Despite some of the evidence and claims that I present in this volume, it should be noted that, as Cutchin (2025, p. 346) reflects, the vast majority of cases of homins (as well as other humanlike entities) simply describe them as watching us. However, the mere *observational* presence still seems to elicit deep anxiety, unease, and fear within the humans whom they watch.

Sasquatch are also reported to stand and sway back and forth while watching humans (e.g., Short, n.d.), a behavior which is associated with anxiety in the face of a potential threat. A prototypical description of this behavior is given by long-term investigator Todd Neiss who observed three of these beings on a road (Eichenberger, 2022).

Other characteristic themes in the literature include *bluff charges* (e.g., Godfrey, 2016; Prince-Hughes, 1997), which are threat displays that are also utilized by primates and other mammals. The bluff charge tends to be defined by the entity exhibiting a quick rush toward the interloper(s) before stopping suddenly or retreating, accompanied by at least one of the following behaviors: (a) extremely loud yelling or shouting; (b) vigorously shaking trees in the vicinity of the interloper(s); (c) uprooting trees and throwing them toward the interloper(s); or (d) breaking sticks and throwing them toward the interloper(s).[21] In Carpenter's *The Sasquatch Awareness Project*, he provides a useful summary of the bluff charge:

> There are hundreds of encounters where Sasquatch will make a ferocious display. Campers, hikers, hunters, fishermen, home owners, farmers, have experienced what is described as a "scream-roar."[22] The vocalization is so loud and fierce that it can be felt and vibrates the witness's chest. Many times, this is accompanied by the sound of large limbs being snapped in two, trees being pushed over, or large boulders being thrown.

> These displays have caused witnesses to flee the area, leaving valuable equipment and possessions behind[,] never returning to the location to retrieve them. Some have lost control of their faculties, while others went into shock and were unable to move.
>
> These displays by the Sasquatch are meant to scare and cause the person to leave the area.[23] In a large percentage of these encounters the Sasquatch does not show itself[;] instead it stays hidden[,] relying on the fierceness of the display to force the person out of the area.
>
> These encounters can cause long term negative effects on people, including Post Traumatic Stress Syndrome (PTSD) and an extreme fear of being outdoors. Despite these harrowing displays, no one is physically harmed. My friend Steve Isdahl has said many times, "If a predator wants to harm you, then you will never hear it coming or have a clue it is in the area." He is correct[;] if the Sasquatch wanted to do these people harm there would have been no one left alive to make the sighting report.
>
> Though it is disturbing, if you have had or do have an experience with a Sasquatch like this, the intention is/was not to harm you but to move you out of the area as fast as possible [Carpenter, 2022, pp. 53–54].

Conventional wisdom states that quickly walking—not running—to exit the area, not making eye contact with the entity or entities, and not brandishing weapons may help to deescalate the situation. With that said, following data reported elsewhere by Carpenter (2019), Baranchok (2021) has asserted that bluff charges occur at a higher frequency than true or actual charges. It is important to note that dealing with ambiguity is often part and parcel of navigating the world of human affairs: developing a solid theory of mind of why other people function as they do can be challenging, and the cultivation of emotional intelligence can prove difficult as well. As such, moving into the world of human-homin relations makes such considerations all the more challenging.

Additional related behaviors include experiencers reporting *stalking*. In these accounts, the experiencer is typically walking along a road or trail lined by trees and hears what sounds like a large, bipedal entity who walks alongside them on a parallel trajectory. If the experiencer stops or starts, the entity follows suit. Typically, the encounter ends when the experiencer decides to quickly exit the area. It should be noted that the stalking behavior is associated with other entity encounters as well and generally speaking, Sasquatch experiencers do not actually see the being who is stalking them.

In addition to the above distinctions, homins are said to be fond of human children for various reasons. We will consider the more nefarious purposes later on in the text, but for now, we consider some more benign encounter narratives. A contemporary encounter involves a family with a 3-year-old child who has conversations at night with a Sasquatch outside of her bedroom window. Around an hour into the *3-hour Bigfoot Marathon December Giveaway* episode, the narrative begins with the father getting up from bed to use the restroom when he hears what sounds like his daughter talking to someone:

> The windows were open, and we were getting a good breeze, and we all went to sleep. Sometime in the middle of the night, I woke up needing to use the bathroom. Now, there were night lights in the hallways and in the bathroom, so I didn't have to turn on any lights. And I didn't want to because I might wake someone up. So, I was standing there and just as I started to do my business, I thought I heard talking. I thought my daughter had heard me get

> up. When I finished washing my hands, then I stood quietly in the hallway to see if she had gone back to sleep. But I heard her clearly jabbering away again, then I heard something else jabbering.
>
> I thought maybe there was a toy she was playing with that was making that noise, and just as quick, I knew she didn't have any toys that sound like that. It was a completely different sound—definitely a toy—and it didn't sound quite human. Guttural is the only word I know, but the sound was fast and fluid. It was all nonsense, and I couldn't make any of it out (either hers or the other's replies), but whatever it was, it was talking really fast. The pitch was lower than a human, but I wouldn't say it was a deep or heavy voice or pitch. It sounded squawky and guttural all at once. I'm sorry I don't have any words to describe it. Mostly, it just sounded wrong, and it scared me to death.
>
> I didn't even think beyond thinking someone was in the room with my daughter. I ran in and I flipped on the overhead light. I remember I was yelling something. As I did so ... I woke the whole house up and my daughter started crying. It was then as I did all of that and my eyes were scanning the room that I saw something move away from the window right after I flipped on the light. My daughter was sitting at the end of her bed by the open window. With the whole house up, I quickly handed my daughter to my wife. I got my shotgun, and I went outside to confront someone, but there was no one out there [Smyth, 2023, October 1].

The encounter described above was one of several recounted from the same family wherein the father kept getting fleeting glimpses of a large bipedal being moving swiftly away from the house whenever he investigated. They eventually moved out of the house, renting the place to their nephew instead. It is noteworthy that after the nephew moved in, he never experienced any visitations from Sasquatch. The father ended up attributing that to the fact that his family member had no children in the house with him. He states: "Maybe it saw our daughter one day when she was out playing. Maybe it was a female that lost a young one and was drawn to her" (Smyth, 2023, October 1). After their daughter turned four, she commented about "missing George" (a name that she had often used to refer to the figure who visited her at the window at night) while looking at a book of *Curious George*. At this point, the parents realized just what (or rather, who) had been keeping their daughter company previously. Further, during a chance daylight sighting of the homin by the family barn, the mother estimated that the being was around eight to eight-and-a-half feet tall. After their daughter got older, the parents asked her if she remembered George, but to their relief, she had no recollection of her nighttime experiences with the large, hairy figure.

Another narrative that deals with a Sasquatch looking in a window on a crying baby one night is shared by Marc DeWerth, founder of the well-known Salt Fork Ohio Bigfoot Conference and former BFRO investigator, during an episode of *Untold Radio AM*. About 43 minutes into the episode, Doug Hajicek then poses the possibility that these window peekers may tend to be female Sasquatch due to their "curiosity with children," and Marc concurs that a Sasquatch mother who may have lost her own children would potentially be interested in checking in on a crying baby (Hajicek & Hajicek, 2024, March 14).

Following the matter of potential reasons for such window-peeking behaviors, author and veteran field investigator Thom Powell (2015) ponders:

> In my mind, the question is not whether the sasquatch are interested in kids, but why. Perhaps it is simply because the sasquatch, while equally interested in all humans, recognize that kids are inherently less threatening and more trustworthy than adults. Another possibility is that the sasquatch are looking toward the eventual maturation of the human race to the point when humans no longer shoot at, or even fear the sasquatch. The current generation of adults is already too far gone, but the next generation is not. Also, the sasquatch are consummately patient. They may be working the next generation since they are a more promising prospect for eventually achieving a spirit of mutual acceptance between sasquatch and humanity [Powell, 2015, p. 134].

Powell's comments are rather intriguing and should not be taken lightly, especially when considering overlap between his thinking and the multiplicitous narratives of Indigenous Americans. It is important to note that, despite Powell's own consummately positive tone here, the fear and anxiety that he refers to in adults is precisely the kind of trigger for problematic relationships, and since adults largely control their children's circumstances, any Sasquatch that fall under the above rubric would have to be excessively patient indeed. And as one final example among many potential episodes involving this particular thread of Sasquatch interest in children comes from veteran investigator Tony Green, who has been involved in field studies into Sasquatch since 1989. He says the following of a general pattern that he has noticed:

> When we had kids in camp, [Sasquatch] wouldn't come as close. They would keep at a distance and circle [the camp]. When there wasn't a kid in camp, they would get in closer. So that leads me to believe ... there's ... protective tendencies on children [Jackson, 2024, May 4, 1:20:40].

Green's intuition here jibes with reports such as those above that deal with some Sasquatch having a keen desire to be especially careful around young humans. Indeed, as Green also notes, the general thinking is that homins tend to also be quite protective of their own young as well. The investigator also speculates that when it comes to Sasquatch being said to kidnap children, that said behavior may arise from this protective instinct (e.g., if the child is in danger).

If it is true that humans have an at-times partially confrontational history with homins (even if that history is largely forgotten, repressed, or suppressed in some segments of the population), then any approach behaviors from homins toward children, even if those behaviors are not intended as threatening, may be met with disdain, suspicion, or even panic. While there are exceptions to that scenario, generally speaking, negatively valenced emotions toward children interacting with or being seen by Sasquatch seem to predominate, at least in those reports that I am familiar with that come from Western witnesses.

Associated with stalking as well as with the previously mentioned behavior of peeking is the oft-reported feeling of being watched. All manner of experiencers, from hunters to campers to hikers and more report the eerie sensation that they are being watched or even hunted. An experiencer named Dick reports to Robbie Knievel about having this feeling before a Class A sighting: "All the time I was there, I had this feeling—you know, you get the feelings? [Robbie Knievel replies in the affirmative] I had the feeling: somebody is up here watching me, but I'd look around and I could never see anything." (Croyle, 2021). This sensation of unease is sometimes accompanied by piloerection (aka goosebumps and hair standing on end), and other physiological responses. While some experiencers tend to rationalize or explain away the feeling (e.g., by blaming the feeling on being observed by unseen wildlife), others respond to it and exit the area as quickly as they can.

Rock throwing is another common theme in Sasquatch narratives (e.g., Gymlan, 2022, March 20), and it involves pebbles, stones, or larger rocks being tossed or hurled toward the interloper. In the cases of trees, branches, or rocks being thrown, the object typically does not actually hit the eyewitness or eyewitnesses but lands quite close, thereby generally leading witnesses to remark on the precision of the unseen thrower and to believe that the act is designed to run them out of the area rather than to hurt them. However, a small minority of accounts involve experiencers actually being hit, such as in the back while facing away from the assailant (Peters, 2024, May 19).[24] Generally speaking, as some such as field investigators Scott Carpenter (Carpenter, 2022, pp. 53–54) who noted as much above, and Michael Mayes (2022, pp. 233–234) has stated, the so-called aggression that Sasquatch exhibit appears to be nothing more than a ruse to get interloping humans to leave the area. While throwing of objects may overlap with bluff charges, with bluff charges being utilized if throwing projectiles does not deter human interlopers, throwing is reported often enough in the absence of threat displays that it can reasonably be treated as a distinct behavior. Further, throwing of lighter objects such as pinecones is at times perceived by the experient to be playful rather than aggressive. And while people have not generally seen Sasquatch making them, all manner of tree structures—from tree breaks, to tree or stick structures,[25] and even stick glyphs—are often associated with homins, and are hypothesized to be used as territorial or directional markers.

In all, the disciplines of hominology and cryptozoology present some fascinating evidence for the consideration of the collective psyche. That very same collective psyche is arguably mutually constituted of a deep death anxiety and egoic desire for control; therefore, those actual or perceived destructuring (Hansen, 2001), Othered objects of potential discovery (or, per Bayanov's [2014] thesis, objects of re-discovery) are the same objects that are constituted in the Shadow of the collective.

Arguably, the tentative ambivalence and thinly veiled impotence in statements such as "Are we alone" (e.g., Loeb, 2021, p. 89)—a question which very much can be converted into cryptozoology and hominology through the Single Species Hypothesis—simultaneously conveys a desire to find other intelligent lifeforms in the cosmos, while also projecting a fear of encountering said lifeforms at the same time. Hence, the ambivalence.

Indeed, according to Dawson et al. (2024), several polls taken in 2018 and 2021, 21 percent and 24 percent of American adults, respectively, believed in the existence of Bigfoot (p. 471). Moreover, according to a survey of 1,032 adults that the authors themselves conducted from August to September 2021, 46 percent of north American adults either believed (34%) or strongly believed (12%) that Bigfoot is real, while 55 percent of the same sample either disbelieved (35%) or strongly disbelieved (20%) in the existence of these beings (p. 476). Moreover, other findings indicated that in the same sample, 41 percent of adults either believed (12%) or strongly believed (29%)

that the yeti is real, while 59 percent disbelieved (39%) or strongly disbelieved (20%) the yeti is real, respectively. Finally, the authors point to the following conclusions:

> By providing plausible portrayals of hidden creatures, the medium may help perpetuate belief in the sorts of monsters that have long occupied a prominent place in folklore. Yet it is also important to note that paranormal reality/documentary viewing and news use predicted belief in cryptids whereas overall television viewing and science fiction viewing generally did not [Dawson et al., 2024, p. 485].

Thus, the medium of television shows focused on these subjects can potentially help to open up people to possibilities regarding the paranormal, cryptids, and homins.

Moreover, homins are at times described as protectors of the forest, as with the basajaun of Spain (e.g., McGrath, 2005)or the yowie of Australia (e.g., Harrison, 2020, July 27, 11:00). One narrative of an extended encounter involves a marked increase in threatening behavior on a property after the owner began clear-cutting the old growth timber (Byron, 2023, August 28). According to an experiencer named Wade (who is the son of the property owner) we learn the following of a group of Sasquatch who appeared on the property in Rainier, Oregon, after logging began in the area:

> And dad had hired a company to come in and start cutting down, uh, trees that were enormous within themselves. They're—you know, the kind of logs you'd only be able to put two or three on a logging truck. And that's when, uh, things changed quite a bit. Umm, they would just come out and stand there … away from the tree line by a few feet. They—they were quite unafraid. All four of them. Uh, they would stand most the time motionless. They had … no fear of us whatsoever—at least to us, the family … everybody was hassled [Byron, 2023, August 28].

Here we have a clear indication that the destruction of the trees led to the threatening behavior of the four Sasquatch (i.e., one adult male, one adult female, and two juveniles). However, it is important to note that in the narrative, at no point did Wade indicate that anyone was physically harmed, despite the fact that the size, strength, and speed of the beings described would have likely allowed them to dispatch the anatomically modern humans with all deliberate speed. He repeats on multiple occasions that the entities were quite curious of the children and never harmed them, even though they terrorized the older workers. Based on a second-hand description of the largest male Sasquatch from one of the workers on the property, he was described as at least 10 feet tall and at most 1,000 pounds in weight. Wade was rather young during these events and may not have been able to present as reliable an estimate of the height or weight of the being. Even though he and his siblings were not physically harmed, he feels that his family was psychologically traumatized by these events and has not been the same since. The harassment got so bad at one point that his sisters ended up moving away from the property.

Following this theme of logging evoking aggression from Sasquatch, Byron [JB] reports elsewhere that podcast host Jim Harold [JH] clear-cutting his property in Nashville, Tennessee, ended up incurring the wrath of Sasquatch:

> **JB:** This one gentleman shared a story where … he had these … workers putting in an air strip, yeah, east of Nashville on his property. And, ah, it got so bad that the workers were … run off the property, and-
>
> **JH:** Wow.

JB: —when they were putting in this airstrip. So, ah, usually ... if you're in an area where there could be Bigfoot and you start clearing wood, ah, brush (which is fine, it's your property), but be aware you could be potentially angering a Bigfoot.
JH: Yeah, you're messing with their habitat [Harold, 2024, February 6].

Byron's brief reflection is important in that it substantiates both the idea that Sasquatch and other homins have been viewed as protectors of natural environments and also specifically ties the beings to trees. Further, in a lecture titled "The Bigfoot Mystery," Jeremiah reflects:

Is Bigfoot a friendly creature or an aggressive and not-to-be-messed-with creature? I think the answer lies there with, "Is a bear an aggressive creature or a friendly creature? Is any animal kind or aggressive?" I think it ... has a lot to do with the area that the creature or the Bigfoot lives in. If mankind is taking away its habitat.

There's a lot of reports that I will take where the creature has started to get more aggressive, and that's because the landowner has started to clear out their property, cutting out all the trees creating all these trails through the property. And I've taken reports ... recently in the Uwharrie National Forest part of North Carolina. And also, there was a Tennessee report where a landowner moved out from Nashville into Wilson County, started building a runway for their airplane cutting down lots of brush.

And to be quite frank, when we take away the habitat of the Sasquatch or the Bigfoot, that's when they start to become very angry. So, I can see how some reports are shown as the creature being aggressive, while some of them are more the forest protector or the kind creature [Sprague, 2024, April 4].

In general then, there are two rather distinct (yet at times overlapping) characters painted of Hairy Man: one of the volatile, giant, and one of the protector of the forest and even of people. Both personalities are shared within oral and written record and thereby persist in present memory.

Famous Footage

In terms of videographic or photographic data, the 1967 Patterson-Gimlin film (e.g., Meldrum, 2012) is widely regarded as the gold standard. It was filmed by rodeo rider, field investigator, and author Roger Clarence Patterson (1933–1972) along with cowboy and horse trainer Robert "Bob" Gimlin on October 20 of that year.

Due to the relative ubiquity and salience within the collective consciousness of the PGF and its iconic subject given the name "Patty," it is helpful for us to briefly[26] consider some context and findings regarding the film. It cannot be overstated that the oft-repeated claim that the 1967 Patterson-Gimlin film has been debunked (e.g., Klement, 1975) is not only untrue (e.g., Green, 2004a), but that such a narrative grossly and maliciously misrepresents the decades of actual scientific and technical research that has gone into examining the data (e.g., Meldrum, 2006; Murphy, 2010, Tian et al., 2022):[27] research which has been published and peer-reviewed and which either has determined that the film subject is genuine, that the film would be near-impossible to hoax, or that the film is inconclusive in its depiction of a bipedal primate of non-human origin. Indeed, the PGF has been studied with great regularity, detail, and depth across the more than half century since it was originally filmed, and far from being debunked, its authenticity has actually been affirmed.

In addition to the PGF, another extremely compelling piece of videographic evidence is the 1994 Freeman footage (M. Freeman, 2022).[28] Paul Freeman has received the honor of being called "the ultimate bigfoot field researcher" (p. 262) by Thom Powell in the *Freeman Bigfoot Files* anthology (Powell, 2022). Freeman's work in the Blue Mountains of Oregon—and specifically, in the Mill Creek Watershed (p. 263)—over a 15-year period evidenced his painstaking commitment to unearthing clear evidence of the existence of Sasquatch. The tracks that he cast as well as the now well-known footage that he shot are testaments to his dedication and are parts of his legacy that cannot be taken away. Freeman had been conducting field investigations for about a decade before his fateful encounter in Deduct Spring in the Blue Mountains. In late summer of 1994, he was in the area every day the week prior to his encounter looking for trackways and other sign. On the way home from helping his daughter with her car, he checked the area—albeit hours later than he normally went—and managed to film a large, bipedal homin walking in front of a copse of trees before potentially linking up with a juvenile and disappearing into the woods. In the words of one of Paul's sons, Michael Freeman, during an interview on *Sasquatch Odyssey*, the following occurred when Paul Freeman (described by Michael as 6'5", 275 pounds, and the toughest man he ever knew) came home immediately after the sighting:

> He's shaking, and he's pale ... and he's sweating ... and he is just ... all over the place, back and forth, you know. Uh, just hyped up, nervous, you know, those things. And then his eyes are as big as saucers ... and he's telling [me and my friends]... "I've got it. I've got it on film finally.... I'm not crazy" [King-Sharp, 2023, February 3].

Indeed, many experiencers seek to confirm that they are "not crazy" (e.g., King-Sharp, 2024, April 14). Michael continues that his father put the tape in the player and that they all sat there and watched the footage about 10 times. They were a hunting family and knew what it was not. Similar to the PGF, there was sign (e.g., footprints) that was present on the scene. Additionally, some of Freeman's previous evidence included casts of one right foot and one left foot that contained dermatoglyphics. According to Michael Freeman, those casts are housed at the Smithsonian (Sharp, 2023, February 3).

Aside from the PGF and FF, other potentially compelling videographic and photographic evidence has persisted in the Bigfooting community. Among them are the 2015 Russian "yeti" video[29] (e.g., Bigfoot Tony, 2017, July 26), purportedly filmed by Yevgeny Anisimov and his father in Kemerovo, Siberia (Sykes, 2016, p. 250), the two Myakka Skunk Ape photos (Blackburn, 2023, November 3),[30] the Stacy Brown Footage (Brown, Jr., 2012, December 1), and the Yowie thermal footage taken by the Australian Yowie Research Organization (Yowiehunters Witness Reports, 2021, October 17). Additionally, the so-called Bigfoot mugshot photo is either a nigh-immaculately conceived hoax or is the clearest and most compelling photographic evidence of Sasquatch that has been taken to date (StrangeSpotting, 2024, March 2). Anecdotally, the photograph has been met with what seems to be a moderate-to-high degree of cynicism within the Bigfooting community. Appearing similar to what might be expected of a National Geographic cover shoot, the photograph depicts a subject with a wide face with what may be a pensive expression, a moderately thick brow ridge, conical head,[31] broad nose, thin lips, and brown hair of varying lengths. The general description conveyed in some reports of Sasquatch as a humanlike ape-man seems to be conveyed in the image.

The above sources summarize the general characteristics and evidence within modern Sasquatch lore. Further, lest the connection between the themes herein and the homin teem be lost, we can see that many of the patterns that have appeared in the oral and written history can serve as potential cause for the development of homin teems while also serving as potential triggers of those teems within the collective human psyche. For the unaccepting or unwilling, such footage and images beg cognitive if not emotional accommodation, or what we might think of as a so-called seat at the table in the halls of mainstream science and in the minds of debunkers, deniers, and cynics.

View It from the Bridge

Herein, I have discussed various terminology including the term "Sasquatch" to foreground the Indigenous American-derived mythology as well as the European American influence of this phenomenon. This chapter has also begun our discussion of the deep and multifarious evidence in support of Sasquatch by focusing on narratives about homins. Establishing the evidence is important to elucidate where the split emerges between mainstream Western culture and the fringed narratives and information that comprise support of homins within hominology and cryptozoology. The classification procedure (i.e., Class A, B, and C) used by the BFRO and adopted by various experiencers, field investigators, and enthusiasts was also discussed. Some of the more iconic pieces of evidence regarding homins in North America was considered, and that includes the Patterson-Gimlin film (PGF) and the Freeman film (FF), among others.

Before moving on, I would encourage you to pause and consider at least one of the reflective prompts on cognitive, emotional, somatic, or conative matters that I have posed in the introduction.

3

Liminal Entities and The Cannibal

The entities that are our focus of inquiry occupy a particular space within the psychological and physical landscape—the forests of the mind and minds of the forest. A number of reports occur at liminal sites such as windows, doors, roads, cemeteries, power line cuts, and at the edges of forests just within the tree line, further indicating their liminal status at or within physical thresholds.

Further, Cutchin (2020a) offers that tales of hairy ghosts are actually rather common within the folkloric literature. In general, these are matters along with dean of integral education and esteemed integral educator Sean Esbjörn-Hargens's (2020, July) *ontological indeterminacy* (i.e., conveying a kind of fluidity in terms of what forms and functions entities assume), which may hold great value for future theory-building around exceptional experiences in general, and entity encounters in particular. Such a point is taken up by scholars such as Joshua Cutchin and Greg Bishop (e.g., Cutchin, 2025), as well as Henry Franzoni (2023) and Erik Bard (Eichenberger, 2023), who state that the phenomenon may essentially adopt any form it so chooses or that is perceptible by us (e.g., via co-creation). Such is an indication of the high strangeness of entity encounters that is at times explicitly noted by experiencers, captured in trace evidence, or recorded in audio or video recordings.

Indeed, in a manner that is evocative of the kind of liminal status that such a being may hold in the minds and perceptions of those who come in contact with homins, April Lynn provides the following poignant commentary about a being who she and her friend saw while walking on the beach around sunset at Houda Point, California, in fall 2007:

> We saw it in all its detail, and we watched it for a good long while. We felt like we saw almost, like, a glimpse into a different dimension or another world, you know, because it didn't look like anything that makes sense with what we know in this reality. You know, it—it went from moving like an animal on all fours, to walking almost like a person on two legs, and then just kind of casually swimming away. Like, it—it just kind of made us both (and we've talked about it many times over the years)—it definitely put a sense of *awe*, you know, in me.
>
> I will say once it stood up and started to walk into the water, the feeling of fear kind of came in, 'cause that was when it was like, pretty sure this isn't something that we can classify. And that definitely made us both, I think, fearful, but fearful in more of ... a curious way. Like, I didn't ever get a sense that it wanted to harm us. You know ... it didn't give us any kind of aggressive feeling. It just—but it just was something— something really different [chuckles] than—than what you think exists in this world [Eichenberger, 2024, April 24, 3:44–5:05].

Lynn's reflection on what she and her friend encountered is in line with the idea that not only is it unclear what Sasquatch is (i.e., in reference to ontological ambiguity), but one reason for that ambiguity may be because Sasquatch can essentially shift the way that they present or show up to us. For example, it is said within some Indigenous American communities that Sasquatch exist in two worlds (Croyle, 2021).

These entities straddle the psychological and physical boundaries between human and Other, civilization and unspoiled nature, consciousness and unconscious, culture and the crude, and especially between what we hope for and what we fear, including unbridled life and agonizing death. As mentioned previously, the relationship between UAP and other liminal entities such as homins becomes clearer when one examines the extant literature. As a poignant example, Vallee and Davis (2005) outline *six layers of UAP characteristics*:

a. physical, as in obeying known laws of classical physics;

b. anti-physical, as in demonstrating perversions of classical physics (e.g., anomalous effects on time like missing time, time dilation, etc.);

c. psychological, wherein cognitive and behavioral measures are enacted to maintain mental poise or equilibrium (e.g., attempts to explain away an encounter);

d. physiological, as disrupting overall body's sensory, interoceptive, and tissue equilibrium (e.g., demonstrating burns, nausea, tinnitus, smelling odd odors, etc.);

e. psychic, wherein the experient develops or demonstrates momentary reception of information outside of classical five sensory modalities (e.g., having precognitive dreams, receiving messages telepathically, being healed, etc.); and

f. cultural, which deals with the larger societal implications and responses to the idea of UAP (e.g., media portrayals thereof, mainstream attitudes toward the possibility of disclosure, etc.)

What the authors have outlined here is a useful framework for understanding the ways in which liminal entities—or at least those who seem to leave behind physically or otherwise perceptually observable evidence—in the modern world can be characterized.

As such, these very same layers can be applied to the homin phenomenon, which is constituted of the totality of direct and indirect causes and effects of the six layers in relation to homins (i.e., Sasquatch, yowie, yeren, etc.): physical (e.g., footprints, vocalizations, etc.); anti-physical (e.g., so-called "cloaking," being seen in the presence of orbs, etc.; Cutchin & Renner, 2020a; Galán S. & Koren, 2024; Moneymaker, 2024, April 9); psychological (e.g., self-denial of an encounter); physiological (e.g., smelling sulfuric or otherwise malodorous aromas, the feeling of being stared at, etc.); psychic (e.g., receiving information telepathically, poltergeist phenomena, being healed, etc.); and cultural (e.g., stigma attached to the subject, popular portrayal of homins in film and television, etc.).

Liminal Entities

The subject of the present chapter generally deals with the matter of *liminal entities*: manifestations of transitory states of the psyche, natural world, or both that appear as physical beings, subtle forces, spirits, or some combination thereof. As a group, *liminal entities* occupy those aforementioned forests of the mind (Bayanov, 2012; Pruitt, 2023, p. 276), representing the many things that any number of humans have come to perceive as anti-structural, as denaturing to modern life, as unnatural, unclean, or even as immoral. They are therefore often the stuff of nightmares, of campfire stories, and are the things that go bump in the night as well as within the psyche.

Importantly, anything or anyone representative of the liminal occupies space at the threshold: those literal and/or figurative doorways, crossroads, and edges that populate the physical and psychical tapestries of our world. In the case of Sasquatch and homins in general, we see what Hansen (2001, p. 407) states simply: that these entities occupy the space between ape and human.

Such descriptions are precisely the kinds of encounters that breach the seal of one's normal ken and allow the extraordinary to seep into present experience, potentially rupturing one's worldview beyond repair. Further still, Joshua Cutchin's (e.g., 2020a) contention that a large segment of contemporary Sasquatch lore (e.g., apports, rock tossing, rapping on walls, etc.), at least per Class B encounters, can be classified as analogous to poltergeist reports. His neologism, the *wildnisgeist*, is a wilderness poltergeist (Cutchin, 2016, 2020a). This thesis is quite intriguing, as it fits much of the observed data that people report (e.g., King-Sharp, 2025, January 9, 24:41).[1] One interesting matter that arises in relation to this idea is as follows: "Speculation that bigfoot may be ghosts (perhaps of *Neanderthal* or *Gigantopithecus*) finds support in some Native American legends, as well as modern sightings and occult practice" (Cutchin, 2020a, p. 200). In the time since the publication of Cutchin's position paper on the wildnisgeist, other Fortean authors such as W.T. Watson have taken the same line of thinking, elaborating on the correspondences between Sasquatch and poltergeist phenomena (Watson, 2023). For example, Watson suggests that Sasquatch researchers themselves, through spontaneous psychokinetic action on the physical environment, may themselves actually manifest phenomena such as so-called wood knocks. In this scenario, field investigators who are frustrated with their lack of solid evidence may find those negative emotions boiling over, thereby being displaced into the space around them.[2] Such a proposition is an intriguing possibility and follows upon the research and theory that have been produced within the field of parapsychology.

In addition to the above abilities, Sasquatch is said to exhibit more exotic abilities in some reports that tend to be associated more with experiencers and enthusiasts who find themselves to be open to ontological categories that go beyond the flesh-and-blood alone. One such ability is *tagging*, otherwise known as being *marked* (Roehl, 2022, May 16), which either exists as a kind of psychic marker or a physical (e.g., scent-based) one: after a person has contact with a Sasquatch, that individual may be able to found or observed more readily by other Sasquatch regardless of where that individual is, while the individual also seems to become more keenly aware of when they are in the presence of a Sasquatch (even if the human percipient cannot see them; Carpenter, 2022). For Thomas of the Tlingit and Haida, an extended experiencer interviewed by Fred Roehl (2022, May 16, 23:50–24:34), marking is due to Hairy Man recognizing the particular scent of fear that a person exudes after encountering one of them. Any Sasquatch thereafter can sense "the fear they invoke in us" and can therefore identify and track that person, even at great distance (24:15).

Further, extended experiencers such as Rich Germeau and Thom Powell (Powell, 2015) have reported such a phenomenon. Powell, for example, reports one rather interesting occurrence after having unsuccessfully spent the previous evening attempting to elicit a response from homins at a site by engaging in his own tree knocking. After driving himself back home to Oregon early in the morning due to a midday affair that he had to attend later in the day, amid several brief yet helpful power naps, he finally arrived at his house and pulled into his driveway. The following narrative is from Thom's account in *Edges of Science*:

> At 5:05 am, as the tiniest hint of daylight illuminated the eastern horizon, I rolled into my driveway in a zombie-like state. I shut off the engine, let my heavy eyelids fall, and said a prayer of thanks. I almost slept right there, but a cozy bed beckoned only a few steps away. I peeled my weary bones from the seat of the Tercel. Stumbling to my feet, I took in a deep breath of the cold pre-dawn air. I softly shut the car door, took my first step toward the house, and at that exact moment I got one of the biggest surprises of my life. From the woods at the back of my rural property, six hundred feet from where I had just parked the car, came three, loud, crisp, resounding knocks!
>
> Despite my intense fatigue, the irony of the situation was abundantly clear. I had been whacking trees all night, always in triplets, only to be greeted with the identical triplet of tree knocks upon my arrival home. And, the responding knocks that I'd been trying to coax from the woods all night finally came at the precise moment when I was absolutely too exhausted to walk any further than the bedroom. Even if I did have the stamina to detour in the direction of the woods, I knew what I would see back there: NOTHING [Powell, 2015, p. 19].

While alternative hypotheses cannot be ruled out in this instance, such as Powell unconsciously evoking his own macro-PK-induced wood knocks73F or some ill-defined, exceptionally odd coincidence, the idea that Sasquatch or perhaps some wildnisgeist[3] phenomenon à la Cutchin had tagged him is not beyond possibility. Of course, at the very least, his experience would be synchronistic due to the seemingly acausal and meaningful coincidence of it all. And further, the seemingly trickster nature of the phenomenon is apparent in Powell's reflections on his physical state (i.e., unable to investigate the source of the knocks due to his great fatigue) and the fact that all of his efforts the previous day had gone unacknowledged until he drove hours to return home. Regardless of the ontology of the tagging or marking phenomenon, systematic analysis of this characteristic of the lore has not been advanced to date. As such, there is room for researchers to examine this fascinating yet haunting aspect of the homin phenomenon. It should be noted that his liminal, hypnagogic state might have played a role in his experience. However, such altered states of consciousness are often part and parcel of high strangeness and exceptional experience in general.

At least a subset of extended experiencers may tend to have intergenerational contact wherein their parents, grandparents, and/or children also have contact with these beings. Additionally, as can be the case with exceptional human experiences in general, some individuals (e.g., those who Esbjörn-Hargens refers to as *super experiencers*; e.g., Esbjörn-Hargens, n.d.) may tend to experience other phenomena in addition to Sasquatch. For example, about 21 minutes into an interview, the following exchange occurs between field investigator, content creator, and author Tobe Johnson and his colleague and fellow extended experiencer Darrell Adams:

> **TJ:** They're almost describing something supernatural. They're describing seeing something that moves so quick, it's not natural. It's like it's in fast forward on a camera or VCR ... it looks like it's digitally manipulating 'cause it's not fully there sometimes. It's in-between in *Predator* zone. It's just pixeled out of view and then it comes back in. And then, the use of no sound. Things moving and running should make a tremendous sound, but a lot of times, uh, people describe not hearing them move at all. Silently coming.
>
> **DA:** Yeah ... it almost looked like it was floating and running at the same time [Eichenberger, 2024, June 2].

Johnson's point is that these experiences can be "*tailor-made*" and "are just enough for [experiencers] to notice, but not enough to go brag about it to your neighbors." Johnson's comment is quite apropos, as it invokes the trickster nature of the continuum of phenomena that are related to encounters with apparitions, NHIs, and homins alike. Moreover, while falling outside of this remit of this text, the tailor-made characteristic, which can very much invoke conscious intent and perception of synchronicity, can be applied to other entity encounters as well. The intrepid reader would do well to consider the tailor-made character of the trickster. Indeed, Johnson and Adams report a number of bizarre and hard-to-explain occurrences in Johnson's text *The Owl Moon Lab* (2023) and other media. The idea that the phenomenon can essentially home in on experiencers and follow them home (i.e., the so-called *hitchhiker effect*) is documented by Johnson as he considers the various experiences that he and Adams had after the two cast an impressive pair of knee impressions in Oregon and brought them home to the lab. *Apports*, which are spontaneously appearing objects often associated with hauntings and poltergeist cases, became rather frequent afterward, including a toy stegosaurus, rocks, and other objects appearing in and around Adams's property thereafter.

The *deep weird* (Hunter, 2023), or the body of phenomena that utterly shatter any preconceptions about the world in which we live being anything but exceptionally strange, may evince an integrative "connecting principle" (p. 7) that interweaves all that exists to everything else. One might say that the weird reminds us of the true essence of reality and extends what is possible beyond the normal ken. For example, Simeon Hein comments on a conversation that he had with Igor Burtsev about a psychokinetic incident that Burtsev shared with him regarding the Sasquatch:

> When Igor Burtsev presented at the Bailey conference a couple of years ago (ah, the *Sasquatch Outpost* conference in Bailey, Colorado), you know, corresponding with him—and he mentioned this in the talk ... there were cases of psychokinesis when some of these cryptids, he says, were near their van. And I asked him specifically what he meant. He said little coins would start floating. Things would start moving around. They even had the car engine start by itself, even though they had taken out the battery. They were using it for heating or something like that.... It started anyway.
>
> To me, that seems a lot like this psychokinesis [PK]. Anyway, guys, you know my point of view on this. These are a spectrum of phenomena that overlap, and we're dealing all with the

> same sort of fundamental process that expresses itself as things do in our universe in just a myriad number of forms: whether it's cryptids being around you and having sort of strange electromagnetic effects, or even things that float, to people that can do PK, to these apports, to remote viewing [Eichenberger, 2024, April 5, 45:13-46:13].

Hein's point about there being a continuum of phenomena and entities is poignant and speaks to a broader epistemology that conforms to what more traditional, non–European models of knowing. In other words, there is continuity rather than discontinuity present in the cosmos. Moreover, researchers, speculative theorists, and authors alike such as Michael Persinger (1945–2018) and Mac Tonnies (1975–2009) have speculated that manipulations of the electromagnetic field around and/or within percipients could produce effects akin to entity encounters. If Sasquatch is capable of somehow producing effects that mimic or draw upon such factors, then some of the overlap between Sasquatch encounters and other entity encounters could indeed be based on a more essential electromagnetic—or even plasma-derived—foundation (Tonnies, 2019).

These phenomena can shake the experiencer out of a sense of normalcy into a knowing that the cosmos is much odder than one previously thought. For example, Thom Powell, science educator and veteran Sasquatch researcher, hailed as one of the first European American researchers to seriously pose the potential *paraphysical*[4] nature of Sasquatch (Ambrose-Meyer Entertainment & Educational Channel, 2024, March 10), proffers the following commentary:

> Right now, I think there's a lot more people than ever before who are willing to entertain the idea that the Sasquatch is one member of this community—this ... collection—of creatures that ... all operate on the fringes, the margins, of ... human existence [Ambrose-Meyer Entertainment & Educational Channel, 2024, March 10].

Thus, to an extent, those *super natural* (Strieber & Kripal, 2016) abilities that are so perplexing and even fear-inducing are actually within the purview of human capacity: in such cases, we may be afraid of our own innate capacity.

High Strangeness

That notwithstanding, astrophysicist and ufologist J. Allen Hynek's (1972) Strangeness Rating together with his Close Encounters categorizations have proved to be quite useful in helping to provide some degree of structure when it comes to analyzing or grasping events that seem to defy the very attempts at classification. Hynek's rating defined *strangeness* as indicative of the number of elements of oddness in an experience that may strain what he considered to be common credulity. As such, he states the following:

> The Strangeness Rating is, to express it loosely, a measure of how "odd-ball" a report is within its particular broad classification. More precisely, it can be taken as a measure of the number of information bits the report contains, each of which is difficult to explain in common-sense terms. A light seen in the night sky the trajectory of which cannot be ascribed to a balloon, aircraft, etc. would nonetheless have a low Strangeness Rating because there is only one strange thing about the report to explain: its motion. A report of a weird craft that descended to within 100 feet of a car on a lonely road, caused the car's engine to die, its radio to stop, and

> its lights to go out, left marks on the nearby ground, and appeared to be under intelligent control receives a high Strangeness Rating because it contains a number of separate very strange items, each of which outrages common sense [Hynek, 1972, pp. 24–25].

Thus, the variation between *low strangeness* to *high strangeness* is a useful marker of how much an event defies one's sense of what should be able to occur in their reality, and the latter term is one that is often used in fringed disciplines and communities. Parapsychologist George P. Hansen (2001, p. 404) notes that, contrary to what may be popular opinion, the classifications of so-called paranormal phenomena (i.e., ETs, Sasquatch, demons, etc.) are not per se discrete and distinct and that they in fact overlap: Sasquatch have been seen during UFO flaps and in people's bedrooms, for example, indicating what could reasonably be called a degree of high strangeness. And adding more fuel to this anti-structural fire, these phenomena tend to be *unbounded*, experienced by a large number of people across time and space (p. 210).

Further, woo woo, or simply *woo* (e.g., Bader et al., 2017, p. 244), is typically used both inside and outside of the Bigfooting community as a term to not only define, but also to derogate, dismiss, and deny accounts of high strangeness and those who pursue them, as well as any paranormal accounts of reality, generally speaking. That said, it should be noted that how one defines what is "odd-ball" or, conversely, what is "common-sense" as Hynek offers, is theoretically constrained by the fundamental culture or even hegemonic tendencies (Boykin, 1986) that constitute one's dominant worldview or perspective.

In terms of exceptional human experiences, what is odd for one person in one time and place may not necessarily be for another person in another time and place. What's more, even if an experience is deemed as odd by multiple people, how they choose to define or label said event may be greatly influenced by their background. In terms of the homin phenomenon, an entity encounter may be variously viewed as demonic, alien, flesh-and-blood, interdimensional, or as representative of some other ontology entirely, depending on one's position and worldview.

To help illustrate this high strangeness, we turn to an example from one witness known simply as Brandy. She reports having heard giggling outside of her 3-year-old son's window, as well as tapping on the window, muddy footprints in their home, the front door being left open, and more (Smyth, 2022, December 2022, 1:59:00). All of these encounters occurred as soon as Brandy, her husband, and their three children moved into a new home in the Ozarks. In retrospect, she states:

> We've had every weird Bigfoot activity happen to us as well: rocks thrown onto the roof, window taps, weird calls and screams from the woods at night. I'd even hear the flipping doorbell ringing, but the sound came from outside. We're still recalling all the weird things we ignored so easily [Smyth, 2022, December 2022].

Many if not all of these behaviors are potential invitations for Brandy and her family to cross a threshold, moving out into the space beyond the house into the realm of the Other. And understandably, such narratives of these entities being heard at physical thresholds such as windows and doors add to their status as liminal entities.

It is interesting to note that other homin-related figures such as the menehune[5] of Hawaii are known for leaving their footprints behind and at times interfering in the efforts of humans when humans transgress on their territory. Similar behavior is known all around the world and is at times attributed to humanlike beings of diverse sizes and statures. Moreover, we find in the above list that Brandy has provided a number of characteristics that are traditionally associated with poltergeists or hauntings. In the absence of a visual confirmation, there is no clear information providing a hint to Brandy of what the ontological reality of the phenomenon is. With that said, her 3-year-old son did report to her that he had seen a big, hairy man outside of his window, but neither Brandy nor her husband had seen the being themselves.

At this point, we return to the phenomenon of the Oz factor. Generally speaking, the factor refers to a constellation of occurrences in the ambient environment, including an odd or even inexplicable silence, a kind of electric feeling in the area, and odd weather such as fog, mists, or storms that seem to appear out of nowhere. Let us consider several examples of how this Oz factor manifests for Sasquatch entity experiencers.

First we turn to Amanda, who is a Forestry Department worker in Texas and had a Class B encounter in a national forest in 2008 after Hurricane Ike made landfall. While walking through the woods with one of her good friends, the two women suddenly had an intense feeling of being watched, experienced a deep silence that seemingly came out of nowhere, and were stalked or pursued out of the area by a bipedal entity. Each of these elements is commonly reported in the oral and written literature regarding Sasquatch. Amanda shares with host Wes Germer [WG] the following of her encounter about 25 minutes into an episode of *Sasquatch Chronicles*:

> **A:** When there's predators in the woods, those things that are prey animals—they fall silent. They're going to be quiet. They're not gonna reveal their-you know, they don't want to be eaten. They're—they're not gonna reveal their location. But when … even the very crickets go silent, it makes me wonder. That's something else. Like, that even the crickets won't make a noise. A bird won't fly. That's bizarre to me.
>
> **WG:** It is bizarre. It is bizarre—
>
> **A:** Yeah.
>
> **WG:** 'Cause nothing else does that [Germer, 2023, November 24].

Given her outdoors experience, the meaning that she makes of the encounter is telling. In other words, her interpretation of the silence should not simply be accounted for by assuming lack of knowledge of the behavior of local fauna in the presence of an apex predator. Sasquatch lore suggests that, without humanity's implements of war, weaponry, and (at times) wits, there would be no contest between humans and homins: our hairier brethren would be able to defeat us in shows of physical strength, cunning, stealth, and speed at every turn.

As field investigator and author William Lunsford relates, he has experienced the following odd sensation during an encounter while with his wife and son: upon prompting from his wife, Will realizes that "all the noise had just quit—it was … a noise that you could—a quiet noise that you could *feel*" (KayDee, 2024, August 18, 51:51), to which host Duke Sullivan replies "it's so quiet your ears start ringing" (52:08). While these kinds of descriptions may sound inexplicable to non-experiencers, they are rather common within the annals of the Fortean (Fort, 2008).

Next, we consider what experiencer and field investigator Old Bear says of a particular area of Summersville Lake, West Virginia, an area that yahoos have been known to run hunters out of: "it's quiet. Eerily quiet" (Byron, 2023, December 18). Such silence is quite common in Sasquatch reports. Animals that stay in the area don't make their typical noises, and other animals such as deer quickly move through the area. Or, as Fred Roehl—member of the Curyung Tribal Council and host of the *Subarctic Alaska Sasquatch* YouTube channel and website—relates the encounter of an Alaskan bush pilot referred to as Buck, we hear the following about Buck's experience after dropping off some brown bear hunters and landing his plane:

> He decided, "I'm gonna grab my day bag, and I'm gonna walk over to those [black spruce] trees over there and just check it out," 'cause he said … it was more silent (…he's been to some quiet places, just quite general), but he said it was *very* quiet when he got out of the plane, which he found odd. He thought maybe his ears needed to pop [King-Sharp, 2024, May 5].

As we can see, Buck's description via Roehl fits the unsettling emotional tone that can come along with the kind of unexpected silence that can accompany the Oz factor.

While the odd silence can be associated with wildlife going quiet when a predator is in the area, for those seasoned hunters, hikers, and outdoorspeople, the added quality of often feeling like something else is off is included with the experience. For example, in Buck's case, we find a classic narrative of this aspect of the lore. As he continues to walk toward the copse of trees, he begins to feel like he's being watched:

> So, he's just looking all around, trying to figure out, "why am I feeling this?" No one is there. He knows no one is there because he flew over the place. There was no one there that he saw: no other planes, no tents, no hikers, no hunters. None of that [King-Sharp, 2024, May 5].

The feeling of another presence in the area who is observing the experiencer is a common aspect of the lore that is one of the most common features of homin entity encounter narratives. A deep sense of unease typically accompanies it.

Further still, an experiencer known simply as John Turner relates his encounter in a Chicago forest preserve in August of 1967 with a tall, hairy, dark-colored biped. Emily Durante narrates Turner's encounter:

> He noticed another odd thing too which was that the park seemed to go oddly silent during the encounter. There were no sounds from any animals or birds. It was just the creature, the river, and me. The astute will recognize another case of the Oz factor [Godfrey, 2016, chap. 24].

As another example, Rich Daniels—field investigator and experiencer—shares a narrative about when he and fellow investigator Craig Sulk were looking for sign in the field one morning after Daniels had a Class B encounter. About 21 minutes into an episode of Barnaby Jones's *Monsters on the Edge*, Daniels states:

> We got about halfway down this road looking for different footprints and different types of you know anything that we could. And as I stood there I stopped and I realized that everything had stopped. Everything was quiet. It was like standing in a vacuum, and that you know of course tells me there's something big around. There's something that nothing wants to be revealed it's presence to right? Not hearing anything, you know, one of us, you know, had a side arm for this thing like that. And we could very—very well be walking into a situation that

> wasn't good and we agreed ... right then and there that we should turn around and go back [Jones, 2024, May 6].

In addition to the unease caused by their mere felt presence, the manner in which Sasquatch and their kin are said to move seems to almost defy the laws of physics. They are reported as gliding over the ground as though they are not touching it, moving at incredible speeds, and seeming to disappear or reappear out of thin air (e.g., Powell, 2018). And reports of telepathic communication with homins have begun to come increasingly into discussion within the Bigfooting community (Noël, 2019).[6] Indeed, avant-garde author Joshua Cutchin (2023a) poignantly notes that many of these overlapping phenomena seem to tell us something profound about life, death, and our place in the cosmos in what he terms an *ecology of souls*.

In general, the extent to which Sasquatch is evocative of other so-called anomalous, observable phenomena that are not easily understood within the Western paradigmatic milieu cannot be overstated. For example, those behaviors and perceptive abilities commonly known as psi challenge notions that individual humans are entirely and wholly separable from their environment and from other people. Parapsychologist George P. Hansen notes:

> Our society promotes rationality and leads us to view ourselves as discrete, independent entities. Psi challenges that idea by subverting the distinction between subject and object. Psi is intrinsically paradoxical, and paradox models are needed in conceptualizing psi phenomena; reflexive models provide them [2001, p. 278].

Indeed, both psi and Sasquatch are subjects that can get rather messy quite quickly, and when the two are placed together, we have high strangeness. The intrepid investigator may find that the rabbit hole of research is ever-deepening and ever-widening. Scientists and scholars who wish to maintain rather clear parameters around the nature of their topic should not pursue such fringed matters.

Cannibal Spirit

Before we get into the definition, mythology, and history around the subject at hand, at the outset of this consideration, I must note that the very fact that I have explicitly named Hairy Man and am herein discussing the cannibal spirit, or CS (i.e., *wétiko*)[7] as well is a transgression, as it is taboo across various segments of Indigenous America to speak of these matters. Speaking and writing are powerful acts that can manifest the reality being spoken of, drawing the entity or force to the speaker. Perhaps to this very point, the manner in which Hairy Man and CS are taken up within the largely European American Bigfooting community do not rely on the same tenets toward taboo. Indeed, seeking out a liminal entity is viewed as either inviting danger to oneself or to one's community *or* as being essential to the process of discovery. Paying respect to these two methodologies in tandem is quite challenging, but there are those who attempt to do so. I would posit that, given the state of the Bigfooting community over the past century, the proverbial cat was let out of the bag a long time ago. That is to say that the advancement toward scientific and personal discovery of homins, particularly within European America, has persisted. Additionally, the public service that individuals such as Curyung Tribal Member Fred Roehl and the late Scott Carpenter have done to educate people about the potential threat that homins can pose to humans is an important one, particularly due to the pursuit of questions about the homin phenomenon. Given this broader context, I decided to discuss the cannibal spirit in this volume to express some of the ways in which the larger homin phenomenon has shown up in the world and how it impacts—and is impacted by—the human psyche.

That said, *wétiko* (also known as *witiko*, *wendigo*, *windigo*, etc.; e.g., Forbes, 2011; Johnston, 1995; Peters, 2023; Short, 2024, p. 89) is a liminal entity offering an intriguing and illustrative case of how culture, spirituality, and entity encounters—both homin and otherwise—can overlap significantly, and particularly within an Indigenous American context. Indicative of its shape-shifting nature, the CS is variously conceived of as a supernatural entity, a sociocultural condition, a human beset by a cannibalistic affliction, or some combination thereof (e.g., Forbes, 2011; Peters, 2023).

The fear of physical cannibalism which is tied to the CS potential indicates the consumption of the flesh of one's own group or species. As I have posited elsewhere (Mitchell, 2023), the dual threats of cannibalism of and sexual assault on anatomically modern humans is clearly illustrated in narratives such as that of the Shoshone giant consuming a granddaughter and her grandmother (Strain, 2012). Arguably, the uncanniness with which these beings are described paints them as more human than not, and as capable of visiting great violence upon us. The relationship between us and Other thus becomes further complexified.

As Pfaller (2016) states, for example, narratives of the cannibal spirit are derived from the Algonquian-speaking Tribes of North America:

> "Wendigo" (as well as other variants of the same name such as; "Windigo" or "Witico") is the most prevalent Native American name for the creature commonly described as Bigfoot/Sasquatch from among some of the different area tribes in Eastern North America [Pfaller, 2016, p. 9].

The fact remains that the subject of the CS has been taken up in popular culture, horror fiction, the Bigfooting community, and in other sectors of non–Indigenous American communities since at least the time of Algernon Blackwood's creative fiction on the subject, and the idea of the negative mental effects of being afflicted by this force have persisted since the times of early European contact with Indigenous cultures.

With that said, from one vantage point, the cannibal spirit can be viewed as a rupture with what the Iroquois term the aforementioned longbody, the wendigo potential is an ever-present psychological, physical, cultural and spiritual threat that manifests through human beings (e.g., Levy, 2013, 2021; Strozier, 2022) who can affect the Indigenous community. Jack Forbes (2011) suggests that the CS is a "sickness of exploitation" (Forbes, 2011, p. xix): an affliction of exploitation, evinced by disregard, disrespect, and transgression upon other beings and the environment, such as through colonialism, chattel slavery, and capitalistic hyper-consumption. The extent to which Western culture-as-cannibal-spirit evinces a threat to the global longbody and, ultimately, even to itself, might lead one to consider that Europe exists in a rather liminal geographic state appended to the western edge of the Eurasian continent. As Mussi (2015) offers, "Europe extends at the outskirts of the enormous landmasses of Asia and Africa, outside the tropics inhabited by primates. At first glance, the geography of the continent is badly designed to accommodate any relevant evidence related to human evolution" (p. 30). Welsing (2004) has contended that the European psyche developed precisely because an archaic population of albino, or melanin-deficient, humans was exiled from, and thereby denied access to, sub-Saharan Africa: the otherwise fertile lands of the birthplace of humankind. That group came to comprise the ancestors of Europeans. While there do indeed appear to have been numerous migrations out of and back into Africa across the epochs, there is little archaeologic evidence to support the historical truth of this claim at present date; notwithstanding that, the narrative truth at least behind Welsing's position is still a potent one. Indeed, it is the challenging climatic conditions provided by this terrain and ecological niche that scholars such as Diop (e.g., Allen, 2008; Wobogo, 1976), Bradley (1991), and others have focused upon regarding the development of the particular cultural armaments and aggressive predilections of the Western collective psyche. Such a threat has attempted to consume the traditional and non–European psyches of the world, just as it has come to consume itself. Such is the modus operandi of the cannibal spirit. Mussi (2015, p. 30) concludes:

> Europe's secluded geographic position, at middle to high latitudes, actually prompted adaptations and solutions tailored to specific local characteristics during the Pleistocene. This even includes the local evolution of a hominin species or subspecies, the Neanderthals. Over a million years or so, humans again and again left evidence of being able to adapt to highly seasonal environments that went from rather cold to extremely cold, and furthermore, was characterized by uneven light time throughout the year, with scarce or no vegetation in winter. Developments in both technology and social organization were needed to succeed. A vast and sophisticated knowledge of natural resources, which happens to be different over short distances, built up through time and became an asset. In the end, the small continent is a kind of yardstick allowing to gauge changing human capacities, notably around 1 million years, when hominins first settled there, stably adapting only 500,000–600,000 years ago; and some 30,000–40,000 years ago, when Homo sapiens eventually took the place of Neanderthals.

Thus, the technological and social prowess of the populations that were the predecessors of modern-day Europeans helped them to stave off and conquer the harsh environment. Equally important, those same cognitive structures and cultural artifacts may well have contributed to those populations overcoming the Neanderthals that had predated them on the terrain and were likely better physically adapted to those harsh climatic conditions. The liminal collective had found purchase in this new home by unseating and at least partially consuming (i.e., through genetic introgression and, perhaps, even through a kind of *culturophagy*[8]) the former reigning champions in what is now Europe or western Eurasia: the Neanderthals. Such is the nature of the cannibal spirit.

Pushing this matter further, Brightman (2015, para. 6) posits the following:

> The four, sometimes blended, causes of metamorphosis were dream events, sorcery, spirit "possession," and prior logistical (e.g., "lifeboat") cannibalism. Of the symptom-indexes, the most windigo-specific are anthropophagous ideation or desire, freezing of the heart,

> and perceptions of humans as game animals. Also commonly described are anorexia (or its inverse, gluttony) and demeanors characterized as "melancholia" and "mania."

Thus, variously conceived as a psychogenic, sociocultural, spiritual, and even supernatural presence and threat, contemporary as well as older accounts from Indigenous American sources speak of a consumptive, even cannibalistic force that preys upon a people's minds, bodies, and ultimately the families, communities, and spirits of the people. This energetic force is a psychic and cultural illness that consumes all that it touches, manifesting in myriad ways at both the individual and larger collective level, and which needs to be dealt with and excised immediately lest it threaten to overrun the populace.

That force is exemplified in the mindset and actions of colonizing Europeans who brutalized the land, people, and flora and fauna of North America. Such a worldview successfully projected a vision of wildness and savagery onto all that they touched. Forbes (2011, n.p.) states:

> Various terms, such as "wild," "savage" and "barbarian" have been used frequently to refer to violent, crude, brutal, cruel, destructive and aggressive behavior. Ironically, such terms have often been used by European writers to refer to non–European peoples whose customs were different and were therefore (because of that element of difference) called "wild" or "savage." The irony stems from the fact that few, if any, societies on the face of the earth have ever been as avaricious, cruel, violent and aggressive as have certain European populations.

By this formulation, the CS represents a split from a sense of communion with the natural world (i.e., *connectedness to nature*; Mayer & Frantz, 2004) at the deepest levels, just as it projects that split onto Othered non–Europeans such as Indigenous people. From contemporary psychology, the loneliness and despair of the "false self" (e.g., Canty, 2022, p. 93) as well as the consumptive character and personal emptiness of the "empty self" (Cushman, 1996, p. 6) overlap quite well with the construct of the cannibal spirit. Additionally, the *preta* (or *hungry ghost*) of Buddhist and Daoist lineage (Wangyal, 1998), *Yurugu*[9] of Dogon cosmology (Ani, 2007), and *Set* of Kemetic cosmology (Plutarch, 2003) are ancient concepts that also share similarities with this consumptive, controlling force. Arguably, each of these personifications has at its core a lack of understanding of its true identity, a chasmic split between ego and Self, and thereby incessantly seeks out truth, power, or identity outside of itself. Arguably, this is the nature of Western culture.

As aforementioned, the CS also manifests through the actual consumption of flesh via the cannibalization of another human via a psychotic manifestation within the individual. But for historical context, consuming human (or homin) body parts has been enacted amongst different geographically dispersed peoples and is thought to confer beneficial health effects. Indeed, the practice of *medical cannibalism*, wherein deceased human or homin bodies are utilized for purported health benefits, was a relatively common practice in places such as medieval Europe and Asia.

Medical cannibalism includes the consumption of crushed mummies imported from places such as Egypt or of the boiled grease of enslaved African bodies (e.g., Woodard, 2014), consumed or utilized as fetishes by genteel European American society.[10] However, the matter of consuming body parts of homins or humans is by no means relegated solely to European culture. For example, particularly relevant to our subject of discussion is a well-known story within the lore of the Bigfooting community involving a particular tooth. While visiting various apothecaries in China in the 1930s, anthropologist Ralph von Koenigswald came across a large molar (Meldrum, 2006, pp. 89–90). While it was labeled in the store as a dragon's tooth to be crushed up for medicinal purposes, the researcher investigated it and came to name the specimen from which it came *Gigantopithecus blacki.*

Additionally, other cases of medical cannibalism come from Asia and include what Porshnev has found to be a rather insightful if not curious inscription in a 19th-century medical atlas. Porshnev includes the original text as follows: "The mi-gyo lives in the high mountains, it is a kind of bear with human form. It has extremely great physical strength. Follow the instructions for medical use of its meat and organs" (Porshnev, 2000, p. 32). Interestingly, Porshnev also comments that "there is no contradiction" between the text itself and the inclusion of an image that does not look like a bear in the slightest. Here, the subtext indicates that the imminent hominologist has equated the mi-gyo with a homin and has also included the harvesting of its body as a form of medical cannibalism. One potentially illuminating question that one may come to ask themselves is: at what point is an upright bipedal, hairy being no longer human or humanlike (able to be cannibalized) and simply an animal (capable of being consumed)? While the question goes beyond the remit of this book, it has rather important ethical implications.

But to return to the matter of medical cannibalism of anatomically modern humans, xenophobia along with its racist and/or ethnocentric manifestations has produced a situation wherein people have been demonized, terrorized, and brutalized and perceived as less than human. It is clear that in places such as the antebellum South in the United States, African Americans provide one example of such an Other to be feared, as a population legally codified as not being fully human (i.e., as three-fifths human). Ironically, as Woodard comments on the fear of being cannibalized by Europeans that was suffered by some enslaved Africans upon their capture, he states the following: "Even worse by way of reputation than the Portuguese were the English, whom some African groups understood to be an even more vicious species of cannibal" (2014, p. 32). Further, as stated by Michael Press when he states that usage of mummies was the most common form of medical cannibalism in Europe, he also proffers the following:

> In 1586, John Sanderson, an English merchant, bought 600 lbs of mummy and brought it back to London to sell to the apothecaries. In Europe, mummy found eager consumers. It was used at the English court of Edward IV. Francis I of France was reported to never go anywhere without some mummy combined with rhubarb. By the late 17th century, Russia—which had been a late holdout—came to embrace mummy too.
>
> Mummy was not the only form of dead human that Europeans believed possessed valuable medicinal qualities. Medical books from the 16th and 17th centuries mentioned drinking blood and ingesting moss growing on skulls, among other remedies [Press, 2020, August 6, para. 4–5].

It is insightful to note that Press argues that these practices did not eventually wane because people had misgivings about consuming human flesh, but because European physicians doubted its health-promoting properties.

On the matter of mummies, an illuminating passage from Porshnev (2017) is related. Porshnev's translator Lars Thomas found the latter's notes about a "supposed wonder drug" of "mummy" being unrelated to the subject of homins and decided to essentially omit the entire chapter from the final published translation (Porshnev, 2000, p. 265). This situation is quite unfortunate, as it denies the intrepid reader from being able to judge the merit of Porshnev's commentary on the subject of Asian medical cannibalism for one's own through that particular translated text. However, fortunately, Thomas notes that anyone curious enough can read up on this drug in another of Porshnev's books titled *The Struggle for Troglodytes*. The now out-of-print book was thankfully republished in 2017 in the *Relict Hominoid Inquiry* (Porshnev, 2017), and provides the following account:

> One of the main sources was the kichlak (village) of Khakimi, in the Karatagh valley, long a nursery of wild men. The name of the medecine, *mumieu* comes from the Iranian *moum*, meaning grease or wax, and from the Tibetan *mi-eu*, or rather *mi-gheu* which, as we already know means "wild man." In the Middle Ages, the Arabs sold in Europe a similar balm, and in ancient Egypt, the word mummy ended up designating the embalming itself. The particular color and the properties of the original substance have passed in the popular tongue to describe a tincture, or a hue, called *mumiya* in Russian [Porshnev, 2017, p. 138].

Thus, we see an explicit as well as implicit etymological connection between the existence of homins and the practice of medical cannibalism via consumption of mummified remains. But to return now to the particular matter of consumption of darkly melanated *human* bodies (e.g., Africans), I assert that the very threat of consumption that Africans feared of Europeans was archaically the same threat that humans in general (and what would become Europeans specifically) felt about homins. Moreover, history suggests that this fear has become so palpable within the European collective psyche that it had to be displaced upon others, xenophobically labeling other racial groups (and even other Europeans) as cannibals and savages. Fundamentally, this death anxiety is of the same emotional tone as that of Vendramini's Neanderthal teem, and would necessitate psychological, sociological, and cultural means of ameliorating it.[11]

Further, among the Amskapi Pikuni (Blackfoot), KJ Bear Medicine tells of an incident from the late 1800s or early 1900s wherein a woman with hairy arms and legs was invited into a family's home and was allowed to spend the night. She did not speak, but the family heard her making sounds throughout the night as though she was eating something. The next morning after she left, they found that in her place were the bones of a baby. Horrifyingly, she had apparently been chewing on the small body during the previous night (Bear Chief & Upham, 2023, May 7).[12] Her behavior and physical appearance smacks of the cannibal spirit. And among the Cree, this cannibal spirit is said to be a giant who consumes humans, growing with each meal yet staying ever-emaciated, always pursuing its next victim (Levy, 2021, p. 8). And further still, Gayle Highpine of the Kootenai Tribe avers that among the Turtle Mountain Ojibway (North Dakota), the CS may be a sign of psychic rupture within the community and might be equated with Rugaru (aka Loup Garou), the werewolf-like entity that preys upon human victims (Meldrum, 2006, p. 83).

These cases demonstrate the cultural significance of the CS for the community and its varied manifestations as consumption of one's own people, absent other extreme inciting events such as famine (Brightman, 1988). Brightman (1988) states:

> The noun *windigo* [Ojibwa *wīntikō*, Cree *wihtikow*] refers to one of a class of anthropophagous monsters, "supernatural" from a non-Algonquian perspective, who exhibit grotesque physical and behavioral abnormalities and possess great spiritual and physical power. Either many or all windigos were once human beings, transformed, usually irreversibly, into their monstrous condition. In some cases the transition was conceived as rapid while in others the condition could be covert and volitionally disguised. The phrase "windigo psychosis" refers in academic literature to an Algonquian-specific psychiatric disorder whose sufferers experienced and acted upon obsessional cannibalistic urges [Brightman, 1988, p. 337].

Given this conceptualization, the cannibal spirit may, at least at times, be viewed as the result of what Grobbelaar (2020) terms "false separation from the archetypal Self" (p. 25), thereby evincing a "heart of ice" which is then visited upon others in brutal fashion. CS is therefore tied to a number of separate yet overlapping ontologies (from the subtle energetic to the wholly physical), and yet it arguably exists solely in none of them, occupying a liminal if not trickster position.

Cannibal Spirit Psychosis

Through its varying and even shapeshifting manifestations, the CS can be tied to cultural artifacts that have consumptive effects. As scholars such as Levy (2013) suggest, to think that one has a full grasp on what cannibal spirit psychosis is, is foolhardy, and may even result in negative outcomes to those possessed of this notion. Levy (2013; 2021) has been greatly influenced by such Indigenous accounts and, like Forbes (2011) before him, has extended discussion of the disease into contemporary critique of Western culture. Defining the CS as a *malignant egophrenia*, or ME disease, he posits that it is a "cannibalizing force" driven by an all-consuming and never-ending hunger, which is at war with—and notably, in fear of—all that is, including itself (Levy, 2021, p. 9). The impetuous nature of this disease is such that, to use a phrase, it will cut off its own nose to spite its face. It stifles cultivation and development and freezes its host in the very image of its own egoic faux glory; furthermore, it displaces all that is disliked or disdained within it onto Othered beings, places, and things that exist outside of itself, thus violating the communal longbody (Aanstoos, Fall/Winter 1986; Porter, 2008), the interdependent web of those people, places, flora, and fauna with which we are connected. Moreover, Levy reinforces the idea that the disease evinces a trickster nature, constantly shapeshifting (Levy, 2013, p. 10), keeping people at least partially unaware of its true nature. Culturally speaking, it is thereby hegemonic, informing actions through reactive, unconscious behavioral programming that both blinds its host to self-awareness while simultaneously masking its presence.

The incessant greed—even psychosis (Levy, 2021)—which characterizes its manifestation is the result of lack of awareness or knowledge of one's own nature (Levy, 2021, p. 13). Similarly, in his discussion of psi censorship, Cardeña points to "egocentricity of knowledge" (2015, p. 612), which indicates extreme cognitive biases, logical fallacies (e.g., cherry-picking data), and myopia. Taken to the extreme, these characteristics are evinced through *psychic blindness* (Levy, 2013). Elsewhere, as Dr. Michael Adamse (Eichenberger, 2022) states in *A Flash of Beauty*, a state of mind wedded so firmly to fixedness, not seeing out of the box, and not seeing potential, is a hallmark of psychosis. Arguably, to not even consider possibility, to deny the narratives and experienced realities of others, or to vilify those who have a differing worldview or experience, may indeed be representative of a deep split from a fundamentally relational sense of self.

The CS is sometimes represented in the form of a Sasquatch who may appear as an omen that the eyewitness or community needs to course-correct, as they have lost their connection to Spirit. Thus, even in the most harrowing of encounters, a lesson may be learned. Following the narratives of Algonquian speaking Tribes, Meldrum (2006, p. 84) reflects that Sasquatch-as-cannibal-spirit represents a potential that is feared among Indigenous people, despite Sasquatch being viewed as an Elder Brother. In a sense, one might consider Elder Brother as providing us with a service in this case, demarcating a line that must not be crossed. We might further posit that he is an omen to hold true to ourselves and not turn from each other: to abide by the longbody. If Sasquatch-as-cannibal-spirit appears to a person, the person is being shown that they have, perhaps unwittingly, strayed too from their beliefs (i.e., psychologically), from civilization (i.e., socially or physically), and/or from their humanity (i.e., ethically or spiritually), and that they must return from whence they came with all deliberate haste and care. To not physically, psychically, or spiritually consume one's brethren and sistren is evidence of one's harmonious place and persistence within the longbody, as it is evidence of one's status as one of the people. Conversely, to engage in such cannibalistic and parasitic acts is indicative that the "icy heart" (e.g., Cooper, 1933, p. 22) of the CS has consumed the person's soul. Cooper views the icy heart as a figurative reference to the extreme conditions that can produce a CS-afflicted human: that is, the persistence of exceptionally cold winters and therefore the threat of starvation among the people. The cannibal spirit psychosis, therefore, is the constellation of behaviors that involve, specifically, a person desiring to consume human flesh, or more generally, a person turning against their own community and manner of enacting their humanity. Those who have an icy heart do not see themselves, nor do they see the world, as it is. Indeed, the icy heart evinces a split from one's communal and divine nature, and therefore indicates that a threshold has been crossed, and an essential taboo has been broken.

The fact that so many "isms" (e.g., racism, sexism, capitalism, etc.) and other extreme violations of dignity and humanity in our contemporary society are evinced by just such consumptive, cannibalistic acts is precisely what Jack Forbes (2011) wrote about in his reflections on Western culture, colonization, and consumerism. For example, he notes that Anglo-American imperialism has cannibalized Native bodies, land, and resources. Further, racism, sexism, and capitalism are among the most vile and virulent forms of what some scholars have termed the wétiko psychosis (Brightman, 1988; Forbes, 2011). Or as Spanish oncologist and researcher Salvador Harguindey (2000, p. 141) opines, "The overwhelming materialism of the modern world has become extremely cunning in disguising novelty as true progress." Indeed, narratives involving the CS are, at least in part, dire warnings about the pervasive corruptive force that European colonialism and enculturation have posed for Indigenous American people.

However, it is also clear in this particular case that the cannibal spirits mentioned here exist in the physical realm and are either people who have been possessed of the desire to consume human flesh or are actual giants threatening to consume human flesh. Of course, both instances would represent significant threats to the survival of the people.

The concepts of both the CS and the longbody persist along a continuum within the Weltbild of the Iroquois and other First Nations people, indicating two poles of a dimension of reality that indicates one's relative connection to creation (or life-affirming action) and to one's community. In interpretations from Roll (1987) and Aanstoos (Fall/Winter 1986), this fundamental connection to others allows for the development and promulgation of various psi abilities (e.g., telepathy) that are both practically useful as well as theoretically interesting, but which might also be frightening or threatening in their implications. One might rightly remember that if Sasquatch are also able to exhibit psi abilities such as *mindspeak*,[13] that humans and homins are connected in ways that go beyond the mere physical. Indeed, some Indigenous communities erect totems where these entities are depicted. Conversely, lack of connection to the interdependent and interpellated larger world is precisely what may eventually result in the manifestation of the cannibal spirit.

But to consider historical cases of cannibal spirit psychosis, we turn to 19th-century accounts such as those found among Algonkian (aka Algonquian) speaking peoples and include the *Kakisikutchin* (*Swift Runner*) and Ducharme legal trials, respectively (e.g., Brightman, 1988; Peters, 2023). The Swift Runner case has come down historically as a significant illustration of this psychosis:

> Swift Runner, together with his wife, six children, brother, and mother, separated from his wife's father during the fall of 1878. In the spring, Swift Runner returned alone, claiming that the other members had starved, committed suicide, or dispersed. He subsequently led a party of police to his winter camps where evidence of cannibalism was found. Swift Runner subsequently confessed to killing and eating six of his family. At his first camp, the eldest son had died of starvation and was buried; the police recovered the emaciated corpse. At the second camp, Swift Runner killed and ate successively the next eldest son, his wife, and the remaining children; he disavowed knowledge of his mother and brother who left the group earlier in the winter.
>
> Famine was an evident catalyst. The corpse of the eldest son demonstrates that Swift Runner's claimed illness and the famine that ensued were not fabrications. Possibly the famine was induced by an immobilizing psychiatric disorder afflicting Swift Runner, although an objective scarcity of game may be indicated by the inability of his wife or the older sons to provision the camp. Some collaboration of the victims in the murder and consumption of their predecessors is indicated by the fact that the serial murders were not at any stage successfully resisted. Although starvation may have prompted the first murder, it cannot explain the others. Swift Runner's winter camp was no more than twenty-five miles from the Hudson's Bay Company post at Athabasca Landing [Brightman, 1988, pp. 353–354].

Swift Runner was ultimately convicted of murder and was executed in 1879. Brightman further identifies cannibalism as a potential precursor of windigo behavior and also points to famine as a possible precursor to such behavior. As Peters (2023) indicates, "Swift Runner's friends and family members ... regarded his cannibalistic rampage as undeniable proof that he had indeed been possessed by the Wendigo, the evil man-eating spirit of the North" (p. 275). Whatever one's interpretation of the CS, the problematic is taken very seriously due to its potential to negatively impact Indigenous American society and has for better or worse been partially absorbed into European American popular culture.

As a poignant example, we learn the following from Meldrum (2006), which points us to another manifestation or even ontological narrative about what the CS actually is:

> Even among those eastern Algonkian tribes to whom Bigfoot represents the incarnation of the Windigo ... his fearsomeness comes from his very closeness to humans. The Windigo is the embodiment of the hidden, terrifying temptation within them to turn to eating other humans when no other food is to be had. He was still their "elder brother," but a brother who represented a human potential they feared [pp. 84–85].

A question that may therefore arise among a people is, "If Elder Brother can turn against and consume his own kind, am I not capable of doing the same?" Indeed, if Vendramini's (2009) proposition that Neanderthals cannibalized early humans carries any truth, then early humans may have felt quite similarly about our hairy, bipedal cousins. In fact, it would not be difficult to conceive of how phenomena such as a curse of Bigfoot (or of any other homin, for that matter) could manifest and persist among a people, even if there were no super natural (Strieber & Kripal, 2016) ontology behind such phenomena. Of course, if there were mechanisms at play that went beyond the normal ken into high strangeness or the deep weird, then the mere sighting of a hairy, bipedal being could evoke or trigger a great deal of existential tension. It would be imperative for a community to establish taboos to not provoke these beings and to stay within the clear demarcations of convention and tradition.

These considerations are extremely important for both existential as well as purely practical reasons, since every facet of the community hinges upon every other facet in order to maintain healthy continuity and, therefore, survival. Moreover, this fear of a force that presses against one's community, one's family, or oneself, is not constrained only to Indigenous America. In fact, it is a concern that is found elsewhere around the world, though the threat may be expressed in different ways.

For example, in the case of a somewhat obscure narrative that was brought into the Western world due to Japanese occupation of the Solomon Islands during World War II, lore has it that some of these soldiers were killed and cannibalized by violent, large (i.e., eight to 15 feet tall), hairy homins, and that some of the Indigenous inhabitants of the islands also used to engage in cannibalism (Lamana, 2023, October 12). Morehead (2024, p. 126) suggests that these homins were true giants, per Coleman and Huyghe's (2006) taxonomy. As we learn about 15 minutes into an episode of *Wartime Stories*, the host of the show, Luke Lamana, shares the following about field research conducted on this subject by archaeologist Nikolaus Cox:

> Because the giants themselves are also thought to be cannibalistic, some islanders believe that their native ancestors *were* cannibals because their culture was influenced by their prolonged contact with these violent, man-eating giants. While many of the islands in the Solomon Island chain are said to have no giant population to speak of, Nik was told that the island of Malaita is replete with giants. Bizarrely, a local man named Ishmael claimed that he himself

> was descended from these giants, and that among his family lineage was a particular giant who was a notable figure: a celebrated warrior from a tribe of giants on the island of Malaita who lived during the colonial period when headhunters still thrived. Ishmael explained that, while many giants lived in the jungles, others like his ancestral line, lived in the cave systems. Despite being separated on the surface by miles of ocean, there are locals who even believe some of the islands are linked by these extensive cave systems [Lamana, 2023, October 12].

It is noteworthy that there are similarities in the above account and others (e.g., Short, n.d., p. 31, pp. 281–282) that speak of hybridization between humans and homins: a matter which we cover elsewhere in this text. Further, if an accurate, deep memory can persist among the Indigenous people of Oceania for tens of thousands of years (Nunn et al., 2024), and if homins have indeed existed alongside humans for at least that length of time, then it is reasonable to expect that valid information about homins—as well as their ecological niche and their intermingling with anatomically modern humans—would have persisted into the present day. Further still, Lamana goes on to say that "As for the ancestral origin of the giants, among the Solomon Island people exists an understanding that, although they are a distinctly separate creature, whatever the original lineage of these giants is, it was borne out of humanity" (Lamana, 2023, October 12, 16:30–16:42).

But to return to the matter of the violent and cannibalistic tendencies that humans and homins alike have maintained, it might be helpful to consider one perspective provided from anthropology. In his introduction to his text *The Human Animal: A Personal View of the Human Species*, anthropologist Desmond Morris proposes, "We are sometimes monsters, sometimes magnificent, but always animals. We may prefer to think of ourselves as fallen angels, but in reality we are risen apes" (1994, p. 6). Reflecting on one's capacity to do harm to others can lead to the depths of despairing rumination or to the heights of collective aspiration, but if one chooses to deny any consideration of such matters, the urge toward *Thanatos* (i.e., the *death drive* per psychoanalytic thinking; e.g., Webley & Zackariasson, 2023) may overtake one's being and express itself in unhinged and unanticipated ways.

Illustrative of the power of such images, whether they be held in autobiographical memory in the oft-hidden recesses of deep memory, these are the stuff of dreams and nightmares. For many Indigenous peoples, it has not been enough to sustain narratives that are purely symbolic in epistemology, in ontology, or in axiology. For example, according to scholars such as the late Vine Deloria, Jr., of the Standing Rock Sioux (Lakota), there had to be a *practical ethic* to any worldviews espoused by First Nations (Deloria, Jr., 2022). Elsewhere in the literature, reflecting on the work of anthropologist Levy-Bruhl, Hansen (2001) remarks on the necessity of "exceptional memory found among primitives" as well as the lessened need for abstraction (p. 354). Therefore, recognizing the potential of the CS was not simply a collective thought experiment but could help to unite the community, reminding its members of the very real danger that could come from transgressing communal dictates.

As is the case with many depictions of the cannibal spirit or even of homins elsewhere (e.g., Forth, 2007), it has been difficult for scholars to determine the potential nature of such beings or entities; indeed, physical (e.g., Meldrum, 2006), sociocultural (e.g., Evans, 1979), psychological (e.g., Brightman, 1988), spiritual (e.g.,

Forbes, 2011), fable/parable (e.g., Bindernagel, 2010, p. 233), and other ontologies have been asserted for them throughout oral and written literature. Given the range of accounts on the CS and CS psychosis, it may be wise to focus on broad implications as well as the specific instances of the construct in the material and metaphysical worlds, instead taking a kind of non-dualistic approach to the subject while still being able to appreciate its particulars within Indigenous and other affairs. To use a phrase, perhaps it is helpful to not lose the forest for the trees (behind which the CS may hide).

Moreover, the aggressive denial of the possibility of homins within mainstream science runs parallel to the threat of the CS in that both potentials are, at least theoretically, borne out of fear, and both potentials can result in defensive actions taken up by a collective.

View It from the Bridge

This chapter has dealt with the matter of homins being liminal entities as noted in various segments of the oral and written literature. Specifically, it has dealt with aspects of high strangeness discussed in oral and written literature, including the Oz factor and the interesting matter of overlap between homin narratives and those of poltergeists. This chapter has also presented the subject of Sasquatch-as-cannibal-spirit, a liminal entity symbolizing the limits of humanity (e.g., cannibalism) that are not to be transgressed. We have also considered examples of the manifestation of cannibal psychosis in humans, as well as other relevant liminal entities and their relation to human-homin contact.

Lastly, before moving on, I would encourage you to pause and consider at least one of the reflective prompts on cognitive, emotional, somatic, or conative matters that I have posed in the introduction.

4

Sasquatch and Sight, Sasquatch and Sound

Following our consideration of high strangeness and the general liminal nature of homins, we now consider some of the characteristics of the homin phenomenon that involve sight, apparent manipulation of shape and/or how they are perceived, as well as how the phenomenon involves sound and acoustic energy to communicate and manipulate the human response.

Light Absorption, Light Reflection

Yet another reported ability is known simply as *cloaking* (e.g., Carpenter, 2022; King-Sharp, 2025, January 9, 16:45). Perhaps one of the oddest pieces of compelling videographic evidence is the "cloaker" or "Predator" video filmed by field investigator Barbara "Barb" Shupe (e.g., Eichenberger, 2023). It illustrates what members of the Bigfooting community have, at least informally, come to call the *Predator effect* because it is defined by the perception that a Sasquatch "cloaked," as Shupe stated, similar to what is demonstrated by the eponymous character in the *Predator* franchise or to what the Klingon warships are capable of doing in the *Star Trek* franchise.[1] Such a description of cloaking has been given by other experiencers and members of the larger Bigfooting community as well (e.g., SunBôw TrueBrother[2] via Bignell, 2023, October 19; Warren, 2023, December 1).[3] Despite the reports of cloaking by witnesses in the field, Shupe's is the only recording that I am aware of that appears to have actually captured the effect. Regardless of how the effect is achieved, it is worthy of further study as the phenomenon may be able to elucidate something about human perceptual capacity.

In other matters regarding unexpected homin characteristics within the visible light spectrum, experiencers often report Sasquatch demonstrating *eyeglow* during encounters. When prompted, many eyewitnesses will clarify that the eyes are not demonstrating eyeshine, as nocturnal animals tend to do when light is shone on them; instead, witnesses report homins having eyes that seem to generate their own light (i.e., self-illuminate), shining from within. Colors said to be emitted by homins that have been reported in the oral and written literature include but are not limited to red (e.g., Bear Chief & Upham, 2023, May 28, 7:36; Shackley, 1983, p. 129), blue (B. Ann Slate as cited by Lamana, 2024, June 8; Brost, 2023; Eichenberger,

2024, August 15, 32:12), amber (e.g., Irwin, 2024, April 20; Brost, 2023; King-Sharp, 2024, April 14; Palacios, 2024, June 24, 2:45), green (Lynn, 2024, May 4, 49:02), orange (Short, n.d., p. 140) and even reddish-brown (Jones, 2021). Aside from dark black or brown, eyes the color of red that seem to be internally generated (Alley, 2018) or self-illuminated arguably tend to be reported most often in the available eyewitness reports.

Notably, homin entity encounter narratives suggest that not only can these beings notice emissions such as infrared that lie outside of the visible light spectrum, and that they tend to not want to be photographed or videotaped, but that artificially generated light is actually bothersome to them.[4]

One related aspect of the homin phenomenon involves the idea that they are sometimes reported as being blacker than black, exhibiting *light absorption*, are unsettling aspects of encounters that seem to defy the flesh-and-blood hypothesis.[5] For example, one report submitted to *Subarctic Alaska Sasquatch* states that a couple "saw this dark figure on—uh, it was—the only reason they knew it was, uh, on two legs is because it was blacker than the darkness there…" (Roehl, 2023, February 8). Indeed, Fred Roehl has stated that during his own encounter in Alaska with his elder and his cousin, that one of the large, hirsute entities looked like it was absorbing light. He describes this being as follows as it stood behind an outhouse:

> It was at least 13–14 feet tall. Every bit of five-five and a half foot wide, right? Hulking. Big. But what was scarier than its size is it was absorbing the light. No eyeshine back … it was like … the darkest shadow you ever seen just absorbing light [Irwin, 2024, March 8].

Roehl goes on to say: "It felt—in that moment, it felt like that big, black nothingness was there for us, and I can't even quantify into words … how disheartening it felt to—to see that" (Irwin, 2024, March 8). It is reasonable to assume that the apparent light-absorbing quality of the subject did not add to Fred's sense of safety in the least but instead added to the visceral nature of the harrowing encounter.

An experiencer named James describes the aftermath of a one-night encounter that occurred decades ago between a homin and James's grandmother as well as her father and uncle:

> From where uncle lit [the homin] up with the [flash]light, they found a small hair sample containing five strands. My grandma still has two of the samples. She described them as all black, absorbing nearly all light that illuminate them. The only way to clearly make it out is by putting it behind a much lighter surface. She showed the samples to me, and they were long: one, four inches, and the other, being six [Warren, 2024, April 19].

James's grandmother's own sighting of the being whom she had named "The Man from the Fog"—indicating the homin's black hair and dark skin—as well as her uncle and father's encounter, corroborate the conclusion that the sample belonged to the homin and the peculiar relationship that some of these beings seem to have with visible light.[6]

As one final example, we consider the following reflection from *Bigfoot Case Files* wherein experiencer Anthony comments on his return to the site of an encounter that he had one night. At the very end of the episode, he offers these words:

> The following day, I returned to the area with my wife and son, and noticed a clear, large, open pathway of sorts through the thick brush. No actual animal trail, however, created by hooves or anything like that—just matted down brush where something large had matted down a walkway. Lots of berries in the area,[7] and a stream within 20 yards, and mountainous cliffs ascending to impenetrable territory just beyond that.
>
> Something comes down out of those mountains at night and eats at those berries. It does it with enough regularity to create a pathway. It does not have hooves. It is eight-to-nine feet tall, and dark enough to soak up the light from a spotlight. It is alive and does have eyeballs that reflect light. There it is: my closest so far encounter [Smyth, 2024, April 25].

Such descriptions can be found from time to time within the oral and written literature on the homin phenomenon, and they paint a picture of a group of beings that clearly tests one's understanding of reality.

Anomalous Trackways

Let us now consider some other, odder aspects of homin phenomena in due turn. Due to the fact that Sasquatch and other homins are so often known by the tracks that they leave behind, we begin this somewhat cursory review by considering cases of vanishing tracks. Oddly enough, cases made by otherwise credible witnesses of trackways that seem to suddenly stop with no apparent egress occur frequently enough to merit some consideration. These *vanishing trackways* have become a subject of intrigue for many (e.g., Cutchin & Renner, 2020a, 2020b). For example, Tobe Johnson states the following of a site where a long-term experiencer who was a Navy Seal had had encounters:

> When things started to occur, like the first extended experiencer that I was allowed to go on their property and [their] tent [was] moved 49 feet and stuck in a tree: I had to pay attention to that. There was really no good explanation. It was a Bigfoot area where tracks and Sasquatch and lights have been seen, and not only tracks, but tracks disappearing in the snow, which I'd heard from the fringe side of things. That these tracks will suddenly be there and then they will disappear [Eichenberger, 2024, April 3].

Despite the seemingly bizarre nature of such occurrences, they are by no means the strangest characteristics of the factors and finds that comprise the Sasquatch phenomenon. Or, as Holland (2024, April 1) reflects, "this is this track that there's no way to fake it, but this track set now goes into a dry creek bed and then just stops. How do you explain that? So, you don't get to cherry-pick your data." The recurring theme of people not being willing to consider data that falls beyond their *boggle threshold* (Haynes, 1980) is a matter that often arises in the pursuit of such fringed phenomena. The threshold is the psychological point beyond which information cannot be accommodated or assimilated into one's schema—that is, moving beyond that threshold boggles the mind. It is insightful to note that the very term "boggle" may be derived from the bogle or bogey, the evil spirit, which animals such as horses are said to be able to see (McLuhan, 2024, March 29; Tréguer, n.d.).

With regards to another example of vanishing tracks, we turn to Thom Powell, who states the following:

> Sasquatch tracks in mud, dirt, and snow have all been observed to abruptly end. There is not simply explanation for how this is done, but there is a definite pattern to this observation, made over many years by many field researchers: track ways do mysteriously and abruptly end, as if the creature that made them disappeared into thin air [Powell, 2015, pp. 136–137].

Further, the book series *Where the Footprints End: High Strangeness and the Bigfoot Phenomenon* authored by Cutchin and Renner speaks to the high strangeness of the Sasquatch phenomenon through more than just its title. For example, in the first chapter of Volume I, a series of odd encounters in 1978 on the property of the Hilsmeier family of York County, Pennsylvania, are included in the following account:

> Allen Hilsmeier and his sons found weird three-toed footprints crisscrossing their land. The tracks were each 16 inches long and six inches wide. The depth of each footprint seemed to indicate that it was left by something with a considerable weight. The stride of the creature was measured at about five feet. This stride did not vary—even when going up steep hills. Each footprint fell in line with the previous—they were not offset by human tracks. Some 2,000 tracks were left in the icy snow around the Hilsmeier farm across two miles of rugged terrain over barbed wire fences, through the woods, across the Creek, and over a distant hill. The trackway terminated strangely in the middle of a field with no indication of where the creature went from that point [Cutchin & Renner, 2020a, p. 4].

If one sought out to test the alternative hypothesis of hoaxing, how might such a feat have been accomplished? Proposing methods such as being airlifted into and out of an area simply to fool whoever might stumble upon a trackway seems as preposterous as some say that claims of high strangeness are. Not only did the report involve a "large, bipedal, hair-covered creature" (p. 4) undocumented by modern Western science, but it also inexplicably involved sightings of three-toed tracks. There appears to be no precedent in the fossil record for three-toed bipeds within the hominin line, though there is evidence of tridactyl locomotion elsewhere in the evolutionary tree.

Even so, this apparent dactyl oddity is actually repeated elsewhere within the annals of cryptozoology: reports of the famous Fouke monster of southwest Arkansas as well as Momo the Missouri monster, and others, also contain mentions of three-toed impressions (e.g., Cutchin & Renner, 2020b, pp. 143–144; Slate & Berry, 1976, p. 72). By definition, to attempt to study such incidences, one's boggle threshold would arguably have to be relatively high. Cutchin and Renner (2020a) suggest that the traditional cryptozoological community focused on flesh-and-blood accounts would necessarily fall outside of such endeavors.

As another example, bowhunter and experiencer Mark Parker (Eichenberger, 2023, December 23) shares the following reflection on encounters that he has had with the hairy giant:

> I wanted to believe 100% that it was an ape, but.... I don't think it is.... I can track animals with the best of 'em, and there's times where.... I'll follow a set of tracks and all of the sudden the tracks just disappear. Where'd they go? It's ... walking on the same ground, but why is it leaving tracks now when it's leaving tracks that're anywhere from inch and a half to two inches in the ground, and now there's nothing? Where did it go? I don't know.

As another example of this phenomenon, one veteran investigator who has not been timid about wading into the weeds of the weird is Stan Gordon, author of *Silent*

Invasion. In an interview that he conducted for the *On the Trail of Bigfoot* documentary, he states the following of a report of vanishing footprints:

> Several months ago, a family from north Huntington, PA contacted me. They provided me [with] a very clear color video of a series of very strange footprints in their yard. They had awakened in January of ... 2018 to see this unusual series of large 15-inch-long footprints, approximately. About 70 feet of them with about a four-to-five-foot stride between the tracks. And what was so interesting to them was here's a series of tracks going through their yard. It goes over to the children's play area, and they suddenly stop and vanish. There's no more tracks. But also, when they went back to look where the tracks started at, there was no beginning. The tracks didn't just come up—for example, come across the road and come to the yard. They just started out of nowhere: began in the yard, continued for a distance, and disappeared [Breedlove, 2019b].

While the above account is unique in that there was no apparent beginning *or* end to the trackway, attempts to explain away or generally to understand reports of trackways that abruptly stop can be met with a variety of reactions, from incredulity to healthy skepticism and more.

Further, one experiencer who refers to himself as Steve shares the following narrative on the *Bigfoot Michigan Rob* podcast after having found what appeared to be foot impressions in the snow in his and his wife's backyard:

> I continue to follow these tracks for several more yards before they stop. So, up to this point I'm already kind of apprehensive: now I am just flat mystified and felt a little bit of anxiety start to rush through my head [Karnafel, 2023, May 6].

Several months passed and no further evidence emerged until one day when the couple decided to go on a walk together in the snow. Steve continues as follows:

> We were quite a distance from the house when those large (non-animal) footprints seemed to appear from out of nowhere. These were fresh and distinctive. Amy asked, "Steve ... who is walking around out here?" Before I could reply, she retorted: "And whomever it is, is a huge man, and he's crazy! Who walks barefoot in the snow?" We stopped and looked at the tracks, then followed for another 20 feet, when suddenly, they stopped much like the prior tracks I found earlier ... several months ago. Amy and I looked out in the distance for any sign of a person walking around. To our dismay (and maybe, perhaps, kind of relieved) ... we found or did not see any person around.
>
> Now, the most strange and eerie thing that I have ever witnessed was about to happen to me and my wife: directly in front of us, we noticed a bit of powdery snow kind of begin to puff out, as though a person was walking through the snow, causing the disturbance from your foot from the snow tap. [Rob interjects: ...he's seeing footprints starting to appear right in front of his path...] Then even more amazing, the footprints started to appear directly in the snow in front of us ... much like the footprints that had stopped earlier. Amy looked at me in bewilderment. "How can this be?" We both seemed to be in shock, yet for whatever reason, we were not frightened. How can these tracks be formed without a physical presence?
>
> We continued following these tracks as they continued to puff up plumes of snow (I guess "plumes of snow," lack for a better word, Rob) leaving the huge footprints in front of us. These tracks kept appearing. In fact, they continued with Amy and I trailing up the river that ran across the land. The river was not fully frozen, as it was a bit too early in the season, and the river ran briskly and fast. Chunks of broken ice could be seen flowing down the stream with considerable force. This is where the tracks ended....
>
> The story takes one last turn here: at the other side of the river, we saw a manifestation of a huge, humanlike figure suddenly appear on the other side of the river. It was transparent,

> and you could see right through it. This was not a human, yet looked like an animal. It was extremely tall and wide. It seemed to look directly at us with what appeared to be bright, blue eyes that were now more distinguished than the immense frame of the ghostly body. Then it turned from us, took a few steps, and disappeared.
>
> I do not know what this was. I have heard of Bigfoot being a spirit amongst the First Nations' people, but to this day, I am left with an amazing feeling of enrichment in some odd way. And you know, Rob? I am glad this encounter happened. Amy and I have not seen anything since, and we thought it was a rewarding experience [Karnafel, 2023, May 6].

Bigfoot Michigan Rob's response indicates openness to the possibility of what the couple reports. Interestingly, there is indeed literature of entities that some scholars have simply referred to as hairy ghosts (e.g., Cutchin & Renner, 2020a).

Some ideas proposed include homins walking backward in their own tracks, to them taking impossibly large leaps that lands in a location that is far from the rest of the trackway (Cutchin & Renner, 2021a, p. 12). Authors such as Alley (2018, p. 172), for example, points out that bears as well as humans are known to walk in their own tracks from time to time, and it would not be unreasonable to suspect a Sasquatch (presuming they have some primate-based ontology) engaging in such behavior.

As Trees, Into Trees, and On Trees

In addition to the above accounts, we find a variety of patterns in existing lore that involve either witnesses reporting literal *shapeshifting* or the perception of shapeshifting (e.g., Eichenberger, 2023; Roehl, 2023, March 20). A particularly large subset of these narratives involve Sasquatch and *trees*, thus adding to their liminal status. In addition to Sasquatch being reported shaking trees, peeking and hiding from behind trees, breaking trees, throwing sticks, branches, and trees at people or placing them in pathways to block ingress, and making all manner of so-called tree structures, they are tied to trees in a number of other ways as well.

Homins are perceived as having legs that look like tree trunks (Roehl, 2025, March 4, 17:07), as logs lying on the ground six to eight feet from an observer (Brown & Brown, 2025, March 4, 11:39–13:43), or as "deadheads" (i.e., partially submerged logs floating in the water; Alley, 2018, pp. 62–63). Both for posterity and to indicate ways in which this particular theme manifests, I include herein a number of the accounts that have found their way into the Bigfooting community, linking homins—and particularly those in North America—to trees.

In addition to narratives speaking of these entities turning into or looking like logs, stumps, and tree trunks, there are stories of them hiding behind trees, climbing trees, swinging in trees, striking trees, using trees and brush as signs and symbols (e.g., placing trees in the ground upside down; Alley, 2018, p. 248), holding tree trunks and branches in various ways (e.g., Alley, 2018), and using tree stumps for various purposes. Indeed, Bayanov (2012) states that "demons in Russia are found of tree-climbing, swinging on the branches, and diving from trees on the river bank into the water" (p. 32), statements which align from reports of homins elsewhere around the world as well. It has even been stated that Sasquatch have been seen literally moving into and out of trees (Morehead, 2024)—a matter which we will return to shortly. Indeed, as investigators such as Ron Morehead—an elder statesperson in the Bigfooting community—have conceded, there is clearly a relationship between Sasquatch and trees, and it is one that appears to have rather deep roots, if you will excuse the pun. Let us now consider some of these narratives about Sasquatch and trees in due turn.

To begin, we turn to the words of Kelsey Charlie, cultural leader of the Sts'ailes Band in Harrison Hot Springs, Canada, which he shares with his colleague Bob Kronbauer as follows:

> **KC:** I've seen them, yeah. I've seen them.
> **BK:** You have?
> **KC:** So this happened in ... 2002. There was two of them. The big one was squatted in the water, and then the little one was standing beside it. And then the big one gave the little one a drink of the water out of its hand. I seen the footprints. I smelled them. I heard them. But I've never *seen* nothing like that before [Kronbauer, 2017, May 15, 3:34-4:07].

Charlie's reflection that he had never "seen" anything like that before may be a reflection of the fact that at first, what he thought he was looking at was a stump in the water; however, being familiar with the area, he knew that no such object was there. It is interesting to note that people's knowledge of the natural environment (in this case, illustrated in his awareness of the presence or absence of trees in the area) seems to actually act *against* them when sensing and/or perceiving these beings. Such a ruse may well help Sasquatch keep their presence concealed from untrained, prying eyes."

Next, we turn to a brief description from an experiencer called Mr. H who regularly went hiking with his daughter in Stinchcomb Wildlife Management Area after seeing the location featured in an episode of *Finding Bigfoot*. As reported by Ryan White of the Native Oklahoma Bigfoot Researchers' Organization (NOBRO) just under an hour into a documentary about the "White Witch" of Stinchcomb, Mr. H, his daughter, and his girlfriend had the following encounter in July 2021:

> They're hiking towards the back of the park, and they hear ... these thuds. Like, "thud, thud, thud" right off of the trail. And the daughter says, "What's that?" And he's like, "What do you mean?" And the daughter says, "That tree sounds like it's breathing." And so, Mr. H went on to describe that the breathing sounded like this weird, asthmatic-like breathing [Terrell, 2024, May 26].[8]

Herein we find language suggesting that the Sasquatch has, at least to the percipients, turned into a tree that is breathing. Another experiencer, field investigator Joey Hawkins, reports seeing what he at first thinks is a tree one night:

> I started walking down the ... hill. Well ... the moon had come out and I could see the wall. So, then I'd had my flashlight on. Well, I got probably half way down and I saw what I thought from the distance was a tree. And as I got closer to it, I realized there's no tree there. That tree would have been in the way when I was raking hay. It would have been in the way. I wouldn't have, uh, I wouldn't have been able to rake that right there. So, I said, "hm," So I eased on down and got a little closer. Well, as I got probably I would say 40 yards from it, it moved. But when it moved, I stopped. And I had my flashlight in my hand, so I–, I turned my light on, and I shined up. And when I shined up, this creature turned away from me, and stepped down into the creek behind the trees [Evans, 2024, January 3, 9:58–10:38].

Or, in the case of extended experiencer Janice Carter Coy, she reports that when she was about 6 years old, she had run into a "tree" while bringing water to her grandfather one day. She fell backwards and looked up, only to find that Fox, the Sasquatch who she would come to find out had been befriended by her grandfather decades earlier, was staring down at her. Apparently, she had run into his leg (Green & Coy, 2002). For posterity, I include some of Janice's narrative here:

> Along about late June or July of 1972 my Papaw and I were on the back acre picking blackberries. We always carried a water jug with us as we picked, but for some reason it was empty, and Papaw decided I should run back to the house to fill it. I skedaddled back to the house and was returning with the full jug at a dead run to where I had left Papaw at. I could clearly see Papaw through some trees and underbrush up ahead of me. When bam! A big tree moved into my path! At least I took it for a tree at first. I hit it in the back of the knee area. This thing did whirl with lightning speed and backed off a couple of feet. It was a male bigfoot. At the time I didn't realize it was male but do so now. This thing scared me so bad that I screamed and nothing came out. I wet and messed my jeans I was so frightened [Green & Coy, 2002, pp. 11–12].

Her grandfather was able to de-escalate the situation between Janice and Fox, but it is interesting to note that people tend to know that, save a few rare species, trees do not tend to move; however, in the moment, young Janice thought that a tree had moved in her way. Her encounter with the "tree" was part of what would become decades of encounters that she and her sister Lila would come to have with Fox and his family and would set the stage for the publication of what may be one of the most significant natural ethnographies of human-homin encounters in Western literature. We will return to Janice's narratives later in the text.

Further, we might consider the following encounter from 1961 in Citrus County, Florida. The experiencer was a 17-year-old junior assistant Scout Master who was taking a shortcut back to camp after finishing his nightly duties. He recalls:

> The return trip was uneventful, and it seemed unusually quiet for a location normally filled with the sounds of frogs crickets and the occasional bump in the night. I decided to take a shortcut through the forest to bypass a bend in the trail and I came to a clearing with what appeared to be a stump. I reached a distance of about six feet from the object and then it stood up [Smyth, 2024, March 31].

As with the above experiencer, in another experiencer Joe Keske's narrative (which we will return to shortly), about an hour and 16 minutes into an interview, he states that the Sasquatch that he and two other witnesses saw one night was "what looked like a tree stump that was about 25 yards out into the water" in a beaver pond (Hajicek & Hajicek, 2024, March 6). In this case as well, he had interpreted the large, male entity as something other than what he was.

Similarly, another narrative from South Carolina close to the Georgia border deals with a boy not realizing that he is looking at a Sasquatch at first, despite having seen the same homin on numerous occasions prior. The relevant portion of the narrative is as follows:

> Just as before in January, it was there waiting along the pines that lined the driveway. This was my best and closest look at it yet. It was the only clear look I had of its face. He was lit up from the slanting sunlight. I don't think it realized that I could see it at first. If the sun hadn't hit it

> the way it had, I might have taken it for another tree or part of a tree. It stood rock still, and it was looking past me like it was trying to not make eye contact with me, but still keeping me in the field of view [Warren, 2024, January 16, 22:04–22:44].

Again, the idea that human visual perception is hampered when the subject is not moving is illustrated here. Due to standing "rock still," the homin likely aided to the misperception.

But to help make this Sasquatch-as-tree-stump connection abundantly clear, we turn to another example from extended experiencer Arla Williams. She shares the following about a Sasquatch youngling who she surreptitiously views while she is outside gardening one day:

> "Baby girl" [the name that Arla had given the young one] I saw the year she was born. Um, she was already up walking around and was over across the creek from me. And I was cutting briars when I looked up and I thought, "Is that a stump?" And so, I kind of lowered my head 'cause I didn't want, you know, to bother her or to scare her, and actually I was afraid she'd leave. But I would kind of look up every little bit, and there she was: this little, square, dark-colored baby. And, uh, I was just, you know, like, "Oh, my gosh." I wanted so much to say something, but I was just honored that they were there watching me, and then went about my business, you know, doing what it was I was doing. I never want to jeopardize anything with them [Eichenberger, 2024, July 7, 13:31–14:27].

As another experiencer puts it, while waiting for a homin to stand up and walk away after spying the being briefly in the woods, the witness "began to wonder if the animal was in fact gone, and [if] perhaps [they had been] looking at some strangely shaped stump, because it did not move, and [they] could not see it well enough to tell exactly what it was" (Smyth, 2024, April 12, 10:40–10:51).

Yet another encounter is related by a woman named Sherry who, when she was a young girl playing with her Barbie RV outside a cabin one day, saw a large, brown-colored entity who had squatted down to watch her. Sherry, upon being prompted to walk back to the cabin by a friend of the family who had also spied the figure, shares with us the following description about 13 minutes into an episode of *Buckeye Bigfoot*:

> I finally moved when I felt him nudge me on my arm. As soon as I started walking toward the cabin, that tree stump stood up, and it sprinted back up the slope incredibly fast, and it was lost in the trees. You could hear the branches moving, and things breaking as it ran away [Warren, 2022, October 31, 13:02–13:21].

In general, the idea that Sasquatch appear to be trees or tree stumps for concealment fits into what one would expect of beings who utilize the environment to hide their presence. Importantly, some of the work that is currently being engaged in by Michael Anne of the *Tactical Bigfoot Research* team is an interesting and insightful project that correlates visual sighting data from close, clear encounters with the flora in the area. Notably, the research provides a window into whether reported Sasquatch hair color corresponds to the Indigenous or local trees, including bark and foliage, thereby providing ecological validity to the study of the larger Sasquatch phenomenon (Anne, 2023, May 28). The working title for the project is "Terrain and color (TAC): A comparison of subjects and the environment—A look at sighting reports using witness identified color definitions" (Anne, 2024, April 25, personal communication). For this endeavor, Anne and his team use colors that participants can identify through a known and sharable color palette database. Thus, the general configuration of color reported in North America also is relatively well represented halfway around the world as well. Similarly, one might argue that such reports map on rather well to the distribution of color present in the great apes. As odd as it may initially seem, the perception of Sasquatch-as-tree-stump occurs more often than one might expect it to, in my estimation.

As another example, a witness named "John" who saw two homins when he was 11 years old in 1977, out walking with his younger brother and their cousin Brad. John shares the following about his perception. The three boys had just smelled something rather odd and were trying to figure out where it was coming from:

> So, we're looking around. We don't see anything. We're looking around, and I noticed some movement out the peripheral vision. And it was off to my kind of, you know, to my right, and about 40 feet away. And so, I turned and I looked, and I saw about, I don't know, five-foot-five dark brown creature that had its arm wrapped around a tree, I thought. And its head was tucked in, and it was peeking up over its arm. Like if you had like your head down on a desk almost and you just kind of looked up, you know.
>
> So, it was kind of peeking up out of there and then turned its head very sharply back into what I thought was a tree. And I'm looking at this thing. And then I–, I'm looking at the tree, and then I start following my eyes up, and I realized it's not a tree—it's the leg of a–, of a really big creature. And, uh, it was definitely female. Uh, she was 7–8 foot tall. Really—really large. Uh, about four foot across. Large black eyes. She was motionless… [Germer, 2023, December 15, 6:02].

In John's case, he is clear that he perceived the female homin's leg to be a tree, but also indicates that his perception was odd due to the fact that there was nothing else out in the field that should have precluded him or the other boys from having seen her or the young one who was hiding behind her leg. To the time of his interview, decades after the encounter, John was still unsure as to how they did not see the entities sooner. Interestingly, later in the same episode, host Wes Germer comments on another narrative involving what a logger initially thought was a tree stump standing up until it was about eight feet tall (40:57–41:55).

We now turn to several accounts reported by consummate field investigator and content curator Bobbie Short. One involves two young boys named Tommy and Raff, ages 9 and 11, who were spending a weekend with their parents at the Mount Charleston Lodge in Las Vegas, Nevada. They were returning to their cabin after spending a Saturday afternoon exploring the wilderness area when it happened:

> [T]hey saw what they thought was a huge tree shaped like a giant man. The older boy said, "*The tree moved*," and they became "*weirded out*." Still thinking it was a strange tree, they got closer and the tree moved its limbs and at the same time they saw the tree had hair growing on it. Young Tommy looked up and saw the tree had a face that looked like Santa Claus looking down at him, Tommy said he screamed and the tree backed up and moved away walking like a man. They ran all the way back to their parents but the e-mail said their story wasn't taken seriously [Short, n.d., pp. 176–177].

Short opines that either the boys needed eyewear or they encountered a homin that was extremely well-camouflaged, blending into the surrounding foliage. The fact that the boys were not taken seriously is not an indication of the veracity of their sighting as much as it is an indication of the denial and stringency that has persisted in Western culture and Western-affected cultures for quite some time.

Another report from Short involves an experiencer known simply as "R.G." While spending some time with several others in northern California between Arcata and Crescent City in October 2003, the following occurs to the party:

> In the late afternoon the 3 of us ate and were scrambling for some firewood. It was late in the season and the area had been picked clean. We fanned out, and I started away from the creek heading into the deep woods. I looked around and saw large trees and a few big stumps. Suddenly, one of the stumps seemed to disappear. I was about 25 yards from it and could swear that a large redwood stump moved! I went in the direction of it and saw a man walking away into the deeper woods. I saw him for about 10 seconds. I yelled out, but all I got was a "whistle." I could tell he was big because another stump he walked by was later measured about 6-feet tall; he was at least a foot taller than that stump. It was evening, but the light was not gone completely. I thought he seemed to be wearing bulky, dark clothing. I didn't get a clear view of anything except his silhouette [Short, n.d., p. 230].

Due to the waning evening light, R.G. did not realize until talking with the other campers that who he had seen was likely a Sasquatch rather than a really tall man wearing "dark, bulky clothing" (p. 230). The next morning, they searched for sign of human habitation but found none. While R.G. was left still questioning whether or not he had truly seen a Sasquatch, his account jibes with others that report this kind of behavior.

Another account noted by Short (n.d.) involves three campers—a couple comprised of Susan and Lowell P., and a man named Sid Jones—who encountered a being given the appellation the Phantom of Fordyce Lake. While camping one night at Fordyce Lake in Nevada County, California, Susan and Powell were awoken in their tent to the sounds of someone or something rummaging through their camp. After going outside and shining his flashlight toward the sound of heavy breathing, Powell was looking at a stand of trees. He reports the following:

> I keep the light on the area while Susan lit up the Coleman. Then, holding my light steady I think I see this tree trunk move, no kidding the damn thing moved!! I'm thinking okay, "*what the hell is going on*. By the way, I'm sober as a judge" [Short, n.d., p. 352].

Eventually, fellow camper Sid Jones comes to support the couple and help them figure out what is going on, by which point both he and Powell can now see that the "tree trunk" is actually a towering, hair-covered, humanoid. Powell estimates that it is standing at least nine feet tall, with extremely wide shoulders. After realizing who they are looking at, Jones urges Powell to not shoot. Eventually, the being turns around and walks off into the darkness. Given the fact that the couple had been woken up from sleep and there was little to no ambient light, it is not particularly surprising that Powell at first thought that he was looking at a tree trunk within a stand of trees. However, despite the less than ideal visual conditions, the narrative that he and Susan shared still jibed with reports of daytime sightings that include similar perceived features.

In yet another encounter, we turn to the words of Fred Roehl, who shares the following report from a biologist named Timothy who was visiting Canoe Village in Alaska off the Kuskokwim River around 2008 for some field research with several other individuals including a security detail. About six and a half minutes into the interview, Roehl describes the scene:

> They're all standing there just kind of watching ... the way the clouds were moving over the rocks. They were just kind of like, you know, all commenting on how beautiful it looked, like, you know, "Look at the clouds moving." It just kind of has that eerie kind of feel.
>
> And as they're talking about this eerie feel, they notice what they perceive as an old tree stump right up there in the center of this rock outcropping, right? And they're all kind of like... "That's a big ass tree stump." And they're looking around and there's nothing comparable. There's no other big tree stumps or any relatively large trees around, you know what I mean? It's a lot of vegetation, you know ... and so they were kind of thrown off by that, and they figured, "It must be an ancient one. Maybe we should go look at that tree stump ... when we're done with our stuff ... we'll take a little side trip. It's not that high up there ... we'll go and check out this stump, you know, check it..." 'cause it intrigued them ... why this big tree stump is there. And there's no other big trees.... So they made a mental note of that and they're going along.
>
> Now, as they start moving again security takes the lead, you know, telling them... "Listen ... for ... signs of bear moving through the brush, and gruffs and this and that," right? Well, just as Timothy is gathering up the stuff again, he put on his pack, and he had his little pail with his work stuff in it, and he looks back up—just one more glance up—at that tree stump: just kind of like, "Wow." And he notices that tree stump starts moving. And it goes from directly in front of him off to his left and then jumped off the rocks.
>
> Blew him away.
>
> He's stuck there for a second, like "What the hell did I just see?" And then he starts yelling at the group, "Hey, hey, hey! That tree stump just jumped off the ... edge of the rocks!" And so, everyone's picturing, "What's wrong with you? A tree stump doesn't run and jump." But he was so in shock of what he just saw ... the words weren't coming out, right? So, he ... checked himself, so he goes, "It wasn't a tree stump. It looked like a large man. It just jumped off the rock."
>
> So now everyone's attention is got. They back up to this little gap in the brush and they can't see anything: tree stump's gone. So, they're like, "Okay, what the hell?" [Roehl, 2024, May 28, 6:30–8:40].

Roehl's above account from Timothy is followed by the team hearing "the lowest, most reverberating growl he had ever heard comes from the direction this thing had ... leapt off the rocks in the brush out of sight" (9:11–9:21). The cognitive dissonance in Timothy's sighting is clear, as he has trouble reconciling what he thinks he is seeing per his recent memory of the "tree stump."

For anyone attempting to better understand examples of this Sasquatch-as-tree phenomenon or those that follow, one would do well to attempt to distinguish between potential top-down and bottom-up processing of such events, at least when possible.[9] With *top-down processing* (i.e., via perception), an experiencer may use prescribed cognitive schemas to perceive environmental stimuli. For example, Daniela (of Sioux heritage) says of her encounter near Cottage Grove, Oregon, in 2008, that she thought the homin who she was looking at was a fir tree because there were other fir trees in the area; that is, until the "tree" stood up, "unfolded" with arms, legs, and all, and walked away (Byron, 2025, May 18, 13:06–13:13). The fact that other trees were in the area served as a cue through which she initially experienced the Sasquatch as being just another tree, noting that if he had not moved, she probably would not have noticed anything amiss. On the other hand, bottom-up processing (i.e., sensation) more directly relies on the sensory input itself to establish the nature of stimuli (e.g., what it is, where it is located in space, etc.).

As another example wherein a homin appears to be a tree stump, we turn to the words of experiencer Phil who was visiting the Shoshone National Forest in Wyoming. On July 30, 2019, while sitting outside of his RV one evening at a camp site, relaxing and doing a word search, the following occurred:

> I was in the shade from the RV, but the trees in the clearing beyond—they were still bright and lit up with the sun. I would say that visibility was exceptional at that time.
>
> There came a time that I looked up, and through the clearing out between the trees that was right in front of me, I did a double take because I suddenly noticed a really dark tree stump that I hadn't noticed before. It was just in front of the band of trees at the back of the clearing. I looked at it and looked at it, and I shrugged and figured that I just hadn't noticed it before because the sun was only on it now.
>
> I went back to my word search, but for some reason I wanted to take another look at that stump again. "Yep, it was still there." I can't say why I wanted to keep looking at it, but now I wonder if my subconscious somehow knew there was something wrong with it. I took a long look again, but it still just looked like a dark stump at the edge of the trees. Thinking back on it now, maybe my mind had picked up on how much darker that stump was compared to all the other trees around it. Like, maybe the stump had been in some kind of a fire, but there was no evidence of a fire in that area. I still wasn't sure why I kept looking at it, but something was bothering my brain.
>
> Now sure, I could have gotten up and walked over there and looked at it, but I was 68 years old at that time, so I opted to check it out from a distance. I was in good shape, yes, but I knew I wasn't able to outrun anything if it happened to be a bear or something weird. So, I went in and got my binoculars. And you know what? By golly, by the time I got out there, that stump was gone. Huh. Well, I decided to play it safe, 'cause it was surely a bear, right? It had just stayed still and was watching me. So, I picked up all my things quickly and called it an early night and went inside to watch some movies that I had on my laptop [Warren, 2024, August 13, 3:27–5:45].

Phil was not bothered that night but ended up seeing the dark-colored "stump" again the next morning while finishing up his coffee. What made the object's reappearance striking was because not only had Phil not seen it earlier—in fact, he had used his binoculars to scan the clearing earlier in the morning but did not see any sign of it—but the "stump" was now twice as close to his position (i.e., about 50 yards away) as it had been the previous evening. Phil continues that "…even more unnerving was that just as my eyes landed on it, I saw it getting into the stump position" (7:45–7:54). Bringing his binoculars back to his face and adjusting the focus, he now sees quite clearly the face of a Sasquatch, complete with a clear vision of a hooded nose, grayish-brown skin, and even eyelashes. Of course, regardless of what is occurring with this Sasquatch-as-tree stump phenomenon, such a ruse is sure to be quite effective in obscuring homins' presence from humans or other prying eyes, including those of furtive quarry such as deer and elk.

Next on this phenomenon, we consider the experience of experiencer Gina who had an experience in Oklahoma in 1986 when she was 16 years old. After she and a friend snuck out of their houses one night and drove along a dark road to meet up with some friends, the two girls saw the following on the side of the road:

> We were near the last bend of the road where we would turn to get to the lake. Out of nowhere, Miranda, my friend, let out a squeal and asked if I saw it. I was half asleep with both of my arms on the passenger door. I was letting the night breeze hit my face. As she slowed the car down, I looked over in that direction and I saw a shadowy figure on the side of the road. At first, she thought it was a stump, but stumps don't move.
>
> As I looked to the left of the road, all I saw was this huge, broken piece of tree, about seven to nine feet tall. It stood tall until my friend stopped to take a better look at this weird stump. He walked gracefully across the road in front of us, like he was waiting for someone to give him the right of way to cross over. To me, he looked like a huge, massively built man, casually taking a stroll. I didn't think it was a Bigfoot [until later], nor do I recall being afraid. That's probably why I barely recalled it. I do know my friend was afraid. We decided not to go back out that night to not tempt fate. Friends told us they heard knocking noises all night at the lake, and they didn't stay long [Warren, 2023, August 1, 2:47–4:16].

Gina and Miranda's perception of the entity being a stump initially may have been primed by the trees surrounding either side of the road, which provided a thick canopy. Miranda's interpretation of the figure being a tree stump jibes with how other percipients cognize what is essentially an unimaginable experience. From one perspective then, it may, at least in part, be the lack of movement that may fool the brain into perceiving the beings as nothing more than inert flora.

It is interesting to note that this phenomenon is not bound by geographical boundaries. Other reports of Hairy Man appearing as tree stumps come from outside of North America such as Australia (e.g., Harrison, 2023, August 28, 13:21). Herein, the witness recounts walking along a path outside of Houston Golf Course, golf balling (i.e., collecting lost golf balls to sell) in about 1990 in Birkdale, Murri (Queensland). The area that he found himself in was one that his father had warned him not to venture into, though the particular reason for not doing so was not conveyed. The witness states the following:

> And I'm walking along, and I look up, and I could see this big log—looked like an old burnt log—and it was across the path, and I was about probably 20 meters from that.... I had to look up, otherwise I'd trip over that log. And just to the right of that log, there was a stump. There was a stump there about three-foot high, and it looked like that was a tree that had burnt out, fires had gone through there. I'm just thinking, "Something's not right here" [Harrison, 2023, August 28, 7:26–7:51].

He was correct—something indeed was not right. The witness ended up seeing a large, female homin down the path from him with her back to him, attempting to place a log in the crook of a tree. But what was just as astounding was that the "stump" to his right was not a stump at all, but was a small homin who was staring at him:

> To the right of me, I wasn't looking at a tree stump in the ground: there was another one of those buggers, and he was three-foot high, and it was the same color as the big one. And I'm thinking, "Aw, shit. That's the baby. That's the baby of whatever that one is" [13:16–13:36].

Even more jarring was the fact that the witness, now making eye contact with the small, chestnut-colored being standing a few meters from him, could not move his legs to get away. He felt that he was in a trance and that the entity closest to him was reading his mind. I would encourage the interested reader to listen to his account in the video, as it also includes his own drawings of the encounter and those of artist Buck Buckingham of the Australian Yowie Research (AYR) team which depict the beings.

Further, the language used by experiencers tends to be literal (e.g., "the tree stump stood up," as we see above) rather than figurative (e.g., "he looked like a tree stump") when relating Sasquatch to trees. That is, homins are often said *to be* trees or stumps, rather than simply *to look like* trees or stumps, such as we see in a Lummi Nation tale wherein a Hairy Man known as the *Glue-Keek* is said to have legs "as big as tree trunks" and skin that is "as tough as leather" (Short, 2024, p. 29). It is not always clear whether the usage of wording that we have seen above is a rhetorical device to add to the feeling or experience of the story, is due to the oft-times extreme cognitive dissonance experienced in the moment of a homin entity encounter, is the actual result of perceived matter manipulation by these beings, or some other factors. I find it rather interesting that literal language seems to be used so often with this particular tree theme. Indeed, as one witness states, the dissonance can be rather profound, especially during the ambiguity that can occur during momentary encounters.

Moreover, the dissonance that can occur does not per se need to be evidence of an other-than-natural phenomenon, as I am sure many can attest to the fact that natural entities can be exceptionally good at concealing themselves. As my parents and I stood watching a group of harbor seals sun themselves in Pacific Grove, California, one afternoon on New Year's Eve 2024, I noted rather quickly that when they were not moving, they appeared to simply be large rocks. In fact, after my mother pointed them out to me as we approached their position, saying explicitly that they were harbor seals, I perceived them to be boulders (for a reasoned summary of how movement and the freeze response may play a role in this Sasquatch-as-tree-stump phenomenon, see Webber, 2025, March 24). Despite knowing that they were seals, whenever they stopped moving, my mind would immediately revert back to having trouble processing the idea that they were not rocks. Their movement dispelled the illusion. Fred Roehl's narrative of encountering a well-concealed female homin in a clearing while he and others were caribou hunting aptly illustrates this character: "her coloring was such that as soon as she hit those … black spruce, she blended in seamlessly like a … baby duckling in the grass, you know what I mean? Just natural camouflage made it appear that she disappeared, but she was still there. You heard her crash through the trees and stuff…" (Byron, 2023, September 26, 44:27–44:44). Given that homins, whoever or whatever they are, are arguably at least as intelligent as harbor seals, the position that they are true masters of camouflage and subterfuge is a tenable one. Any perception of them appearing to be tree stumps makes more sense when taken from either a naturalist's or from an anomalist's position.

In addition to the above cases dealing with high strangeness and trees, one particular source that Cutchin and Renner draw from is B. Ann Slate and Alan Berry's (1976) informative text simply titled *Bigfoot.* In it, the potential high strangeness of some encounters with these enigmatic and reclusive beings is brought into full view: itself an oddity given the time at which the book was initially published. In one chapter, Slate and Berry begin by focusing on cases that retired detective Ken Coon had investigated. One involved a man by the name of John Parkhurst who had witnessed a "tree" step across the road while he was driving near Lancaster, California, during the spring of 1973 (Slate & Berry, 1976, p. 69). The giant figure turned at the waist to look at the approaching car before disappearing on the other side of the road. Upon investigating the site, Coon noted that there were 18-inch-long footprints at the scene as well as evidence that something had flattened a sage brush. In addition to the problem that there was apparently a large hairy man walking around at night, the matter of where it had gone baffled the then-captain. He stated, "I went to the spot, and although I remember a shallow wash, some brush, and a few Joshua trees, there was nothing to hide an eight-foot-tall giant in just a few seconds. Could he have just disappeared?" (Slate & Berry, 1976, p. 69). Further, other reports of a large, hairy biped also occurred in the area and help to corroborate this sighting.

And lastly, another case involving the connection between Sasquatch and trees is as follows from Stephen Barcelo, proprietor of the Cryptozoology and Paranormal Museum of Littleton, North Carolina. In an interview with Doug and Alex Hajicek on *Untold Radio AM*, he states the following after being asked about what he thinks Sasquatch are:

> Personally, I kind of still lean towards, ah, flesh-and-blood, I mean, just 'cause I'm finding the prints. But, I could tell you stories about some of the guys that're—I've worked with in my group, and … they've come back to me and said, like, "I watched this thing move across, went behind some trees that weren't even big enough to hide this thing, and it was gone." And then they go to the area, like, "Is there a hole there? Is it a,'" you know, 'cause there was gold mining … tunnels and stuff around some of these areas, and—but there's nothing there. There's no place for this thing to have gone. So, how did it just disappear? How did it just blink out? So, they kind of lean towards the interdimensional end. Personally, I kind of—I haven't gone there yet. But I kind of—I trust these guys. I understand what they're—you know, they're honest. They're—they come back and they're uncomfortable [Hajicek & Hajicek, 2024, March 28, 1:52:30–1:53:16].

Following further queries from Doug Hajicek for alternative hypotheses, Barcelo continues:

> I wasn't there, so the sightings they've seen—it's like, [Sasquatch] go behind some trees that are no more than, like, 10–12 inches wide. This thing's four times the size of that. It kind of walks behind and it's gone [Hajicek & Hajicek, 2024, March 28, 1:53:23–1:53:34].

In addition to highlighting the theme of trees that often comes up in Sasquatch narratives, incidents such as these speak to the stranger nature—or at least perceived stranger nature—of some Sasquatch encounters.

In a video on his North American Bigfoot Center (NABC) YouTube channel, veteran field investigator, museum curator, and content creator Barackman and the original witness relate an encounter involving a road crossing. While driving home late one night after getting off work at 12:30 a.m. on April 14, 2021, around Stevenson, Washington, the witness comes around a curve slowly, only to see a tall bipedal figure bounding across the road. Our witness then swerves to avoid hitting the subject, bringing his car to a halt. Directly in front of the car, the figure now appeared to be a "stump," and Barackman relates what then happens:

> …right in front of his hood was a "stump"—a "stump." While the witness was looking at this stump, one side of his brain is saying, "Look at the stump." The other side of his brain is saying, "There is no stump here. I drive home every single night. There is no stump there." And then suddenly, the "stump" stands up [Barackman, 2024, December 12, 0:59–1:22].

The unnamed witness's description is one that likely occurs in the minds of other experiencers of this aspect of the homin phenomenon. To aid potential future understanding of how this aspect of the phenomenon is perceived by witnesses, it may be insightful for researchers to ask experiencers who use this kind of language to elaborate on this aspect of their experience.

Moreover, I would note that a proposed counterpoint to this whole narrative has been put forth by Loxton (Loxton & Prothero, 2013), suggesting that people may mistake a tree stump for Sasquatch, rather than mistaking Sasquatch for a tree stump. The authors reflect on a case wherein two shepherds, Jill Carrier and Jolene Shepherd, who were working on the Alaskan panhandle thought that they had seen a Sasquatch, but remarked that it was probably a tree stump instead. Upon examining the site later, the author and the witnesses found that it was indeed a tree stump.

On this point, there are several hypotheses that may be advanced to explain the reports wherein Sasquatch are perceived to be tree stumps. An oft-cited comment both within and outside of the Bigfooting community is that *pareidolia* (i.e., the tendency to unconsciously perceive meaningful patterns in otherwise ambiguous stimuli) can account for misidentified sightings of Hairy Man. Pareidolia may help to explain what happened with Carrier and Shepherd's experience. However, it does not explain the vast majority of cases wherein experiencers report seeing Sasquatch as trees and tree stumps. In fact, in most spontaneous and single-encounter narratives such as those that we are considering at present, the experiencer has no interest or belief in Sasquatch or is not looking for Sasquatch in the first place (e.g., experiencer Dee's account that he "was not looking for Bigfoot" when he and his son had their encounter; Byron, 2024, May 10, 14:05–14:07). That is to say that in these cases there is no real reference point, conscious or otherwise, for perception of a homin. There are alternative hypotheses that have been put forth by some members of the Bigfooting community, at least some of which overlap with Indigenous American accounts of these beings. Extended experiencer and field investigator Chuck Jacobs summarizes some of these points, including Sasquatch being able to project mental images into the minds of the observer (i.e., through mindspeak; Jacobs, 2024, May 30).

To further discuss competing hypotheses of this aspect of the phenomenon, we turn to a narrative from a woman who is half–Choctaw. She recalls an evening around the fire when she was younger, spending time with the Choctaw side of her family a few miles from Lake Sardis in Oklahoma. As people were getting ready to go to bed, one of the uncles of our unnamed experiencer asked her to fetch some water from the hand pump to put out the fire. At about 12 minutes into the episode, she describes what happened after she heard a "a sharp, barking, grunting noise" from the tree line while getting the water:

> I had no fear, even when I heard this strange, barking, grunt sound. I knew well what a buck sounds like, and although I had never encountered a bear, I somehow was certain this wasn't a bear I was hearing. But then my flashlight shined on a very large, reddish outline that was about nine feet tall. I thought it was a broken tree that had red bark on it, though I knew of no such trees. Then, it moved so that it could keep the flashlight off of its face. I held my breath when I saw that big shape outlined in the light. This was a big and very furry humanlike gorilla thing. I didn't know what else to call it then. I had heard of Bigfoot and Sasquatch, but for some reason, I didn't equate what I was looking at with them. It was nine feet tall, and it was four feet wide at the shoulders [Warren, 2023, August 1, 11:57–12:59].[10]

The above experiencer had prior knowledge of Sasquatch but did not equate who she was seeing with these beings. Additionally, contrary to many of the "other" narratives that we are considering here, she uses language to refer to her perception of the event (i.e., that she "thought" that she was looking at a broken tree). Her narrative therefore presents a different perspective from that which Loxton offers—namely, that people can have awareness of Sasquatch and yet still not make the connection between the stimuli they are sensing or perceiving and a homin until later during the encounter or even much, much later. The psychocultural claim that people are primed to perceive Sasquatch due to the prevalence of the trope in popular culture and thereby perceive what they are primed to perceive is a claim that could use further research to test, but it is not one that seems to be borne out by eyewitness testimony as of yet despite the presence of figures such as the Jack Link's beef jerky mascot, Harry in the film *Harry and the Hendersons*, and others (King-Sharp, 2024). Many experiencers simply do not think that these entities exist and end up being quite surprised and shaken at their encounter.

Further still, bowhunter Joe Morris tells of an encounter when he sees a large, black tree stump where there should be no such thing (i.e., at the base of a receding glacier). He realizes that as he is walking down a trail that he has traveled quite often and recounts the following to Jeremiah Byron [JB]:

> **JM:** I look at this stump, and I'm thinking, "Well, I'm gonna go sit on it. What is this thing? It's weird. It shouldn't be here." And I walk towards it, and my feet get tangled in the brush. I look down, you know, get 'em untangled and keep going.
> **JB:** Mhm.
> **JM:** And I look up, and it's gone.
> **JB:** Oh, boy.
> **JM:** And one thing I hadn't told you is, while I was watching this stump before I walk towards it, it opens its eyes. So, on the side of the stump, its eyes opened.
> **JB:** *Really?*
> **JM:** And, I was shocked. I'm like, "*What* is this?" So, I thought whatever it was would get up and run away. That's why I was standing there slowly smoking this cigarette, looking at this thing. And it was probably—it wasn't far at all. I don't know how many feet. It was a ways, you know. I'm a bow hunter. It would be an easy shot, so, 25–30 yards. Um, so I'm like, "Well…" And then it closed its eyes and it turned into a s—you know, you couldn't tell it was anything else. So, I'm like, "Well, I'm gonna go find out what it is."
> **JB:** [chuckles]
> **JM:** so, I … got a gun on [inaudible] no big deal. So, I walk towards it, get stuck in the brush a little bit, look up, it's gone. No sound at all [Byron, 2024, July 29, 17:14–18:37].

Morris's encounter is insightful because it adds another wrinkle to this aspect of the homin phenomenon. If his narrative exemplifies historical truth as well as narrative truth—that is, that it not only "actually happened" but that Morris also perceived it so—it would suggest that some entities may be able to partially shift between two entirely separate physical states and back again: that of fully inanimate tree stump and that of animate Sasquatch (if a homin was indeed the object of Morris's perception). Further, this case suggests that the shape-shifting character that some experiencers and mythologies have attributed to Sasquatch or Sasquatch-like beings is not simply the result of misperception or even of images being projected into the mind of the observer or witness. A tree stump that sports a blinking, winking eye and that also can disappear (or at least move so rapidly as to be indistinguishable from vanishing) would definitely be situated under the rubric of high strangeness, if not the deep weird (Hunter, 2023). Indeed, regarding high strangeness, the inquiring reader should note that tree stumps and logs are found elsewhere in Fortean folklore as objects to deceive humans or to stand-in for humanoid entities (e.g., Fae folk).

On the matter of Sasquatch and tree stumps, I would be remiss if I did not point to the oft-noted behavior of Sasquatch being perceived by their human observers to use trees for cover. In one particularly riveting story, a large male Sasquatch interacts with a tree during an experience that is, in my opinion, one of the most intriguing encounter narratives that I have heard. Sybilla Irwin—artist, field investigator, and host of the *Sketching Encounters* YouTube channel—illustrates experiencer Marc's recollection in a two-part interview during which Marc recounts a nighttime encounter two Sasquatch (one male and one female) outside of his cabin window. Marc recalls the following after having briefly lost sight of the large male while his attention was occupied by the female Sasquatch:

M: Where's the big guy: what happened to him? I don't see him, but where—I, I know he's not far away.

SI: Yeah.

M: Last I saw, he went over the edge [of the deck], so I look up. I–, I look over the side and I look up, and the trees that I had pruned along the side of the cabin there, I'm looking at the trees. That's all I see, but one of them is way too big [laughs]. It's really wide, and I knew I'd pruned that tree. [Sybilla places illustration on screen of Sasquatch behind tree] And here's this big, wide tree, and I'm looking at it, and I'm going, "Oh, yeah." And he was standing right, so perfectly in line with that tree, and he even showed, like, a couple little stubs or something, you know.[11] I'm looking at it, and I'm going, "I took all the branches off that tree. There's not ... supposed to be [inaudible]—"

SI: Oh my gosh, that's incredible.

M: I knew I took all the branches off all those trees. And yeah, so here he is, standing in there like that. And the minute I saw him, he steps out. He takes one step out, and I see his leg and I thought, "Yeah, there he is." And then, he kind of makes a, "Omph," and steps out again completely. [Sybilla places illustration on screen of Sasquatch standing beside tree, hanging onto it with his right hand] And he's sort of hanging on the tree. He looks over at me, and he's just kind of, uh, you know, just like, "Omph," and he's looking at me—not super aggressive or anything—but, uh, to give me a full view.

SI: Yeah.

M: Everything they did that night was in the light. The way the moon was coming, and everything else, they could have been in the darkness or in the shadow, but they chose what they were doing and where they were standing. I'm sure of it. It was in the light, and it was, you know, you could just see them [Irwin, 2022, September 12, 17:10–18:55].

The entirety of Marc's encounter, which spans two episodes on *Sketching Encounters*, is an extraordinary one to say the least, and I would encourage the inquiring mind to give it a listen. Marc's perception that the Sasquatch had somehow temporarily hidden himself behind the tree, making parts of his body appear to have merged with or be part of the tree evokes the trickster character of these entity accounts. As one example, the subject captured in the Freeman Film displays some intriguing and often overlooked behavior. As Thom Powell notes in his poignant reflection on the life of Paul Freeman, when the homin continues to walk after Freeman exclaims "Jesus!," she moves behind a "small grand fir tree and stops," "rendering it indistinguishable from the tree in front of it" (Powell, 2022, p. 267). Having seen the film countless times myself, I find Powell's assessment to be quite accurate. Notwithstanding the fact that the slightly grainy quality of the film may contribute to what may be a visual illusion, the perceptual effect portrayed in the film is, in my opinion, quite reminiscent of eyewitness reports of Sasquatch disappearing into trees, disappearing behind trees, or turning into trees.

As another example of the hiding behind trees theme, we turn to an account from a fisherman. About 24 minutes into an interview on the *Blurry Creatures* podcast, another encounter related by a fisherman to *Expedition: Bigfoot! The Sasquatch Museum* owner David Bakara speaks of a similar theme of "hiding" behind trees (Henry & Rodgers, 2023, September 27). The fisherman had been staring in awe at a Sasquatch for some time when the latter suddenly realized that he was being watched. According to Bakara, the following is how the fisherman had related the end of the encounter to him:

> [The homin] just kind of got a panicked look and [the fisherman] said this thing ... took a couple steps behind him to a tree, and [the fisherman] says... "It backed up against the tree and tried to blend in with the tree." ...Now, this thing is 7-foot ... usually trees are dark. These things are reddish-brown. He said, "It tried to blend in with the tree, and when he realized it wasn't working," he said, "It turned and it tore off up this hill" [Henry & Rodgers, 2023, September 27, 25:23–25:57].

With regards to the noted behavior of Sasquatch seemingly hiding behind trees, I would argue that things are not necessarily as they seem. It flies in the face of reason to suggest that Sasquatch seem to be able to evade prying human eyes quite easily (e.g., by engaging in rock throwing and bluff charging without being seen), and yet cannot seem to figure out that they cannot elude human vision by standing behind a narrow tree, by hugging a tree that does not conceal their bulk, or by crouching beside a tree yet still remaining in a human's line of sight. While some may disagree, the proposition that homins attempt to hide behind trees that are wholly inadequate to conceal their size is, in my opinion, similar to the idea that they hit trees to create so-called wood knocks or tree knocks: both ideas are likely to be either oversimplifications or utter misconceptions of what is actually happening. It is quite possible, if not plausible, that something else much stranger is going on with this aspect of the Sasquatch-tree phenomenon. As unbelievable as it sounds, some of the available narratives seem to indicate another possibility: perhaps cases wherein Sasquatch seemingly hides behind trees that are much too small for them are times when the process of entering or merging with a tree are incomplete or unsuccessful. Ron Morehead shares:

> While living in Washington on the Olympic Peninsula, I met a woman who reported that she had seen one of these beings move in, and also out of, a tree. There is also a man, whom I have known for several years who lives in that same state and swears that they move in and out of trees. Native American mythology says that they live in two worlds, that they are spirit beings who can disappear. What do we do with these reports? Indigenous people who have been inhabiting this continent much longer than outsiders. So, shouldn't we ponder these reports? [Morehead, 2024, pp. 111–112].

Morehead's poignant remarks here align with other contemporary reports of Sasquatch sightings wherein the entities seem to simply vanish behind or into a tree. As odd as these accounts are, simply dismissing these reports outright as spurious or misinformed sightings might be a mistake for those who wish to pursue the truth behind the larger phenomenon of Sasquatch. Indeed, Morehead even suggests that the sound of the wood knocks could be that of homins' "energy leaving the tree" (2024, p. 113). But a more mundane proposition proposed by field investigators like Janice Carter Coy (Szilagyi, 2025, April 18, 1:46:14–1:47:16) and Les Stroud is that the sound is coming from inside of the tree, produced by homins hitting the inner surface of a hollow trunk (Stroud, 2020, December 14, 36:16–38:31).

Further, as is reported in the documentary *The Bigfoot of Bailey, Colorado, and Its Portal*, several of the narratives involve Sasquatch and trees. In one narrative about halfway through the documentary, its creative team consisting of Ronald C. Meyer and Alan Megargle have an encounter while meditating with a tree upon which their hands were placed. In an altered state of consciousness, Ron perceived there to be a Sasquatch standing directly behind Alan as the group stood there at the tree, while Alan sensed the strong presence of an entity behind him with his eyes closed. The implication of this particular narrative is that it was the group's intentional contemplative exercise at the tree that led to the homin entity encounter. Ron is quite willing to concede that, despite being a shared experience, it was an "anecdote of anecdotes," suggesting that there was nothing other than their word and memory to validate the encounter (Meyer, 2023, 28:51). Of course, the narrative truth of what can come of these experiences lies at the center of our present discourse. an exploration of a particular spirit/prayer tree in the area that has been apparently "verified by shamans of the Ute tribe" (Meyer, 2023, 22:48). Further, while using a structured light sensor (SLS) camera (i.e., the Kinect platform from the Microsoft Xbox) to film the tree, the outline of an image seemed to be moving inside of the tree: an image that eyewitnesses perceived to be a Sasquatch. The narrator summarizes that "a humanoid figure, invisible to the naked eye, appears to be *dancing* in the tree. Has the Bigfoot of Bailey actually shown up for us?" (Meyer, 2023, 32:24–32:34). Regardless of one's impression of the accuracy of the SLS technology being utilized—a device that has become popular in ghost hunting circles and legend tripping—and even with confirmation bias potentially contributing to the group's perception that Sasquatch was present in the tree, the larger pattern linking Sasquatch to trees still holds in the variety of narratives that have persisted about this connection.

In some cases, Sasquatch and other homins, overlapping significantly with the wild man trope (e.g., the *Green Man* or *woodwose* of Europe; British Cryptids, 2023, January 1; Cutchin & Renner, 2020a) are more or less synonymous with the trees themselves. At times, homins are reported as being quite comfortable in trees (i.e., arboreal), and thus as being seen swinging, hanging, or sitting from or on branches. For example, community confidante and Sasquatch historian, Stan Avery, shares an account wherein a purported Sasquatch was photographed sitting in a tree (Eichenberger, 2022). Additionally, Christopher Noël (2021) has had a significant encounter at night involving two entities scaling a tree a short distance away from where he stood along a trail in an area that he frequented. Elsewhere, on May 23, 1997, in the Catskill Mountains, Doug Pridgen filmed a potential youngling in the background behind a campsite that he and friends were staying at for a music festival. In the twilight, the subject appears to be swinging in a tree in the distance, while what may be an adult is seen briefly on the ground below the tree (History, 2024, March 9). According to the History Channel show *The Proof Is Out There*, some noted personas in the Bigfooting community such as Cliff Barackman and Jeff Meldrum have assessed the film as offering potential evidence of a genuine homin, save it depicting something like a young chimpanzee instead.[12]

Various Vocalizations

Having considered some of the more iconic aspects of how light and vision are involved in the homin phenomenon, we now turn to the matter of Sasquatch and sound.

First, regarding audio and otherwise potentially linguistic or symbolic data (e.g., glyphs, tree structures, etc.; Baranchok, 2023, December 18), it is my opinion that such forms of evidence will continue to exist at the frontier of research on the homin phenomenon. Despite being the present underdog to videographic and photographic evidence, these forms of data can be more readily collected or examined through relatively noninvasive means.

Similar to the most impressive videographic evidence, there are only several sources of audiographic evidence that stand out within the annals of North American homin lore. Those include the *Ohio Howl* (BFRO, 2002; MelBlanc222, 2016, December 17) recorded by lawyer, co-host of the *Finding Bigfoot* series, and founder of the BFRO, Matthew Moneymaker, and the *Berry-Morehead Tapes* (aka the *Sierra Sounds*) recorded by Ron Morehead and Alan Berry in 1972 and 1974. These data offer some of the best evidence for the existence of beings who are related to humans and yet who exhibit a distinct language of their own as well as a vocal range that goes beyond what humans can produce (Cosper, 2018; Cutchin & Renner, 2020b; Eastburn, 2023, January 18; Morehead, 2013). Mark Matzke of the *Small Town Monsters* team states:

> In late autumn of 1994, Matt Moneymaker of the Bigfoot Field Researchers Organization captured a recording that would come to be regarded as the epitome of Bigfoot vocalization. Near the wooded banks of the Ohio River in Columbiana County, just across the river from West Virginia, Moneymaker obtained audio with two distinct signatures: one of them, a barking dog; the other, an unidentified howler in the distance making a series of three long moaning calls.
>
> In the years since, credentialed analysts have ruled out known animal sounds, as well as a mechanical device like a siren as the source of the rising and falling tones on the recording.

> What's more, there have been many instances in which people from around the country, having heard strange sounds of their own, have listened to the Ohio howl online and found in it confirmation of what they heard in their location. It's become a Bigfoot touchstone of sorts.
> Perhaps that's why some investigators have concentrated on creating a library of audio recordings. Such collections are helpful. They have properties that can be analyzed. And it may be the most common evidence of an uncommon creature [Breedlove, 2025, April 23, 32:37–34:05].

The intent behind creating an audio library is, in my opinion, one of the most significant steps forward in better understanding not only these entities, but potentially their effects on the physiology of anatomically modern humans as well.

Despite some debate regarding the nature of the subjects in the Sierra Sounds recording (e.g., Pyle, 2017), analyses by individuals such as retired crypto-linguist R. Scott Nelson suggest that the sounds evince a non-human language (Eichenberger, 2023, December 17; Kirlin & Hertel, 1995); furthermore, they map onto what other experiencers report (e.g., Byron, 2025, March 7, 38:08–39:29; Byron, 2025, April 15, 5:54–6:10).

Though there was no visual observation made at time of the recordings, and despite claims that the vocalizations in the recordings were either hoaxes or misidentifications of known animals (e.g., Stollznow, 2014), the fact remains that other eyewitness reports of verbal communication among homins have been made, some of which overlap significantly with the prosody and phonology demonstrated in the Sierra Sounds tapes (e.g., Byron, 2025, March 7, 7:48; Germer, 2019; Hajicek & Hajicek, 2023, April 26; Hudson, 2020, 1:55:00). Indeed, while acknowledging that claims of pseudoscience have been leveled at Nelson's work, scholars such as Bader et al. (2017) have stated, "Should Nelson's analysis have cracked Bigfoot language, it is a scientific feat worthy of great note" (p. 216). The authors' claim is hard to overstate. Importantly, these sounds have been said to be reminiscent of human speech, albeit at a much, much faster cadence than our own (Jackson, 2024, January 28, 12:25–14:00). Moreover, other written and oral literature suggests that homins are capable of using written symbols as well as glyphs that may be indicative of language (e.g., Green & Coy, 2002; Lapseritis, 1998).

As is often the case with more formal disciplines, members of the Bigfooting and cryptozoological community have developed their own jargon to refer to various aspects of the Sasquatch phenomenon, coining or adopting several terms that speak to the larger mythos around Sasquatch and their potential abilities. In addition to the characteristic hirsute appearance of the beings, perhaps the most commonly reported acoustic features of encounter narratives include wood knocks (or the less-reported *rock clacks*; e.g., Alley, 2018; Breedlove, 2025, April 16, 34:58–35:17; Brown & Brown, 2024, October 5, 3:15–3:25),[13] *whoops* and *howls* (e.g., the Ohio howl; BFRO, 2002), growls, and grunts.

Fo example, wood knocks have become such a universally reported feature that many field investigators have incorporated methods into their repertoire to produce similar sounds, employing baseball bats (or "knockers"), wooden sticks, and other devices that they strike against wood in order to hopefully elicit a response. While these methods have been used quite frequently to varying degrees of success, while the wood knock is a common feature of Sasquatch lore, and while there is general agreement that the knock is a form of intraspecific (i.e., within species or within group) communication among Sasquatch, there are different hypotheses as to the mechanism of sound production. Those hypotheses include but are not limited to the following: (a) wood-on-wood: the striking of a tree with an object; (b) hand-to-hand or hand-to-body: rapping hands against each other or against the body (e.g., chest) to create the noise; (c) tongue-to-teeth or hands-cupped-to-mouth: Sasquatch creates the sound with the mouth.[14] And despite the nigh ubiquity of acceptance of the wood knock-as-evidence-of-Sasquatch within the Bigfooting community, complicating the matter further is the fact that most experiencers do not actually see Sasquatch producing the sound in real time, thereby indicating Class B encounters. To add to the phenomenon of the wood knock is the increasing interest within the Bigfooting community that Sasquatch may have air sacs that contribute to their vocal capacity and volume (as David Ellis, Jeff Meldrum, and others have suggested; e.g., Myers, 2024, April 17), as well as the idea that Sasquatch may articulate sound on the in-breath as well as the out-breath (e.g., as Scott Nelson avers; Eichenberger, 2023, December 17), as opposed to just on the out-breath as in anatomically modern humans.

At this point, we turn to a subset of vocalization reports attributed to homins: those that are said to resemble air raid sirens. One narrative containing such a description is detailed in the *Bigfoot Case Files* as related by narrator Shannon Morgan. On July 31, 1976, in Rocky Mountain National Park in Colorado, a young couple had their tent set up that summer night and decided to go to sleep. The two awoke to the sounds of someone or something approaching them from up the canyon. Morgan relates the following:

> A light rain was falling, and Liz was fast asleep. I laid there for a while, listening to the rain on the tent and wondering why I was awake. I then heard the creepiest sound I had ever heard in my life. There was a siren in the far distance, but you could tell it was being made by something alive: a person or a creature. It definitely wasn't mechanical. It's hard to describe, but it was just like something with really big lungs was imitating an old air horn or a raid siren, like in the movies. I laid there listening, thinking I was dreaming, as I swear, it was getting closer [Smyth, 2023, December 30, 8:12–8:50].

This general description of the Sasquatch making loud noises to warn of an impending flood due to a storm maps precisely onto what McGrath (2020) has said of the hairy basajaun in Europe. Such reports are also indicated elsewhere in the available literature. For example, investigator and *Small Town Monsters* team member Heather Moser relates how several Class B witnesses in the Ohio area have recalled hearing vocalizations like the noted Ohio howl or similar to a "siren-like howl. That's exactly how they described it: like an ambulance siren" (Breedlove, 2025, April 13, 3:37–3:41). Additionally, if they are genuine, a series of exceptionally clear vocalizations documented on March 15, 2012, in St. Louis County, Minnesota (which I am referring to here as the *St. Louis Sounds* in homage to the famous Sierra Sounds), are some of the best audio recordings of homins available (Sasquatch Confessions, 2022, August 6).[15] Arguably, they are second only to the Sierra Sounds themselves. While the question remains as to whether or not the Ohio howl and St. Louis sounds were actually produced by a homin, there is a clear corroboration between Class B reports such as these and other Class A cases like the above report by Liz and her boyfriend.

Further, a series of such howls clearly illustrates this character and is included in a documentary produced by the *Small Town Monsters* team (Breedlove, 2025, April 13, 34:34–36:19). For example, an interesting note is made in the documentary by experiencer and field investigator Doug Cooper, who states that he had received an audio clip from a colleague based in southern Ohio that the former man describes as follows: "It was kind of like the Ohio howl, but there was a siren from an ambulance or something going by, and you could hear them both at the same time" (Breedlove, 2025, April 13, 59:35–59:45). Further study within bioacoustics, linguistics, cryptolinguistics, symbology, cymatics, and related fields may well prove to be quite useful in helping to establish convergence or distinction between synthetic human-generated and homin-generated sounds as well as the purpose, meaning, and effects of the latter. I posit this at least in part because I am of the opinion that humans seem to be able to capture audiographic evidence without nearly the same kind of difficulty that seems to be part and parcel of capturing videographic or photographic evidence. As Timothy Renner suggests (Cutchin, 2025, p. 298), perhaps we are "permitted" to capture the former. I tend to agree.

Furthermore, I speculate that the alerting whoops of air raid sirens in particular, if not also police and firefighter sirens in general, may serve as useful alarms precisely because they are a close analogue to reported homin whoops. Moreover, if this were indeed the case, then human-made air raid sirens could trigger deep memory (e.g., via homin teems) of human-homin contact at a very visceral and unconscious level, provoking immediate and subcortical response within the percipient. In other words, if these sounds activate something like a homin teem (or more specifically, a Neanderthal teem), then humans may be essentially hardwired to orient toward and react to these auditory stimuli. As Matzke (Breedlove, 2025, April 13) poignantly notes as he closes out the *Small Towns Monsters* documentary, humans "tend to treat strange sounds with appropriate vigilance. It stands to reason that if Bigfoot exists, then it would generate sounds that awaken wariness in us—a factor that Sasquatch may, in fact, exploit" (1:03:54–1:04:11). Indeed, such wariness is part of a broader discussion of how humans respond and react to homins (e.g., Baranchok, 2021) and lies at the center of our topic of discussion.

Following this train of thought, if deep memory of archaic human-homin contact has persisted into the present, and if some of that memory has encoded the emotion tied to homin-generated sounds, then perhaps it is not homin vocalizations that sound like air raid sirens, but it is instead air raid sirens that resemble homin vocalizations. One can potentially imagine such a scenario when one hears recordings like those that I have noted above or the audio that expert tracker and field investigator Robert Kryder and his team have recorded (e.g., Kryder, 2024, September 10, 46:21). Again, if something like Vendramini's (2009) Neanderthal teem is activated by such acoustic stimuli, then critical consideration of sympathetic nervous system response triggered by these sounds would be further warranted (Baranchok, 2021).

In addition to the above cases, we find reports of sirens being associated with homins elsewhere. For example, Roehl's descriptions of air raid–like screams reported by experiencers include the statement that a vocalization was like "an air raid siren up to high pitch" (Roehl, 2024, October 3, 17:00), while experiencer John associated "some weird air raid siren or something that was broken" (Germer, 2023, December 15, 20:51) with the homin phenomenon. Further still, the narrative of the Cowman of Copalis Beach (i.e., a hairy humanlike being reported in Grays Harbor County, Washington), has been associated with a "loud, moaning cry, kind of like the siren on the volunteer fire department" (Blackburn, 2024, October 3, 21:15).[16] These descriptions illustrate the salient nature of this vocalization type and elucidate how hearing such a thing could be jarring, unsettling, or generally warning for the percipient.

Thus, for a human psyche that may have access to memories of human-homin conflict from the deep past, any perception of these sounds could prompt sympathetic nervous system arousal (i.e., fear, disgust, panic, or paranoia). Interestingly, this is precisely what occurs, both in neutral and ambiguously valenced encounters, as well as in beneficent ones as well. The tendency is for the human being to respond in fear, only to later realize that the Sasquatch likely meant no harm at all or was actually attempting to help. Given Vendramini's (2009) proposal that fully modern humans may have access to archaic emotional memories of being predated by powerful, hairy, bipedal beings, such a response is not surprising.

Infrasound and Zapping

In addition to the large variety of vocalizations tied to homin encounters (e.g., Alley, 2018; Mayes, 2022), these entities (e.g., the *jack-muh-lantern*; Cutchin & Renner, 2020a) are also said to draw unwitting people toward them, as well as to stun or even hypnotize people. Another matter that has become intimately interwoven with Sasquatch reports is that of *infrasound*. Infrasound is a low frequency vibration below the range of human hearing (i.e., less than 20 Hertz) and which has the capacity to produce a variety of physiological and psychological effects (e.g., Meldrum, 2006, pp. 198–199). Those effects include but are not limited to torpor, paralysis, disorientation, unease, memory loss, feeling of dread or panic, blurred vision, hallucinations, nausea, and loss of consciousness (e.g., Carpenter, 2019, p. 141; Eichenberger, 2024, April 3; Meldrum, 2006). Experiencers also often report feeling their bodies vibrating (e.g., Germer, 2024, May 8). While speaking of bush pilot Buck's encounter in the Alaskan tundra, Roehl provides the following description of this dread as "uncomfortable fear":

> something came over him: a feeling of dread that he said he never felt before. Even being in the presence of polar bears, charged by brown bears, charged by moose, he never had that kind of uncomfortable fear. He—he said he felt uncomfortable in his skin. Like every … like I stated before: every part of you wants to run, and you don't know why [King-Sharp, 2024, May 5, 6:51–7:13].

The soundwaves are felt rather than heard and are known to be produced by organisms such as certain large predators (e.g., tigers) and large mammals (e.g., giraffes and elephants), and also by large engineering and machinery.

However, most relevant to our present discussion, infrasound is also said to be produced by some homins. The iconic puckered lips of the female wildwoman, known as the *dzonoqua* (alternatively spelled *dsonoqua*, *dzoonokwa*, *dzunukwa*, etc.)[17] among Tribes such as the Kwakwaka'wakw in the Pacific Northwest, have been associated with the production of infrasound. We will return to this discussion of infrasound in due time, but for now, suffice it to say that Sasquatch and related entities are associated with the generation of sounds that are said to have powerful, even hypnotic effects on people.

For example, there is a segment of narratives that include mention of *humming* sounds that seem to be made by Sasquatch that are similar to the beating of humming bird wings (Hajicek & Hajicek, 2024, April 17), the drone of bees (Hajicek & Hajicek, 2024, April 17), the sound made by playing a digeridoo (Cutchin, 2022, p. 82), or Tuvan throat singing (Timothy Renner via Cutchin, 2022b, p. 82). David Ellis has referred to the humming as the *Bigfoot purr* (Hajicek & Hajicek, 2023, April 26), which I believe is quite an apt name for the phenomenon.[18] One experiencer has reported to Ellis the following repisodic (i.e., the same event occurring on multiple occasions) account, which Ellis shares about an hour and eight minutes into the episode:

> **DE:** There was a gentleman—Mike Mullen—that when he was five years old, um, had a Sasquatch coming through and he—he said that he always knew that they were going to be approaching, because he would hear … this buzzing sound like, uh, the nest of a bees. So, he was … fairly calm throughout this process … a Sasquatch (when I'm 4–5 or six years old) comes up to my window, I'm gonna be … yelling and screaming. But he said that this sound seemed to have a calming effect on him, and he was able to … go through the ordeal and not be frightened. So, there seems to be something to the nature of this vocalization that has a calming effect.
>
> And [another experiencer] Paul Graves actually spoke to this. He said that he couldn't believe how after hearing the sound how … kind of had a euphoria if you will and … was very at ease and fell right back to sleep—
>
> **DH:** Boom.
>
> **DE:** [inaudible] after … the ordeal that they went through with something coming through camp and creating all that ruckus, then this particular sound had a calming effect on him. So there seems to be an association with that as well [Hajicek & Hajicek, 2024, April 17].

Elsewhere in the homin literature, following reference to some of Bobbie Short's work, Cutchin notes that Indigenous American lore indicates that Sasquatch and other entities are able to induce altered states of consciousness such as hypnotic trance in people and prey (Cutchin & Renner, 2020b, p. 83). Another tale of homins seemingly attempting to abduct women comes from the state of Alaska. During an interview on the *Bigfoot Society* podcast (Byron, 2023, September 26), Fred Roehl shares the following narrative:

> I get accounts all the time from the villages … where out berry-picking, these things have been known to try to lure women away, you know, with this slow-motion wave.… I've had a young lady in her early 20s share with me not too long ago where they were just checking the conditions of the berries to see if they're almost right for picking (her and her little cousin), and they're in the wide open—wide open tundra, nothing around. They get to this … horseshoe-shaped trail. They get to the apex of it roughly, and all of a sudden there's this Hairy Man about 70ish feet away, roughly.

> And initially she said she was almost in a trance-like state … she felt peaceful with this thing waving at her. And she's on a four-wheeler with her little cousin. So … the trail they were on was well-defined … and she veered off and she bumped her knee getting off of that trail, and it snapped her out of that trance. And she saw it for what it was and realized the danger and, you know, skedaddled out of there [Byron, 2023, September 26, 32:29–33:49].

Regardless of the actual intent of the homin, such a narrative seems to again indicate the potential danger that these entities may pose to the unwary or unscrupulous.

Importantly, the humming may be felt as much as it is heard and therefore may be tied to infrasound. Indeed, Cutchin (2020b) reports cases wherein the humming sound is associated with a child seeming to be sent into an epileptic fit—a fit that witnesses thought was caused by infrasound (p. 82). As such, it may be that the intensity (and perhaps intent) behind the infrasound serves to act either as a defensive deterrent (e.g., Cutchin & Renner, 2020b; Neely, 2020) or as a means of inducing a healing or beneficial effect (e.g., Hajicek & Hajicek, 2024, April 17). Either way, the connection between infrasound and experiencers engaging in activity wherein they appear to be hypnotized (e.g., led away from the site, as in Scott Carpenter's case; Carpenter, 2022), these infrasonic effects can be potent.

Additionally, in the argot of the Bigfooting community subculture (Bader et al., 2017, p. 216), being *zapped* is a term that overlaps with the negative physiological effects of infrasound and consists of the person feeling physically drained, nauseous, and disoriented (e.g., Bear Chief & Upham, 2025, February 1, 12:35–13:40).[19] Some reports even involve the unique side effect of people experiencing significant burning in the quadricep muscles due to lactic acid buildup in those tissues.[20] At the more extreme level, the late Scott Carpenter's son Travis Carpenter who goes by the appellation "T. Carp" has stated publicly that he thinks that his father being zapped by Sasquatch may have contributed to his death due to ruptured aneurysm (Carpenter, 2024, April 15). In *The Sasquatch Awareness Project*, Carpenter provides the following description of zapping:

> A phenomenon that may be related to infrasound, the person who experiences zapping feels an electric like shock go through their body. This shock can stun, disorient, and is extremely unpleasant. The physical effects include nausea and in some cases blood in the urine [Carpenter, 2022, p. 56].

He also states that he believes that he was the recipient of zapping himself on multiple occasions, leading to memory loss, missing time, and even the receipt of telepathic suggestions (i.e., via mindspeak) to leave the area. The latter psychic impressions were so strong that they led to what he felt were subsequent, inexplicable behaviors. Interestingly, it should be noted that seemingly out-of-context actions (e.g., falling asleep or not being able to be woken up in the presence of entities) are associated with homin as well as ET entity encounters.

Further, about 11 minutes into the documentary *Believe It or Not*, *uNcomfortable* podcast host Erick Szilagyi states the following of his own apparent encounter with infrasound: "I know what people mean when they say that got zapped, because it was in the best of my … recollection … electrical manifestation. Whatever it did to my body felt electrical" (Penford Media, 2024, April 16).

What is possibly the most well-known, or at least widely televised, potential encounter with homin infrasound involved field investigator and content curator Ryan "RPG" Golembeske. During the inaugural episode of the popular reality television show *Expedition Bigfoot*, he experienced debilitating physical symptoms that track onto what is generally noted with being zapped, leading him to attempt to recover in his tent on site. Unfortunately, his headaches were reportedly so severe that he had to bow out of filming and be replaced by another team member (i.e., Ronny LeBlanc) as a result. His former teammate Bryce Johnson has commented that while he was not willing to stake anything on the idea that infrasound caused RPG sudden downturn, he was also not willing to rule it out either, given the fact that the symptoms overlapped with homin experiencer reports (DMAX UK, 2025, February 4). It should also be noted that the idea of targeted infrasound being used by homins to distract or deter interloping humans from entering an area has been posed, at least anecdotally, by some within the Bigfooting community.

In addition to such an example, we might consider the insightful words of the late Sonya Vivianna Zohar (1967–2024), anomalous researcher, extended experiencer, and empath, who shares the following general description of the trauma response that can occur following the impact of infrasound on the human body:

> I've had two experiences of what I call the fear experience, and the fear experience is something so frightening that it ... lives inside your body. It never leaves you. The moment I start to talk about it ... my throat starts to tense up.... I mean, I guess that would be the definition ... what a traumatic experience is, but it's still not the same. It's distinct [Eichenberger, 2024, January 1, 14:48–15:08].

Zohar's description is illustrative of the extent to which the memory can become embodied and potentially reactivated at later dates given the proper trigger. Of course, at a much broader level, the same kind of response can be discussed in terms of deep memory as far as what scholars such as Vendramini (2009) have posited. Sonya describes the following of one of her sightings that she had which involved likely contact with infrasound during a Class B encounter:

> Now, I'm sitting there, and I'm starting to feel it as I'm talking about it. I was just exhausted. Everything just caved. I just had no energy in me, and I wasn't afraid. And then I just went to bed. And I got in my sleeping bag, and then about 2:00 in the morning, I wanted to get up to go to the bathroom, and it hit, and it was this paralyzing bodily fear. And I'm naturally claustrophobic a bit, and I don't really put my head under the covers, and I literally just forgot about having to go to the bathroom. I pulled the sleeping bag up, I crawled in a fetal ball, and I stayed there until ... sun came up.
>
> In the morning, Dr. Meldrum and I had a flight out. We had to leave. And I got up, and the first thing I noticed is that the tops of my thighs [points to her quadriceps] were on fire with lactic acid, like I'd done about—I don't know, 100 squats the night before, and ... we hadn't hiked that much ... we were riding Argos and taking very gentle hikes. We had ATVs to get us around to and from spots ... so there was no reason that my legs should feel that way, but they did [Eichenberger, 2024, January 1, 19:55–21:12].

Zohar goes on to describe how her physiological response, which included shortness of breath, tiredness, and a prolonged feeling of burning in her thighs, was still persisting two weeks after the encounter. This state of affairs lead her to seek out the services of a medical professional, who "took [her] vitals. She said, 'You seem fine, Sonya,' but ... 'I think what happened is you were scared to the core'" (Eichenberger,

2024, January 1, 22:13–22:16). This kind of response from a medical doctor is, in my opinion, rather profound, particularly when I consider what seems to be a large number of experiencers who report being scared or traumatized and yet never seek out the services of a trained professional for fear of ridicule.

Zohar then reflects that at that very moment while she was being filmed during the interview, she was having some of those same symptoms return to her, including tightness of the chest, and places her hand over her chest. To conclude her story, she moves us forward a year into the future:

> I'm back in Nordegg. I'm with ... Dr. Susan McDonald from the University of Toronto. She's a wildlife ecologist. She runs ... a chimpanzee site, an elephant site, and a raccoon site ... ongoing research sites. She came out to the forest with us. We showed her the physical evidences ... and she said if she didn't know better, she would believe that she was at a gorilla site in Africa: that the bedding down sites, the tracks ... the stick breaks, the minimal types of structures ... she said it looked just like a gorilla site. That night, as we were talking, I told her about the experience that I'd had, and that the weakness that I had had for weeks following, but the oddest thing of all was the burning sensation on the top of my thighs.
>
> And when I said that, she became very serious, and she goes, "That's infrasound ... at my elephant site, I was charged by a bull elephant, and I was hit from infrasound, and for some reason it makes the lactic acid rise in the top of your thighs.... I've experienced that too." So as far as I know, I don't know what in the forest would actually hit you with infrasound, but that's exactly what I was hit with immediately following talking to something that was in the woods... [Eichenberger, 2024, January 1, 22:39–24:04].

The late empath and experiencer's account is not just evidence of Sasquatch potentially using infrasound. Perhaps more importantly, it is in part an explanation for the deep, intense, and persistent fears that experiencers can perceive during and after encounters. Additionally, the extent to which some of these experiencers (e.g., hunters, hikers, etc.) inadvertently come in-between Sasquatch and a hunt or kill (e.g., Byron, 2023, December 18), if Sasquatch is using infrasound to hunt and these people end up in the line of fire, then some cases wherein fear and negative physiological responses are induced may be unintentional byproducts of the situation rather than intentional or directed effects.

Of course, Zohar's encounter is not the only one within the Bigfooting community that demonstrates the potent effects of what infrasound might do. For example, the late Scott Carpenter shares the following:

> I had a very odd encounter, during which time, I captured a brief video of a Bigfoot, and then inexplicably walked away. I have no recollection of seeing the Bigfoot or taking the video. I was shocked when I reviewed my video and found footage I did not remember recording. Doing an analysis of the audio track from the video, I found strong infrasound being produced, presumably by the Bigfoot [Carpenter, 2019a, p. 135].

The ability for infrasound to influence human physiology and psychology that the above experiencers note falls in line with research literature on the effects of infrasound, which include drowsiness, fatigue, fear, and even inner ear damage (Moyano & Leczano, 2020). Interestingly, the same literature suggests that optical illusions can result from exposure to infrasonic frequencies, and that hippocampal neurons can also be impacted. At least theoretically, the noted illusions may relate to at least a subset of the visual oddities that are reported in some sightings, while the hippocampal effects may relate to reports such as Carpenter's narrative above wherein memory is affected. Such hypotheses are technically testable though studying such effects of infrasound on the human body is not particularly ethical. With that said, retrospective mixed methods studies that include corroborating evidence on the presence of infrasound could be helpful.

Interestingly, in addition to infrasound, while there is Indigenous American lore about homins making noises to announce their presence (e.g., Dsonokwa, revered wild woman of the Kwakwaka'wakw Tribe), the sounds typically discussed are *whistling*, which seems to be distinct from the knocks discussed elsewhere in the literature. The whistling of the Dsonokwa is said to presage her arrival, and children especially are taught to stay away from her and to hide. Moreover, it is ill-advised for anyone traveling through the woods to whistle, as it could draw the attention of the wild woman. Whistling is reported in encounters from Americans of European and Latine ancestry as well (e.g., Warren, 2024, April 19).

One of the physiological aspects of homin entity encounter narratives that are most compelling—as well as most difficult to explain away—deal with their auditory characteristics is the matter of people reporting their viscera vibrating due to frequencies being produced by homins. The typical report is as follows: the eyewitness inadvertently gets too close to a Sasquatch, the Sasquatch yells at them so loudly or growls at them so deeply that the person's organs vibrate, and the experiencer exits the area posthaste, potentially having urinated and/or defecated on themselves. Euphemistically, the tones produced that lead to these latter effects are referred to as the yellow note (i.e., that may induce involuntary urination) and the brown note (i.e., that may induce involuntary defecation). In general, North American homins are said to produce a number of sounds that can have various, often noxious, effects on those of us relatively hairless humans who hear them.

Mimicry and More

In addition to the above sonic characteristics of homin entity encounters, the sounds of baby cries or like someone is being murdered are particularly haunting elements associated with homins that appear in the literature (Byron, 2023, September 26; Cutchin & Renner, 2020a; LeGro, 2024, May 16). For example, the eerie noises that renowned lepidopterist Robert Michael Pyle heard one night in the Pacific Northwest were curious enough to pique the interest of the prolific author and biologist, prompting him to later write a book on the subject of Sasquatch.

From another source, Curyung Tribal Member Fred Roehl and his cousin Ms. Elizabeth Cook recount an upsetting encounter from 1969 that happened to her. Fred provides the context here, sharing that, at the time, Ms. Elizabeth and her family lived on Unalaska Island:

> No trees. It's a windswept Dutch harbor. You know, it's just windswept. You may get some scrub brush, but that's it.... They had a neighbor: [a] Native woman who had a child out of wedlock at the time with a fisherman. The fisherman went away and she was left with this baby, and so she would always ask for help from her neighbors and whatnot. But this baby's

> cry: everyone knew it, because it was a colicky young baby and the mom didn't know what … she was doing, you know. And so, she would ask for help [Byron, 2023, September 26, 34:33–35:05].

Therein lies the setting for the incident. On the night of the encounter, as Ms. Elizabeth and another cousin of hers were taking care of their own children at home, it was getting dark,

> And they heard this baby crying outside. They *knew* the cry and they *recognized* it. Well, they go outside to look to see what was going on with the baby cry, you know? Making sure the baby didn't need help. And, they get outside—they go around, they don't see anything. And they're going back into their little apartment, and right in front of the bay window—10-feet away, looking at them—is this Hairy Man imitating that baby cry to a *T*: to perfection.… She said that it sounded identical to the baby cry [Byron, 2023, September 26, 35:06–35:45].

I can only imagine the kind of uncanniness that such a sight would have elicited, but in Ms. Elizabeth's own recounting during an interview with *Small Town Monsters*, she says:

> …what drew us to look outside—it made some kind of noise. And it was all quiet outside because everybody was sleeping. And the bar was closed. We could see the bar lights from where [my cousin] lived, and everybody was gone from there. And it was very quiet, and then we heard this … sound like there was a *baby* out there. And it did make—uh, loud enough for us to hear through the walls [Breedlove, 2023, December 31, 34:34–35:00].

She recalls that the dark-colored, hirsute entity seemed to be about 8 feet tall as he stared down at them with red, bloodshot eyes from just on the other side of the window. Given that the two women had children to protect and were afraid that the being would break through the window, they quickly retreated into the bedrooms and tried to get another neighbor to come help them, but to no avail: the neighbors did not want anything to do with Hairy Man.

Thankfully, after some time, the homin apparently just walked away. Still, the ordeal was traumatizing enough for Ms. Elizabeth, who reflects: "I never, ever, ever want to see it again in my whole life. It's so real. It's horrifying" (Breedlove, 2023, December 31, 37:30–37:39). Her emotional state during the interview still seemed to be quite palpable as she recounts the event, despite the fact that it occurred over half a century ago.

Her cousin Fred reflects these sentiments by stating that despite the many decades that separate Ms. Elizabeth from that day, when she talks about it, she still sometimes gets a "shellshock"-like expression on her face (Breedlove, 2023, December 31, 38:48). Such a reaction falls in line with the profound ways in which these experiences can trouble witnesses, even if the experience was brief. Lastly on this particular incident, I share Fred's own reflections on the mimicry:

> Now, to me, that's a level of cunning that is just *unreal*, because they're literally using a woman's natural instinct against them. They're using that baby cry to lure them out. That's—man, that is some cunning stuff, man. Just cunning [Byron, 2023, September 26, 35:45–36:02].[21]

I do not disagree with this assessment; however, I would note that it is almost certain that the encounter could have been easily escalated by the Hairy Man should the entity have desired to do so. Despite the persistent negative psychological impact of the encounter, neither the women nor their children were physically harmed that night. On the other hand, regardless of the intent behind the homin's actions at the time, the potential threat posed by such behavior is not hard to imagine, especially in light of the ambiguity of the behavior.

Arguably, the ambivalence that can arise from such an encounter is not easy to deal with, but having access to cultural context (e.g., knowledge of Hairy Man via oral history) and preserving such experiences for perpetuity can potentially help a great deal. A large part of Roehl's stated mission is to do just this: to provide a public service to the people of Alaska, sharing information about Hairy Man to hopefully minimize negative human-homin contact.

View It from the Bridge

This chapter has dealt with sightings of Sasquatch and how these entities seem to utilize light to befuddle or intimidate their human counterparts, including narratives of them seeming to absorb light, to seeming to "cloak," and to even apparently vanishing. Moreover, particular attention has been paid to narratives involving the interesting case of Sasquatch being perceived to be trees or parts thereof. This chapter has also dealt with some of the primary ways in which homins have been reported using or being associated with sound. Wood or tree knocks, which have an ambiguous provenance, are commonly reported, while other behaviors including potential use of infrasound (i.e., zapping) are also found in the literature. The noxious or generally disorienting effects of infrasound have been summarized conceptually and via a sampling of narratives. Additionally, whistling, such as is part of the lore associated with Dsonoqua, is a clear marker of Hairy Man activity. Narratives shared via oral tradition and other methods have served a practical purpose, helping to keep the people safe from negative homin contact.

Before moving on, I would encourage you to pause and consider at least one of the reflective prompts on cognitive, emotional, somatic, or conative matters that I have posed in the introduction.

Section II

Trauma and Taboo

As we begin Section II, know that at least some of the material herein may be emotionally or somatically triggering, as it deals with trauma and some of the deep, unconscious burdens that it seems that humanity has been carrying within its collective longbody since our archaic past. Given the weightiness of some of the material that we will consider herein, it may be helpful for us to consider the words of author and somatic abolitionist Resmaa Menakem at this juncture: "If your body simply won't settle, remove yourself from what's happening for a few minutes. Find a relatively quiet and private spot; resettle your body; and then return" (Menakem, 2021, p. 244). Therefore, if at any point you notice any tension in your physical form, take time to step away from the text to allow your nervous system to reset.

5

Violation and Attraction

Content warning: This chapter makes explicit reference to sensitive topics including abduction and sexual assault.

We now begin our consideration of the transgressive acts attributed to Sasquatch with what are perhaps the most challenging to hear about: the varied cases of homin interest in abducting women and children, and at times, men (e.g., Roehl, 2023, March 3). Indeed, in order to prevent such abduction, many Indigenous traditions have explicit taboos against transgressing into Hairy Man territory (e.g., Roehl, 2024, February 17, 14:49–16:24)

Regarding the potential for human-homin contact, authors such as Arment (2019), Neely (2020), Cutchin and Renner (2020a), and Strain (2008) have noted the fact that reports of abductions of young females and children abound, as do tales of sheer curiosity toward these two populations (e.g., Hajicek, 2004). General interest that homins seem to have in these two groups is worth noting first. For example, from the 1800s comes a report out of the *Gazette* of Morristown, Tennessee, which is shared in Arment's (2019, pp. 344–345) *The Historical Bigfoot*:

> Editor of the Banner—Dear Sir: The horrible sight of a hairy man has been seen in Fannin County, Georgia. He is wild and monstrous—he has been seen in houses carrying off women and children. He is eight feet high and is covered all over with a black curly hair. He started from a house lately with a woman in his arms, but by the approach of two men she was released. The settlement was alarmed and pursuit given on horseback.

This report carries remarkable similarities to other narratives, including the fact that upon men pursuing the entity, a man named John Haircrow was killed and a horse's tail was pulled off. The being demonstrated such strength and ferocity that it was left alone.

Further, the general description of a group of potential homins known as the *Tschäggättä* of the Lötschental region in Switzerland is such a common depiction of the tensions between humans and dark-skinned or dark-haired homins that one would be hard-pressed to find a group of humans who has had significant contact with homins that does not maintain some kind of oral or written tradition around the stealing away of women or children. Additionally, le Noël posits that these homins were Eurasian Neanderthals: the same kind of Neanderthals who Vendramini (2009, p. 20) has suggested were the group that predated upon early humans in the Levant. Indeed, the scenario that le Noël paints regarding the conflict between humans and Eurasian Neanderthals in prehistoric Switzerland is precisely the kind of situation that Vendramini suggests occurred when Cro-Magnons hunted Eurasian Neanderthals down west across Europe and into Spain.

Regarding further intertextual overlap, the comment about the Tschäggättä having flat teeth like humans and/or like horses is important to note due to the fact that elsewhere in Eurasia as well as half way around the world in North America, the same narratives are also found in association with homins (e.g., Alley, 2018; Cundiff, 2021, September 27, 43:30; Palacios, 2024, June 24; Shackley, 1983, p. 119).[1] While le Noël emphasizes the potential pre-historic origins of the Tschäggättä as a population of homins who were eventually subdued by encroaching humans, assistant professor of European ethnology Konrad Kuhn (2015) focuses on the symbolism of the Tschäggättä as representative of death and horror and the continuity of what has effectively become a counter-narrative of history that is maintained by the people of the Lötschental. Speaking of a carnival tradition among the people of the Lötschental culture which involved adult males donning masks and other costuming that lent them the horrific personage of these hirsute beings, Peters states:

> Perhaps, as the prescribed behavior of the Lötschental carnival participants seems to imply, the *Tschäggättä* preyed on lone women and children who strayed too far from their kinsmen. Whatever the case, the confrontation must have been intense. Lötschental tradition indicates that the wild men were physically robust creatures, well-suited to their mountain environment, and capable of scaling cliffs inaccessible to humans. However, they lacked effective weapons, resorting to rudimentary branches or rocks. Facing them were less robust *Homo sapiens* who communicated through speech and employed strategic thinking, wielded effective weapons like spears and flint axes capable of penetrating flesh and inflicting fatal wounds on vital organs. The humans likely had knowledge of rudimentary medicine, unlike the hairy beings. Moreover, they were almost certainly experienced in interclan warfare and could defend themselves against attacks [Peters, 2024, April 14].

Again, the description overlaps significantly with other narratives in oral and written tradition, including narratives about attraction between humans and great apes and/or ape-men that blur the lines between fact and fiction (e.g., Dodds & Wessels, 2011).

Abduction Cases and Lore

While modern cases of missing people may not necessarily involve Hairy Man, they do tend to overlap with the tone and tenor of oral history and lore about homins abducting people. *Missing people cases*, and particularly those that involve national parks in the continental United States, are a keen interest of certain members of the Bigfooting and other related, fringed communities. Author, content curator, and retired police officer David Paulides, famous for his *Missing 411* series, has become more or less synonymous with the subject of missing people and high strangeness. Herein we consider some cases from Paulides and others that have become associated with Sasquatch; however, it should be noted that even in instances when evidence for such a connection is at best circumstantial, it would be helpful to keep in mind that the human psyche may still tie together homins and missing human persons.

One disturbing case is that of Billy Pope which comes from Alaska. The 16-year-old teen went missing in January of 1975 one day after visiting his girlfriend about three hours away. After a search for the teen was put into motion, it was discovered that he appeared to have set up a fire away from a group of trees; disturbingly, also found around that fire were large, humanlike footprints. Decades later, about 57 minutes into an interview with *Small Town Monsters*, Jonathan Durr, a friend of Billy's, recounts:

> It was so strange because they found where Billy ... had stopped. And he had ... built a fire, but ... where he built the fire was, like, a lone tree ... way from the rest of the forest. He had, like, been breaking off branches like this [cups hand to indicate diameter of branches]. I mean, it was a place that, you know, it made no sense to stop and start a fire.
>
> And then ... they found the prints ... the Bigfoot prints. [The Bigfoot] had been circling where he had built this fire. And, like I say, it had been snowing and kind of raining, so everything was a little distorted. And some people had gone through on the search, made a mess of things ... but they had clear evidence that he was being surround—you know, circled. And ... they think somewhere in there is where this—uh, this Bigfoot ... apprehended Billy and killed him.
>
> And, you know, I think ... he wanted a line of vision, 'cause he knew he was being followed. And ... he had to be scared to death to be snapping off those branches. And that's the last they saw him [Breedlove, 2024, June 2].

Durr also provides the following account of his own experience talking to Pope's father. He states:

> Picture this if you will: it's a stormy night. The rain's pouring down, and I'm sitting with—uh, with his father. And I say, "Well, I gotta know: what happened to Billy?" And he says, "Oh, it was Bigfoot. We didn't tell the press that, but we all know it was, and we found tracks" [Breedlove, 2024, June 2, 59:00–59:17].

While other explanations have been put forth to explain Pope's disappearance (e.g., that he had been the victim of a massive snowstorm that had swept through the area), questions still remain as to what happened to his body, or why he and so many others like him have gone missing in Alaska and elsewhere. Additionally, there have been a number of cases that relate people being spirited away by these entities in ways that run parallel to fae as well as extraterrestrial lore.

Another unsettling and unsolved missing case involves 12-year-old Jared Negrete who disappeared on July 19, 1991, while on his inaugural hike with a boy scouting group in the San Bernardino National Forest. On the way to the summit of Mount San Gorgonio, he fell behind the rest of the troupe and the leader. At one point, another group of people hiking saw Jared as he was making his way back down the mountain, cutting across switchbacks. They warned him against doing that, urging him to stay on the trail, and upon reaching the summit, informed the scout leader that they had seen Jared. The troupe made its way back to base camp and the leader spent the night searching for the missing preteen, but to no avail. *Strange Outdoors* reports:

> At least 70 officers, some of whom were airlifted by helicopter into the forest and horseback riders as well as helicopters with infrared, were deployed. Over the next two weeks, as many as 3,000 people had logged 45,000 hours scouring 50 square miles of the San Bernardino National Forest from Angelus Oaks to Whitewater Canyon. A blue water bottle was found,

> but this was confirmed not to be Jared's and had probably been washed down the mountain by flash flooding during the search [Strange Outdoors, 2017, November 25, para. 9].

Jared's disappearance could have been due to predatory behavior from humans or a carnivorous animal, but no evidence corroborating these hypotheses was found in the area. To make the incident odder, Jared's backpack was found along with a camera that he had apparently used to take pictures. The images were processed, and it was found that all but the last picture on the roll were of the local landscape; however, the final picture was a close-up image of Jared's face with someone or something else that appeared to be immediately behind him and to the side. Without formal analysis, it is quite difficult to determine who or what seems to be standing behind Jared, but Justin Chernipeski—host of *Mountain Beast Mysteries*—suggests that an eye as well as part of a nose and a mouth belonging to a dark-colored face are visible (Chernipeski, 2024, January 3, 4:15–5:28). Justin has further proposed that the figure might be a Sasquatch. Before such speculation is pushed aside with calls of gullibility or spurious claims, several matters should be considered: (a) the claim that an eye and perhaps the possible, partial outline of a nose can be seen behind Jared is, in my opinion, a reasonable one to make; (b) other people have gone missing in the same park, and (c) sightings of Sasquatch have been reported in the area as well. If you are interested, I would encourage you to look at the picture yourself, to consider Jared's case, and to come to your own conclusions.

As mentioned earlier, the general phenomenon of missing people dovetails with homin narratives from oral history (e.g., the Nakani of Dene and other northern Indigenous traditions; Peters, 2024, December 1); further, the cases of Billy and Jared that we just considered also smack of homin lore via another factor: interest in children or younger persons.

For example, there is a class of homins called "*visiting demons*" (Bayanov, 2012, p. 32) that includes regional variants such as the *leshy* and *rusalka* who are said to live around the Black and Caspian Seas. Such "demons" are discussed in the following manner:

> Folklore is insistent that demons love human children. Hiding from adults, they often come in view of children and even play with them when adults are not around. They are also said to calm down crying babies and, inevitably, as a result of such fondness occasionally take human children with them. In Bielorussia, a wood goblin was "charged" with stealing a cradle with a baby and hiding it in a birch tree. In the Novgorod province, a boy of 13 was kidnapped by a wood goblin. Four years later the boy returned naked and unable to speak [Bayanov, 2012, p. 33].

Importantly, Bayanov clearly notes here that some homins may be so fond of young humans that they are led to abduct them, at least at times. However, without further information from homins themselves, it would be presumptuous if not foolhardy to make inferences about the intent behind their actions. Interestingly, Christopher Noël suggests that a pattern of behavior which seems common among Sasquatch is a tendency to be rather obsessive and compulsive in their actions in a manner that is not entirely intentional but is more or less innate within them (Noël, 2021, October 11); as such, they may be led to act in ways that are not always beneficial to the humans who capture their interest.

For example, in a narrative shared on *Buckeye Bigfoot*, an extended family was out picking huckleberries when two of the children, Robert and Tilly, had a harrowing encounter with a "bear" that the adult men ended up shooting and running off. Later that evening after the children got in their tents to go to sleep, the following occurred, as recounted by one of them (i.e., "Grandma") decades later:

> Robert and Tilly were also in the kids' tent, but all they got was Robert saying that the bear had started out being very nice, gave him huckleberries to eat and everything. Then it suddenly grabbed him and Tilly, and then it wasn't such a nice bear anymore. He said that when Uncle Ezra shot the bear, the bear suddenly dropped them, but he kept running. They said Uncle Ezra shot it several different times with his rifle, and they saw the bear fall down. This was an incredible story to be sure, Grandma said. A bear fed them berries? Ran off with them? And then their uncle just shot it? Something seemed wrong about that story even at her young age [Warren, 2024, March 12, 13:09–13:56].

The person who wrote the story was getting this information secondhand from his grandmother who was recalling the encounter from when she was about 10 years old. Unfortunately, while Robert and Tilly were saved from being carried off by the "bear," several Sasquatch had apparently visited the basecamp that night, with one of them attempting to abduct Grandma from in front of the children's tent. While she was saved thanks to some quick thinking from her Uncle Ezra, the encounter—one that I would encourage the inquiring reader to listen to in its entirety—is a powerful illustration of the age-old theme of children being stolen away at night by the bogeyman. Following the evidence that we have considered thus far, this literally and figuratively dark figure is all too real, rather than simply being a manifestation of overactive imagination or misperception. Indeed, some of the lore tells of human children being led away from adults of their kind by homins, only to be unable to survive in the way that homins can, or eventually being left behind (Bayanov, 2014).

It follows that around the globe, narratives of homins kidnapping and/or forcing themselves upon anatomically modern humans abound. Actor and experiencer Elaine Miles, enrolled member of the Umatilla Reservation (Cayuse and Nez Perce), summarizes some of the common knowledge that was shared with children by elders, including to not whistle, to not go out after dark, to close the curtains over windows in the house, and to be careful while berry-picking, or Hairy Man might find and steal you away (Eichenberger, 2024, February 14). Similarly, as stated by Cutchin (2016), for example, "people the world over tell legends of giant, smelly, hirsute wildmen, fond of abducting women and devouring human flesh" (p. 184). Or, as Paulides (2017) asserts, "There have probably been hundreds of attempted abductions of women by bigfoot across.... North America" (p. 428). Still, in the Western world, such subjects are relatively taboo (Coleman, 2003) or go unspoken among many of those who investigate the homin phenomenon. Potential reasons for this discrepancy are in line with my central thesis dealing with the threat of death anxiety that homins pose. Because sex is first and foremost procreative, as well as the fact that homins represent a potential threat to the survival of anatomically modern humans, any recognition of Sasquatch sexuality is life-affirming for homins and symbolizes the opposite for the anatomically modern human.

We continue this consideration of abductions with a narrative shared by Carrie

Lynn Bear Chief of the Pikuni Aunties, who recounts the following tragedy related to her by another Indigenous woman simply referred to as "Sue":

> When ... [Sue's] sister was about 17–18 years old, um, she came up missing. And she had left that residence—her and her cousin—and they were going to hitchhike back into town. And so, they left and it was at night time. And Sue said, "My ... sister and cousin headed out. And they were gonna go into town, but then the cousin got scared because it was so dark and everything. And they made it to the road, and then the cousin said, 'Let's just turn back. I don't want to. I don't want to hitchhike. I don't want to go ... on the road. Let's just go back home.' And then the sister said, 'No, I'm gonna go to town. You can go back if you want, but I'm going to town.'"
>
> So, the cousin turned around and went back home. Well then, a day later when the sister didn't come back home, they started to get worried. And now, this was kind of normal that they would hitchhike to town, you know (...And I know how that is, 'cause I lived 7 miles out in a community. And it was common for people to hitchhike from our little community back into Browning.) So, where they lived it was ... kind of common for them to just hitchhike to town. And—and so they didn't think too much of it. But when their sister never returned, they began to search for her and look for her.
>
> And at the time that Sue told my mom and dad the story, Sue is about in her maybe mid-30s by the time she's telling the story, uh, to my mom and dad. And she felt like (at the time she told my mom and dad) she felt like Sasquatch had taken her sister. Because up to this day, her sister has never been found. And they never did find her sister. And so that was the story that stuck with me as I grew up.... And that story never left me. I always remembered Sue's story that she told my mom and dad. And what really stuck with me was the heartache of not knowing what happened to ... her sister. And that was all she could blame: she felt like maybe Bigfoot/Sasquatch/Sabe had taken her.... And for many years we would always talk about this story [Bear Chief & Upham, 2024, September 20, 9:51–12:24].

One might be left wondering why Sue attributed the loss of her sister to Hairy Man than to, say, nefarious human interference or animal predation. Around five years prior, the two girls had had a harrowing nighttime encounter with a large bipedal being who was scratching his back on the side of their house.[2] It is important to note that despite the fact that Sue and her sister were from a different Tribe, similar knowledge of Sasquatch has been maintained in these Indigenous communities—knowledge that typically explicitly or implicitly relates respect and caution when encountering these homins or when moving through their territory. The cultivation and maintenance of such practical wisdom would be expected in the presence of real rather than fictional, purely symbolic, or imaginary beings. Those who remain dubious about the prospect of homin abductions would do well to remember that some Indigenous scholarship has stated that imaginary or fanciful tales typically have no place in Indigenous American lore, as practical knowledge tends to be prioritized in such communities (Deloria, Jr., 2022)—communities that may also hold salient narratives about Coyote, Raven, or Beaver, all of which are beings that are known to modern Western science.

Further, in *Tribal Bigfoot*, David Paulides reports on the following information that was conveyed by aforementioned Gayle Highpine of the Kootenai Tribe about a woman of the Lilloett Tribe who was kidnapped by a Sasquatch, became pregnant, and gave birth to a hirsute baby who died soon after birth:

> Ms. Highpine's story shows that bigfoot/sasquatch abductions and rapes have occurred in Canada as well as the United States. You would assume that stories like this regarding females

> in a small tribe would be something that most would be very tight lipped about. The woman probably wouldn't want the entire tribe knowing she was having a Sasquatch baby. The number of stories similar to this that exist is much too large for all of them to be fabricated [Paulides, 2017, p, 430].

Paulides's reflection here is worth noting and may well bear significance for those who have been direct witness to such horrifying events. Other lore tells of harrowing encounters between homin males and human women. One tale as tragic as it is legendary comes from the Choctaw Tribe and tells of the birth of LeFlore County in Oklahoma as well as its connection to a group of predatory homins. In *Wartime Stories*, Lamana sets the narrative in 1885 after the Choctaw were forcibly removed from their ancestral homeland during the horrific Trail of Tears. Joshua LeFlore (of Choctaw and French heritage) and other Choctaw men including the renowned Tubbee warriors banded together to pursue the mysterious marauders who had begun to steal away livestock, women, and children from their peaceful community. After tracking the thieves for days, the warriors finally came upon a ghastly scene, which Lamana describes as follows:

> Nothing could prepare them for the nightmarish reality they had quite literally stumbled into. Bodies—dozens of them: loved ones, barely recognizable through mutilation and decay. Their flesh had been ripped away in chunks, devoured by what appeared to be a pack of rabid animals. Their bodies—what was left of them—had been stacked in a putrid pile at the far end of the clearing. Clouds of fat, gluttonous flies swarmed over them as their droning buzz reached an impenetrable din. Further adding to the disgusting horror of the scene, piles of excrement lay scattered about the den, further spoiling the flies.
>
> Snapping the Choctaw from their horrified gaze, the telling sounds of footsteps drew their attention to the clearing's far edge. The cowards, it seemed, were fleeing from the very fight they had started. But before LeFlore could muster pursuit, the true face of their enemy stepped into the light of day.
>
> What LeFlore and the Tubbees were confronted with was no human adversary. Like *nothing* they had ever seen, these beasts were manlike, but far more massive [Lamana, 2024, March 18, 18:07–19:25].

As Lamana tells it, the ensuing battle was quick and fierce. The melee left the heroic Joshua LeFlore and other men deceased, but the hirsute hunters were also felled by those men who remained. It was a pyrrhic victory, though the aforementioned county in Oklahoma now bears LeFlore's name as the family's legacy remains.

Yet elsewhere in Indigenous America we find other narratives of the abduction of women with varying outcomes. Chronicled by John Walter Burns and reproduced in places such as Short (2024), the story of Chehalis woman Serephine Long is perhaps one of the most well-known abduction narratives within hominology. Indeed, it has become rather embedded in Sasquatch lore (e.g., Bayanov, 2014; Cutchin and Renner, 2020a, p. 24). She was 17 years old in 1871 when the incident unfolded. As Ms. Long relates, while she walked along a tree-lined path thinking about her betrothed, a powerful, hairy arm and hand shot out of the brush and grabbed her. The being was big, powerful, and hairy, and placed pitch over her eyes so that she could not see. He took her to a cave and kept her there for a year. He impregnated her and, as the months wore on, she became ill and deeply homesick. She attempted to communicate this to her captor, who eventually relented and, placing pitch on her eyes once more, returned her to the outskirts of her village. She went to her people and told them what had occurred. Soon after, she gave birth to a boy, but the baby did not survive through the night. Similar to Ms. Serephine's narrative, there are also those accounts that depict tragic fates for the offspring sired by homin-human coupling.

For example, Georges Dodds (2007) shares numerous versions of a narrative from around the world that speaks to the atrocities that homins can potentially commit, or at the very least, the implicit psycho-sexual threat that they may pose to humans. In this particular article, Dodds relates a legend that he labels *the monkey-spouse tale* which has persisted in Russia, central Asia, southeast Asia, the Middle East, and the Americas. The tale is essentially encapsulated as follows: a human becomes marooned; they are found and saved by a hairy humanlike being who eventually coerces them into sex; a child is produced; the human escapes; discovering that the human has escaped, the homin gives chases; but, unable to retrieve them, the homin rips their child in two, throwing half of the corpse at the departing parent. Typically, the human is female and the homin is male; however, some versions contain the opposite gender pairing.

One Portuguese version of the narrative has the female human be rescued only to be "condemned to death for her sins, but her sentence is commuted to ending her days in a convent" (Dodds, 2007, p. 86). In this story, the apparent moral inequity of her encounter is extended by the sentences imposed on her by her own people, with the great irony of her escaping one tragedy to be confronted with another being a parallel to contemporary experiencer narratives wherein those whose encounter becomes known are often ostracized or suffer in other relational ways.

Moreover, a Honduran version of the monkey-spouse tale is about *el sisemité* (or *sisimite*),[3] which is a homin known to Indigenous and Latinx inhabitants of Central America and southern Mexico. As follows, Dodds (2007, p. 95) shares the story as related by a secondary source:

> "My grandfather told me that he ran into the Sisimite around 1912, up there on Pico Bonito. It walked like a man, had a very hairy body and was very tall," said Don Manuel Mejöa, an octogenarian living in the village of La Union, scant kilometers from La Ceiba. "[...] These monsters would kidnap women and take them to their lairs. It is said that man-apes were born of these matings," added the old man. The story of a woman who managed to escape from one such Sisimite abode is still discussed among the mountain villagers: the creature pursued her, carrying with it the three offspring they had had together and showing them to the mother, who had fled to the other side of a river, in hopes of attracting her to her children. Its efforts were in vain, and the troglodyte mortally threw the inhuman infants into the water [Mausó, 1999].[4]

One of the matters that may be reflected upon in such narratives is how sex, physical security, and the offspring are used as power plays to entice the abductee into staying with the hirsute host or abductor. Indeed, Dodds and Wessels (2011) expand on these themes in a collection of tales dealing with this theme of forced sexual (or, at times, consensual and amorous) human contact with hairy primates. It takes no real leap of imagination to see how a less explicitly violent version of the legend plays out in popular tales such as the popular animated Disney rendering of *Beauty and the Beast*, wherein the Beast essentially abducts Belle,[5] or even in ancient portrayals of the saga between Persephone and Hades.

Other narratives with similar themes include that of the *ocho kochi* of Abkhazia (Porshnev, 2000, p. 196) and the barmanu of Pakistan (Coleman, 2009; McGrath, 2022), for example. Referring to his archival research on hirsute liminal entities of Japan, author of the text *Hibagon: Japanese Bigfoot* Kyle Brink provides the following summary of one historical narrative about the *oni* (often read: demon), which he treats as a more general term for the hirsute hibagon:

> The one name I would say is general all throughout Japan is oni. Back to the 900s. And ... this is in the national—or imperial archives ... there were oni extermination campaigns. So these are incidents where a bunch of the local oni (which, again, I'm going to finger as "hibagon") get too rowdy. They get too bold. And they come into town. They come into these villages. And they take women. And they kill people. They kill livestock.
>
> And word of this would reach the emperor. And he would send out ... a military force with a general at its head. And the general is named in the document. Dates are there. The places are there.... They went to such and such mountain because such and such village was complaining, and they go up and ... search out these oni and destroy them [Documentaries—Crash-Course Cryptozoology, 2023, October 9, 10:16–11:26].

To this day, the oni hold a prominent place within Japanese communicative memory (e.g., within popular culture via *anime* and *manga*) and are often depicted as assuming generally human form and as enacting mischievous, dangerous, or even murderous intent toward humanity. One would be hard-pressed to not recognize in these narratives echoes of other accounts such as the Choctaw war, half a world away.

Similarly, in these accounts are seen implicit allusions to Heuvelmans's conceit: that is, that a race of "sub-men ... were descendants of our rivals which were once near to exterminating us and which we may hardly have exterminated" (Heuvelmans, 1959, p. 87). To be sure, in the second edition of his book on the hibagon, Brink presents the following simple and unambiguous warning: "Beware of hibagon—they take people" (Brink, 2021, p. 5).

Returning to indigenous North America, we find these same themes to be present. According to Bobbie Short, for example, since at least the 1600s, narratives have persisted within Sioux tradition of the *Cee-ha-tonka* (aka Citonga) abducting Indigenous women and children at times:

> ...when the *Cee-ha-tonka* giants become men, they leave their mother and father and strike out on their own to find a woman and start a family; sometimes they steal Indian maidens and carry them to distant places in the mountains, sometimes they steal children to raise as their own [Short, n.d., p. 136].

Elsewhere in North America, we find the following narrative from the Lake Band of the Colville Indigenous Americans, related as follows by anthropologist Ed Fusch (1992):

> Back around the turn of the century (1885–1900) the Indians set up a fishing camp near Keller on the San Poll River.... In the evening the men would return, tired and hungry, to camp with their days catch. The women would work all evening processing the fish and putting it on drying racks to dry. While cooking dinner one of the women, a recent bride through bride-purchase, took a kettle and went off after water. Minutes later she was heard screaming. The men rushed to the scene but could only stand and watch as Skanicum carried her off. They knew that Skanicum was very vengeful and if harmed the captive may be injured and the mountains would not be safe for any Indian. As she was carried away, the captive tore off

> and dropped pieces of her white slip leaving a trail for the men to follow. She was with Skanicum all summer, or at least a couple of months, when the men searching for her on horseback saw her gathering wild potato roots.
>
> Skanicum was asleep nearby. Upon seeing the men she emptied her lap of the potatoes, crept quietly to them, leaped on one of the horses behind its rider, and thus escaped. Upon return to camp all of the Indians immediately broke camp and hastily departed the area. During her stay with Skanicum the woman had gathered roots, etc., which they shared. Skanicum eats anything other people eat but lives primarily on roots such as that of the thule (tooly) or cattail plant, which they gather, dry, and store in caves. They build fires with flint stone and steal hides from Indians, which they use for bedding and to cover the entrance to their cave [Fusch, 1992, p. 19].

Fusch's retelling of this narrative suggests the persistence of knowledge about Skanicum among the Colville Tribe: knowledge which dictates taboos to be followed as well as other behaviors that humans tend toward in relation to homins. The author goes on to explain that viable offspring are produced through intercourse between the woman and Skanicum. Not only that, but several generations are related in the story, wherein some of the physical characteristics of the homins tend to be retained in the children and grandchildren of the sexual pairing. And further still, others such as Bobbie Short (n.d., p. 155) who painstakingly saved Fusch's work with his blessing, have stated that the anthropologist has indicated that descendants of *hybrid* human-homin offspring still live in places such as on the Colville Indian Reservation. Such an account is quite remarkable and opens up fascinating ontological questions, and yet the gist of the narrative still jibes with other contemporary reports that are told of homin sexual violence toward, abduction of, and/or attraction to humans. To be sure, Renner (Cutchin & Renner, 2020a, p. 245) reflects on the work of Jim Brandon known as *Rebirth of Pan*, wherein he suggests that one of the binding features of anomalous entities—Sasquatch included—is their interest in human sexuality.

Following this line of inquiry, one of the most oft-told abduction narratives within the Bigfooting community is that of Muchalat Harry, a member of the Nootka Tribe of Vancouver Island who was said to be an experienced trapper and in excellent physical condition, often venturing off for weeks at a time to go about his business (Bigfoot Encounters, n.d.; Byrne, 1976). In autumn of 1928, Harry set off deep into the bush for a solo venture in a location he knew well: the Conuma River, at the head of Tlupana Inlet. One night while he slept in his blankets within his lean-to, while dressed only in his underwear, he was abducted and carry away by a large, male Hairy Man. He was brought several miles away to a place where a group of Hairy Men had made something of a camp. Harry's ordeal thereafter proceeded as follows:

> The males to the front of the curious group[,] females behind them[,] and young ones to the rear. Muchalat Harry was frightened at first and his fear grew to terror when he noticed, he said, the large number of bones lying around the campsite. When he saw these he was convinced that the Bigfeet were going to eat him.
>
> The Bigfeet did not harm him in any way. Occasionally one came forward and touched him, as if feeling him, and when they discovered that his "skin" was loose—it was in fact his woolen underwear—several came forward and pulled at it gently.
>
> While they looked at him and examined him, Muchalat Harry sat with his back to the rock wall and did not move. He was cold and hungry, but his thoughts were only on escape. Some

time in the late afternoon, curiosity on the part of the Bigfeet seemed to slacken and with most of the Bigfeet out of camp, probably food-gathering he thought, there came the opportunity that he needed. He leapt to his feet and ran for his life, never looking back [Bigfoot Encounters, n.d., para. 5–7].

Muchalat Harry returned to his people to tell of his tale. Father Anthony Terhaar of Mt. Angel Abbey, who learned of the event while nursing Harry back to health over about three weeks, later related the narrative to popular field investigator and author Peter Byrne. Apparently, the ordeal had stressed the Nootka man so badly that his once black hair had turned to white. Of note, Byrne shares the following of the aftermath of the encounter:

> Not only did [Harry] never return [to his encampment]; according to Father Anthony, he never left the settlement at Nootka, never went in the woods again for the rest of his life. He preferred to lose all of his valuables and probably hard-won possessions rather than risk another encounter with the Bigfeet [n.d., para. 10].

Harry's behavior following his abduction maps on well to that of other abductees and experiencers who have the fortune of returning to civilization.

That said, another well-known abduction account within the Bigfooting community that is on the surface quite similar to that of Muchalat Harry is the rather extraordinary narrative of Albert Ostman (1893–1975). Coming to light in 1957, 33 years after it is said to have occurred, the narrative is of Ostman's abduction by the apparent patriarch of a family of four Sasquatch (i.e., mother, father, sister, and brother) and his subsequent stay with them for six days before his escape (Green, 2018; Patterson, 2018).[6] Cryptozoologist Loren Coleman (2003) notes that, per the work of both John Green and Ivan T. Sanderson, Ostman felt that he had been abducted to pair with the young female Sasquatch. Indeed, the same claim is recounted in Short's (n.d.) text, wherein she states: "Ostman felt the reason for his abduction was that he was a potential mate for the daughter of the hairy hostage taker" (p. 263). Further still, Short's own reflections on this matter are as follows:

> If not repulsed by the idea of intercourse with a hair-covered bride, surely Ostman's performance would be hindered by the stress of a captive situation. The idea also occurs to me that the Sasquatch apparently thought Ostman one of his own species; a man of his own kind otherwise why did the dominant Sasquatch bring Ostman back to camp as a potential husband for his daughter? [Short, n.d., p. 263].

Thus, the subject of human-homin sexual compatibility and viability is again considered, just as it is in various narratives from Indigenous America (e.g., Short, 2024) and elsewhere. On the matter of Ostman's own perception of the young female homin whom he felt he was intended for, he offers:

> The girl would not hurt anybody. Chest was flat like a boy—no development like young ladies. I am sure if I could get the old man [Sasquatch] out of the way, I could easily have brought this girl out with me to civilization. But what good would that have been? I would have to keep her in a cage for public display. I don't think we have any right to force our way of life on other people, and I don't think they would like it. (The noise and racket in the modern city they would not like any more than I do.) [Patterson, 2018, p. 119].

Ostman's words are noteworthy. He seems to be indicating that the young female's demeanor was amenable enough to have allowed him to bring her with him.

Or perhaps he is indicating that the girl seemed to be interested enough in him to have allowed him to have brought her along when he inevitably attempted to make his escape. Either way, he seems to be suggesting that the female homin (as well as her family as a whole, for that matter) was not entirely behaviorally incommensurate with the human experience, particularly since at no point during his forced stay was he physically harmed.

I must note at this point that when I first heard of Ostman's encounter some years ago, similar to my initial reaction to Janice Carter Coy's testimony, I was rather incredulous. It seemed to me at the time that such extended contact with humans was utterly implausible. However, upon further investigation into the matter, which included considering the words of others familiar with Ostman or his narrative (e.g., Dahinden as cited in Short, n.d., pp. 263–264), and seeing parallel themes in Ostman's and Coy's accounts elsewhere in the homin lore, I have come to think that at the very least, the gist of these narratives bears historical, if not just narrative, truth.

Sexual Aggressions

While not all of the aforementioned abductions of humans result in forced sexual contact, sexual contact and violation is often reported in these narratives. Here we consider some of these matters more concertedly. Similar to one implication of the Cherokee Tsul'Kalu narrative, it cannot be overstated that in a very real biological sense, if two beings are able to have sexual union and procreate, then they are technically members of the same species. One remaining question is whether or not the offspring is sterile, but as has been stated elsewhere (Vendramini, 2009), Neanderthals and early humans were sexually compatible. Due to the fact that Neanderthals have been said by some to be predecessors of the modern-day almas or almasty, the rather incredible tale of Zana of Abkhazia is one narrative which provides some perspective on this matter.

The (in)famous legend of Zana has found rather fertile ground in the collective psyche of the Bigfooting community. The story is a rather divisive one, with varied interpretations presenting themselves. Some interpret the implications of her saga as reflecting the ills of racism and slavery, reading Sykes's work in particular as suggesting that Zana was simply a sub-Saharan African who ended up in the Caucasus due to the greedy and rapacious conceits of humans. Author, mountaineer, and sailor Graham Hoyland, for example, posits that Zana was a modern African woman who had been imprisoned and raped in the Caucasus (2018, p. 155). Still, others including Sykes (2014) himself have pointed to Zana's archaic African origin, suggesting that she was likely from an African lineage so ancient that she and her people were descendants of archaic humans. This latter scenario would support a legacy of sexual procreation between anatomically modern humans and homins. Zana (which, according to Sykes, means "black" in Abkhazian; Sykes, 2014, 2016), was said to be an almasty of African heritage who was captured in the southern Caucasus Mountains in the mid–1800s. Sykes contextualizes Zana's story as follows:

> In many ways Zana's is a classic tale of a wild creature part-human, part-animal, captured and tamed. And so it would have remained, a story, and we would have known nothing more about Zana. What has kept the story alive is that she had at least four children with local men. The circumstances are unclear but there are tales of drunken orgies and curious men being granted access to her in exchange for money [Sykes, 2014, p. 296].

Zana is said to have been kept inebriated with alcohol for much of her enslavement, thereby easing the sexual abuse forced upon her at the hands of her "curious" captors.

Various researchers, including noted hominologists Marie-Jeanne Koffmann and Boris Porshnev, studied Zana's story and found it to be entirely credible, as it left behind various types of testable forensic, genealogic, as well as folkloric evidence. Sykes also includes a genealogy of Zana's four generations of her descendants, including her great-granddaughter Indira who was born in 1974 (2014, p. 316).

Elsewhere in the literature we find other examples of sexual viability between humans and our hairier kith and ken. For example, among the Zulu people of southern Africa, Vusamazulu Credo Mutwa speaks of the tale of Amarava, the last remaining member of the Red People, and the demonic Odu, the last of the sub-humans. They are commanded by a deific figure, the First Goddess *Ma*, to consort with one another and to repopulate the earth after a great flood is brought down onto the earth (Mutwa, 1964).

Or in the Caucasus, Bayanov reflects on the following, thereby providing grounds for his position that tales of sexual relations are found in folklore the world over:

> In Circassian [Sunni Muslim culture of the North Caucasus region] folklore it is said that the shaitan and his female partner jinne can be caught. However it is not advisable to catch a shaitan because he will offer strong resistance. Jinne is a different matter. If caught, she can be used as a woman. Sometimes she herself is seeking sex with humans, coming to herdsmen for the purpose [Bayanov, 2014, p. 62].

Indeed, Bayanov's assertions fall in line with the general amorous, lustful, or lascivious behavioral nature ascribed to some jinne (aka djinn, jinn, etc.), and it should also be noted that some other rather peculiar traits (e.g., backward-facing feet) are at times attributed to homins.[7] However, lest it be misunderstood that the matter of attraction is said to come from the human side as well, Bayanov's (2012, p. 38) report of a horse herder cohabiting with a female almasty and having three children with her stated: "Be it a shaitan or a human, it doesn't matter," apparently referring to the diversity of the herder's own sexual appetite, his ability to procreate with both types of people, or both.

Notably, terms such as shaitan and its variant satan (Porshnev, 2000, p. 188) have been used to refer to homins like the almasty and are etymologically meant to convey moral distance from the divine or to characterize an adversarial nature. In other words, there is a connotation of physical and/or moral disconnection not just from humans but from divinity—a matter which is explicitly noted in various narratives about homins. For example, in one telling of how the lai ho'a of Indonesia came to be, they were the result of an incestuous relationship between a human brother and sister pair. Once other members of the village found out about the unclean affair, they banished the pair into the forest to live among the animals (Forth, 2022, p. 85).[8] The siblings thus became the progenitors of the lai ho'a, a group of entities said to be physically unattractive, a feature attributed to their moral repugnancy. Such narratives seem to carry a good deal of narrative truth wherein those who attend to them often find practical meaning in them. Perhaps these stories serve as some cue to the deep memory residing in the collective human psyche.

At this point, we turn to 20th-century examples of sexual violation and attraction between humans and homins. In 1915, as the Southern Pacific rail line was being cut between Eureka, California, and other large cities, one of the rail workers went missing. The tale as follows was told by one of the man's co-workers, Theodore Spagopoulos, and was related to his daughter, Esther, and her siblings:

> Three, and then four, weeks passed from the original disappearance when one two-man team on their way back to their site found the missing line worker naked and delirious in a pit near one of their work sites. They made a small litter and carried him to camp. Theodore was on the trail and saw the line worker and heard his statement. The worker was partially alert and could speak, and said a female ape kidnapped him and held him in the pit against his will and he was forced to have sex with it. The ape licked his hands and feet until they were raw so that he couldn't walk and escape. Theodore stated that he saw the worker and could see that his hands and feet had no skin on them at all, and he could easily see red, raw, bleeding flesh on both hands and feet. The workers carried the employee back to the main camp where limited medical aid was available. He was suffering from severe wounds and hypothermia, and died late that night [Paulides, 2017, p. 195].

In 1993, Esther conveyed the above narrative to her son, John Lewis, who had asked her if she had ever seen any Sasquatch in the Pacific Northwest during her time living there. She shared that she had not, but that John's own grandfather had told her about a strange incident involving his fellow rail worker that had occurred about 70 years prior. Subsequently, John Lewis shared this information with David Paulides. The tragic story follows a pattern that we see across time and space, wherein homins steal away humans for sex.

Later in the 20th century, another incident involving rape occurred: this time, with a male homin abusing a female human. As recounted in *50 Years with Bigfoot: Tennessee Chronicles of Co-existence* (Green & Coy, 2002), Janice Carter Coy relates how she and her family had regular, continued contact with a family of Sasquatch thanks to the efforts of her grandfather many years earlier to resuscitate and heal the young male who would become the patriarch of the family unit. Coy says of Sasquatch, "I know they rape women because they raped a girl from here in our area, at least the young one, Blackie did. It caused her to go crazy. She is in Moccasin Bend in Chattanooga still and may never be right again. It happened over 20 years ago" (p. 158). The girl had been walking home from her boyfriend's place when she was pulled into the bush and assaulted. Coy states:

> All I know was that she was around thirteen at the time and used to walk up and down our road to go see her boyfriend who lived behind our place. She was on top of our hill and the young male grabbed her. It dragged her into the woods on the neighbor's side and tore her insides really bad having sex with her. She was never in her right mind after that.
>
> It was Uncle Strange and Bill his brother that found her. They took clubs and got the young male away from her or so they told afterwards. It was just awful. They brought that girl to the

> house to help her clean up a bit and called her parents and the law about her. The law called the Forestry Service because they didn't believe any of us on the matter. They thought we were making up one big story to save the boyfriend being prosecuted for the charge of rape against him because it was determined that some animal did rape her out in the woods.
>
> It must have been near 1980 or so but it happened so long ago and I was probably around 8 years old, so I can't be certain. I don't think they put anything in the paper about it being an animal that raped her either, but I could be wrong. I know they did a write up on it as being the boyfriend who raped her at first. Her boyfriend still lives in the same old place next to his parents. They dropped all of the charges against him when they arrested him after lab tests proved that he was not the one who raped her. I heard the lab tests proved that it was an unknown animal's semen and not a human's.
>
> Uncle Strange and Uncle Bill died a long time back. They were the brothers to Birdie and Henry and all of them are dead now so therefore I do not have any real proof in this matter. It may be written up in the newspaper[9] though about the boyfriend raping her and then possibly about the charges being dropped against him [Green & Coy, 2002, p. 159].

Following what Coy shares above, this young girl paid a terrible price for Blackie's depravity. Rape is one of the most violent and vile of all transgressions. Blackie was one of the children of the male Sasquatch, Fox. Fox was the patriarch of a family of Sasquatch. He was just a youngling when Coy's grandfather nursed him back to health after a tree fell on him. As Janice tells it, Fox and her grandfather, Robert Carter, Sr., spent the rest of their lives in a respectful relationship with each other, and Fox would eventually bring his own family to live in the woods on the family's sprawling property.

In an interview, Coy stated that the girl who was raped (whose name she never divulged in order to protect her identity) was institutionalized for 40 years following the assault, due to the extreme toll that it took on her mind and body (Totherow, 2020, November 9). In the same interview, Coy also pointedly remarks that she feels that Blackie (who was apparently the only dangerous offspring of Fox and his consort Sheba) was a psychopath, and points to an incident wherein her own daughter had an encounter with Blackie when she was younger: at the time, the homin telepathically (via mindspeak) showed her what he had done to the girl who he had raped.[10]

As it is, rape by a human male is a horrid affair, but when it occurs by a being who is not supposed to exist according to popular Western wisdom, the devastating and fracturing effects that the act would have on the mind and body are quite surely extremely difficult to cope with or heal. Unfortunately, as we have seen, such narratives of homin-human sexual violence seem to be rather prevalent around the world (e.g., Short, n.d., pp. 389–390).[11]

For example, tales of the Ucumar of Central and South America (e.g., Bolivia, Ecuador, etc.) are quite telling. The beings are said to be quite large (up to 15 feet 7 inches, or 4.8 meters), black-haired, and bipedal, and to leave behind humanlike footprints (Newton, 2005, p. 470). Similar to the monkey-spouse tale (Dodds, 2007), some accounts of the Ucumar state that the entity abducts men rather than women (Coleman, 2003), while others depict attraction to and abduction of women instead (e.g., McGrath, 2022; Newton, 2005; p. 470). While there is some debate as to the ontology of the being (i.e., some reports potentially being of the spectacled bear rather than a homin, while others purport an extant Gigantopithecus; McGrath,

2022), and despite the contradiction in the gender of the abductee, the matter of adults being abducted for sex particularly is not one that is so easily explained away as encounters with ursine abductors. Following the idea that Indigenous narratives tend to contain practical rather than fanciful concerns (e.g., Deloria, Jr., 2022), the notion that stories of bears kidnapping people for sex strains credulity. Moreover, it does not seem necessary to add sexual predation to these tales in order to encourage women and children to be cautious. In my opinion, it would be a rather superfluous detail, straying away from a more grounded "danger dictum" to, for example, simply not be eaten by predatory animals.

While the majority of the narratives that we have considered thus far involve male homins and human men, women, or children, I have not explicitly dealt with the matter of female homins very much. Interestingly, the fact that some of the most famous Bigfooting lore involved human men and female homins, which is a potentially interesting theme, in my opinion: (a) Patterson and Gimlin tracking and filming Patty for the PGF; (b) Albert Ostman being brought as a mate for a female homin; (c) William Roe observing a female homin; d) Paul Freeman tracking and filming a female homin for the FF (e.g., P. Freeman, 2022; Powell, 2022); (d) human men abducting and imprisoning Zana. One might speculate that such encounters (absent the Ostman case) may have been at least in part due to the female homin allowing the men to get close due to interest or curiosity, the loss of her own mate or consort, or due to being used to the men's presence in the area.

To return briefly to the matter of hybridization, broadly speaking, one subset of the Bigfooting community has advocated that Sasquatch are Nephilim. Taken up by some members of the community as evidence of interbreeding between humans and some other humanlike being (Carpenter, 2019), the narrative dovetails with a nigh-unending variety of myths, legends, and folkloric accounts of humans mating with demi-divine and/or demonic humanlike beings to produce a hybrid race. While the Nephilim hypothesis seems to be viewed with derision by some segments of the Bigfooting community, it dovetails with other folkloric and mythological accounts such as those that Bayanov (2014) and Porshnev (2000) report regarding the dev, deva, domovoy, or other homins, wherein they are reported to represent a demonic or angelic ontology. Such a narrative may not fit well with Western secular convictions, but the Nephilim idea is by no means an outlier when it comes to mythological, cryptozoological, or hominological accounts.

As scholars such as Welsing (2004) aver, a great deal of psychological tension can develop around the subject of sex and sexual propagation. After all, one's progeny are not just representative of one's *symbolic immortality* but are determinants of the survival of the species. Any threat to their ability to grow and thrive is a threat to the species as well as to the individual progenitor. Due to the argument that organisms only have a finite amount of physical resources to cope with stress (e.g., as evinced in Hans Selye's General Adaptation Syndrome), as well as the argument that one's conscious ability to consider information is also finite (e.g., the concept of *cognitive load*), a fair amount of material available to the psyche must thereby be suppressed or repressed into the unconscious realms of the mind. If we were to couple this with the psychodynamic assertion that sexual acts, libidinal desires, and sexual propagation can be an enormous source of tension, we can arrive at a conclusion that, absent any other selective pressures in the environment, the average person's psyche could contain at least some unbidden sexual tensions.

At this point, we return briefly to the particular taboo of incest, given that it is a sex-related theme that occurs within some homin narratives. Gregory Forth provides the following origin story of the lai ho'a of Indonesia:

> An elderly brother and sister became involved in a sexual relationship. The sister was long past childbearing age. One night a younger relative spied on the pair, saw them engaging in intercourse, and told others about this. Following their transgression a terrific storm arose, with thunder and lightning. Fellow villagers then realized that, to stop the storm, they would have to formally banish the transgressors. As part of the procedure, the villagers exclaimed, "you will become a kind of animal, what kind of animal is up to you." Their kinsmen further declared, "you are no longer our relatives, you will become lai ho'a (ape men)." They then chased the elderly siblings out of the village and into the forest, where they mixed with monkeys [Forth, 2022, p. 85].

As illustrated by the above narration from Goda, a Lio elder who related the tale to Gregory Forth, another taboo concern relevant to our present discussion is incest concerning both humans and homins themselves. Goda's narrative contains themes of the incest going against natural order, that behavior and character—and particularly those related to sex—are what make someone human (or generally *Homo*). As he concludes his book, Forth (2022) reflects that the Lio ape-men of Indonesia are thereby said to be the result of "transformations of misbehaving humans" (p. 246) who were expelled from their communities for their moral depravity and eventually came to live in the wild. One reading of this narrative speaks to the kind of cultural divide that may persist between homins and humans, with the former tending to observe different rules about what constitutes right behavior as opposed to that expected of an oppositional character (e.g., shaitan, satan, etc.).[12]

Earlier, Forth (2022) also states that Goda's above statements indicate the physical appearance of the lai ho'a (who are said to look like old people), their closeness to humans, and also overlap significantly with a Lio myth on the origin of monkeys. It cannot be overstated that, significant among these themes, is the fact that improper comportment is equated with the nature of animals rather than humans.

It is important to note that sexuality and its expression are by no means singled out here by mere happenstance. From the *hieros gamos* or holy union of the ancient world and beyond to the transpersonal sex of contemporary times, sex stands alone as a means through which human beings can experience the purest and most unifying of states as well as the basest, most vile of passions. Thus, the full continuum of human experience from *peak experiences* to nadir or desolation experiences can be expressed through sexual acts. In this way, sex, power, and identity are linked quite tightly to one another. Indeed, scholars such as Jenny Wade who has written extensively about transpersonal sexual experience, suggest that such an encounter can help resolve the seeming dichotomy between the spiritual and the profane, between holiness and one's worldly desires (e.g., Wade, 2015). In this sense, one's sexual acts and views toward sex can very much reflect how they view themselves and the world in the most fundamental way.

In all, the ways in which homins may threaten violation of the human body and/or psyche can be problematic if not outright dangerous in terms of psychological or physical safety. Existential danger generally needs to be addressed.

We end this discussion of violation and attraction with the words of Curyung Tribal Council member Fred Roehl as he reflects on his most harrowing encounter: "I felt like food. When it looked at me in the window, I felt like food. I–, I felt like a rabbit went in a hole with wolves around that hole" (LeGro, 2024, January 12, 48:00). To put it mildly, such an experience would surely be threatening, and its emotional trace would be preserved in the psyche for posterity, ideally to aid in his survival and that of his community.

Sexual Anatomy and Arousal

Following the general train of thought that we have been on in this section thus far, we continue with further consideration of sasquatch sexual anatomy, sexuality, and attraction to humans.

While there is some diversity in accounts of male and female Sasquatch sexual anatomy, this is to be expected when considering the relative variety of the same among human men and women. A narrative from 2013 offered by experiencer Jason Miller contains a clear description of uncircumcised male genitalia and scrotum at close range during which the juvenile Sasquatch was said to be watching the witness's daughter who was walking with Jason, while sitting happily eating huckleberries (Hajicek & Hajicek, November 29, 2023; King-Sharp, 2024, April 14).[13] And if *50 Years with Bigfoot* is indeed a genuine accounting of human-homin interactions, which it certainly seems to be, then it stands as one of the most significant pieces of ethnographic literature on the subject that has ever been written. In addition to recollecting general behavior and individual personality traits of a family of Sasquatch, Green and Coy (2002) discuss some particularities of sexual anatomy and sexual functioning. For example, Coy recounts various sizes, degrees of erectness, and position among a sample of several male Sasquatch that frequented her grandfather's farm, as well as the admission that female Sasquatch have something akin to a menstrual cycle that occurs about every 6 to 8 months, that these beings tended to prefer privacy when they had sex, and that they performed sex in the missionary position (Green & Coy, 2002, p. 138).

Additionally, from relatively droopy to fuller breasts, female homin secondary sexual anatomy is described in various ways as well. The females found around the property in Tennessee are described by Coy as having breasts that are not as full as those demonstrated by "Patty" from the Patterson-Gimlin film. William Roe's daughter's illustration of the female homin from his 1924 encounter (Bigfoot Encounters, n.d.a.; Green, 2018, p. 26) as well as what is visible of "Patty's" mammary glands in the 1967 PGF both indicate fuller breasts.[14] Patty and the subject of the William Roe encounter have relatively robust mammary glands in relation to reports from elsewhere in North America or around the world. For example, in Albert Ostman's account of his abduction, he notes that both the old and young females were rather flat-chested (Green, 2004b). Or, as noted by Shackley (1983, p. 104) of reports of the almas of Mongolia, the females are generally noted as having long, droopy breasts that can be flung over their shoulders to feed the young ones nursing on their backs. Similarly, in Bobbie Short's (2024, p. 24) own northern California (i.e., by the Smith River) encounter from 1985, she notes that the female homin who was quite close to her had breasts that were "hanging empty, nipples up" and that "moved with every step she took."[15] In other literature such as Forth's (2022, p. 35)[16] work on the more diminutive (i.e., around 3.3 feet, or one meter, in height) lai ho'a of Indonesia, the females are generally said to have breasts like human women but smaller, and nipples resembling those of a dog. Further still, Bayanov (2012) notes that among those "devils" of Eurasian lore, females' breasts are said to be "'huge' and even 'frightening'" (pp. 31–32).

During a 2001 conference presentation, Loren Coleman (2003) discussed a case involving an eyewitness reporting a male Sasquatch having intercourse with a cow, and he also considered whether the incidence of homosexuality among Sasquatch mirrors the incidence among *H. sapiens*. Regarding the cow incident, it has assumed a rather special position within the annals of Sasquatch studies and comes from a book by Jan Klement titled *The Creature: Personal Experiences with Bigfoot*. The text provides a series of autobiographical accounts around Klement's encounters with a large, hairy male hominoid whom he nicknames Kong. During this particular encounter, we learn the following:

> As I approached the bottom of the hill I could see the cows in the pastures on the other hillside. There was a noisy commotion among the cows and when I ... walked over I could see Kong. He was mounted on a large Holstein cow and was shoving away. The cow would start to walk away, and Kong would lift his legs and hang on with his hands cupped against the side of the cow until it would stop and then he would begin working his buttocks rapidly again...
>
> Kong continued his activity for what ... was probably about five or six minutes. I ... returned to the cabin.
>
> I was sitting on the porch when Kong returned to the cabin. He was visible in the light rays beaming from the cabin and I could see his penis dripping... [p. 83].

Klement also comments that shortly before the cow incident, Kong had appeared at the former male's cabin with a fully erect penis. Of course, following the above account of bovine bestiality, Kong appeared soon thereafter to have satiated his sexual appetite.[17]

Though there are other accounts in the annals of Sasquatch lore which indicate that an erect penis may be a threat display [e.g., Coleman, 2009] or may simply be an indication of sexual desire, in either case, physiological arousal is presumed.

In one account from Nance Warren's *Buckeye Bigfoot* (Warren, 2024, February 2), a female experiencer named Anne of age 23 at the time of the encounter shares a harrowing ordeal that occurred while she was camping alone in northern California. An extremely large male Sasquatch (which she estimates was at least 10 feet tall) gently rocked her pickup truck and stared in on her while she lied on her air mattress one night, clutching one of her guns. Quite understandably, she lost control of her bodily functions and urinated on herself.[18] The witness then shares the following account as the entity walked around the outside of the car, sniffing the air:

> It would stand up straight and bend down, looking as it walked around. I could *definitely* tell that it was a massive male. I saw it was very aroused as it went around the corner of the pickup. It definitely knew that I was a female, I'm guessing by the smell of my urine. It stood, sniffing at the partially open vent on the roof cover camper over the truck bed. It wasn't a camper exactly, just a type of cover, but I forget the correct word for it. I'm sure you'll understand me.
>
> It stood for another five minutes, sniffing, and I was thinking, "Go away. Leave me alone. I don't want to shoot you." It finally started walking away and went back into the woods after about 20 minutes of circling me [Warren, 2024, February 2, 10:10–11:00].

Reflecting on the incident later in her thirties, she writes, "That Bigfoot maybe wasn't being too aggressive, but it did rob me of the joys of the outdoors," and states that in her investigations thereafter she found that Sasquatch sometimes engage in unsavory behavior with women (Warren, 2024, February 2, 12:10–12:15). Her experience is indicative of one of the major themes found within the oral and written literature on homins.

As another example, Scott Carpenter (2022) indicates two encounters that were brought to his attention by women who were approached by male Sasquatch, and he brings these to the attention of the reader in order to clearly and proactively warn women to be particularly careful if they are in the outdoors by themselves. In one case, a woman who was living with her mother and son had been privy to rather consistent Sasquatch activity on their property (e.g., her mother and a Sasquatch waving at each other in their backyard). On one occasion, the woman was in her kitchen when she heard her wind chimes rattling. Upon inspecting the reason for the occurrence, she reported the following to Carpenter:

> Before I knew what was going on I saw a movement out of the corner of my eye to my right. I look and walking slowly toward me just a few feet off into the yard is a light brown colored Bigfoot. He never looks at me just kept slowly walking, no he was strutting past me. When he was directly in front of me, I saw that his penis was hard and fully out. I was stunned and scared to death!! I jumped back, grabbing the door trying to open it to go back in, but he never made a move at me, he just kept walking, never looking at me once [Carpenter, 2022, pp. 112–113].

The woman's encounter may indicate a kind of mating display meant to demonstrate his prowess, as it were, to her. If so, the kind of feigned disinterested behavior of the strutting male is something that is quite human, in my opinion. The male homin's usage of her backyard as his own personal catwalk is also striking, as it indicates a degree of comfort that is characteristic of a being who is quite cocksure, if you might pardon the pun.

Further, Carpenter (2022) notes two other cases reported to him by the same person. In the first, a woman and her husband had engaged in sex at a remote outdoor location in an attempt to get her pregnant. They did not bring any materials to freshen up afterwards, and as they were making their way back to their car, they were followed by a white male Sasquatch who had apparently smelled their lovemaking. She reports, "He could smell us from where we had made love, I know he could smell us, he was sniffing the air, and grunting, and yes, he was aroused. It was very easy to see because he was not that far behind us" (Carpenter, 2022, p. 115). The Sasquatch's attraction to or at least curiosity in the sexual relations that she and her husband had just engaged in was clearly perceived by the experiencer. The same woman was followed several years later by a visibly aroused male Sasquatch who followed her out of the woods along with another Sasquatch as she made her way out of the woods after hiking alone (p. 114).

Narratives such as these that Carpenter has collated are among the few in print that I am aware of that deal with sexual attraction between homins and humans. Moreover, Carpenter's aim to provide a public service announcement to the Bigfooting community through his publications and YouTube channel—an endeavor that his son Travis "T Carp" Carpenter has continued in his stead—has been as insightful as it has been well-intended. This is particularly the case regarding the potential dangers of being a woman while engaging in Bigfooting, and especially when one considers that these kinds of stories do not tend to predominate among the non–Indigenous Bigfooting community in the lower 48 states. Indeed, as memorykeepers such as Fred Roehl (Curyung Tribal Council) have stated, places such as Alaska do not tend to hold narratives among the people of Sasquatch being friendly forest giants—quite the opposite, in fact. Unfortunately, narratives of abduction abound, and women (as well as children) are advised to be especially careful when spending time outdoors.

Elsewhere, a rather odd encounter is reported to have occurred after a *Playboy* centerfold camera shoot in northern California. What has come to be known as the *Redwoods video* or the *Playmate footage* is thought to depict a large, bipedal being displaying a large, erect penis walking across the road in front of the film crew's bus (e.g., Matthews, 2024). As Coleman (2003) and others have noted, the fact that the context of the footage was a shoot during which those present (including eyewitness Anna-Marie Goddard, a *Playboy* playmate at the time) were in a state of revelry, coupled with the apparently erect phallus of the Sasquatch, have not done much to advance the standing of this footage in the eyes of many of those who are aware of it (My Talk Show Heroes, 2016, May 4). However, as Coleman (2003) suggests, the hominological and cryptozoological communities are going to have to get over their embarrassment of the subject of Sasquatch sexuality to better understand the larger phenomenon as a whole. Forgive the phallic pun, but I would argue that embarrassment is just the tip of the matter, and that what Sasquatch sex represents within the collective psyche lies at the heart of the problem.

Another encounter involving an erect homin phallus and a potential threat display deserves mentioning here, and that narrative is the incredible tale of Claire that we considered previously. It is shared in episode 515 of the *Sasquatch Chronicles* podcast and is discussed elsewhere in the literature (Cutchin & Renner, 2020b; Germer, 2019, July 31). Claire reports having been visiting the central California coast by Carmel in 1989 when she had an evening encounter with a group of Sasquatch on the beach. After she accidentally dropped part of her camera kit while trying to take some photographic evidence, the large male noticed her, became quite agitated and aggressive, and bellowed at her. During this exchange, Claire notes that just before she blacked out, she remembers, "feeling incredibly sick. And—this thing: mouth wide open, big pink mouth. And it—it was obviously male. It had an erection, and it was urinating, and that is all I remember" (Germer, 2019, July 31, 16:15–16:34). The large male seemed to be arguing with what appeared to be the elder female, and then screamed at Claire, at which point she "could feel [her] insides vibrating," just before she lost consciousness (35:15–35:18). When she awoke later, she was lying down in the parking lot with bruises on her body, and her camera was nowhere to be seen. She was able to get back in the car and drive away to seek help. The host of the show, Wes Germer, also added that other guests on his show have reported the same kind of threat display wherein the being has an erection and is urinating.[19] In retrospect, Claire's sense was that the large female prevented the large male from not harming her further, and then dragged her back to the parking lot after she blacked out.

In all, given the potential threat of dark-colored, hairy beings that is contained in narratives such as those above, it would be a salient and essential need among humans to easily identify other humans and protect them (and particularly to do so for women and children). Interestingly, as Vendramini (2009) states of the threat of Neanderthals, according to his Neanderthal predation theory, this dual necessity could have generated a rather specific cultural development among humans:

> Clothes were vital for concealing the anatomical features that attracted Neanderthals. By covering the genitalia (particularly those of females in oestrus) clothes provided an adaptive functionality (they saved lives) and so attitudes towards them became an innate proclivity [Vendramini, 2009, pp. 150–151].

If homins, at least at times, have posed a threat that was similar in intensity to what Vendramini posits was the case with Neanderthals, then the same adaptation to clothe may have been influenced by the presence of said homins around the globe whenever they interacted with humans.

On a related note, the bodily fluids of human females may well be attractants to Sasquatch and their kin, as scent is not only a powerful means of identification but is also able to be projected into or impressed upon the environment in a variety of ways.

As a case in point, we turn to the matter of menstruation. As primatologist Esteban Sarmiento states, for example, females who are either on their menstrual cycle or who have just had it, tend to encounter Sasquatch quite often (Halloran & Halloran, 2024, June 24, 27:30). Sarmiento reflects that while he had been familiar with this pattern previously, that theme had been corroborated by Rhonda Morehead, Ron Morehead's daughter, who is an extended experiencer. Indeed, elsewhere Rhonda has spoken about a sighting during which she was on her menstrual cycle (Squatch Zone, 2016, August 15).

Further corroborating this theme, Scott Carpenter notes the following in his text *The Sasquatch Awareness Project*: "Dave Paulides found through statistical work that 90% of the full-bodied daylight sightings that are reported come from women. Also, note that a majority of those women were on their monthly cycle when the encounter happens" (Carpenter, 2022, p. 109). We note that such encounters can be considered to be Class A sightings and therefore occur wherein the observer is able to see the entity and to identify him or her in a relatively unambiguous manner. Further, while the gender of the homins is not mentioned in Carpenter's citation of Paulides's work, one can make a reasonable assumption that the attendant Sasquatch tend to be male. The inquiring reader is left to consider that, given the fact that modern human females do not provide clear visual signal of their menses as is the case in other primate species (e.g., Vendramini, 2009), without visual confirmation of the source on the part of the homin, it is likely the hormonal flux and/or blood produced during menstruation that is initially detected by the curious homin (Carpenter, 2022, p. 115).

Moreover, as an illustrative example of this theme, we turn to Vendramini's (2009) insightful remarks that, due to being targeted by Neanderthal males, "young Paleolithic girls were at increased risk of Neanderthal sexual predation once they began menstruating, [and thereby] the onset of menstruation was inevitably associated with increased anxiety, stress and depression" (p. 406). Poignantly, the literature suggests that these same Neanderthals may be one precursor source of homins (e.g., the almas) of central Eurasia in modern times (e.g., Bradley, 1991). Moreover, Vendramini notes the problematics of such interspecies contact, wherein Skhul-Qafzeh females would have to stifle their inborn drive to enhance in-group genetic diversity through sexual pairing with other viable hominins because these particular hominins (i.e., the Eurasian Neanderthals) were so dangerous to be around; moreover, he asserts that the females' male counterparts would not have looked kindly on such pairing (Vendramini, 2009, p. 57). I suggest that this threat of violent sexual encounter between human and homin(in) is very much still alive today, and not just because of the persistence of Vendramini's Neanderthal teem. The extent to which male humans could be hyper-reactive to the perception of female humans engaging in extra-group sexual intercourse is something that both Vendramini and I suggest has been retained in deep memory into the present.

Additionally, Timothy Renner's statements bear further insight:

> Could bigfoot be attracted to menstruating women, not because they can *smell the blood*, or associated pheromones, but for some deeper, stranger, or more mystical reason? Is it a primal attraction of a different sort: one based not on the old trope of the weak female being carried off by the monster's blood, but instead on arcane feminine power associated with menstruation? [Cutchin & Renner, 2020a, p. 246].

Renner's remarks are quite telling and open the doors wide for considerations about the reasons for such attraction. His further considerations around the association between Sasquatch and apparitions (specifically, Women in White) is both figuratively and literally haunting, as he ties both phenomena to representations and harbingers of death. Regarding menstruation (and entry into puberty) and death, both are rites of passage into a new identity or plane of existence. Indeed, an encounter with Sasquatch presages the same for many people, entirely upending who they were prior to the event.

And as one final example of how menstruation may play a role in human-homin interaction, we turn to a story from the southeast United States credited to the Indigenous Cherokee Nation (Wells, 2014). Cherokee member Paul Buckner (Lancaster & Lancaster, 2020) and Wells agree that not many homin narratives exist among the Cherokee Nation. In the Cherokee narrative—a story that predates the arrival of Europeans in the area in 1823 (Lancaster & Lancaster, 2020)—the *slant-eyed giant* (known as Jutaculla, Judaculla, or Tsul'Kalu) is a master hunter, tall and immensely strong, who can be fearsome to behold and has the ability to read minds (Wells, 2014). He woos a woman by reading her and her mother's minds and bringing them gifts that they desire, including deer meat and uprooted trees for wood.[20] His only requirement is that they do not look upon his face. However, eventually, the woman convinces Tsul'Kalu to let her see him, and she accepts his appearance; however, her mother also eventually would come to see his face, but she runs away in fear. Angered, Tsul'Kalu leaves for a time and only returns when the woman begins her monthly cycle: the mother disposes of the blood in the river, the scent of which ends up attracting him back to them.[21] He and the woman reunite and she eventually bears his child, after which he takes them back to the home of his ancestors, Tsunegun'yi, which is thought to be located at Tennessee Bald in North Carolina. They come to live there among his people.

While the Wells (2014) retelling of the Tsul'Kalu narrative does not contain any supernatural elements per se, another version of the story tells of the slant-eyed giant speaking in wind and thunder, and of the home of his ancestors vanishing after his wife's family does not pay proper tribute (i.e., by fasting for seven days in order to see him; Strain, 2008, pp. 228–229).

The Tsul'Kalu narrative bears consistencies with many others in the general description of the size, strength, and intelligence of homins as well as their prowess for psychic capacity, in this case, mindspeak or telepathy (e.g., Cantrall, 2013, p. 114–115; Cutchin & Renner, 2020b, pp. 86–87; King-Sharp, 2023, April 14, 40:54; Noël, 2019). Of course, the main theme of sexual union here is important in that not only are Tsul'Kalu and the woman able to have sex, but their offspring is presumably viable. As is indicated elsewhere, Indigenous lore, such as in Colville tradition about the hairy giant S'cweneyti, describes homin male interest in the scent of virgin females (Fusch, 1992, as cited in Short, 2024, p. 83). Thus, following the flesh-and-blood hypothesis, both Tsul'Kalu and the S'cweneyti would have actually been members of the same species as the human women to whom they were attracted.

But regardless of the reason for the persistence of the narrative—that is, if due to a desire to procreate or to draw on the intrinsic generative power of the menstrual cycle—the idea that male homins are attracted to female humans is one that occurs and persists throughout the world, present in contemporary encounter (e.g., Byron, 2024, January 12; Szilagyi, 2024, August 6, 43:50; Warren, 2024, April 2)[22] as well as older folkloric or mythical narratives.

Cannibalism Redux

At this point, we return to the matter of cannibalism that was introduced in Section I, broadening the conversation beyond the CS and cannibal psychosis and considering other ways in which the human psyche is impacted by the threat of the cannibal Other. Some narratives involving the hirsute cannibal giant or giantess contain what may seem to be fantastical elements while others seem particularly grounded in what some may consider to be a reality that conforms to classical Western physics.

As one insightful example of how cannibalism is contained within the human psyche, the hairy *Glue-Keek* pursues Lummi Nation women who pick berries at berry patches (Short, 2024, pp. 29–30). Finally tired of his advances, the people trap him and set him on fire, but before he dies, he curses them and says that he will return to feast on their blood. As he is burning, the rising smoke turns into "swarming blood-sucking mosquitoes" (p. 30), enabling Glue-Keek to figuratively cannibalize the Lummi people.

Elsewhere, among the Shoshone, we find the aforementioned narrative (Strain, 2008) as particularly illustrative of this cannibalistic character as well as homin sexual appetite. Here, I reproduce the cannibal giant story in full from an earlier source (Smith, 1993, p. 37):

> Once there lived an old woman and her granddaughter. They went out every day to gather pitch from pine trees. One day the Cannibal Giant found them. He chased them around. He can run fast. He chased them around a big tree. The grandmother and her granddaughter thought it was fun to have the giant chase them. They laughed. Soon they tired. Then he caught them. He flicked his fingers at their nipples. Their breasts swelled up. Then he killed them and took them home. He ate their bodies, all except their breasts, which he cut off and hung up to dry. The grandfather went out to look for his wife and granddaughter when they didn't come home. He found the giant's tracks and followed them to his cave where he found the giant asleep. He had his bow and arrows with him but he could not kill the giant. So he shot at his penis and that is how he killed the giant. The giant is like a rock.

While there is no mention in this narrative of the giant being hirsute, his large size, stamina, and near-imperviousness to physical attack (i.e., being rock-like similar to the genoskwa or stone giants), as well as his sexual and carnivorous appetites, make it a good candidate for at least demonstrating significant overlap with some of the more nefarious and frightening tales of hairy homins.

Further, the Shoshone tales of the spear-fingered giantess, *Tso'apittse*, carry with them similar threats of such deviance (Smith, 1993, pp. 137–139). In one narrative, a female Tso'apittse abducts a young boy from his mother and takes him to her cave. The boy grows into a man under her captivity, with his abductor sexually abusing him the whole time. After he grows up, he runs away from his captor whose ravenous sexual appetite eventually ends up getting her tricked by a rock wren who had decided to help the young man. The bird fashions a fake phallus and entices Tso'apittse to have sex with it within a shelter that he made, wherein she becomes trapped and unable to escape, her sexual appetite having thus led to her imprisonment.

Elsewhere in Native American lore, we find the tale of the aforementioned Dzonoqua of the Kwakwaka'wakw people of the Pacific Northwest (e.g., Alley, 2018, p. 151). She is depicted in totems and on ceremonial masks as having puckered lips and an open mouth, and at times as having her arms outstretched in an embrace. The Wild Woman of the Woods, she is typically said to be a hairy female giant known for abducting children and taking them away either to be eaten or to be brought up as her own (e.g., Strain, 2008). However, similar to what we see in the monkey-spouse tale (Dodds, 2007), in some narratives she is said to have children of her own, at times as the result of mating with a human man. Strain (2008, p. 153) tells of how in one narrative, she stole dried fish from a Kwakwaka'wakw man who then caught her. They fell in love and Dzonoqua eventually had a son with him. The son was named

Bukwas,[23] who is also said to be "in the habit of striking trees with a piece of wood" and being shy (Strain, 2008, p. 154), both of which are behaviors associated with Sasquatch. Though abduction was not involved in this particular tale, stealing or theft and sexual relations were indicated quite clearly.

A brief and relevant aside is that conflation and misinterpretations of Indigenous narratives by European American investigators and enthusiasts is not something to be dismissed. Some scholars and authors (e.g., Loxton & Prothero, 2013; Nickell, September/October 2017, para. 8), for example, suggest that cases such as the Dzonoqua are not indicative of a species of hirsute bipedal hominoids, but are instead either pigeonholed narratives taken from Indigenous lore or are more synonymous with legends of a single entity such as that which we find in the tale of the witch who attempts to cannibalize Hansel and Gretel. However, there are in fact narratives indicating that there are multiple entities in existence and that they represent flesh-and-blood reality (e.g., Pyle, 2017). One example is the Kwakwaka'wakw tale of a Dzonoqua abducting boys and girls to feed to her own children (Strain, 2008, pp. 158–160). Such a narrative feature may be more representative of what one would expect from a naturalistic account rather than one that is purely meant to keep children from going out in the woods at night. Moreover, given the tendency for Dzonoqua and other homins to be represented as thieves of food (e.g., dried fish), this also represents a detail that one might expect from a set of beings that have actually been encountered. Indeed, as scholars such as Bindernagel (2018, p. 122) and Pruitt (2023) aver, accounts of theft of food stores come from all across Indigenous North America as well as from eyewitness reports. If such reports are evidence of ongoing and historic challenges posed by real beings, it would be wise to encode such information in narratives that instruct about such matters—particularly for communities living in regions where food provisions may be hard won and scarce. This is more or less what we see in tales of the Dzonoqua, but any contention that these narratives do not represent beings that exist in the physical world exacerbates ontological ambiguity rather than clarifying it.

View It from the Bridge

The preceding chapter has dealt with quite sensitive material, including the subject of homins violating human psychological and physical barriers, namely through abducting, raping, and/or cannibalizing humankind. However, we have also considered some examples of the opposite case as well. Narratives of these interactions come from oral history, folkloric, and eyewitness narratives the world over, including Tschäggättä, Tsul'kalu/slant-eyed giant, Zana, abduction, leshy, rusalka, the monkey-spouse tale, and curupira. Generally speaking, the matter of homin sexuality seems to evoke various reactions within humans, least of all being fear and anxiety.

Before moving on, I would encourage you to pause and consider at least one of the reflective prompts on cognitive, emotional, somatic, or conative matters that I have posed in the introduction.

6

Anxiety and Ambiguity

Some experiencers such as Mark Barton and Sonya Zohar—each of whom had frightening and soul-shifting experiences with Sasquatch and other liminal entities—have literally stated that contact with homins is *toxic* (Arnold & Agliolo, 2020, August 1; Byron, 2024, November 11). I am reminded herein of the literally noxious terms used to identify homins or the areas that they are associated with (e.g., Sulphur Spring Road, California, or Sulphur Creek, Alabama; Cutchin, 2016, p. 235).

For example, Zohar, who until her passing in 2024, felt nigh-impelled to pursue the homin phenomenon since 2007, had not been able to rule out the development of her cancer to her previous close encounters with Sasquatch (Byron, 2024, November 11, 1:43:26–1:44:46). Sonya's reflection, which was prompted by Byron's poignant inquiry about the potential connection between her cancer and her pursuit of Sasquatch, was not absent the recognition that there have also been reports of Sasquatch helping or even healing people. Notably, these emphatically opposed perceptions of homins add to the ambiguity, anxiety, and ambivalence that humans can experience in their presence. As of the time of the recording of their interview on November 4, 2024, Sonya had been rapidly deteriorating due to advanced breast cancer and had been making the necessary arrangements for her transition. Even so, she notes at the end of the interview that even if her contact with Sasquatch *had* led her body to develop cancer, that she would still have pursued these beings if she was given a chance to go back in time.[1]

Trauma presents humans and other organisms with a number of salient physiological and psychological features. Physiologically, the body tends to recruit internal resources to cope with the threat in the moment. Traditionally, these resources include a coordinated response between the central nervous system (i.e., the CNS), the peripheral nervous system (i.e., the PNS), the smooth and skeletal muscles, and the viscera, in order to aid in the survival of the being in the face of danger. Typically, the body responds with one of the *six f's* of sympathetic nervous system response: that is, *fighting, flying/fleeing, freezing* (i.e., ceasing movement with body rigid), *flopping* (i.e., ceasing movement with body going limp), *fawning* (i.e., adopting a pleasant or friendly posture toward the threat to diminish it), or *friending* (i.e., seeking out social support to help deal with a challenging event). This cluster of non-conscious responses to a perceived or real stressor immediately prepares the body to fight its way out of the situation, to flee from the situation, to freeze in place (e.g., to play dead), or to placate the potential threat and potentially get it to leave.

Every one of these behavioral postures can be adopted by humans when it comes to aiding experiencers' chance of surviving or extricating themselves from onetime or long-term encounters. Fighting may involve shooting at a homin with a firearm so that it leaves the premises; flying/fleeing occurs when experiencers quickly walk away from or run from homins; freezing and flopping may each occur, wherein the experiencer "clams up" or collapses in the presence of a homin; fawning happens in cases wherein people being harassed by homins attempt to placate them (e.g., with gifts); and friending may involve enthusiasts bringing other people along with them when they do field investigations in order to help calm their nerves and increase their sense of safety.[2]

If we are to view from the bridge, as it were, the proposal that since the dawn of our species, humans have had at times violent contact with hairy beings who look and at times act like us, if we are to observe the various compunctions towards approaching or avoiding the subject of the homin phenomenon that have been adopted among the many cultures of the world, and if we are to note that among them, Western culture stands out as the exception to the rule of accepting and orienting toward coping with the phenomenon, then we might open ourselves to a singular possibility: that worldwide for many millennia, humanity has likely been coping with the equivalent of a species-wide encounter with death at the hands of our hairy kith and kin.[3] According to this narrative, we were brought to the brink of death, revived, and survived with renewed vision and vigor.

If the threat is substantial enough, what is essentially an emotional memory of the energy recruited by the nervous system during the endangering event can be stored within the organism and triggered by environmental stimuli later on. Information about the event can even be passed on to subsequent generations (e.g., via teemosis, epigenetics, etc.).

PTSD

At this point, it would behoove us to consider a particularly potent threat that the trauma associated with negative homin contact could cause within the individual and/or collective human psyche. Specifically, we consider the matter of post-traumatic stress disorder, or *PTSD*. Per the reflections of eminent cognitive neuroscientist Daniel L. Schacter:

> The most common post-traumatic symptom is unbidden recollection of the trauma which occurs in the context of emotional disturbances and spotty memory problems. In a few instances in which follow-up studies have been done months or years after the trauma, available evidence suggests that the frequency of intrusive recollections tends to diminish but not disappear [Schacter, 1996, p. 203].

The "unbidden recollection" that Schacter speaks of is an example of what he elsewhere terms a "sin of persistence" (Schacter, 2001, p. 161), which occurs when a memory—typically of a physically and/or psychologically traumatic event—remains with us and arises without warning or conscious intent. Indeed, such recollection can be quite challenging for those who suffer from PTSD, for example, to cope with effectively. Schacter further describes persistent memories as being debilitating and states that negative events may tend to be remembered in a more elaborative or detailed manner than positive events are (pp. 164–165), thereby suggesting that there may be adaptive value for humans (or even organisms in general) to have memorial access to information about negative, potentially threatening stimuli. This claim falls in line with the general thesis that noxious stimuli—especially those that produce unbidden death anxiety—tend to be retained in individual, if not also within collective, memory. One experiencer named Dorothy reports about her consistent refusal to return to the garbage dump that was the site of her close encounter, thereby potentially reducing the risk of coming into contact with the homin again (Boulier, 2017, p. 94). We might further consider experiencer Kaitlin's hyperarousal after a nighttime encounter during a camping trip (LeGro, 2024, May 16), or how an unnamed experiencer continuously made sure that the outside lights were on before going to bed and his anxiety when thinking about a homin entity encounter. This last case occurred in 2014 at Carl Mountain, West Virginia, as the eyewitness saw the Sasquatch chasing deer (Jones, 2021).

Of course, efforts to integrate the negative experience in certain ways can provide positive sense of agency for some experiencers. As one unnamed male experiencer says of his multiple encounters, "I know it sounds odd to have PTSD, yet [to] go looking for the one thing that gave me my PTSD. I don't know how to describe it, but I'm conflicted. I never wanted to see the creature again, yet I did. Again, I know that sounds weird" (LeGro & Hopf, 2019, chap. 8, 1:25–1:42). These examples provide a clear window into the dissonance that can arise when experiencers and enthusiasts alike are faced with the presence or potential of liminal entities like Sasquatch. Further identifying what kinds of trauma-induced sequelae people can experience and how they may manifest, the *Diagnostic and Statistical Manual of Mental Disorders* (DSM-5) outlines symptoms of PTSD (post-traumatic stress disorder) during or after the trauma-inducing event. The appendix includes those symptoms in addition to potential correlates with what Sasquatch entity experiencers tend to report of their encounters and/or the aftermath. For instance, intrusive states of hypervigilance, anxiety, and fear related to the traumatic incident persist for a significant amount of time (i.e., for at least one month) following the event. In addition to the aforementioned accounts, the case of extended experiencer and "sensitive," Kaitlin, provides an exemplar of such a case:

> It has messed with me over these last years. I have went camping after, and I will say my anxiety is a lot higher. I don't enjoy it as much, especially at night. I don't know. It—it did change my life. It really did [LeGro, 2024, May 16, 1:03:35–1:03:53].

Given the terror that often accompanies homin encounters, Kaitlin's heightened anxiety is not surprising, regardless of whether the fright is intentional or not on the part of the other party. Additionally, the fact that such extreme changes in behavior and outlook on life can occur from relatively brief encounters is evocative of the anti-structural nature of the incident.

It is interesting to note that previous versions of the DSM (e.g., the DSM III) included the stipulation that the trauma-inducing event lie outside of the range of normal or typically expected situations or experiences (e.g., Cahill & Pontoski, 2005). That criterion would most definitely apply to Sasquatch entity experiencers, some of whom exhibit *out-of-context emotions* or behavior during the encounter (e.g., Cutchin, 2025, p. 169; Eichenberger, 2024, January 1; Neely, 2022), after the encounter, or both. Sonya Zohar states that such emotions are an insightful aspect of the encounter that many experiencers take note of (e.g., Eichenberger, 2024, January 1), while Cutchin (2023b) notes that some experiencers will "inexplicably" (p. 322) go back to sleep after seeing Sasquatch outside of their windows. As an example of the emotional oddness that can transpire, Mike, a golf course owner, shares the following experience:

> And then, the last sighting: I was coming home one night late again. General vicinity. And I saw… I didn't know what I saw. It was actually between two of my neighbors' houses, right next to me. And, um, I thought it—first of all, I thought it was a ghost. And then I go and I told my wife, like "I–, I don't believe in ghosts, but what I saw was a ghost. It was something…" And she's like, "How big was it?" And I told her. She's like, "That's the gray one Chuck saw." So, right away, I ran to the back porch, and it was—whatever it was, was down in the woods behind our house.
>
> But the weirdest part about that experience was, I lost my emotions. I started uncontrollably crying. I wasn't sad. I wasn't afraid. I wasn't anything, but I could *not stop crying.* And I felt nothing. I mean … my emotions were weird. And I actually went out. I mean, I–, you know, I ran off the porch, going down to look at it. My wife's like, "What are you *doing*?" And—and there was no fear. There was no—there was no anything. But the emotion was the weirdest thing I've ever experienced in my life [Breedlove, 2025, March 2, 20:20–21:43].

Mike's explanation is a key example of how such out-of-context emotions can manifest, as well as the ineffable or unknowable manner in which the homin phenomenon is often experienced (e.g., Cutchin, 2025, p. 406). Upon further prompting, he indicates the inexplicable nature of that "highly emotional state" (21:54) that was unlike anything he has experienced before or since then.

Further, about 25 minutes into his previously mentioned interview with Barnaby Jones (Jones, 2024, May 6), field investigator and experiencer Rich Daniels speaks of the psychological overlap between what youth with emotional disturbances—those individuals with whom he had worked with in his former paraprofessional mental health work—and Sasquatch entity experiencers report:

> I was working with kids that had behavior issues. And a lot of those kids—their behavior issues were … resulting from emotional disturbance and trauma [from] the situations they had been through before. And in the course of doing my everyday job working with these kids (I mean, some of these kids, I'd be around them eight hours a day), and you get to know them and you get to understand how these things affect them. And … you end up treating the side effects … the aftereffects, just so they can get through their days, and … be able to make it through it.… I was working with them in a classroom situation, and we still had to … take care of those issues.
>
> But, then I started to make the connection in my mind, because at the same time I was doing my research training (you know, just like any other Bigfoot researcher), trying to find out more. I'd been out in the field, you know, a good bit at that point. And I started to realize that some of the people that I talked to that were Bigfoot … witnesses complained of some of the same things that the kids I was working with on a daily basis were doing. Uh, mostly sleep disruption, sleep deprivation, those type of things. Um, night terrors, nightmares … anybody … who's ever … had a night terror can understand just exactly, you know … what … it's like

to wake up yelling and screaming at the top of your lungs in the middle of the night, and just to be shocked out of it from just a single image in your mind. Just that single thought ... that gets you.

And I started to find that connection, and Craig Sulk was actually one of the first guys I talked to about it.... And I asked him, I said, "Do you think there's something to this?" And he said, "There's definitely something to this," 'cause he had talked to a lot of witnesses that have been really shaken up as well. And we all have. As researchers ... we've all come across these folks, and we know how greatly affected they can be. And then I started to realize just how underserved ... that this was in our research community [Jones, 2024, May 6, 25:10–27:11].

Daniels has conducted one of the only qualitative studies (formal or otherwise) that I am familiar with that examines Sasquatch entity experiencers in any kind of systematic way. During a later interview with Doug and Alex Hajicek, they introduce his work as "something no one else has ever done ... actually interview[ing] witnesses for the purpose of studying their trauma and the effects that their encounter had" (Hajicek & Hajicek, 2024, July 17, 51:00–51:07). While it may come as a surprise, as far as I know, that is in fact the case: no systematic, consistent efforts have been made to support Sasquatch entity experiencers in the aftermath of their encounters. Indeed, as I have stated previously, that recognition is in large part what led to the production of this volume and the book chapter that presaged it. This striking paucity is particularly relevant within a community that largely does not have access to mythological or folkloric structures that give ontological credence to the existence of Sasquatch and other homins.

All told, after vetting and interviewing participants at least twice via digital and/or in-person communication, and excluding data from anyone who had a history of mental illness or with inconsistent retelling of their account, Daniels culled an initial sample of 408 down to 112 men and 36 women for a total sample size of 148 participants who had had Class A encounters. One hundred forty-one of them reported encountering a Sasquatch, while the remaining seven reported encountering other NHIs. Discussing his key findings, he states the following:

The pain that they were feeling. The discomfort that they were feeling. Some of these folks had been more than 20 years since their encounters and they were still feeling effects from it, and that was profound to me ... that is one of the striking things about that ... study, was ... the lasting nature of these effects and how pervasive it got into their lives.

And ... one of the gentlemen that I spoke with ... he had not ... ever spoken to anybody about his encounter. And he had it when he was 23. He talked to me when he was 58 [Jones, 2024, May 6, 31:02–31:40].

One important ethical note is that those who interface with experiencers and enthusiasts do what they can to properly hold space and not further traumatize those who may already have been negatively impacted by the phenomenon. That said, the Bigfooting community and the few academicians who have publicly studied the Sasquatch phenomenon have focused almost exclusively on (re)discovery of homins rather than on the psychological implications of encounters with them, as Daniels has discussed and others such as Baranchok (2021) have emphasized. Such a stark discrepancy within a broader culture that generally disavows the subject leaves experiencers with few if any resources to draw from post-contact.

In this sense, the Bigfooting community has much to learn from other populations such as UFO experiencers—a group that has for better and worse been connected to the Memory Wars, psyops, support groups, and mental health professionals for decades. Unfortunately, people holding in the pain and discomfort for years if not decades is by no means uncommon. There is a clear and present need for any and all people who are dealing with homins and/or with homin experiencers in their work to do so through an overabundance of respect, restraint, and rapport-building. While Daniels's words here do not deal directly with the matter of ethics, I would argue that there is nothing that is more important when it comes to the intersubjective nature of this work.

The importance of this thrust of work is twofold: (a) affording a space for people to share their encounter and to be heard without judgment, and (b) disseminating that information in a systematic way with the ability to define and potentially explain the effects that entity encounters can have on people. Others who are formally trained have followed a similar line of thinking that Daniels has stated. Clinical psychologist and parapsychologist Thomas Rabeyron, for example, has shared the following:

> Many people prefer not to speak about their anomalous experiences and feel a form of culpability, or even shame, toward intimate experiences they prefer to keep secret due to their fear of not being understood. This fear is not totally irrelevant given that most of the clinicians have not received a specific training in this domain [Rabeyron, 2022, p. 2].

As Hein (2022) states, "We don't hear about these cases because in many cases, the people are severely traumatized, having encountered something they can't describe or didn't believe in" (p. 210). And Baranchok (2021) insightfully notes that even positive experiences with Sasquatch may require a resetting of the nervous system, potentially induced by techniques that he overviews including self-hypnosis and breathing exercises. Thus, the potent potential that homins have to induce states of unease, worry, and fear is part and parcel of the threat that they pose to the human psyche, both individual and collective.

Paleotrauma and Death Anxiety Redux

As biotraumatologist, biologist, and psychologist Peter A. Levine suggests, *trauma* is the body being stuck in the act of dealing with a present threat without fully resolving the action. Whether the organism is a gazelle running from a leopard or a human running from a pursuer, the body needs to complete the act of shaking off the energy that can become stuck in the various tissues. For anyone who has received a massage and was surprised at the presence of a knotted muscle—a condition that had previously entirely escaped conscious awareness—Levine's definition may resonate. He further states:

> When we are unable to flow through trauma and complete instinctive responses, these incompleted actions often undermine our lives. Unresolved trauma can keep us excessively cautious and inhibited, or lead us around in ever-tightening circles of dangerous re-enactment, victimization, and unwise exposure to danger [Levine, 1997, p. 32].

It may be unsurprising that the above characteristics of trauma can potentially lead to distortions in memory retrieval, particularly when eyewitnesses are asked to rely on higher-order processing to describe what occurred. Relatedly and rather poignantly, retired senior special agent and chief, Russell W. Strand, states:

> Good solid neurobiological science routinely demonstrates that, when a person is stressed or traumatized, inconsistent statements are not only the norm, but sometimes strong evidence that the memory was encoded in the context of severe stress and trauma. In addition, what many in the criminal justice field have been educated to believe people do when they lie (e.g., changes in body language, affect, ah-filled pauses, lack of eye contact, etc.) actually occur naturally when human beings are highly stressed or traumatized. Science of memory and psychological trauma must be applied to interview approaches and techniques [Strand, 2017, p. 2].

Arguably, the trauma that Levine discusses can persist in ways that Strand summarizes above, regardless of the source of that trauma: that is, whether it is primary, secondary, vicarious, historic, or even what we might simply call *paleotrauma*. Levine's commentary on unresolved trauma can technically be applied to each one of these types of trauma. While there may be more than one source of paleotrauma within the human lineage that has been preserved within deep memory, here I use the term to refer specifically to the results of negative emotional memories produced by archaic human-homin contact. Moreover, following the theme of Vendramini's (2009) teemosis, I suggest that something akin to a homin teem serves as a cue for arousal (e.g., hypervigilance, sympathetic activation, etc.) in the face of perceived potential threat and can shut down the human psyche and body to further experience that may evoke said perception. In the most extreme cases wherein paleotrauma or other forms of deep trauma persist, it seems that manifestations such as *Cartesian dualism* (i.e., the philosophical separation of reality into sections, the most prominent of which is the mind-body split) may occur which allow for some sense of management or warding off of the threat.

In the case of contentious or dangerous human-homin interactions that have occurred from the deep past into the present, I suggest that paleotrauma and primary trauma serve as the most important forms of trauma for us to consider.[4] *Primary trauma* is experienced in first-person by the organism under direct threat. Importantly, it can be physical, psychological, or both. What Curyung Tribal Council member Fred Roehl, his cousin, and his late elder experienced as a result of being under siege by a group of large, menacing Hairy Men one night in Alaska is an example of primary trauma: they all experienced the event directly and had to deal with the aftermath in their own ways. However, if anyone who Roehl told about the event after it took place experienced negative psychological effects themselves as a result of hearing about the harrowing encounter, then they would be said to have suffered from either vicarious trauma (i.e., in the immediate aftermath of him telling them) or secondary trauma (i.e., much later on after him telling them). *Historical trauma*, which is similar to *collective trauma* (Brave Heart et al., 2011), is passed from one generation to the next, while paleotrauma deals with the transgenerational persistence of trauma across a multitude of generations and proceeds from the deep past. The origins of paleotrauma may lie in the birthing and growing pains of humanity (à la Grof's previously mentioned basic perinatal matrices, or BPMs; Grof, 2012) as well as in our earliest contacts with other humanlike beings—beings who may have mirrored as well as mired our perception of ourselves. Thus, historical trauma and paleotrauma essentially occupy two opposite poles along a temporal continuum of traumata that can occur to or among a group of people. While historic trauma can persist across generations and starts in the relatively recent past, I conceptualize paleotrauma as persisting across many millennia and starts in the remote past. However, it is important to note that both historic trauma and individual trauma can resonate with paleotrauma (e.g., through teemosis and the activation of said teems), thereby potentially amplifying the experiential, even ineffable, quality of said trauma in the present.

Therefore, given our consideration of deep memory and its manifestations, be they ameliorative or anxiety-provoking, we now consider the primary threat that homins present that I posit has become encased, imprisoned, and maintained within the Shadow of the collective Western psyche. Broadly speaking, that threat is death anxiety (also known as the previously discussed thanatophobia, from the Greek *thanatos*). Described as the emotional and cognitive tension that can arise because of attending to the potential (e.g., imagined) or real approach of mortality, death anxiety can have extreme negative consequences for the healthy functioning of people on individual as well as collective psychological levels (e.g., Ani, 2007; Yalom, 2011). Indeed, as existential psychiatrist Irwin Yalom has proffered, adults in the Western world have not been taught how to confront what he terms "the icy chill of mortality" (2011, p. 117). Further, the father-daughter psychologist duo Ross and Rachel Menzies reflects:

> During the early life of a child the spectre of death slowly seeps into the psychological marrow. By the end of the first decade of life, death has become "the worm at the core" of the human psyche, nibbling away at our sense of security. Like our shadow, it is an ever-present companion that darkens the scenery [Menzies & Menzies, 2021, p. 9].

I assert that the paleotrauma from the threat of violent human-homin contact has contributed to this "worm at the core" of our collective psyche. Further, following other scholars such as Bradley (1973, 1991), I posit that this death anxiety is strongest within the Western psyche, and that such a situation may be due to our species' early years fending for survival in Eurasia, and against other humanlike beings such as Neanderthals (e.g., Vendramini, 2009).

As eminent psychiatrist and thanatologist Elizabeth Kübler-Ross has stated, the very thought of death can be perceived as nigh-inconceivable, a "malicious intervention" (1969, p. 2) by some outside force. Arguably, when one considers the relative lack of Western master narratives that treat existential anxieties in ways that are both cohesive and ameliorative, death anxiety and the Shadow end up being undesired realities in said collective, and both are often shoved into the farthest recesses of psychic awareness. While the authors above offer a bleak outlook on these existential concerns, their writing helps to contextualize what we have been considering thus far in this text. If the source of said fear (i.e., homins) are acknowledged as ontologically real, then the fear must be confronted more directly. If homins remain marginalized on the fringes of scientific discourse, then the unbidden existential threat that they pose can continue to be ignored, allaying the unbidden triggering of any paleotrauma (e.g., via homin teems).

While study of death anxiety has not been applied in any systematic way to homin entity experiencers, it is a scientifically valid and heuristically useful construct for us to consider here speculatively and may provide ample gist for future intervention and research. Elsewhere in the scientific literature, the concept has been studied rather extensively. For example, the foundational Templer Death Anxiety Scale or TDAS (Templer, 1970) as well as the newer Scale of Death Anxiety or SDA (Cai et al., 2017), provide opportunity for self-report of perceptions of mortality. The TDAS includes items such as "I am very much afraid to die" and "I fear dying a painful death," while the SDA contains items such as "In the past month, I have often thought of my own death" and "In the past month, whenever thinking of death, I have often felt scared" (Cai et al., 2017, p. 6). Cai et al. (2017) say the following of the development of their SDA:

> Previous theoretical and empirical literature discussing death anxiety, anxiety, and related constructs (e.g., fear of death, death attitudes, and anxiety disorders) and currently available measures of death anxiety were reviewed to generate items. Considering the behavioral consequences and nature of anxiety, Death Anxiety was defined as the state in which an individual experiences physical symptoms of being upset and nervous, and dreaded feelings of worry and fear related to one's own death and dying generated by an imagined threat to one's existence. Specifically, it included four dimensions as follows: (1) physiological nervous reactivity; (2) recurrent thoughts about death and dying or death-related events; (3) feeling worry and fear when thinking about one's own death or dying; and (4) avoidance of thoughts and events associated with death and dying [Cai et al., 2017, p. 3].

Relevant to our present discussion of potentially fear-provoking homin entity encounters from the archaic past to the present, each one of the above dimensions of death anxiety is important at both individual as well as collective levels of the psyche. Physiological resources tend to be drawn upon when an individual enters a fight-flight-freeze-fawn mode of action, wherein the sympathetic nervous system prepares the body to respond to a potential or actual threat. Heart rate increases, pupils dilate, blood vessels constrict, breathing rate increases, and blood gets shunted away from the viscera to support the functioning of vital organs. During states of hyperarousal, such as when a person experiences PTSD, these very same physiological responses can be activated, even if the actual threat is not present (e.g., Baranchok, 2021).

Moreover, an important distinction must be made at this point between fear and anxiety. As Baranchok (2021) reminds us, at the level of physiology, there is essentially no difference between an anticipated threat and a current one. Therefore, when we consider the threat that homins might produce within the collective Western psyche—a collective that may have experienced contact with homins since its own archaic past—both fear and anxiety may play a role; however, anxiety is the likely more relevant threat for the vast majority of people within this group, since despite the large number of first-person reports, it is reasonable to posit that most European Americans have never had a face-to-face encounter with a Sasquatch. Still, that does not mean that unbidden anxiety related to large, bipedal, dark-haired, dark-skinned beings does not persist within the collective unconscious of this group or within the unconscious of all of humanity.

Force and Fright

As one of our unnamed experiencers who perceived a homin crossing the road to seemingly turn into a tree stump reflects, the fear that the encounter evoked within the man was quite palpable:

> ...I never knew that all my body could shiver in different directions ... the hairs on the back of my neck ... everything in my body was telling me I need to get out of that area ... you know, like, it was engrained in my—like, in our genes, like [laughs nervously], "We don't want to be around this" [Barackman, 2024, December 12, 5:20–5:35].

His words are rather chilling and surely are illustrative of what many, many others who encounter these beings experience. If Sasquatch and other homins have produced death anxiety within us, then the persistence of memories of negative contact with these beings can be viewed in a broader explanatory context. Moreover, an important point is that, if Vendramini's (2009) assertion that Neanderthal teems (or the more generic homin teem that we are considering) persist in humanity, then a variety of otherwise ambiguous stimuli may lead to activation of said teems. As Baranchok (2021) states, for example, real or imagined threats in the environment can result in arousal of the sympathetic nervous system; further, activation of teems for large, dark, and hairy bipedal beings can be achieved through real or imagined stimuli as well. Experiencer Amanda, a Forestry Department worker from Texas, states of her own Class B encounter:

> Even though I didn't see anything, that day is so vividly etched in my mind. Like ... it's crazy. Like, I can remember every detail. And I can remember the utter silence that—as this thing started following us—that fell over the woods [Germer, 2023, November 24, 31:27–31:46].

Amanda describes the eerie silence as "unnatural," the Oz factor adding to the sense of unease that she felt during the experience and further cementing the event in her memory.

Or elsewhere, field investigator and experiencer Nathaniel Bronis, shares the following about his post-encounter experience:

> Ever since then, I went through about ... a year of ... completely being mortified about being outside in natural spaces or couldn't even feed the animals at night. Couldn't ... walking past a sliding glass door at night was too much.... All the lights had to be on, and ... you couldn't bring yourself to do anything outside after dark [White, 2022, December 16, 16:47–17:06].

Eventually he began to recover by learning more about great apes and Sasquatch themselves, lessening what he felt was a fear-inducing encounter of an unknown monster and contextualizing what happened as something that could be evoked by a being that is natural in the environment.

Indeed, it is precisely the kind of threat noted here that is present within homin narratives. For example, in Arment (2019), Peter J. James of the Lummi Tribe shares the following narrative from the *Province* newspaper of Vancouver, Canada, on June 3, 1928. The story deals with the *Seeah-tiks,* or Stick Indians, large, hairy homins of the Pacific Northwest:

> [He] recalls hearing of the fight between the Duwamish tribe and the Seeah-tiks from his mother who, it is said, witnessed the struggle. According to the story the Seeah-tiks, who were also referred to as "the Indians of the night," formerly raided the coast tribes, stealing women and children. The Duwamish warriors retaliated and killed some Seeah-tiks. Then down from the mountains came the giants and seized young men and with their bare hands tore them asunder....
>
> Again, there is a story current about Comox that the Puntledge tribe, once a powerful band, but now numbering so few that they have been merged with the Comox by the Indian

> department, were practically wiped out, only one or two families escaping, about seventy-five years ago, by the invasion in the night of a way party of strange, unknown natives who swarmed down from the mountain heights of what is now known as the Forbidden Plateau, a few miles from Courtenay. Today Coast Indians can not be induced to venture to this scenic wonderland where, beneath towering peals, luxuriant grasses and beautiful wild flowers grow beside cool lakes that swarm with trout… [Arment, 2019, p. 182].

The above narrative vividly captures the threat posed by these homins. Two Tribes are brutalized by beings who give no quarter, affecting revenge horrendously when the warriors fight back or when the townsfolk are, apparently, simply trying to survive. As another example of the threat that Stick Indians might pose, we turn to Lyle Blackburn's summary of the matter, wherein he shares the following about 31 minutes into the "Bigfoot Attacks!" episode of his *Monstro Bizarro* podcast:

> For example, the Salish Tribe of the Northwest refers to these beings as Stick Indians. Stick Indians are described as malevolent and extremely dangerous forest spirits who resemble a large, hairy, manlike creature. In some stories, Stick Indians have the power to paralyze, hypnotize, or cause insanity in hapless humans, while in others, they merely lead people astray by making eerie sounds like whistling or laughter in the woods at night. In some stories, these creatures even eat people, kidnap children, or molest women. They also take revenge against humans who injure or disrespect them. These are a far cry from the image of Bigfoot as a benevolent forest creature who walks casually along creek beds [Blackburn, 2022, September 13, 31:02–31:57].

Following this discussion, theories such as Terror Management Theory (TMT) have emerged as means to further investigate and explain the manner in which death anxiety can be understood, the contexts in which it arises, and the means through which it can potentially be mitigated (e.g., Greenberg & Arndt, 2012). Specifically, under the TMT, *mortality salience* (i.e., increased awareness of one's own finitude) can evoke death anxiety and people engage in behaviors to help lessen that salience and therefore reduce the anxiety.

More to the point, even the most casual observer of Sasquatch oral or written literature will quickly become confronted with mentions of these homins' overpowering smell: a stench that is, at least implicitly, associated with death and decay (e.g., "sulfur and sewage"; Germer, 2018, September 28, 21:22). Turning again to Cutchin (2016), we find the following characterization: "It is an understatement to say the hedonic associations are not pleasant. A majority of these smells fall under the larger umbrella of 'decaying odors,' though one could argue that the true unifying factor is the presence of sulfur…" (p. 187). As such, death and decay are tied together through the homin phenomenon in several ways: (a) through the smell that these beings are often reported to produce, (b) to the potential physical threat that they pose, and (c) through their association with death (e.g., in association with the archetypal Shadow). Any instincts or inclinations to avoid rotting flesh, garbage, feces or urine, or other items that smell rank or putrid, are meant to preserve us.[5] If any such unconscious inclinations are themselves preserved via teemosis, then we have evidence in support of Vendramini's (2009) central position.

On the matter of how Sasquatch and other homins smell of death and putrefaction, Cutchin (2016) further contends:

> Garbage odors are inextricably tied to smells of decay. Although the odor of the Minnesota Iceman was attributed to its putrefaction, it is unclear whether the beast would have

> smelled any better alive. Alongside wet dog and sulfur, rotting meat is described in Sasquatch encounters with great regularity. Witnesses often find themselves under the false assumption that they have stumbled upon a dead animal, or driven over some particularly rank roadkill, just prior to seeing Sasquatch [Cutchin, 2016, p. 221].

Cutchin also states:

> Though outliers certainly exist, the stench of Sasquatch is usually compared to wet dog, urine, feces/manure, garbage, cabbage, musk, sweat, body odor, and, naturally, sulfur. Icthyc (fishy) smells are reported occasionally, though with no real regularity [Cutchin, 2016, p. 187].

Due to the deep association that smells have with the physical realm and with memory, the above scents tend to indicate that something is not long for this earth or something that has already passed: therefore, approaching the object emitting the smell or prolonging exposure to it may invite death itself to the experient. The noxious smell is a sign that one has come into contact with something or someone associated with decay, the anti-structural, or liminality; or, at the very least, a clearly unpleasant episode, with the scent itself inducing the watering of eyes, gag reflexes, and vomiting (Cutchin, 2016, p. 190). The idea that the undesirable associations with Sasquatch may be associated with their oft-reported provoking pungency is also noted by Pfaller (2016), as he reports a narrative from Navajo lore of the *Big Ye-I*, a Sasquatch-like entity. He states that, according to the book *Origin Legend of the Navajo Enemy Way* by Father Berard Haile, the deity was the progeny of a woman who had covered her genitals in excrement with a river rock during estrus, and that this act made Big Ye-I ever associated with rivers and a rank smell among the Tribe (Pfaller, 2016, p. 135). Thus, we find in the Navajo narrative a potential association between the scent of the entity and taboo (or at least, self-injurious) behavior, in this case the mother-to-be rubbing feces on her vagina, thereby leading to the birth of the Big Ye-I.

Following this line of thought regarding breaking taboo and scent, in multiple reported encounters, the human in contact with the homins is described as ending up smelling as they do, unable to get rid of the scent (e.g., Cutchin, 2016, pp. 191–192). Importantly, as authors such as Cutchin (2016) posit, it may be that homin encounters that evoke animalistic scents are of actual flesh-and-blood beings, while those encounters that evoke a sense of sulfur are evidence of something else entirely—something supernatural or paranormal in nature—that is essentially donning the guise of those biological beings. Generally speaking, the contention that there are multiple types of beings reported around the planet—various kinds which bear entirely physical traits, some which blur the boundaries between physical and supernatural, and some which seem to be wholly spectral in nature—may warrant further consideration. In short, it is no wonder that homins are often associated with death and denial of life, as these odoriferous aromas themselves can provoke extremely visceral reactions, including watering eyes, vomiting, and any and all psychological sequelae that manifest as a result. Further, the fact that narratives of homins would persist in some form or fashion within the collective psyche in order to persist as a warning of the potentially monstrous[6] nature of Elder Brother may be better understood in such context.

One exceptional account from *Buckeye Bigfoot* is shared by James Fournier of Edmonton, Canada, who is the great grandson of a man known simply as Grandpa Mort. We hear of Grandpa Mort's travails with the Hairy Man and of what he learned about these beings during his travels. While visiting a town in western Canada after his first encounter with a Sasquatch around the early 1900s, Grandpa Mort learns the following about Hairy Man from a man of Cree descent:

> He said that the First Nations man told him … to never ever trust them, and that they worked often like a pack of wolves: one would make eye contact with you (that's the one trying to keep your attention), while the others are moving in closer to attack. He said they are always violent, though at first they will seem friendly. They are known to be takers of men, women, children, horses, livestock, dogs, and anything they can take. He said one thing to know and understand about them is they are known to eat their prey before killing them. Grandpa Mort said, "What does that mean?" He said they will eat their prey and they will eat it alive. They do not kill it first. They will find the animal or the human, break legs or arms (whatever they must to disable it), then they start eating their prey alive. Their victim dies from blood loss and shock—typically not a broken neck. They will sometimes kill very large animals, only because it is harder for them to hold down and control while they eat it alive—things large like a cow or a horse. Then, they will try to snap its neck. The more he talked and the more he listened to that man, the more Grandpa Mort said he shuddered when he remembered that night that the thing came into his camp.
>
> Then the next thing that the Cree man told my grandpa scared him very, very badly. The First Nations man said that sometimes once they get the scent of a particular man, if they are successful at getting something from that man (whether it's food, an animal, or a shiny object,[7] or if that man has something they want to take) they will keep that man's scent, and they will follow him to the ends of the earth [Warren, 2022, April 1, 19:47–21:52].

Narratives such as this that paint a picture of Sasquatch as extremely dangerous, quite cunning, and exceedingly patient. Grandpa Mort's full narrative is well-worth listening to, in all of its bittersweetness, and it is no surprise that his stories stand among Nance Warren's favorites.

Due to the interaction between Christian influence of European colonizers and Indigenous American accounts (e.g., Pruitt, 2023), names that indicate "devil" or "demon" are also incorporated within some Native American names (Pyle, 2017). For example, Newton (2005) states that the "hairy-faced dwarf" or *memegwesi* of Algonquin tradition may be the same being as the devil monkey (p. 291). Or further, Strain (2008) lists *chenoo* from the Micmac Tribe as meaning "devil cannibal" (p. 273), or *skookum/skukum*[8] among the Chinook and Quinault Tribes as meaning "evil god of the woods," "mountain devil," or "devil of the forest" (p. 275). Negative and noxious names for homins that have been used among European Americans include boogeyman, booger (e.g., Arment, 2019, p. 86), hillbilly (Powell, 2015), skunk ape (e.g., Blackburn, 2023, November 3; Moore, Jr. & Blackburn, 2024), ABSM (Sanderson, 2008), and mountain devil (Patterson, 2018, p. 79). Moreover, for a bit of interesting history, terms such as "booger" and "wood booger"—used in southern states like Alabama and within Appalachia—are a colloquialism for "boogeyman" (e.g., Reinhardt, 2024, January 22), which is, of course, literally the stuff of nightmares. Indeed, in his illustrated *Encyclopedia of Legendary Creatures*, McGowen states, "British goblins were also called Bogles, Bogeys, Bogeymen, Bugbears, and Bugaboos" (1981, p. 27). Furthermore, "boggle" may be derived from the bogle or bogey, the evil spirit, which animals such as horses may be able to perceive (McLuhan, 2024, March 29; Tréguer, n.d.).

Additionally, there are a number of ominous entities found within folklore that invoke doom and gloom: entities who are either synonymous with Sasquatch or happen to exhibit behaviors that overlap with those for which homins are known. Cutchin and Renner (2020a, pp. 96–97) cite a narrative by Sikes's (1979) which states that in the late 1880s, "negroes of the southern seaboard states" would tell of the jack-muh-lantern, an immensely strong and swift hairy biped who would lure unsuspecting victims into the swamps to die. And, as Powell (2015) asserts, "According to Kentucky researcher and author Bart M. Nunnelly, the term 'hillbilly' was originally coined in Appalachia to refer to ominous beings that confronted explorers of the remote, densely forested hills and steeply forbidding hollers in the mountainous terrain of the eastern U.S." (2015, p. 53). One particular sighting of these beings led to local folklore regarding the "Hebbardsville Hillbillies" (Coleman, 2006, December 27; Nunnelly, 2006). Nunnelly (n.d.) states the following of an encounter with them:

> just across the mysterious Green River from Reed and Spottsville, [Kentucky] ... I had learned that, in early winter 2004, two stargazers were parked on Negro Hill, located on Pleasant Hill Rd overlooking the Green River bottom lands, when they spotted two figures in the field below them pulling up old corn stalks and apparently eating the roots. The creatures were large, apelike and hirsute, one having brown hair and the other white. Returning to the scene the following morning, signs of the beings['] presence, in the form of uprooted corn and tracks, were reportedly found.

Included in the report is a wonderfully drawn image of one of the entities by Nunnelly himself, with its upper torso and head pictured from behind after having pulled up some of the roots (Coleman, 2006, December 27). While this particular narrative did not include any particularly fear-inducing imagery, the fact that the homins were called "hillbillies" is a likely callback to the original meaning of the term.

Moreover, some of the locations where homins have been sighted are possessed of appellations indicative of liminality, or in more extreme cases, a veritable hellishness, such as Sulphur Spring Road, California, or Sulphur Creek, Alabama (Cutchin, 2016, p. 235), or further, Devil's Elbow (Roehl, 2024, April 11), Devil's Ridge, Devil's Lake, or Skookum Meadow of Oregon (Powell, 2015, p. 369).

Still elsewhere within North American Sasquatch lore we find the following: (a) the Nahanni Valley, also called the Headless Valley, which is known as a place where the heads of human interlopers are ripped off by the hairy inhabitants of the valley (Coleman & Huyghe, 2006, p. 52); (b) Portlock, Alaska, known as a town in the bay of Port Chatham where the entire town may have been vacated in part due to the continued aggressions from a group of Sasquatch (Baxter, 2021; Breedlove, 2024, June 2); (c) the aforementioned Ape Canyon, wherein a group of miners was assaulted after one of them shot a Sasquatch (Beck, 1967); (d) Honobia, Oklahoma (Powell, 2015), known for the so-called "Siege of Honobia," during which people were aggressed at by Sasquatch (BFRO, n.d.); and (e) Headless Holler of Alabama, known as a site where European men settling in the area were found with their heads ripped off (Rienhardt, 2024, March 18). We will return to the subject of homins decapitating threats shortly.

In order to effectively kill others in such a manner, immense strength and size is necessary. Corroborating such an idea, we turn to several narratives which explicitly mention perceived or observed strength. For example, as experiencer Steve states of a brief but fright-filled encounter that he and his friend Ross had in Minnesota, the homin "looked so incredibly powerful … just the—just the thought of it … getting a hold of you is the most terrifying … feeling that I have even to date" (Ramirez, 2024, June 26, 23:18). Despite the briefness of their event, it profoundly affected the two men thereafter. While Ross did not have much of anyone to talk to besides Steve, Steve thankfully had his parents to share the incident with as well.

Further exemplifying this theme of perceived strength, Fred Roehl shares the harrowing personal encounter that he and two family members (i.e., his cousin and elder uncle) had with these beings in 2006 along the Nuyakuk river:

> I shot one of these things with a 30 aught 6 [high-powered rifle], 50 yards away. It did nothing. Uh, it stopped moving forward, but it didn't buckle or anything, and we use that identical rifle—same one—to kill walrus, you know, 2,000-pound walrus within a shot or two, and this thing didn't even flinch [LeGro, 2024, January 12, 15:45–16:08].

The extreme death anxiety that can be brought up by such events can and has been life-changing for many experiencers. Or, similarly, in the same interview, Roehl shares:

> It's especially spooky when you're in an area where there's, uh, a 10-inch diameter spruce tree that had been twisted 180° and pushed over—not broken—but forced over with a perfect bend and … broke tree roots… [LeGro, 2024, January 12, 17:34–17:50].

As a seasoned outdoorsman, Roehl's reflections on his experiences should be taken seriously. My own position is that narratives like his should be enough to lead open-minded skeptics to consider the potential ontological reality of these entities as well as the potential physical threat that they may pose when we transgress. And lest we forget, the tremendous strength of the great apes known to Western science far exceeds that of their relatively hairless human kin, and even gorillas are said to be considerably smaller than some of the largest homins reported in the literature. Reflecting on the difference in raw power between orangutans and humans, for example, Menzies and Menzies (2021) opine that it is entirely clear who would a fight between an orang and a human if the two were to meet in a dark alley.

Providing another example, Jeremiah Byron offers the following account when interviewed on the *Mythical Legends* podcast about what occurs after an experiencer's initial encounter:

> A few nights later … the side of the trailer is actually hit so hard by something that it was knocked off the blocks, which that's extremely hard right? And … [to] complicate things even more, the next morning when they open the door to go outside, there was a bear's head just sitting there in front of the door by itself—no attached bear body [Barnett, 2024, April 21, 10:02–10:29].

Narratives of bears with heads ripped off are associated with Sasquatch, just as are stories of the sides of trailers and other physical structures being hit so hard that they are rocked off of their foundations, the rafters shake, or objects—even beds—that are in contact with exterior walls are knocked or thrown from them. Of course, without anyone seeing the culprit, the wildnisgeist hypothesis (Cutchin, 2016) applies just as well here as any other. Needless to say, it takes a great deal of force to achieve these feats.

Taking this theme of brute strength further, one encounter related by founder and director of the New York State Sasquatch Organization, extended experiencer Alfred "The Squatchfather" Santariga, involves a Sasquatch ripping the head off of a Brahma bull (Hajicek & Hajicek, 2024, February 28). Santariga shares with the Doug and Alex Hajicek the following information about the encounter that he experienced with some of his family members in Florida when he was younger:

> **AS:** We follow the sheriff and the cattle rancher back to his place. We get back to his property and, um ... the sheriff is panning the pasture, and there in the middle of the pasture is this white Brahma bull bleeding out with no head. It's got no head [inaudible]
> **DH:** A Brahma bull?
> **AS:** Brahma bull.
> **DH:** Those things are *massive.*
> **AS:** Massive. And they are mean too. They are mean bulls [Hajicek & Hajicek, 2024, February 28, 1:20:36–1:21:07].

This brief part of the exchange between Doug Hajicek and Alfred Santariga indicates the incredulity that such a feat would have been able to occur, where both Doug and Alfred are familiar with the size, strength, and aggressiveness of these immense bovines. However, the narrative does not end there. After sharing a bit about the fact that he is so familiar with the physicality and character of these bulls, Alfred continues:

> **AS:** And so, it's bleeding out, and I'm ... in disbelief. I can't believe this bull is bleeding out. And ... so the sheriff is panning the rest of the pasture and like 100 yards away at the other end of the pasture is the head. This creature just ripped the head off of this bull and then just threw the head away. Now, the only thing I could think of—
> **DH:** Okay, good night everybody.
> **AS:** [laughs]—the only thing that I could think of was maybe that creature was in the pasture to get a calf or something, you know, and the bull seen it, and attacked it, and you know, may the best man win. And at that point, this cattle rancher was going absolutely *nuts* because this bull must have cost him a fortune [Hajicek & Hajicek, 2024, February 28, 1:21:33–1:22:21].

Or, as noted in another interview on said podcast, field investigator, experiencer, and author Rich Daniels states that five years after sighting a huge, hulking figure one night about 40 feet from him as he brought items in from a car, he realized who he had seen while watching a show on Sasquatch that he thought would help him fall asleep. While Sasquatch was not previously part of his cognitive schema, now as he watched the show, it dawned on him that the being he had seen five years prior was a 95 percent match to the description that a witness was discussing in an interview:

> I got—I got a cold chill. I broke out in a cold sweat. My hands were shaking. And I went into the bathroom to splash some water on my face, and all the [moves hand in front of face] color had drained from my face.
>
> The thought of what had been in front of me just 40 feet away, and what it could have done to me had it wanted to—I mean, let's face it: these things are huge and they're powerful and that thing could've waltzed across those 40 feet and pulled my arms right out of the sockets and there's *nothing* I could have done. And, um, that was *terrifying* [Hajicek & Hajicek, 2024, July 17, 59:31–1:00:05].

Daniels's encounter and the experience that followed are part of a constellation of events in the larger Sasquatch phenomenon that are reported quite often. Regardless of whether they are terrified, in awe, or both, experiencers tend to be struck by the visceral perception of potential strength, size, and/or speed of these beings.

Ontological Ambiguity

It is important to note that if an inciting event is strong enough in terms of its psychological impact, then it can bypass the typical multiple-treatment exposure that is necessary for classical conditioning in learning (i.e., in the case of Pavlov's famous studies conditioning dogs to salivate without the presence of food). If a single event is potent enough, such as encountering an entity whom one does not think exists, then it can be impressed in one's memory indelibly. As clinical psychologist Michael Adamse states (Eichenberger, 2024, February 19), such a phenomenon is known as *one-trial learning*, and it has arguably impacted people's reactions to homin encounters the world over. Adamse states:

> It's not like they saw it 30–40 times. In some cases, they only saw it once. In some cases, they saw it a few times. But it was such a powerful experience (and we call it one-trial learning) that that's all it takes. Example: a child puts … his or her hand on the stove once when it's hot, and the parent says "Don't you do that. It's freaking hot." They put their hand there and it burns: they won't do it again. One-trial learning. "Don't put your finger in the socket. It's not a good idea." One-trial learning. And we find this in life. And I think with respect to … what you're investigating, I think one trial learning, this is a robust example of that. I think that Bigfoot is a great example of something once again that people can't categorize [Eichenberger, 2024, February 19, 21:29–22:14].

In Adamse's reflection, one-trial learning wonderfully encapsulates how homin encounters can impact people profoundly, even if the sighting or incident is brief and happens once. Moreover, if people have trouble determining what they saw, then ontological ambiguity is at work, present in the various hypotheses that have been put forth for reports and encounters. Ontological ambiguity is defined as lack of clarity about the nature or origin of a particular subject of study. Ontological ambiguity is the perceived quality of a thing wherein the observer or percipient does not know its nature or where it comes from. This lack of clarity about how to categorize or qualify a phenomenon can lead otherwise interested researchers or scholars from investigating or proceeding with discovery of said subject (e.g., Hurn, 2017). According to Kripal (2016, p. 84), we hereby come to an important matter relevant to people's understanding of the nature of reality: "*completely* anomalous experiences would in fact be 'meaningless' in the simple sense that we would have nothing else to compare them to, no context in which to place them, and so no way of understanding what they are or how they are functioning." Functionally speaking, all entity encounters of the kind that fringed disciplines—from ufology to hominology and beyond—discuss are rendered "meaningless" in this sense, as mainstream Western culture has generally refused to accept evidence presented in favor of those encounters as genuine.[9] This is the larger epistemological frame within which Sasquatch entity experiencers, enthusiasts, investigators, content creators, and scholars have been living since the very inception of the phenomenon as a popular Western culture icon in 1958.

With that said, we turn to the words of Navajo Nation member Huk, who relates the following to Glen Boulier:

> One thing, Glen, which I entirely agree with you on, is the strangeness behind the differences in the geographical climate involving this being. Where we live in the southern United States, there is more of a mystical tone to the creature that we know. To the north, those indigenous tribes believe this spirit to be more as the flesh of the Earth. Who is right? Can it be both? I think it is so, as I have heard many things. You researchers are not alone in knowing this. Which of these would make more sense? In the north, where would this creature's place of origin be? I have asked myself this before. It exists, but where have they come from on both counts? [Boulier, 2017, p. 433].

Huk's reflections are evidence of the fact that there is not a single monolithic depiction of Sasquatch among different groups of Indigenous American people; however, the lack of agreement is expected if there are any regional differences in the human-homin interaction and in their overall ecology. We also learn from David Rains Wallace that among the Klamath People, the term "Omah"—although often used to describe hairy bipeds—is also "a word applicable to many uncanny phenomena" (2003, p. 73). Indeed, elsewhere, Cutchin (2016, p. 236) posits the following:

> Like the weirdness associated with UFOS—some aspect of the Sasquatch phenomenon operates in a much weirder, twilight realm, a space where modern science is unable or afraid to go, where something tugs at frayed strings from the fabric of reality.

Following our earlier consideration of the liminal status of homins, this twilight realm is fundamentally, or at least epistemologically, at odds with the mainstream scientific establishment, disallowing and disavowing any sense of consistency within the pursuit of Kuhn's (2012) normal science. It is the search for consistency that is often thwarted by these fringed phenomena, leaving the pursuer in a state of ambivalence about what exactly it is that is being pursued, what the character or temperament of these beings is, or both.

However, further regarding ontological ambiguity, Pruitt (2023) discusses such lack of clarity of the subject when he states that proponents of studying the subject "don't agree on what the sasquatch phenomenon represents" (p. 251). As a quite poignant example of ontological ambiguity, Bindernagel and Meldrum (2012, p. 82) share the following:

> As noted in an 1891 eyewitness account from northern California (*The Daily Democrat* of Woodland, California. April 9, 1891), a sasquatch was described in a newspaper headline as "An Unheard of Monstrosity," even though the animal was initially thought to be "a man clothed in a suit of shaggy fur." Elsewhere in the article, the animal was variously described as "some kind of monstrosity," "strange creature," "unnamed animal," "non-descript," "strange beast," "creature with the strength of a gorilla," and, finally, returning to the monster theme, a "peculiar monstrosity."

Thus, homins can take on various personages in the minds of percipients, adding to their perceived ontological ambiguity.

As one final, extended example of ontological ambiguity, we turn to a brief case study of the matter of the aptly named *stone coats* or *stone giants* (e.g., the *Ge no skwa* of the Iroquois such as the Seneca; Pfaller, 2016; Strain, 2008). By one account, the narratives discussing these beings refer to them as what Coleman and Huyghe (2006) would refer to as true giants, as veteran investigators such as Duke Sullivan have stated that the stone giants tend to be over 15 feet tall (KayDee, 2024, August 18). Such a claim still places the stone giants in the realm of homins.

However, other claims state the stone giants are *actually* rather than figuratively made of stone (Loxton & Prothero, 2013). The authors state the following: "For example, Bigfooters routinely cite tales from eastern North America that feature man-eating 'giants' whose bodies are literally covered with stone" (Loxton & Prothero, 2013, pp. 65–66). Loxton and Prothero also suggest that anthropologist, author, and famed Sasquatch researcher Grover Krantz (1931–2002) also did not think there was "any physical referent at all" between the stone giant and reality (p. 66). Loxton and Prothero are right in their broader point that cultural appropriation of Indigenous American narratives is damaging, uncritical, and much can get lost in translation, though their approach to the stone giant is not one that appears to hold much water.

As we will see though, there is little to suggest that anyone who has seriously commented on the stone giant either inside or outside of Indigenous American and/or the Bigfooting community has suggested that the entities were literally made of stone. If this were indeed the case, these beings would fall under the rubric of the purely fantastical. In scenarios when European and European American scientists think the subject to be of purely imaginary origin or due to misidentification by the narrator, said subject can be easily dismissed as not worthy of study. This kind of scenario has often occurred throughout the history of Western academic disciplines when it comes to traditional and Indigenous cultures and is a salient example of epistemological imperialism. Such events are also useful sleights of hand to avoid or deny subjects that may arouse a threat response within the collective psyche of the European colonial diaspora.

With that said, more typical accounts of the stone giants treat them as very real beings who have hides that are *like* stones rather than being actually made of the material (e.g., Gymlan, 2023, January 29). For example, we learn from Nick of the StrangeSpotting channel the following, as he draws from texts such as *The Iroquois* by historian Barbara Graymont:

> Apparently, the Iroquois knew that these giants were not really made of stone, but that they had devised a way to make their bodies impenetrable to arrows. They would spread tree sap on their skin, roll on sand and gravel, and repeat the process until they were indeed covered by a stone coat.
>
> It's very important to mention that while the Native Americans' reticence to share their Tribal knowledge with outsiders is well-known, those who gain their trust manage to access more information about specific legends and beliefs. And it is a generally consistent fact that while legends are a way to collect and pass on their knowledge from generation to generation, they often do believe in the real existence of creatures that those outside their society consider mere imagination, and the Iroquois make no exception [StrangeSpotting, 2023, July 15, 2:38–3:34].

Further, we learn from Leon Pfaller the following:

> Bigfoot/Sasquatch-like creatures are referred to in English as Stone Giants, or "Stone Coats" because it has been described that they would roll themselves in the sand over and over again

until they appeared to have a texture similar to that of stone. Much [*sic*] similar to tales told among other Eastern tribes (See—Cherokee, Cree, and Penobscot). As well as some Western tribes which are less specific, yet seem to have vague suggestions and similarities of this same sort of detail (See—Paiute and/or Apache) [Pfaller, 2016, p. 16].

This "stone crusted pelt" (Pfaller, 2016, p. 129) would be a very useful means of further protecting the already robust physique of the Sasquatch: a point which the author notes is quite an intelligent adaptation to potential threats such as those that tool-using humans would present. Moreover, turning to the Tete-de-Boule (otherwise known as the Atikamekw Tribe), some of these entities (in this case, given the aforementioned cannibal spirit name) are said to be figuratively made of stone due to coating themselves in pitch (i.e., tree resin) and then rolling in sand or gravel, thereby resulting in a significant hardening of their hair, for example (Cooper, 1933; Sullivan, 2023, December 17). Cooper clearly (p. 23, emphasis added) states:

The Tete-de-Boule *Witiko* "used to rub himself, like the animals, against the fir, spruce, and other resinous trees. When he was thus covered with gum or resin, he would go and roll in the sand, so that one would have thought that, after many operations of this kind, he was made of stone." A similar habit is ascribed to the Passamaquoddy *Chenoo* who used to rub themselves all over with fir balsam and then roll themselves on the ground so that everything adhered to the body.

The statement that "one would have thought that" the beings were made of stone indicates that the homin thus named is a being whose hide, hair, or skin is *like* stone rather than actually *being* stone. Indeed, as we learn in *Outfoxing Fear: Folktales from Around the World*, Iroquois lore tells of a group of beings "whose skin *seemed* to be made of stone" (2006, p. 116, emphasis added). Moreover, Brian "Duke" Sullivan (2023, December 17) states that by using pitch and then rolling in gravel several times, stone giants would essentially be impervious to flint arrows made by Indigenous American hunters and warriors, at least until European colonists brought their guns. And further still:

According to Cherokee traditions, all tribal dances and songs came in a single event. This was the slaying and the sacrifice of a monster called Nun' Yunu Wi (translated by early European settlers as being Stone Coat or Stone Man); so named for his skin of solid rock appearance. He is reported as being big of stature. My source tells me that this monster was hairy all over and that he was covered in dirt the color of stone, hence the name, by way of appearance from being caked in this dirt [Green & Coy, 2002, p. 179].

And yet again, content curator/creator Bob Gymlan has this to say of the stone coats, herein referred to through the example of the Beast of Seven Chutes:

Personally, I don't think the term "stone coat" or "stone giant" has anything to do with actual stones. Humans all across the board tend to give names based on the most notable attribute. And we're typically inclined to do so through metaphor, meaning "stone coat" or "stone giant" is in reference to perhaps the most applicable feature that concerned the people who encountered them: made of stone, as far as penetrating them is concerned, which is quite a frightening thought, if you ask me.

The implication of the nomenclature, as far as I can tell, is indicative of the toughness of their hide more than actually being of stone much like how this frog is not related to, made of, or wearing leopard [shows picture of a leopard frog], this bird does not elect the pope [shows picture of a cardinal bird], and this bird does not in fact become the senate [shows picture of an emperor penguin].

> Though "stone-coat" or "stone giant" could also reference the coloration of stone, I think. Or maybe even a curious habit of remaining very still and being unnoticed [shows inlaid picture of the Beast of Seven Chutes], as if it were merely a stone, which to me is perhaps far more intriguing than "pebble armor."
>
> The Iroquois maintained that the stone coats were not the threat they once were, due to a successfully waged war on their Tribe. This is a common story in North America. But they said that historically speaking, the stone coats would raid their villages for humans.
>
> There were four features that were mutually agreed upon regarding the Genosqua: they stank—they smelled like a mixture of skunk and decay; they were three- to four-times the size of a human; they took people; and lastly, that their preferred method of combat (and their telltale sign) was a specific way that they would decapitate their victims. It seems they would twist the head off: not pull off. Not knock off. But twist the head free of the neck, which seems like a specific thing to mention. And of course, Parc de Sept Chutes is right on the edge of Iroquois territory, which I thought was worth a mention [Gymlan, 2023, January 29, 17:14–19:15].

Gymlan's interpretation seems to me to be a reasonable one. I would also note that the lore surrounding the Nahanni Valley and other narratives involving decapitation elsewhere in the world (e.g., the *poluchelovka* of the Western Pamirs, as discussed in Porshnev, 2000, pp. 116–117) as a manner of dispatching threats jibe with his reflection. Additionally, while the facial characteristics of the Beast of Seven Chutes are in line with what Coleman and Huyghe (2006) classify as the giant monkey type, the potential size of the Beast is more in line with what they term the true giant (i.e., up to 20 feet in height) and what Gymlan says of the Iroquois description of the genoskwa (StrangeSpotting, 2023, July 15). And given that these beings were already said to be quite large, coating themselves with pitch, pebbles, sand, and the like, may have been as much to prevent damage when fighting each other as it may have been to defend against other out-group threats.

Further, following our earlier consideration of the cannibal spirit, scholars such as Cooper (1933) suggest that the stone coats (i.e., "blood-thirsty cannibal giants"; p. 23) of the Iroquois and the aforementioned *chenoo* of the Micmac are synonymous with that entity. Additionally, the Algonquian name of that spirit is said to be the likely origin of the term "stone giant" that came to be known to European settlers as they traveled through Indigenous territories (Short, 2024, p. 37).

Before returning to Loxton and Prothero's assessment of the stone coat lore discussed above, we consider one last comment made by Gymlan which is worth noting. Given the oral culture of Indigenous Americans such as the Iroquois, he notes that any information preserved would have to be functionally important rather than simply fictitious or fantastical. This assessment is in line with what Indigenous American scholars such as Standing Rock Sioux (Lakota) member Vine Deloria, Jr. (2022) have stated as well.

Given these perspectives, and though it may be presumptuous of me, if the stone giants' skin were in fact made of stone, then why would the bulk of the narratives not simply state that their skin *was* made of stone? Still, Loxton and Prothero (2013) clearly postulate that cryptozoologists have mistaken tales of literal stone giants to be conflated with narratives about Bigfoot or Sasquatch. Unfortunately for this claim, Sasquatch has been referred to throughout Indigenous American and European American accounts as being nearly impervious to harm: a trait that fits well figuratively with the idea that they would be made of stone, which is of course a material that is exceptionally hardy and resistant to wear.

One might further consider that Sasquatch reports tend to favor the following anti-structural characteristics, which may also increase this perception: (a) observed subtle or covert behavior (e.g., tossing or throwing of objects without being seen) rather than overt behavior; (b) indirect (e.g., from perches; Jones, 2021) rather than direct observation of humans; (c) perceived auditory mimicry of other beings rather than using overt signaling; (d) perceived physical mimicry of and/or being mistaken for other entities and/or objects; and (e) ambiguous trace evidence, much of which has been attributed to other organisms (e.g., humans and animals) by skeptics, pseudo-skeptics, and even members of the Bigfooting community.

For example, as veteran Fortean investigators Tony Healy and Paul Cropper have found through their decades-long observation of the Yowie phenomenon in Australia, the flesh-and-blood hypothesis does not account well for the depth and breadth of the way the phenomenon presents itself. Similar to the manner in which the subject has been taken up elsewhere in Western culture, the co-authors posit that two other possibilities exist: that either the reports are the result of some kind of mass hallucination, or that they evince a group of "psychic phenomena that are capable of taking physical form" (2023, p. 5), a hypothesis that falls in line with various non–European Indigenous narratives throughout the world, including those of Sherpa, Native American, and Indigenous Australian origin. Further, remarking on the similarities between their findings and the work of other scholars such as Powell, Lapseritis, and Cutchin and Renner, the authors suggest the following:

> having interviewed many more witnesses and having perused hundreds of additional cases, we have come to accept that a significant proportion of reports contains details that smack somewhat and often considerably more than somewhat of the supernatural. Although most remain convinced they've encountered real, flesh and blood creatures (about ten to fifteen percent of witnesses make a point of mentioning very weird details), and some firmly believe their entire experience was decidedly uncanny. Specific "high strangeness" details crop up time and time again strong: unsettling feelings of being watched, cessation of all bird and insect noise, levels of fear out of all proportion to the situation, post-sighting nightmares, sightings of "black panthers" and other odd creatures, floating lights and electrical malfunctions [Healy & Cropper, 2023, p. 5].

The high strangeness that these various authors report from different regions around the globe from various timepoints are very much in alignment with each other and indicate a pattern that transcends not only space but also time. Content curator Bob Gymlan provides an apt description of what the experience of ontological ambiguity can look like for experiencers:

> For every sensational story, there's a thousand more minute and vague encounters hanging out in the ether. Not to mention, for a creature that matches the description of the subject in question—that is, a creature that is cryptic and cunning—it makes sense to me that accounts like this one would make up the overwhelming majority of human-Sasquatch interaction: events that are *ambiguous*. Big in the moment, but not much to write home about. Perhaps earth-shattering to one, but only mildly out-of-the-ordinary to another, running the gambit [*sic*] between mind-bending and imperceptible, entirely dependent on a plethora of minute detail [Gymlan, 2024, August 8, 19:39–20:17].

Due to our focus on the treatment of the subject of homins within Western culture, it might be helpful to ponder what historical—and even evolutionary—contact the Western psyche in particular may have had with said homins over the course of millennia.

Considering these stated or hypothesized contacts between *H. sapiens* and homins, it may do us well to briefly consider some of the appellations that humans have used to describe or refer to homins. Here, we consider North America specifically. These beings exist at the intersection (i.e., the confluence or liminal zone) where Native American, European American, and other (e.g., African American) cultures meet, clash, and conflict. True to the title of Strain's (2008) text, Indigenous names for homins or homin-like beings often mention the nature or behavior of these beings as hairy (e.g., *sc'wen'ey'ti* from the Spokane Tribe, meaning "tall burnt hair"; p. 274), cannibals, giants, wildmen or wildwomen.[10] And as Hansen states, beings such as Sasquatch occupy a liminal space between human and beast that blurs or mediates that binary (2001, p. 63). Indeed, despite not thinking that there is any evidence worth noting for the existence of beings like Sasquatch, author Colin Dickey (2021) poignantly reasserts the stance that wild men and their modern correlates disrupt the boundaries between clean and unclean, as well as between civilized and uncivilized.

Such statements seem to generally reflect the state of affairs regarding homin entity encounters. Following this matter, we briefly consider elements of a narrative from aforementioned experiencer named Claire that took place on the central Californian coast in 1989—an encounter that we will cover in more depth later (Germer, 2019, July 31). Claire states of the large, hairy male that stood not more than 20 to 30 feet from her:

> If it wanted to kill me, it could have killed me—no two ways about it. Nothing I could have done ... it would have snapped me like a twig [Germer, 2019, July 31, 32:29–32:36].

This brief excerpt from her story simply and effectively articulates the threat that homins—and particularly those who are larger than anatomically modern humans—may be perceived to pose to us. By her account, Claire was lucky to have survived the harrowing event.

As John Baranchok (2024, March 11)[11] has stated, given that humans are both flesh-and-blood and also exhibit so-called abilities such as psi that fall outside of conventional Western thinking, it is not per se necessary to separate out seemingly advanced capabilities (e.g., telepathy) from reports of encounters with homins, particularly when studies on another group of upright, bipedal, primates (i.e., *Homo sapiens*) has reliably demonstrated that such psi capacity is indeed part and parcel of our mental toolbox (e.g., Bem, 2011; Bem et al., 2015). The necessity only arises if these capacities fly in the face of one's worldview so much that they threaten to collapse it.

As a so-called paranormal example of the anti-structural nature that has been associated with homins, experiencer Barbara "Barb" Shupe's aforementioned "Predator" or cloaker film as well as her experience thereof definitely qualifies (e.g., Eichenberger, 2023).

Ontological Shock

Further, as mentioned previously, exceptional experiences represent that category of events or encounters that contain a quality of high strangeness or that tend to promote shock, awe, or extend our notion of the structure of reality. In other words, exceptional experiences, often belying a quality of ontological ambiguity, may indeed promote a degree of *ontological shock* (e.g., Levy, 2005) in the percipient or experient as a potential consequence. Philosopher Paul Tillich (2011) defined ontological shock as the threat of non-being. He succinctly states:

> The threat of nonbeing, grasping the mind, produces the "ontological shock" in which the negative side of the mystery of being—its abysmal element—is experienced. "Shock" points to a state of mind in which the mind is thrown out of its normal balance, shaken in its structure. Reason reaches its boundary line, is thrown back upon itself, and then is driven again to its extreme situation. This experience of ontological shock is expressed in the cognitive function by the basic philosophical question, the question of being and nonbeing. It is, of course, misleading if one asks of some philosophers: "Why is there something? Why not nothing?" For this form of the question points to something that precedes being, from which being can be derived. But being can only be derived from being. The meaning of this question can be expressed in the statement that being is the original fact which cannot be derived from anything else. Taken in this sense, the question is a paradoxical expression of the ontological shock and, as such, the beginning of all genuine philosophy [Tillich, 2011, p. 113].

Potentially unaware of Tillich's earlier usage of the term yet demonstrating clear convergent evolution of concept, John E. Mack (1995, p. 142) has stated that "ontological shock" referred to "the realization that one's conception of reality does not hold," applied to cases of contact with (and apparent abduction by) non-human intelligences. Indeed, Mack (1995, p. 208) states:

> The intense physicality of this sort of experience may be employed so that [experiencer] Sara and other human beings are forced to acknowledge the reality of entities that our Western acculturation has taught us in recent centuries cannot, even must not, exist. Yet this kind of ontological-physical shock may, in my view, be an essential initial step in the process of human consciousness evolution that seems to lie at the core of the alien abduction phenomenon.

Mack's statements belie an underlying theme that persists within much of the literature from which I draw in this book. That theme deals with the idea that confronting an entity or information that triggers fear, anxiety, or a split from one's former reality, can be a potent catalyst for subsequent behavior, whether that behavior is repression and suppression, or realization and transformation. Indeed, drawing from the work that John Mack conducted in Rua, Zimbabwe (i.e., the Ariel school case), and elsewhere, John L. Roberts (2023) has reflected on the massive schism that can take place when people encounter non-human intelligences, when one may not only experience "intensive disruption of psychic continuity or in the absolutisms of the everyday life-worlds of individuals, but in interruption of the absolutisms that maintain much of the modernist world itself" (Roberts, 2023, p. 240).

It is not just the alien abduction phenomenon but encounters with all manner of liminal entities who have the potential to shake and rattle humanity to the core of our being. Such discordance can either lead to a resonant shift which positively transduces us into a more expansive state, or it can, at least temporarily, cause a cascade of reactive shifts that are focused on survival. Like Mack, Vendramini (2009), Welsing (1994), Bradley (1973), and others have posited that death anxiety and mortality salience, at their core, can produce momentous and long-lasting, even evolutionary, shifts in form and/or function of the human being. It is those out-of-pocket and unanticipated events and encounters—otherwise known as anomalies, generally speaking—that can press an organism into profound and persistent change. Such a shift is cued by ontological shock, Tillich's "threat of nonbeing" (2011, p. 113) that explodes the psyche.

It follows that Kuhn (2012) also discusses anomalous experiences, defining them as "experiences that, by evoking crisis, prepare the way for a new theory" (p. 145).

As Michael Bleuler notes in an episode of *Sasquatch Ontario* with Mike Paterson, "if you ever look at one of these things in the face—eye to eye—it'll change the way you look at the world" (Paterson, 2023, March 28, 57:18–57:23). Further, as a woman who simply refers to herself as Squirt shares of a Sasquatch encounter that she and her husband had at Trinity Lake in California:

> After this happened, my husband and I … did not tell people in our life about it. It's kind of like a trauma that's just too hard to discuss. It's maybe like shell shock in a way. Maybe we should coin a new term. Let's call it "Squatch-shock" [Warren, 2024, February 13, 1:26–1:45].

Squirt's coining of the term above is arguably an accurate if not humorous illustration of what experiencers go through both during and after encounters. The challenge of sharing that experience with others can indeed add to the difficulty in healing from and integrating the incident into psychological structures that make sense for the witness.

Another encounter that involved this kind of deeply disconcerting shock is related by Jeremiah Byron, wherein he states that a hunter in his tree stand witnessed a Sasquatch run down a hog, break its back with its hands, and then hurl the hog into a tree thereby smashing its head. The Sasquatch then slung the hog over its shoulder and made eye contact with the hunter as he walked away with his prize. Byron states that the hunter did not leave the tree for hours, and after he did, he never returned to those woods again. It was an experience that utterly demolished his worldview (Harold, 2024, February 9).

The phenomenon of ontological shock overlaps a good deal with the anomalous experiences or EHEs referred to within transpersonal psychology and parapsychology, since they implicitly invite us to reconsider and redefine how reality works, and particularly within the frames of Western science and academia. For example, let us consider the words of Cardeña, Lynn, and Krippner (2014, p. 4), as they introduce the term anomalous experiences from the standpoint of exceptional experiences:

> The English word anomalous derives from the Greek *anomalos*, meaning "irregular," "uneven," or "unequal," in contrast to *homalos*, which means "the same" or "common." An "anomalous experience" is "irregular" in that it differs from common experiences, and "uneven" in that it is not "the same" as experiences that are "even" and "ordinary." Typically, it is also "unequal" in that it does not draw the same attention, at least in academia, as that given to "regular" experiences. There is one additional sense of "anomalous" discussed by Robert K. Merton (1975) that is particularly apt for our purposes, namely that anomalous observations are surprising because they seem to be inconsistent with prevailing theory or accepted facts. In an important article, Marcello Truzzi (1987) wrote that anomalous phenomena "contradict commonsense or institutionalized (scientific or religious) knowledge" and are "anomalous to our generally accepted cultural storehouse of truths" (p. 367). We define an anomalous experience (AE) as an uncommon experience (e.g., synesthesia), or one that, although it may be experienced by a significant number of persons (e.g., psi experiences), is believed to deviate from ordinary experience or from the usually accepted explanations of reality according to Western mainstream science.

Thus, we see where the uses of "exceptional experience"—the very subject of our present inquiry—and "anomalous experience" are relatively coterminous with each other, though there is some divergence present as well. It follows that for those who do not take mainstream Western scientific paradigms as their starting or end point, the phenomena that we have discussed in these pages may be anything but "anomalous." If people's so-called commonsense (read: hegemonic) notions of the way in which reality works are not offended by the idea of hairy bipedal beings existing at the fringes of society and exhibiting various abilities and behaviors, then there is no need to label them as "anomalous" in the first place.

As a case in point dealing with anomalous experience and ontological shock, we turn to the words of cryptozoological documentarian and founder of the *Small Town Monsters* production team, Seth Breedlove. While paying special attention to the views of a sample of Indigenous inhabitants in Alaska, and speaking particularly to the experience of Ms. Elizabeth Cook whose story we considered previously, he states the following:

> One thing that strikes me about Elizabeth's story of the bigfoot is the way it made her *feel*, even at the time when it happened. Elizabeth, like most witnesses, has spent most of her life in this place. She was familiar with the local wildlife, and yet when she encountered the Sasquatch staring at her window, she was left shaken and disturbed.
>
> This is a creature that seems right at home in its native environment, and yet despite being here for centuries, when a person encounters one, they can hardly process it. Almost as if the creature has altered the way in which we see the places we once considered our domain, or simply our home.
>
> The bigfoot doesn't just appear and disappear without a trace. It leaves behind a shattered perception of what the witness once thought they knew about their environment itself. In many cases it leaves the witness feeling like an intruder in a world they no longer understand, even if that world is once settled by your ancestors over hundreds if not thousands of years [Breedlove, 2023, December 31, 46:20–47:21].

Breedlove's poignant remarks capture much of the tone and tenor of what ontological shock is and how it can affect people. Moreover, he notes that even for those Indigenous folk who may have access to ancient narratives about these homins, the effects of an encounter can still be quite disruptive.

On another note, due to the outsized influence of Western cultural paradigms on the ways in which so many people think about our world and the cosmos, it is necessary for us to consider how this impact has warped and even damaged the ways in which fringed phenomena of study are received. Therefore, that which is perceived as anomalous, extraordinary, exceptional, or even revolutionary, is largely a function of the worldview (i.e., ontology) into which a person is enculturated.

For example, experiencer Lorri who encountered a large male homin in the Blue Ridge mountains of West Virginia, reports having to call one of her sisters after the experience because she "had to talk to somebody":

> I couldn't deal with this quite by myself. I mean, I just couldn't.… I didn't want to be alone with my thoughts. I thought I had done lost my mind. I thought that that they gon' put me in a straight jacket or something, or lock [chuckles] my ass up, because I had—I started doubting, you know, what did I s—you know, I just … maybe I didn't see it. You know, maybe I was just, you know, I don't know, I just—it, it just [pauses] mind screwed me [Byron, 2025, February 15, 8:45–9:15].

When scanning one's environment for potential challenges to that survival (e.g., predators), it is therefore helpful to accurately identify those threats. However, it is typically more advantageous to one's survival, at least in the short term, to overgeneralize potential threats than to undergeneralize them.

Phenomena that are marked by an anti-structural nature therefore also typically exhibit ontological ambiguity, where both are characterized by a kind of liminal status or fluidity in their form and/or function. The trickster meta-myth is necessarily one such example of anti-structure. Functioning variously as mischief-maker and frustrater, clown or fool, guardian of thresholds, and elder sage, the trickster is the ultimate liminal entity and performs numerous roles in one's pursuit of truth, wholeness, and wisdom. If we peer deeply enough into the entity encounters that are pervasive in ancient myth and modern (fringed) narratives, we may clearly see the image of a trickster within (Cutchin & Renner, 2020a; Hansen, 2001; Vallee, 2014).

The Numinous

Following the matter of ontological shock and the extreme inner tension that it can engender, we find ourselves considering other inciting matters that can contribute to such shock. Arguably, the entities that White (1994) identified within her rubric of entity encounters can be either awe-inspiring and/or dread-inducing. Such a character is what Rudolf Otto termed the *numinous* (e.g., Nörenberg, 2017; Otto, 1917). Experiences thus termed put us in the presence of a nigh indescribable and irreducible phenomenon that carries with it an experiential quality of fascination (i.e., *fascinans*) and even fear. It is therefore fundamentally anti-structural (Hansen, 2001) and is experienced through an innate ability that we have which Otto termed our *sensus numinus*. Otto describes part of the character of the numinous as being objective (i.e., outside of and separate from the person), of producing a diminishment in one's self-valuation in the presence of something that is profoundly awe-ful and Other, and of also evoking a creature-feeling, which he summarizes as follows:

> All that this new term, "creature-feeling," can express, is the note of self abasement into nothingness before an overpowering, absolute might of some kind; whereas everything turns

> upon the *character* of this overpowering might, a character which cannot be expressed verbally, and can only be suggested indirectly through the tone and content of a man's feeling response to it. And this response must be directly experienced in oneself to be understood [Otto, 1917, p. 10].

Thus, the sense of trauma and taboo that is the subject of this section may arise from a persistent and unbidden fear of contact with the numinous that Hairy Man can evoke, whether that is via deep memory of paleotrauma, a Class A homin entity encounter, and/or some other factor. In other words, the non-rational, often fear-inducing quality of the numinous can be so anxiety-provoking that it is, intentionally or otherwise, best to simply deny it.

Scholars such as Jack Hunter (2023, p. 23) have expounded on Otto's work, using the numinous as a focal point of entry into discussion of varieties of high strangeness and exceptional experiences. In the case of the bogeymanesque and/or beneficent qualities of homins that seem to have been preserved in humanity's deep memory, there is a clear case to be made for these entities—and the encounters tied to them—being characterized by a numinous quality.

According to Otto, the numinous is characterized by two dually existentially provocative experiences: (a) that of awe, or of the *mysterium fascinosum*, is one that can induce reverence, piety, and elation, while (b) the experience of dread or terror is what he termed *mysterium tremendum*, together comprising what Otto termed the *religious impulse* (Hunter, 2021b, p. 44). However, the so-called negative numinous can manifest an experience that evokes a "daemonic dread" (e.g., Hansen, 2001, p. 356; Hunter, 2023, p. 22).

Moreover, it has been noted that the mystery is fundamentally irrational, and that in times and places such as ancient Greece (from which the etymology of the term "mystery" arises), it was only through myth and rite that one arrived upon meaning and contact with the deities, albeit not through rational means (Benchín, 2022). As I contend, it is contact with the numinous quality of the homin phenomenon that draws enthusiasts, experiencers, and even denouncers (e.g., cynics, pseudo-skeptics, etc.) toward it, continually seeking out or stamping out these entities the world over.

We continue by once again considering the words of Paul Tillich, who states:

> In revelation and in the ecstatic experience in which it is received, the ontological shock is preserved and overcome at the same time. It is preserved in the annihilating power of the divine presence (*mysterium tremendum*) and is overcome in the elevating power of the divine presence (*mysterium fascinosum*). Ecstasy unites the experience of the abyss to which reason in all its functions is driven with the experience of the ground in which reason is grasped by the mystery of its own depth and of the depth of being generally [Tillich, 2011, p. 113].

Here, we find the essence of the threat that homins can pose to the collective unconscious: they can symbolize some awesome expression or approximation of the "annihilating power of the divine presence" of which Tillich speaks, and which are echoed in the words of Rudolph Otto. Further, as Jeff Kripal reflects in the documentary *Love & Saucers* about a man named David Huggins's encounters with otherworldly beings, he provides the following insights:

> ...when a human being encounters the sacred, it's a terrifying experience, and it's an ecstatic experience. You are being split open. So, I'm not surprised at all to see someone like David say

> ... it was scary, and then to paint ... some of these terrifying images, and to insist that it was the most pleasurable events of his life. And he'd do it again in a heartbeat [Abrahams, 2017, 51:08–51:40].

Kripal's synthesis again suggests that ecstasy and terror can absolutely become commingled in encounters with the divine, or even with what we might call the demi-divine or demiurgic powers that have interacted with humankind since time immemorial. Moreover, even though David's experiences largely revolved around intelligences who many would call extraterrestrials, one of the beings who he saw was an upright biped covered in brown hair who had glowing eyes—very much fitting the image of a homin. Encounters such as David's speak to the dual nature of the numinous and are also exemplified by other accounts. For example, in episode 858 of *Sasquatch Chronicles*, experiencer Matt viewed his homin entity encounter as sacred, while experiencer Eugene was utterly terrified by his (Germer, 2024, May 8).

Other than acts of God such as hurricanes, volcanic eruptions, tsunamis, earthquakes, and plagues, modern humans have eradicated most other existential threats, save some of those that are most shrouded in mystery, such as the potential or perceived threat of Sasquatch. As aforementioned experiencer Anthony notes of seeing a particularly large and physically imposing homin called Papa, "it was fascinating seeing him, but at the same time ... it was like a nightmare seeing him" (Germer, 2018, September 8, 49:44–49:49). Or, from another narrative, we find the following reflection from an extended experiencer named James:

> For those of you who haven't had an encounter of any kind—whether it be vocal, or a sighting, or anything of the sort—please don't take this the wrong way, but I don't think you quite understand the trauma or horror that comes with it. Yes, it's cool and fascinating and amazing, but I just feel like you really don't understand what it feels like when you're face-to-face with a nine-foot giant that's ready to tear you apart and can if it wants to. It really is frightening [Warren, 2024, April 19, 2:18–2:49].

The mysterium tremendum aspect of the numinous is clearly evoked in James's description here. Furthermore, reflecting on the works of Otto, parapsychologist George P. Hansen shares the following meditation on the approach to the phenomenology of "liminal (interstitial) creatures," stating that "the dread evoked by such beings can be profoundly disturbing" (Hansen, 2001, p. 66). While the topic of discussion was ghosts, his commentary about the mysterium tremendum can be just as easily applied to Sasquatch. Indeed, some homin experiencers have reported initially thinking that they were looking at a ghost, illustrating the hairy poltergeist phenomenon that is noted in the literature (Cutchin & Renner, 2020a, pp. 37–38). Indeed, Mel Skahan's (Yakama Nation) experience with a Sasquatch that apparently materialized during a cleansing ceremony may be viewed through a very similar lens (Eichenberger, 2024, February 10).

As experiencer Steve reflects on the brief yet impactful encounter that he and his friend had in Minnesota, he states the following of his own emotional and physiological state in the presence of a Wholly Other:

> There's this panic. This fight or flight ... feeling that we both had, that we're no longer in a controlled environment where we can shut ourselves in away from danger, um, and that we're in the presence of ... something that is *infinitely* more powerful than we are. And that, uh,

> you know, kind of like you probably feel very similar if you encountered ... a bear or something. Um, you know, it's just this—this type of fear that— that you want to escape but you don't think you're going to get away. You think you're probably done. Um, then that was, um, that was what that was like for me [Ramirez, 2024, June 26, 30:05–31:02].

His reflection further elucidates the potential manifestation of primordial awe—a deep and primal sense that arguably overlaps significantly with mysterium tremendum. The two men had unintentionally snuck up on a large, dark-haired biped who had his back up against a tree. Steve got the feeling that when the homin turned to face them, his facial expression and body language implied that he was annoyed or even frustrated that they had managed to get so close to him. As of the time of his interview, Steve had not returned to the woods. While he felt that he had largely recovered by the time he interviewed on the *Sasquatch Theory* podcast hosted by Miguel Ramirez, he states that "for most of [his] life since then, [he] wished that ... it didn't happen" (36:30), and reports having had nightmares about Sasquatch for several years after the experience (e.g., seeing them in the woods, having them come upstairs from his basement, etc.).

Or, as Project ZooBook co-founder and Olympic Project member Amy Bue has reflected, "I talk to grown men who will stand there and cry over what they've seen. They won't go back in the woods to hunt" (Eichenberger, 2022, 1:11:11–1:11:18). Understandably, the mysterium tremendum is likely at play in at least some of such cases. Amy has shared this example on various occasions and seems to have been struck by the sincerity of these men in the face of the stigma that can be attached to sharing such narratives.

In general though, the idea that a deific and/or demonic character would be associated with homins may not seem so far-fetched when one considers the fact that myths about them are also similar to myths about Fae folk and aliens (Vallee, 2014), both of which are said to abduct humans for sexual purposes or study, to be relatively capricious, and to possess superhuman if not utterly magical qualities. However, it is also notable that all three of these entity groups are typically described as being generally humanlike in appearance, evoking an uncanny aspect to their being.

Other scholars such as Strieber and Kripal (2016) and Bayanov (2014) tie encounters with Sasquatch (among other phenomena) to experiences with divine entities. Strikingly, Bayanov (2014, p. 23) tells us the following:

> Div (dev, dav) is a common name for the "wild man" in Persia (modern Iran) and the adjacent countries. Initially divs were worshipped like gods by heathen peoples, and this explains the fact that the words in other Indo-European languages, such as "Deus" and "Divus" in Latin, "Zeus" in Greek, "divine" and "divinity" in English, are etymologically related to the word "div." It may be noteworthy that according to Greek mythology, Zeus was born in a cave. With the advent of major religions, such as Zoroastrianism, Judaism, Christianity, and Islam, the heathen gods and their hominid prototypes were condemned and relegated to the status of demons.

It is interesting to consider that, aside from their horns, illustrations of figures from satyrs (e.g., Pan) to Baphomet (i.e., half goat, half man) are archetypally quite similar to the liminal figure of the homin (i.e., part ape, part man) as well as to various depictions of Satan and/or the devil (e.g., Porshnev, 2000, p. 28): all of them occupy liminal spaces representative of the confluence of animal (or perhaps, wild) and human (perhaps civilized or rational) characteristics. Indeed, there are numerous contemporary narratives that exist tying Sasquatch and other homins to demons (e.g., Roehl, 2024, May 8).

Moreover, there are many depictions of people being advised to utilize religious ritual or prayer as means of protecting themselves from these beings. For example, Bayanov (2012, p. 37) notes that in Russia, men are advised to say a certain prayer to banish *rusalkas* back to the forest, while in Lutheran Sweden, "death sentences were passed even in the 18th century for sex with female trolls, called *skogsra.*" Anecdotes suggest that religious rebuke (e.g., via prayer) tends to cause the homin to flee the area forthwith, just as religious conviction is part and parcel of the means by which humans connect with homins, per what Barry Webster, Sr., of the Omaha Tribe, family, and colleagues have demonstrated in their work through *Rez Squatching Research Community.* In my opinion, the whole of this area of concern deserves further study.

As we begin to bring this discussion to a close, I ask you to consider the other aspect of the numinous: that is, mysterium fascinosum. We turn briefly to some narratives that speak to the beautiful, inspiring, or even healing power of these entities. To be sure, some of these beings (e.g., the long-haired, magic, wildmen and wildwomen of the forest) are Sasquatch-like in their appearance, ecology, and power, and are seen as purveyors of wisdom and truth, or keepers of treasure, yet also as potentially trickster in their demeanor—an allusion to the dually fear-inducing and faith-invoking nature of the numinous.

As our first example, in one narrative found among the Indigenous Tule River Nation, the Hairy Man is directly responsible for the birth of humanity and is therefore central to their cosmology, preventing humans from assuming the form of Coyote, and tricking Coyote so that humans could take a two-legged form instead, just like Hairy Man. While some interpretations (e.g., Strain, 2012) of the petroglyph suggest that it depicts a family of Sasquatch, there is not currently consensus on the ontology of the beings depicted on the ancient rockface (Boulier, 2017; Pfaller, 2016; Trey the Explainer, 2024, February 8). Still, I include this as an example because of the fact that the Hairy Man hypothesis surrounding the petroglyph overlaps with other accounts of Sasquatch as being not only helpful, but as elder beings who are inexorably tied to the development, if not creation, of humans. Herein we may assert that an encounter with this Hairy Man would equate to an encounter with a being imbued with divine—or at least, profoundly supernatural—power, being directly involved in the physical form that humans were to take on this earth.

In another account dealing with mysterium fascinosum, we turn to the illuminating documentary *A Flash of Beauty: Bigfoot Revealed.* In the film, an eyewitness has a lifechanging encounter with a homin while out on an excursion in Alaska with his son-in-law. What makes this encounter particularly insightful is not just the fact that the two have a sighting, but that Daryl Wilson had been diagnosed with terminal cancer and the excursion may have been the last opportunity he had to share with his son-in-law in this way. He describes the incredible physical appearance of the being, shares that at one point the two of them locked eyes, and that he and his son were swapping the pair of binoculars back and forth. Finally, the entity departs swiftly and disappears over a hill. Wilson reflects:

> We finally turned around and went back to the boat: the most solemn experience of my life going down that river. Me and God were talking: "Thank you, God. I'm diagnosed to die. Thank you for letting me see such an *incredible* thing and to experience this in the last time of my life." 'Course that was 10 years ago. I am God's miracle [Eichenberger, 2023, December 25, 22:31–23:08].

As he finishes this part of his recollection, Daryl indicates that he is clearly still alive, having overcome his own medically proclaimed death sentence. On the other side of the experience, having stared fear and mortality in the eye, he has emerged and found new faith, new passion for life, and new meaning in the warp and woof of the cosmos. On the other side of us humans lie the Wholly Other homins, within the innermost intimate spaces within our psyches, coupled with those points of light that spread out and connect us to each other. While Daryl did not explicitly state that Sasquatch saved his life, he did find through his encounter an intimately and utterly life-changing event. Afterwards, he began interviewing other witnesses. At the time of being filmed for the documentary, he had chronicled many hundreds of interviews with other experiencers. Clearly, connections were made. But he also shares something that makes the meaning in his encounter even more apparent:

> My purpose in sharing this story with you is to bless those who have not been able to share their story, and who have been mocked and ridiculed and belittled [Eichenberger, 2023, December 25, 38:14–38:26].

Mr. Wilson's awe-inspiring encounter is reflective of the profoundly spiritual and deeply meaningful experience that people have had at times as a result of coming into contact with Sasquatch. His witnessing is a powerful testament to the potentially positive strength of exceptional experiences when they are met with equanimity and grace from both parties. Indeed, his general salutary experience was likely as much about his own state of mind as it was about the Sasquatch who he saw. Despite initially being a self-avowed non-believer of Sasquatch, he engaged in his sighting fully, and eventually emerged from it in reverent prayer, thanking God for this life-changing experience.

View It from the Bridge

Herein we have considered that death anxiety and the threats that it poses have arguably been tied to human-homin contact since our archaic past. What we have been considering is more or less an extended fight-or-flight response due to negative interactions with these entities since archaic contact. The ontological shock, mortality salience, and traumatic response (e.g., in the form of PTSD) that can be elicited have been focused upon herein. These existential factors set much of the stage for the overall negative response that is eventually manifested in the Western collective psyche. This chapter has also dealt with the ability for homins to evoke a sense of the numinous within humans, both through their awe-inspiring nature and their terror-inducing potential. The numinous can be experienced in any number of settings or experiences, from the joy of a glorious sunrise to the birth of a child, to encountering a being who you did not think existed. I have included examples from experiencer narratives, folklore, and other available literature to illustrate these dual qualities.

Before moving on, I would encourage you to pause and consider at least one of the reflective prompts on cognitive, emotional, somatic, or conative matters that I have posed in the introduction.

7

The Relict Complex

Complex Defined

At this point, we begin to crest the summit, marking our return to the beginning this journey. The point of contention, or the problem at hand, has been for us to consider why such reticence has persisted within the Western psyche toward the subject of the homin phenomenon. Here, we consider the words of Marimba Ani who shares with us the following about a prototypical European psyche:

> The individual becomes obsessed with the negative and threatening possibilities of the future—with accident and with death. He lives in a culture diseased with thanatophobia and one that provides them with insurances "against" every kind of physical or material possibility imaginable, yet knowing that no amount of financial gain can redeem his soul. He is truly Faustian man—but he did not choose to be so. The "choice" is already implicit in the *asili* of the culture: the bio-cultural, ideological core [Ani, 2007, p. 380].

Viewed from the bridge, herein we might begin to see some of the origins of a rather tortured collective psyche that can do a great deal of damage both to itself as well as to other cultures with which it interacts. Of course, such is the modus operandi of various liminal Othered entities, including the CS and Yurugu.

In due time I hope to make plain why this is relevant to the matter of the homin enigma, but at the moment, let us return to attachment theory. Of the matter as a whole, Bowlby states:

> The resulting conceptual framework is designed to accommodate all of those phenomena to which Freud called attention—for example, production for example love relations, separation anxiety, mourning, defence, anger, guilt, depression, trauma, emotional detachment, sensitive periods in early life—and so to offer an alternative to the traditional metapsychology of psychoanalysis and to add yet another to the many variants of the clinical theory now extant. How successful these ideals will prove only time will tell. As Kuhn has emphasized, any novel conceptual framework is difficult to grasp, especially so for those long familiar with a previous one [Bowlby, 1988, pp. 25–26].

In Bowlby's conceptualization noted above, what we encounter is a brief treatise on how attachment is tied to a number of phenomena in the unconscious and conscious life that bear great significance for humanity. Moreover, those early experiences are pivotal to forming a proper (i.e., warm and consistent) foundation through which the developing child can cultivate an inner sense of competence, autonomy, and ultimately, a healthily individuated and communally integrated spirit.

In order to properly appreciate the work that we hereby consider, we must first reflect upon the proposed nature of the *complex*, following particularly upon some of the works of Freud, Jung, and Jacobi. The complex is a psychical split which emerges from the unconscious as a constellation of behaviors wrapped around an emotional core. It is formed due to pressures—typically familial, social, and/or cultural—that paint certain instinctual (e.g., libidinal) desires, urges, and the like as unacceptable, even taboo.

In her foreword to her and Jung's (2013) work on Jung's thinking, Jacobi shares the following:

> This fact, that there are well-characterized and easily recognizable types of complex, suggests that they rest on equally typical foundations, that is, on emotional aptitudes or *instincts*. In human beings instincts express themselves in the form of unreflected, involuntary fantasy images, attitudes, and actions, which bear an inner resemblance to one another and yet are identical with the instinctive reactions specific of *Homo sapiens* [Jacobi & Jung, 2013, p. x].

As a result, a set of blueprints for behavior form within the subconscious around a given repressed urge or desire, at times emerging into an expressed form (e.g., the eponymous Freudian slip). In such cases, the scenario or situation may be the impetus provoking the complex into emerging. An uttered Freudian slip may be the result of a tense social interaction and may thereafter evoke a nervous laugh from the individual thus possessed, as a means of further expressing the repressed energies.

The emotions at the core of a complex arise from instincts, which are themselves fundamentally tied to the physical form of the individual: that is, the physical body. In this sense, the purpose of the complex is to better effect the survival of the individual, or species, in question. Libidinal energies are present for a reason: to allow the individual within whom they reside to persist—and if they are consciously suppressed or unconsciously repressed, they must make themselves known in due time. Levy posits:

> "Autonomous complexes," a term coined by Jung, are the psychologically equivalent term for what indigenous people would call "demons," e.g., [the cannibal spirit]. To condescendingly think that we, as modern-day enlightened people, are too sophisticated to believe in something as primitive as demons is to not realize their psychological reality. These unconscious complexes alter our experience of ourselves. The psychic conditions which breed demons are as actively at work as ever. The demons have not disappeared but have merely changed their name and taken on another form—they have become unconscious psychic forces [Levy, 2013, p. 134].

Jung (Jacobi & Jung, 2013) further proposes that there are a variety of complexes which can emerge, and yet which (in his opinion) are rather fixed in their expression and variety within the human species. Those complexes may include the mother complex, which may manifest as the Electra complex, and the father complex, which may manifest in the Oedipus complex. However, there are also other complexes such as the anxiety complex and the inferiority complex, both of which may relate strongly to the proposed complexes that I will discuss shortly.

Complexes can potentially be beneficial in the short term due to their ability to help preserve the individual in which they arise. But their clinical relevance is often focused on their negative, or maladaptive, manifestation. In this sense, Jung stresses that the complexes are daemonic[1] or even numinous in their essence, as they can emerge from a deeper archetypal reality. The daemon is the primal force from which the various desires and drives in life emerge and can be manifested in destructive as well as creative ways. Levy summarizes this force as follows:

> Being an archetypal transpersonal energy that can literally take over and possess a person, group, nation, or species, the demonic announces itself by drafting people into its service, enlisting human beings as instruments of its full-bodied revelation of itself. People so possessed will be compelled to unconsciously act out so as to give shape and living form to this archetypal, demonic energy in the third dimension. The word "daemon," etymologically speaking, is related to our inner voice and guiding spirit [Levy, 2013, p. 305].

Thus, the unconscious serves as a medium through which the daemon can be expressed in the collective or individual psyche.

Ideally, a complex becomes integrated into conscious awareness over time, wherein the formerly splintered personality becomes dissolved back into the sea of the person's soul, thus leading more fully into an individuated character. However, when a particular negative constellation remains unresolved, continuing to operate outside of conscious awareness and therein possessing the individual's ego, this can erupt into more problematic consequences for the individual and for those with whom she interacts. The classic Electra complex involves the desire to displace the mother who comes between the daughter and the daughter's father. When negative manifestations of complexes occur at the larger societal or even racial/group level and remain unresolved (i.e., undissolved into the collective conscious), they arguably can become concretized into a system of belief and enaction, such as racism or sexism.

Moreover, the extent to which the complex is tied to both instinct and to the unconscious necessarily connects it to the deep memory that persists within the human species. Deep memory, crystallized within the unconscious and emerging at times in these particular behavioral repertoires, makes itself known and serves as the vessel through which a profound awareness can emerge. However, when it as well as its source (i.e., *deep source memory* preserved through homin teems) remain unacknowledged, they can cause vast and cutting splinters within the collective psyche that persist and painfully manifest for all. Herein, we re-encounter Heuvelmans's (1959) proposition that anatomically modern humans likely had a prolonged conflict with homins. Such interactions, potentially spread out across millennia, could have absolutely left an indelible mark preserved within our species' deep memory.

And lastly, I would be remiss if I didn't mention the matter of sex and identity. Welsing (2004) states that, "at the most primordial level, sex can be viewed as the reproduction of one's own image, of self and of kind" (p. 7). Thus, there is an extremely important—as well as particularly interesting—element when considering the fact that sexual energy is extremely potent and can manifest in rather curious, if not at times unpredictable, ways. We will keep these points in mind as we move forward regarding the complexes.

Arguably, such a deep memory may pre-date the species and may be an amalgamation of sorts from various salient and meaningful epochs in our phylogenetic history. Following the work of Grof (2012), for example, we might consider that the previously discussed systems of condensed experience (COEXes) are similar to complexes, as both revolve around an unconscious, emotional core and can prefigure behavior.

In the case of all complexes, it is arguable that there is a kind of irrationale, a term that I proffered earlier, that is pervasive in them. They arise from the unconscious and are expressed through body and behavior, potentially leading the mindful among us to better integrate those desires and drives that presage and populate the complexes in the first place. If we can do so wisely, then there may be room for us to advance our own healing. Such a scenario is particularly helpful when one encounters the numinous which, as we have seen, can very much occur when one comes into contact with Hairy Man.

With that said, we now turn to the first of two complexes that I wish to discuss. While the following quote from aforementioned experiencer, Claire, does not deal directly with deeper matters of identity crisis or ontological shock, it does illustrate the manner in which homin entity encounters can significantly shift experiencers' perception of themselves and the world:

> I have traveled the world, been all over the world, never really worried about it. But I have to say: I probably lost an awful lot of *confidence* after that, not surprisingly [Germer, 2019, 39:36–39:48].

Claire's encounter with a group of large, hairy homins dramatically shifted her view of reality as well as how she moved through the world thereafter. Here, we consider the matter of confidence, identity, and how they intersect with the fringed phenomena of homins.

The Cronos Complex

With these matters in mind, we now turn to the late Canadian anthropologist Michael Bradley's *cronos complex*. Bradley suggests that all organisms are concerned with achieving dominance over some modicum of territory within which they can assert their influence. One might view such an assertion, in a crude but very apt biological analogue, instead as *insertion*, whereby a male's genetic (read: ability to produce something) material inseminates an egg. Notably, the psychobiological fruits of such seminal, or foundational, labor may be viewed as helping the individual to establish and thereby perpetuate his identity beyond his physical person. Indeed, Bradley posits that among higher organisms, it is the male member of the species who is particularly concerned with such matters.

Importantly, the organism's *confidence* in their ability to assert said influence is thereby fundamentally equated with their *identity*. For Bradley's decidedly nomothetic approach to theorizing about organismic behavior, "confidence is the same, functionally, as identity" (1973, p. 26), regardless of whether the individual is a shrew, a fish, a dog, or a human. To be sure, if as Smith (2007) states, humans and other primates can tend to be status conscious to a fault, then it would not be out of the question to consider that other beings who are reported to look like upright, humanlike primates would be able to manifest similar behaviors. An individual's ability to assert itself appropriately per the dictates of its group, community, or species is equated to its ability to establish some degree of dominance in some particular arena(s), and that capacity is equated with that individual's confidence and, necessarily, with its identity.

In organisms that do not have a sense of their own movement through time (or perhaps what has been termed an *autonoetic* consciousness, a state of mind wherein self-awareness is exhibited; Tulving, 1985), their only concern in this domain is to assert influence over the dimension of space. However, since humans have the ability to conceive of time, we are positioned to desire to assert ourselves temporally as well as spatially. Bradley (1973) posits that humans in general, and people of European descent specifically, are predicated upon colonizing space as well as time. Moreover, the passage of time coupled with the propagation of the species means that one's identity is ever at risk of being overtaken by others: one's parents and their generation must be overcome by the present generation, and one's progeny must in turn surpass the present generation. Of this *temporal aggression* in humans, he states, "we assert and defend temporal territory as well as spatial territory and social position. Indeed, one important characteristic of human beings is that we use almost all mechanisms to assert identity" (p. 44).

Importantly, Bradley even suggests that mortality salience developed in Neanderthals. And following Vendramini's (2009) position that Neanderthals themselves predated upon early humans and competed for physical territory, it could be insightful to determine whether the degree of that aggression is at all amplified within those humans who carry Neanderthal DNA as opposed to among those humans (e.g., sub-Saharan Africans) who tend to not carry such genetic material. Further, if Neanderthals were indeed aware of their own mortality as has been suggested by some research (e.g., Bradley, 1973) and saw the forbears of anatomically modern humans as threats to their own persistence, they may have focused their temporal aggression on these relatively hairless competitors. Relatedly, one mechanism that asserts such aggression is religion, which is by Bradley's estimation, a recognition of finite time to life and of mortality, and of the connection between past, present, and future. Due to the importance of this contention as well as the fact that, unfortunately, Bradley's text is no longer in print, I reproduce here more of his words on the matter of *Homo temporalis*, what he proposes as the proper species name of anatomically modern humans:

> The idea of temporal territory would be strengthened if it could be shown that temporal assertion had some effect on biological relevance. The struggle for biological relevance, identity, pervades territorial behaviour and dominance. We have seen that this "identity" is not purely subjective. It is very definitely a physical biological thing, for the strength of the animal's motivation to assert himself in territory or society concomitantly determines the survival of that animal's *self* as reproduced in offspring [Bradley, 1973, p. 47].

Herein there is a clear problem: the human (primarily confined in Bradley's colloquial referent to the male gender) is imprisoned by time through what can be conceived as the fetters of biology, producing a definite and ever-present tension to establish confidence no matter the cost. The temporal quandary thus activated is that in its extreme, a cronos complex by necessity produces a delimitation in the degrees of freedom offered to the present generation or to the current individual in question, as that group or person proceed from the present into the future. The solution (or rather, the anti-solution that manifests) is, in essence, a *past-averting* and *future-limiting* process: one which Bradley posits is particularly crystalized in humanity within European and European American culture.

Such an approach and ethos which favors *present-extension* thereby places extreme pressures on other people and the planet as a whole in order to preserve some sense of confidence in one's present ability to remain relevant and in control of one's physical and temporal domain. The recipe thus sets those who enact future-limiting behaviors on a collision course with the environment (Forbes, 2011), with future generations, with past generations, and with one's own ability to retain confidence—and therefore, to assert stable identity—in the face of receding time. This is the cronos complex, a fundamentally destructive force in its most extreme psychological and physical consequences and manifestations. Bradley (1973, pp. 84–85) posits:

> Cronos, of course, is "Time" and we still derive words like "chronology" and "chronicle" from his name. The Greeks rightly understood that the temporal personality is a jealous personality. Cronos tried to surpass the past and deny the future. The Greeks also saw that offspring could survive the chauvinism of the temporal identity only by trickery on the part of fertility. We have seen that our sexual adaptations, the subject of Desmond Morris's *The Naked Ape*, can also be regarded as tricks to tempt a temporal creature to reproduce.

Thus, within the complex there is a direct tie to Cronos's hubristic tendencies to defy life's inexorable impulse that thrusts us forward from birth to death and back again, tied to the longbody and to the natural ebb and flow of life. Bradley's considerations in his text, as well as those assertions from his 1991 follow-up book *The Iceman Inheritance*, suggest that among the various populations of humans, the modern Western psyche in particular (along with its ancestral and even archaic forebears) has had to develop behavioral retrofits (e.g., romantic love) to counteract any future-limiting tendencies. These psychological and cultural adaptations would serve as a counterforce to any thanatotic impulses preserved within the collective psyche, aiming to preserve and protect rather than to diminish and destroy. But again, any perceived threats—be they real or imagined—can become a focus of attention in the collective psyche, even if that threat is unacknowledged at the conscious level.

Generally speaking, though, Bradley (1973) further posits that the cronos complex "is a human affliction consisting of paradoxes and conflicting responses to two different identity demands: physical survival in the material world, and psychological survival in the temporal world. The 'Cronos complex' is characterized by irony" (p. 85). The irony is perhaps seen most evidently in the battle against time, where there are ultimately no winners. Similarly, as archaeological scientist and lecturer Myra Shackley has posited, "There is something in human nature which makes us reluctant to accept that anything (including ourselves) can come to a full stop, leaving no apparent trace" (Shackley, 1983, pp. 165–166). The salient as well as subtle manifestations of this affliction are not easily denied by those who have a high enough boggle threshold to be able to view this development from the bridge, as it were.

Further, due to the consideration of sex as well as gender thus far in our discussion of the human-homin connection, we must at least briefly consider an important homage made by Bradley to the ever-present fear within human males (or at least, those of European ancestry):

> The special temporal identity-threat was initially a male problem. And, because of the female representation of reproduction, I believe that men *normally* have an approach-avoidance attitude towards sex and a *normal* fear of women who represent the mechanism for robbing male temporal identity. I do not believe that this exists in men, especially contemporary ones, only as a psychological characteristic. I believe that this normal fear of sex and women is an unconscious memory of the matriarchal structure of many Neolithic societies, and it is a memory reinforced by the behavior of the Indo-Aryans who destroyed the Matriarchies closest to our own cultural history [Bradley, 1973, pp. 75–76].

Bradley's assertion here jibes with Vendramini's proposal that early male humans would have tended to outcast any women who considered Neanderthal characteristics to be attractive: using Bradley's term, such women may have been viewed as temporal identity-threats for these early men. As such, the mere thought of human women having sexual relations with Neanderthal or other homin males would have been a clear and present threat to human male confidence and, therefore, identity.

Further, as stated previously, the temporal identity-threat is the particular quandary of past-aversion and future-destruction, each of which are tied to a woman's ability to reproduce: there would be no genetic lineage without procreation, and there would be no procreation without a woman's ability to conceive, thus cultivating a fear—unconscious or otherwise—in men thus possessed of a cronos complex via their own temporal intelligence or awareness. The fear is potentially proportional to men's lack of a solid and/or consistent identity, which is per Bradley's assertion, tied to their confidence. And if Neanderthals had similar autonoetic consciousness and ability to process mortality salience, and if Vendramini's (2009) position on Neanderthal males raping human females bears any truth, then it is quite possible that Neanderthal men would have had some ambivalence toward sex as well. That ambivalence could have been processed in sexual violence, just as it has been in anatomically modern human males. Indeed, if a deep memory of a past that was potentially steeped in such violent assaults is preserved into the present day (particularly among European stock), then this scenario could potentially result in heightened psychosexual anxieties and aggression. The resultant behavioral constellation fits quite well with Welsing's (2004) central thesis, speaking to the psychological as well as cultural need to identify and deal with perceived threats to survival—even if those behaviors are maladaptive and disharmonious in the long term.

If Bradley's (1973) contention about confidence and identity has indeed been a factor in the development and behavioral compunctions of humans, then it may well be the case that during some of the early years of *H. sapiens*, confidence and therefore identity were likely at a low due to clear and present threats toward carving out a functional niche within time and space that allowed us to persevere. At the level of the individual psyche, an organism's ability to acquire functional (i.e., adaptive) capacity in its environment, and thereby to react and respond appropriately in order to maximize chances of survival, has been argued to form the fundamental rudiment of behavior. Moreover, due to the potential existential threats such as homins (e.g., Heuvelmans, 1959), there may have been greater pressures placed upon early humans to cultivate such niches. Following Vendramini's (2009) train of thought, it is precisely such pressures that may have contributed to our species' apparently unprecedented predilection to generate technologies—particularly those that are capable of dominating other beings, thereby increasing human confidence in our ability to persist within spatial and temporal domains of functioning.

Relatedly, in Pasulka's text on another fringed subject—ufology and its religious relevance for contemporary America—she shares the following poignant thoughts about technology and pre-human hominids:

> I was reminded of the first scene in the film *2001: A Space Odyssey*. A group of hominid human ancestors are losing a fight with a rival tribe. After a night's sleep, they awaken to find an anomalous object, the monolith. The monolith, and the idea it inspires, drives them to develop one of the first tools of war and is the catalyst for human evolution and dominance. Arthur C. Clarke's insight is compelling: not all ideas are benign gifts [Pasulka, 2019, pp. 76–77].

Per Pasulka's commentary, one might consider that the weapons of war that humans have created may have temporarily assuaged death anxiety, briefly extending the lives of those afflicted by such anxieties, but only at the expense of ever-expanding internecine conflict and destruction of nature—the environment, the flora and fauna, the land which sustains us and, potentially homins as well. That destruction includes our very own human nature, our capacity for creative compassion and advancement of technologies that enhance rather than eradicate communal bonds.

Cannibal Spirit Redux

As a relevant thought experiment, let us consider the aforementioned matters of symbolic immortality and epistemological imperialism in relation to the cronos complex. For symbolic immortality to adhere, the image of the individual and the human species must be perpetuated and propagated across not just space, but also across time. Due to the fact that digital and mental dimensions of reality offer fertile soil within which to plant such seeds, both humanity as a whole and the Western psyche seem determined to colonize the vastness of the internet from the present forward, as well as from past to present, the vital force and manifestations of the human mind and its creative spirit. Still, as both Bradley (1973) and others (e.g., Menzies & Menzies, 2021, p. 15) have opined, the search for such an immortalized legacy may largely be the province of male members of our species. In the specific case of the epistemological imperialism affected by mechanisms such as European colonizing culture, to effectively coerce and compel Othered beings into acculturative divestment of their heritage, traditions, values, and ways of being, is to effectively seed those same beings with the ontologies, epistemologies, and axiologies of Europe and its imperial diaspora. Parasitizing other minds, bodies, and lands not only induces a mass symbolic immortality for the collective European conscious, but it also permits the cronos complex to endure. This is arguably a manifestation of cannibal psychosis (Forbes, 2011; Levy, 2013), of Yurugu's endless wanderings (Ani, 2007), or of the hungry ghost's insatiability (Mitchell, 2022): a mind split off from its transpersonal self and collective roots, thereby wreaking havoc upon all that it touches, including itself. In short, the extreme aggression evinced by Western culture due to the cronos complex is what I have come to call *Bradley's beast*, and it is more or less an analog of cannibal psychosis, Yurugu, and preta. Moreover, these liminal entities can potentially play a role in the manifestation of intentional forgetting, as each of them can contribute to psychological blindness around who we are and how we relate to the world through which we move.

However, the Western mind with its culture of elitism, positivism, and progressivism, has also perceived itself as exhibiting a necessarily superior behavior and stance above all other human beings on this planet. In her illuminating critique of European culture, anthropologist Marimba Ani (2007) speaks of the incessant and insatiable desire to control all of that which is Other, from the world's majority cultures to the environment and more. Moreover, she states that this cultural collusion is a "union of like-minded people, who have cooperated in the creation of a technological giant—or monster" (2007, p. 351). This monster is the spirit of Yurugu: the embodiment of disorder that acts against harmony and balance in the universe, thereby seeding destruction, lack of wholeness, selfishness, and greed. As a result of its own defiance and desire to split off from Source for its own perceived gain, Yurugu is an extreme masculine principle that it is not in possession of inner balance with the feminine principle. He is thereby doomed to perceive lack, incompleteness, and degradation around him, and to generate the same in the world. If the natural world is structural, Yurugu is anti-structural in the truest sense of the word, conveying an axiology of amorality that is opposed to an ethic of broad or universal good. Arguably, Yurugu is a liminal entity—representative of a "devastating spiritual disease" (Ani, 2007, p. 561) as well as a being that has very real implications for material reality—that is quite similar to other similar figures in world wisdom traditions. But as contemplative authors such as Paul Levy (2013) posit, the antidote to—and lesson to learn from—the destructive capacity of these entities is found in their own character. We must become critical and reflective of our inner lives and how they are related to each other as we move through the world—a world that entities other than us inhabit.

Similarly, if we view Sasquatch-as-cannibal-spirit in the same light, there are clear demarcations set within various segments of Indigenous America as to what behaviors are life-affirming and humanity-affirming, and what behaviors are taboo to such a telos. Arguably, by setting boundaries around what we are and what we are not, Sasquatch and other homins—as well as the liminal entities of folklore and myth that cohabit cognitive, emotional, and spiritual space with them—point us toward what makes us who we are. As Turner (2017) posits, "of all cryptozoological projects, the liminal spaces occupied by bipedal, humanlike cryptids may be the richest sites for unearthing explanations of why cryptids matter" (p. 24). Indeed, it is the physical and psychological closeness to us that sets homins and their kith and kin apart from other entities and organisms within the cryptozoological, hominological, and otherwise fringed scientific literature.

Further, in the conclusion to his book *Between Ape and Human*, anthropologist

Gregory Forth (2022) posits that the aforementioned lai ho'a ape-men mentioned among the Lio people of Indonesia (possibly extant or recently extinct relict of *H. floresiensis*) are most likely hominins, but reflects on reasons for his own reticence to accept this plausibility. He states (2022, p. 248):

> Among these is probably a lingering influence of the now increasingly challenged but still persisting unilinear view of hominin evolution, bound up with the nineteenth-century notion of "progress," whose most famous proponent was Darwin, and even older ideas about human perfectibility. Another factor is the stigma deriving from a widespread view of people who entertain the possible existence of creatures not (or not yet) accepted by science as mentally peculiar if not downright delusional!

But why the stigma in the first place? Of course, this present volume extends previous works on the matter (e.g., Bindernagel, 2010) and attempts to proffer further reasons for such deep and abiding reticence. The Single Species Hypothesis, progressivism, human exceptionalism, and the dogmatic stigma associated with the idea of homins, are, arguably, prevalent strategies to maintain some modicum of egoic defense against the onslaught of potential threats to that status: not only could the existence of other hominins throw off this sense of half-baked pride, but they could utterly upset and upturn this worldview.

In addition to their apparent size, strength, and speed far surpassing that of anatomically modern humans, their ability to sexually molest, rape, and potentially sire viable offspring with us is a psychically insurmountable threat—particularly for the global minority, a group that is already at threat by the global majority which is capable of genetically annihilating the former group. And I repeat that it goes without saying that, by biological definition at least, if even one of the many accounts of hybrid offspring are veridical that humans and at least a subset of the homin population *are members of the same species*.

The untenable position for the global minority (i.e., people of European descent) of experiencing numerical inadequacy is that one's whole group could be wiped out by more darkly melanated anatomically modern humans as well as by homins. Following Welsing's (2004) assertion, these pressures would be too great to bear consciously and would have to be displaced into the subconscious levels of the psyche. Moreover, if these threats presented themselves not just across several years or generations, but across millennia, then the pressures could be nigh-unbearable. It thus follows that this tension would not be able to be acknowledged consciously without threat of severe trauma resulting thereafter.

It cannot be overstated that an insecure psyche more easily views Othered beings, situations, and environments as threats. The insecurely attached individual more easily perpetuates and perceives disorder rather than order. Such is the nature of Yurugu, hungry ghost, and the cannibal spirit, for example. By consuming other and moving incessantly in the wrong direction (i.e., away from Source, or away from Spirit), there is a tendency to reify rather than resolve the problem which is, as Wangyal states, the "real hunger we feel … for knowledge of our true nature" (1998, p. 37). Indeed, we see that the hungry ghost state of being is in part an allegory for very real states of mind that are characterized by materialism and split from community (Pope, 2011), or what I have referred to elsewhere (Mitchell, 2022) as "close encounters of the *preta* kind" (p. 86). Such consumption, as Pope states, temporarily satiates a deep and pervasive sense of paucity: that is, "we are actually covering over a tremendous sense of lack, hiding from the fact that we do not exist in the ways we conventionally think that we do" (p. 174). By "we," Pope is referring to those enculturated in—or perhaps imbibing of—Western culture. Thus, it arguably follows that who a person thinks they are, is fundamentally tied to their culture, which in turn helps to direct their cognitive and emotional processes. But one might posit that this sense of lack is fundamentally a result of the lack of confidence—and therefore identity—that Bradley (1973) discusses. By centering one's identity in one's ability to conquer time and space, as it were, the psyche (whether it be individual or collective) situates their sense of "I" fully within the material world, thereby utterly neglecting any transpersonal sense of self.

The Relict Complex

Following this train of thought, as we bring this volume to a close, I hope that a glimmer of understanding something that we might call the *relict complex* has begun to coalesce in your mind or has started to sprout in the well of your soul. This psychological complex is what we might consider to be an at times conscious, though typically unconscious, constellation of approach-avoidance behaviors toward homins that exist within humanity's collective psyche—a set of pre-programmed actions, orientations, and approaches toward Sasquatch and their kin that is predicated on the potential threat that these beings pose and the likely paleotrauma that has been retained within our species' deep memory since time immemorial. It is relict because, as yet, it has persisted as a remnant from our archaic and primal past. It is a complex because it operates relatively autonomously and primarily outside of conscious awareness; yet, when viewed and understood in proper context, it may lead to greater integrity and wholeness within.

I generally define the relict homin complex, or simply, the relict complex, as a desire to either establish contact with or establish control over one's relationship with the physical, psychological, and/or cultural reality of homins. The complex may operate through an entirely unconscious or partially unconscious mechanism of manifestation. Whether they are hairy ghosts (Cutchin & Renner, 2020a), flesh-and-blood beings, unbidden archetypal projections of the human psyche (Prince-Hughes, 1997), some combination thereof, or something entirely different, homins seem to call to us in various forms and fashions across space and time, from the deep past into the present. Indeed, if humans throughout the world have had to develop strategic means of coping with the presence of homins in order to survive, then I suggest that the foundations of such a complex would be borne out.

Further, the relict complex is defined by one thing (e.g., the structural) being consumed by another (e.g., the anti-structural) via a psychic blindness (Levy, 2013) or by a single-minded mentality in a manner that figuratively recalls those narratives—or rather, the proposed deep memory—of homins cannibalizing humans. Though following an irrationale, and particularly one that contributes to intentional forgetting, the individual thus affected is typically either unaware of and complacent, or is aware and complicit, of the complex being manifested through their body, mind, and/or spirit. Thus, the complex emerges from the collective unconscious and acts through the individual in both a manner that is unique to the penchants and proclivities of that person, as well as in more general stereotypical ways that arise, following a path of an irrational, pervasive, and non-local (à la Levy, 2013) potential. Again, we are confronted with the irrationale that may impel us to pursue behavior that from one perspective is utterly incomprehensible, and yet when viewed from the bridge, makes sense within the context of deep memory, death anxiety, and even the cronos complex. It is those more general patterns of manifestation within the relict complex to which we will direct the bulk of our discussion here as we begin to bring our present journey to a close.

In addition to the above patterns that I suggest constellate this complex, it is arguably marked by orthogonally opposed (i.e., approach and avoid) emotions to be close to as well as to distance oneself from homins; competing desires which at times overpower the other or briefly subsume otherwise rational action on the part of the individual thus possessed. These emotions have the potential to influence and yet exist apart from typical cognitions and behaviors. Through the complex, there is deep fear or anxiety of being physically and/or psychologically overpowered by a homin, just as there is great elation or excitement at the prospect of being physically and/or psychologically overpowered by a homin. Herein lies a parallel with our consideration of Otto's (1917) sensus numinus. Such a pattern may be tied to the general numinous nature of encounters with these beings and with their attendant phenomena that are evocative of high strangeness (e.g., light orbs, mindspeak, electrical and equipment malfunctions, etc.). Importantly, this ambivalent attitude toward Sasquatch and other homins may reflect that tendency within our collective deep memory toward remembering, toward forgetting, or toward some combination thereof.

Similar to the manner in which defense mechanisms manifest in general, the relict complex—in its milder manifestations, at least—is neither good nor bad, but is a response to simply living on this planet with other beings who can, at least at times, potentially pose a threat to our survival. At its positive extreme, the complex can be beneficial to more firmly ensconcing humanity in the larger web of life and death, or perhaps in what Cutchin (2022) refers to as an ecology of souls. However, at its negative extreme, the complex may manifest as a psychological split from one's humanity, separating from or denying that interconnectedness in some form or fashion.

On one other general point, the complex is called "relict" for two reasons: (a) due to the position that at least some of the reports of extant homins in the present may be holdovers of archaic humanlike beings, and (b) due to my position that the memory of contact has persisted within the collective psyche from our ancient past. This latter point is one that I will touch on briefly before moving back into the broader, former point. It is the case that, by definition, something that is relict is a remnant of the past that has persisted into the present. In the case of the relict complex, I argue—as do others such as Vendramini (2009)—that a psychological, if not cultural, holdover from humanity's ancient past, a deep memory that for some is consciously recalled, and for others, has been shuttled away into the recesses of the unconscious, only emerging from time to time, unbidden and causing alarm to the percipient.

Moreover, something that is relict is anti-structural in a way, given that not only does it persist from the past, but given whatever the dominant modes of thought, paradigms, or perspectives are as they pertain to the subject of that which is relict, that which persists *should not still exist*. Of course, that is precisely what many European American experiencers of the phenomenon say: that they saw something that should not exist (e.g., Eichenberger, 2022). In this way, the destructuring or denaturing character of the relict Other upsets and threatens to strip away the cultural and psychological structures that individuals, communities, or societies have built up in order to persist in confidence.

To further define what I mean by relict complex, in popular parlance, that which is relict used to be and yet is thought that it no longer should be. It is anachronistic, in a sense, existing in a time in which it should no longer persist. Of course, "should" is not devoid of its own sociohistorical and cultural baggage, perhaps as a kind of residue from Kuhn's (2012) normal science (e.g., the long-accepted contention that the Single Species Hypothesis most readily describes the state of affairs for hominins and their ilk within an evolutionary context). Therefore, the assumption that a species should or should not exist is inherently intertwined with the culture that supports that assumption—the assumption and the culture are what cultural psychologists would call *mutually constituted*. In the case of homins, the oft-repeated perception stated by witnesses, skeptics, and cynics alike that these beings should not exist is a direct and unfiltered example of the fact that recognizing them as real is a threat to the sustenance of a stable individual or collective egoic identity, and that these beings are anti-structural or denaturing to the mainstream tenets of Western science and academia in particular.

Further, that which is relict, in many ways, disrupts formalized and concretized scientific structures, undermining the paradigms of normal science that have come to be accepted within the core, mainstream of those scientific disciplines for which the relict entity is most relevant. Essentially, anything that is relict is treated as anti-structural and is cast out of the Weltbild of mainstream scientific thought.

Moreover, given the progressivist tendencies within the European *utamawazo* (Ani, 2007),[2] there is an abiding tendency within Western culture to supersede, if not conquer, the past, and to incessantly move toward the rational ideal: an ideal that will never be reached. Such a characteristic falls squarely within the impetuous and ever-seeking nature of Yurugu. Therefore, the past itself becomes an enemy to be controlled, defeated, and subsumed so that the future can come into fruition. Indeed, Bradley's (1973) cronos complex implies the same drives and behavioral manifestations, wherein humanity (and particularly its Western manifestation) is in a never-ending battle with time itself. Following this logic, that which is relict must arguably become a casualty of that war, sacrificed to the gods of egoic striving.

Further, due to the deep and abiding reticence of Western culture to accept or possess information about homins, there has arguably been great pressure to suppress or repress any and all desire to recognize these beings as real. Generally speaking, the relict complex is characterized by a desire to possess a homin in mind, body, or spirit: this propensity utilizes the term "possess" in all of its forms and fashions, wherein some aspect of the character or nature of the homin is taken over by and/or overtakes the human psyche.

Again, a pervasive displacement into the collective unconscious does not seem to have taken place in traditional European or non-European Indigenous cultures around the world to the extent that it has in what has become mainstream or popular Western culture: instead, the former groups include those cultures that have developed and sustained legendary, folkloric, mythological, and even cosmological, narratives about homins. Still, there are Indigenous American narratives that are evocative of an abiding psychological need to bond together in the face of opposition toward homins. Hansen (2001) states:

> Bigfoot can be partly understood in terms of projection and paranoia. Anthropologist Henry Sharp, in his book *The Transformation of Bigfoot* (1988), tells of a small Chipewyan society in which tensions between two brothers threatened the group's existence. A hunt for Bigfoot brought them together in a common purpose even though neither had a firm belief in the creature. The hostility within the group was projected outward onto a common enemy, and that strengthened the social bonds. Each brother realized that he needed the other as an ally. The fear of Bigfoot was therapeutic and adaptive [p. 608].

I have commented more thoroughly on the above narrative elsewhere (Mitchell, 2023). However, this Chipewyan case is indicative of the fact that there is potential benefit in becoming consciously aware of and responding to a perceived threat, even if the threat is entirely imagined. Arguably, the primary difference between an instance such as that which is discussed above and what tends to occur in Western culture is the extent to which such behaviors are enacted consciously and with consistency for the sake of ingroup cohesion. In the case of European American culture, the adoption of figurative boogeymen to fear—from folks of African descent to Sasquatch and beyond—may help group cohesion in the short term, but in the long term it appears to be maladaptive for the group itself as well as for the objects of said group's fear. Additionally, it might be argued that the usage of such a strategy as described above is a temporary solution that should not be confused with long-term strategies toward ameliorating ingroup conflict. Given the nature of complexes, one might expect for the expression of the relict complex to be more pronounced in situations and scenarios wherein more repression and suppression is more likely: arguably, that describes precisely what has occurred within the confines of Western culture.

Further, as sociologists Bader, Baker, and Mencken put it simply: "humans generally do not like uncertainty and try to reduce it" (2017, p. 86). In the case of the two brothers (Hansen, 2001), we might suggest that forming a cohesive in-group bond helps to reduce uncertainty. As an example of such uncertainty, there is an entire subculture of people within the Bigfooting community who are focused on the idea that Sasquatch are responsible for disappearances of people in the nation's woodlands—particularly within the national parks. And while David Paulides's popular *Missing 411* work does not explicitly name Sasquatch as the culprit of the missing persons, the implication is that these beings may be responsible for at least some of the mysterious disappearances of individuals in National Parks and elsewhere (e.g., DeGrazier, 2019). Naming the potential threat helps to reduce uncertainty by providing the community with a coherent narrative about the causes of the problem to be addressed.

Overall, I view the relict complex as a potentially insightful, albeit rudimentary, conceptual structure through which to view the ways in which Hairy Man has been accepted or avoided in Western culture and elsewhere, and as a bridge to the considerations of deep memory, paleotrauma, and death anxiety that we have been reflecting upon throughout this text. Additionally, it is another avenue through which Western psychology can at least theoretically bring to bear some of the century and a half of its contributions to understanding of the stranger reaches of human experience.

View It from the Bridge

The preceding chapter has defined the concept of the psychological complex as an autonomously acting splinter of the psyche. Additionally, we have introduced the first of two complexes discussed herein: anthropologist Michael Bradley's cronos complex, which describes the deep anxiety that humanity as a whole and Europeans in particular feel the need to colonize or aggress against time due to awareness of our own mortality. I suggest that the cronos complex can be heightened in the face of existential threats such as the perceived danger that homins pose, thereby leading to the multifarious reactions devised by the conscious and unconscious mind to generate greater egoic stability.

I have also proposed the relict complex as a means of constellating the approach and avoidance behaviors that seem to permeate the human-homin connection and that particularly define the mainstream Western perspective toward the homin phenomenon. While the complex is speculative, it may provide an avenue for better understanding the breadth and depth of ways in which people behave toward Hairy Man and their kith and kin.

Before moving on to the conclusion, I would encourage you to pause and consider at least one of the reflective prompts on cognitive, emotional, somatic, or conative matters that I have posed in the introduction.

Conclusion

I suggest that the shock, fear, and anxiety that may give rise to this posited relict complex may serve as a potent opportunity for that portion of our species' collective—and particularly, the Western psyche—to rediscover, or perhaps, to remember, these otherwise neglected or fringed experiences from the distant past into the present. In short, truly important insights may be drawn from the abiding reticence toward and rejection of the homin phenomenon.

Rather than turning a blind, hateful, or fearful eye toward what (or rather, who) goes bump in the psyche, if we gaze at the homin phenomenon with clear and wide open vision, we might see that our reactions and responses to all manner of Hairy Man the world over—from Sasquatch to yowie to otang to yeren to almas and more—may teach us something not just about them, but about the deepest and most intimate parts of our own psyches as well.

Appendix

Association Between PTSD Symptoms and Features of Homin Entity Encounter Narratives

PTSD Symptoms Per DSM-V	Associations with Homin Entity Encounter Narratives
Criterion A (1 required): The person was exposed to death, threatened death, actual or threatened serious injury, or actual or threatened sexual violence, in the following way(s): • Direct exposure • Witnessing the trauma • Learning that the trauma happened to a close relative or close friend • Indirect exposure to aversive details of the trauma, usually in the course of professional duties (e.g., first responders, medics)	"I felt like food. When it looked at me in the window, I felt like food. I–, I felt like a rabbit went in a hole with wolves around that hole" —extended experiencer and host of Subarctic Alaska Sasquatch, Curyung Tribal Member Fred Roehl (LeGro, 2024, January 12, 47:52–48:01) "It's just this—this type of fear that—that you want to escape but you don't think you're going to get away. You think you're probably done. Um, then that was, um, that was what that was like for me."—experiencer Steve (Ramirez, 2024, June 26, 30:45–31:02) "It's just hard to put into words that experience of having this thing follow me and every time I would turn around it would just be closer and just standing there.... And—and that's when I ... I genuinely thought that I was going to die. I–, I genuinely believed that ... this thing was gonna to kill me.... It's not like ... if someone's had a bear follow them, or a cougar.... Seeing this thing and experiencing it, it strikes in you a fear that.... I've never experienced before." —experiencer Joseph reflects on a solo hike in Big Cypress National Preserve in Florida at age 19 (Germer, 2021, March 24, 17:57–18:38)

PTSD Symptoms Per DSM-V	Associations with Homin Entity Encounter Narratives
Criterion B (1 required): The traumatic event is persistently re-experienced in the following way(s): • Unwanted upsetting memories • Nightmares • Flashbacks • Emotional distress after exposure to traumatic reminders • Physical reactivity after exposure to traumatic reminders	"...I had nightmares ... for several years ... after that ... you know, seeing them, you know ... being out in the woods and all of a sudden there's one in front of me ... having them ... come up from my basement and, you know, just ... my brain just kind of did ... a bunch of weird things after that. But.... I never went to a counselor or anything like that ... but I probably would've benefited if I had. But [chuckles], then again, what am I gonna tell them: I saw Bigfoot and it scared the living 'you-know-what' out of me, and now I have nightmares?" —experiencer Steve (Ramirez, 2024, June 26, 34:28–35:20)
Criterion C (1 required): Avoidance of trauma-related stimuli after the trauma, in the following way(s): • Trauma-related thoughts or feelings • Trauma-related reminders	"I was 13 [during my first encounter] and it altered my life forever. Years after, I have suffered from what must be PTSD. I've had nightmares and a fear that sometimes makes it impossible to even go near the woods" —unnamed experiencer (LeGro & Hopf, 2019, chap. 8; 1:08–1:20) "Ever since then, I went through about a year of ... completely being mortified about being outside in natural spaces, or couldn't even feed the animals at night. Couldn't—walking past the sliding glass door at night was too much ... *all* the lights had to be on, and you ... couldn't bring yourself to do *any*thing outside after dark." —experiencer & field investigator Nathaniel Bronis (White, 2025, February 28, 16:45–17:06)
Criterion D (2 required): Negative thoughts or feelings that began or worsened after the trauma in the following way(s): • Inability to recall key features of the trauma • Overly negative thoughts and assumptions about oneself or the world • Exaggerated blame of self or others for causing the trauma • Negative affect • Decreased interest in activities • Feeling isolated • Difficulty experiencing positive affect	"I talk to grown men who will stand there and cry over what they've seen. They won't go back in the woods to hunt." —experiencer & co-founder of Project Zoobook Amy Bue (Eichenberger, 2024, March 5, 1:11:11–1:11:18) "Like, how come I just had to see this thing and I'm never told about it before, you know? Only as a fairy tale. I never believed in them or anything like that." —extended experiencer & Olympic Project member Rich Germeau (Eichenberger, 2024, March 5, 1:12:47–1:12:22)

PTSD Symptoms Per DSM-V	Associations with Homin Entity Encounter Narratives
Criterion E (2 required): Trauma-related arousal and reactivity that began or worsened after the trauma in the following way(s): • Irritability or aggression • Risky or destructive behavior • Hypervigilance • Heightened startle reaction • Difficulty concentrating • Difficulty sleeping	"Ever since that incident ... now when I go into the woods, if anything is out of the ordinary or I notice anything ... in the air or the air feels different.... I get out. I feel hyper-sensitive to them now, and I just know: if I'm in the woods, I can walk into the woods now (and it took me a long time, by the way. It probably took me 20 years before I went back in the woods). But.... I can go into the woods now, and I can ... feel the woods. It's kind of weird, but I can feel the woods and when I'm walking through the woods if they're nearby, I'll feel them and I'm out. Time to go." —experiencer John (Germer, 2023, December 15, 42:13–43:10) "The term I use for ['Bigfoot on the brain']: PTSD. The sighting has caused them so much stress, so much anxiety, but now they're seeing it everywhere. Just like some of the vets that come back: they hear a certain thing, it triggers them, and now they're seeing the enemy everywhere." —field investigator & content creator Steve Kulls (Hajicek & Hajicek, 2024, April 24, 1:35:50–1:36:08)
Criterion F (required): Symptoms last for more than 1 month.	"I turn 57 years old this year, and I have never ever *willingly* gone camping again. That gave me nightmares for years. When you're 7, and you see something like that, you suddenly know that a world of monsters does exist. They're real. And you become more afraid. I know everyone tells me not to be afraid. They try to tell me they're just friendly creatures. I don't care. The fear of me as a 7-year-old is still alive inside me. I guess it will always be there. I don't care if it was there to make friends with us. It scared me very badly that night. I have never been the same." —experiencer Mr. Carter (Warren, 2024, May 11, 18:17–19:03)

PTSD Symptoms Per DSM-V	Associations with Homin Entity Encounter Narratives
Criterion G (required): Symptoms create distress or functional impairment (e.g., social, occupational).	"Get this: about a month later after I had experiences with…. Bigfoot and so forth, I quit my job [chuckles], because I couldn't handle it. And I kept trying to tell my mom. I said, 'Hey, can I work during the day? Can I, you know, can I do something other than work … really late and then get off and have to drive all the way home … every night early in the morning, you know? Get home about 3 or 4 in the morning.'"—experiencer Emerald Tucker (Aaniiih and Nakoda) of Fort Belknap Reservation after her encounter while driving home from her casino clerk job (Fort Belknap Casino) around 3:30 a.m. in June 2017 in north central Montana (Bear Chief & Upham, 2022, January 6, 41:20–41:49)
Criterion H (required): Symptoms are not due to medication, substance use, or other illness.	"I'm lookin' at this thing, and I'm like, 'Holy-, you gotta be kidding me.' And I … wasn't on no drugs, I didn't smoke anything. I didn't drink anything, so I know I wasn't hallucinating…" and "I didn't have any medicine that day so I know wasn't tripping" —experiencer Bob "Bobcat" Carpenter discusses his sighting in 2017 while walking on the Ohio Towpath Trail (Kruze & Grover, 2024, May 30, 11:03–11:24)

Comparison of PTSD Symptoms via DSM-V and Features of Encounter Narratives. Sourced from the DSM-V, the left column summarizes the clinical characteristics of PTSD (U.S. Department of Veteran Affairs, n.d.). The right column, sourced from the oral and written literature on the subject of Sasquatch, depicts corresponding exemplars of those characteristics related to Sasquatch encounters.

Chapter Notes

Introduction

1. Experiencer Robert Manresa has stated that another term utilized by some groups of Indigenous Americans is "blood-and-skin Bigfoot," said to be a reference to the Hairy Man or keeper of the forests (Horton, 2024, June 24, 6:32).

2. Much of the research on the almasty comes from hominologists, including Koffmann (2015b), Bayanov (2014), and Burtsev (e.g., Margaryan et al., 2021).

3. Thanks to the concerted interest and efforts of herpetologist Terry Cullen (Jones, 2023, January 16; Prescott, 2022, March 16) who contacted Heuvelmans and Sanderson, the original Iceman received some degree of scientific scrutiny before it was apparently replaced with a forged replica. I would encourage those who are interested to listen to Cullen's interviews and published materials on the Iceman (Heuvelmans, Coleman, & LeBlond, 2016) as they are quite insightful and help to answer the oft-asked refrain to produce a body (e.g., Shermer, 2003).

4. For an insightful overview of the various types of entities that are reported in entity encounters that updates some of White's work, I direct the interested reader to the works of exo-studies scholar Sean Esbjörn-Hargens, such as his detailed taxonomy of entities and their potential ontologies (Esbjörn-Hargens, 2020, July).

5. Geography is arguably one defining feature of homin entity encounters. While some reports of homins occur in or near populated areas (e.g., Terrell, 2024, May 26), Sasquatch are physically liminal just as they are phenomenologically liminal, often requiring that experiencers physically and/or perceptually move beyond a threshold, *traveling out* or *looking out* into natural spaces; however, UFOs and apparitions, for example, are often seen where people already live, work, and go about their daily lives, not requiring experiencers to travel beyond their normal ken.

6. A note regarding nomenclature is that I choose to use the term Sasquatch with a capital "s" as it pays homage to the European American folk tradition of hairy homins just as it recognizes the Indigenous American roots of much of that lore. Moreover, I capitalize the term in deference to treating the beings as they are often (or at least, sometimes) treated in these two distinct traditions: as a People, thereby having the right to their collective appellation being capitalized just as any other nation of anatomically modern humans does.

7. You might be wondering why I did not explicitly mention interspecies encounters as being indicative of homin entity encounters. For those unfamiliar with the hominology or folklore about homins, you may be surprised to learn that there is a significant segment of the oral as well as written literature, both past and present, that discusses human-homin interactions which result in viable offspring (i.e. at least some of which are able to reproduce, themselves). By (current) definition, if two beings can produce viable offspring that can procreate, themselves, then the parents of said offspring belong to the same species.

8. Associate professor and chair of gender and women's studies, Mimi Thuy Nguyen, poignantly states: "To be an object is to be determined by another, is a being-for-other (to recall Hegel). However, becoming a subject is also a subjection, because to be a subject is to be inscribed through layered abstractions that render one recognizable, and against those who are not, who are instead alienable" (2015, p. 813). We might therefore consider that being Othered is akin to being made into the object of another.

9. The denotation of the term "pseudoscience" essentially just refers to any person or enterprise that misleadingly purports to follow the tenets of science. However, its connotation and typical usage are much broader than that and, arguably, much more powerful functionally, conveying that anyone or anything referred to with the slur is uncritical, illogical, debased, or gullible, on one hand, or on the other hand, is a bad actor or intentionally disinforming and leading the public astray, and in need of swift and total censorship.

Chapter 1

1. It has been reported that between 2 percent and 4 percent of modern genetic material in anatomically modern humans is of Neanderthal inheritance (e.g., Sykes, 2014). Such a ratio is relatively common in individuals that are outside of sub-Saharan Africa, such as Europeans and Asians.

2. On the other hand, following the unfolding through which Western culture has often appropriated language, myth has become within the European psyche the antithesis of this: rather than being connected to reality, myth is defined by its non-reality or fiction. For example, as field investigator, content curator and creator, and author Brian King-Sharp reflected on a prior conversation with evolutionary anthropologist Hogan Sherrow, he queried the latter scholar about his interest in the subject of Sasquatch. Sherrow had responded by talking "about the mythology and the folklore of Bigfoot," to which King-Sharp considered in retrospect, "He's talking about Bigfoot as being a myth and folklore, so he doesn't believe in Bigfoot" (King-Sharp & Totherow, 2024, March 22, 19:39–19:48). Thus, we have an illustration of how myth, folklore, and the ontologically fictious tend to be equated within this particular collective psyche. In essence, following the insightful words of Cutchin (2025, p. 248), myth and legend end up being both true and fictious at once, while being particularly imbued with the anti-structural within "the colonial mind."

3. Xenophobia is the fear of others, and is related to ethnocentrism (Carroll, 2018).

4. We will return to the matter of teems later in the book, but for now, suffice to say that they are extreme emotional memories (e.g., due to traumatic environmental events) that can become encoded in DNA such that subsequent generations can be more responsive to sensory cues and therefore better able to survive.

5. BPMs, or basic perinatal matrices, are essentially archetypal blueprints for the ways in which the psyche can perceive situations as relevant to confinement or release, specifically defined by four phases of the birthing process (i.e., BPM I–IV), which deal with themes of unity, confinement, struggle, and emergence (Grof, 2012; Roberts & Winkelman, 2015). These themes serve as a bridge to the transpersonal, collective levels of the psyche and provide a foundation for the COEXes.

6. This is the same aforementioned Boris Porshnev/Pourshnev.

7. That position informs my own no-kill position (outside of cases of one's own clear and imminent death) as well when it comes to some investigators' attempts to procure a Sasquatch body. A pro-kill approach is untenable.

8. The author distinguishes between Cro-Magnons, whom he refers to as a transitional stage of modern humans, and present-day humans, or us, whom he refers to as fully modern humans.

9. If there is truly genetic overlap between humans and homins, then *xenogeneic* (i.e., carried over from another species) transmission of infectious diseases may be a significant threat in the case of interaction between these two groups.

10. Malfunctions of electrical equipment are a staple of interactions with non-human entities (e.g., King-Sharp, 2025, January 9, 20:30). The outcome often ends up being the production of evidence that is either inconclusive or non-existent. For example, "*blobsquatches*" are, at least at times, said to be the apparent result of such interference. Blobsquatches are the colloquial term for those pictures of purported homins that are so blurry or grainy so as to be inconclusive if not frustratingly unconvincing as evidence in support of these beings.

11. Importantly, Baranchok (2021, p. 78) states that a better term for the construct than "genetic memory" might be "genetic behavior" or "genetic conditioning," suggesting the following: "So many of the manifestations of so-called "genetic memories" or the collective unconscious are behavioral manifestations. Even those that apparently reflect past knowledge (from a previous life, for example) don't arise out of a conscious recollection but typically are spontaneously displayed or known." Such an assertion dovetails with Vendramini's (2009) teem theory and underlines the typically non-conscious aspect of memorial activation.

Chapter 2

1. In 1996, the journal *Psychological Inquiry* published a special issue (i.e., volume 7, number 2) that dealt with the subject of UFO abductions. Much of the content dismissed the phenomenon to varying degrees by proposing psychosocial or psychoanalytic models of functioning (Taylor & Francis, 1996).

2. This approach is evinced in the pendulum swinging back toward such methods within the ontological turn of anthropology, which concerns the explicit appreciation of non-Western modes of thinking and understanding reality.

3. While the foot measurements were derived from footprint casts, other variables (e.g., height) were estimates based on eyewitness reports.

4. Data scientist Terrestrial has found that, among a sample of 1,600 cases, perceived height is significantly positively correlated with fear reported by eyewitnesses, where as reported height increases, so does the level of fear (Sasquatch Data Project, 2025).

5. Of note, the image that Vendramini and Balseiro present of Neanderthals stands in stark contrast to many of the depictions of these hominins, many of which have presented our evolutionary cousins as slightly different versions of ourselves—hairier, stooped, and less refined, but still clearly human.

6. Hairy breasts are also noted on Patty, the subject in the PGF from 1967.

7. It is not entirely clear here how Green distinguished gray from light in color. Additionally, a considerable number of narratives elsewhere (e.g., in Eurasia) have reported red-haired beings as well (e.g., McGrath, 2022). Following my general thesis, it may be that xenophobic impulses toward redheads that have persisted into modern times are not just due to human-human interactions

within the scope of history and may in part be due to negative interactions with red-haired homins in humanity's deep pre-history.

8. The Class A report is based on potentially verifiable *physical* evidence. However, I posit that an underacknowledged area of inquiry involves those psychic impressions, intentional and otherwise, that are made during so-called mindspeak (e.g., Noël, 2019) as well as visions and dreams involving homins. Further, modification of the current classification system (e.g., borrowing from the Close Encounter classification; Hynek, 1972) may be warranted if enough evidence is systematically uncovered in support of this sub-type of homin entity encounter.

9. Though it does not seem to comprise the majority of color in reports, skin color that witnesses perceive to be more or less the same hue as is seen among the average person of European descent is also reported with at least some small degree of frequency throughout the world (e.g., Harrison, 2021, March 27, 14:47). Further, Alex, a rather prominent and presumably reputable experiencer who has shared his encounters during a number of episodes of the *Bigfoot Society* podcast, has discussed his own childhood sighting of a large, albino Sasquatch with "weird pink skin" and "reddish pink eyes" like those that rabbits with albinism exhibit (Byron, 2023, October 22, 10:00–10:22). The sight "scared the living hell out of" him (10:15–10:18) and was "absolutely friggin' terrifying" (12:22–12:24), and so much so that despite the decades that had intervened since the encounter, Alex apologized to Jeremiah (the host) for sweating and shaking during the retelling, stating "That thing…will haunt me 'til the day I die" (20:37–20:42). This particular experiencer had also been able to meet and network with various luminaries in cryptozoology and hominology. One of those individuals was Peter Byrne (1925–2023) who, according to Alex, thought that his encounter was genuine.

10. The episode in question was episode 708. With few exceptions, each episode of the show is dedicated to interviewing at least one person who shares their experience.

11. Koffmann (2015a) provides a key wherein she states that "k" stands for the regions of Kabarda, Balkaria, Karachai, and the like, "x" refers to undetermined gender, and juveniles are designated by "Δ" (p. 94).

12. The audio clip in the LeGro episode simply referred to as "Come here, Kaya" is described and played just under two hours into the episode.

13. It should be noted that Coleman and Huyghe (2006, p. 150) draw attention to the fact that two types of beings—unknown pongids and what the authors refer to as true giants—are at times given the appellation "yowie," potentially conflating different entities into one.

14. An experiencer's narrative describes the grasping action of the foot that is allowed by the mid-tarsal break in (Cundiff, 2021, September 27, 44:13).

15. While some reports of homins wearing clothes have persisted in the oral and written literature (e.g., Green & Coy, 2002; Short, n.d.), I suspect that these occurrences are not frequent enough for this mention of a "little hat" to literally refer to a hat. An analogy can be seen in the stone giant lore that we consider elsewhere. However, if any homins were known to more frequently sport clothing or other accessories, I would suspect that they would do so in areas such as Alaska and other northern climes like where the Gilyuk are said to live, due to the more extreme cold encountered in such regions.

16. While the term "Bigfoot community" is often used, I prefer to use "Bigfooting community" or even the rather awkward "Sasquatching community" to denote the various enthusiasts, investigators, scholars, researchers, and skeptics who have found themselves drawn to the subject of Sasquatch and dedicate some degree of time and energy into interacting with other individuals who do the same, focusing on engagement (i.e., consumption, production, and/or critique) with social media, articles, video essays, podcasts, documentaries, museums, and other media related to the subject. The term Bigfoot is treated with a gerund (i.e., the suffix, "ing") to emphasize that to be a member of the community requires some degree of relatively consistent action, and also to distinguish those human individuals who pursue the subject of Sasquatch from a group of Sasquatch themselves (i.e., what may be termed a "Bigfoot community"). Lastly, due to the varied epistemological and ontological stances in the community about what Sasquatch is and how the pursuit of discovery should be carried out, as well as the extent to which members do or do not demonstrate cognitive flexibility around their own thinking and that of others, some individuals have found the need to leave said community either quietly or rather publicly.

17. Alley implies that Markotic's word should be given extra weight given the fact that the latter man had obtained two Doctors of Philosophy—one Ph.D. in cultural anthropology, and one Ph.D. in physical anthropology—with each one allowing him to focus on a different side of the question of the existence of homins (Hajicek & Hajicek, 2024, March 20).

18. Chiropractor, author, BFRO investigator, and podcast host Russ Jones notes that *kleptoparasitism* (i.e., the practice whereby one organism intentionally steals food that another organism has procured or produced) is a behavior that is often noted in Sasquatch encounters (Jones, 2021), and may be supported by the use of *perches* (i.e., in Jones' coining, areas that provide opportunity to spy upon humans as well as offer easy egress; Jones, 2021). Such stealthy behavior is noted throughout Indigenous American as well as European American accounts, both old and new.

19. Due to his groundbreaking work on relocating the Ape Canyon site, Marc Myrsell was named the 2023 "Bigfooter of the Year" by Daniel Perez,

editor and publisher of the longest-running periodical on the subject, the *Bigfoot Times* (https://www.bigfoottimes.net/).

20. These are sounds that have been hypothesized to be produced by Sasquatch striking wood on wood or by some other mechanism of sound-production. These auditory phenomena are also called *tree knocks*. As an example, you are invited to listen to the brief audio clip from 1:15:31–1:15:38 in "The Last Frontier" (Breedlove, 2023, December 31).

21. A minority of the reports of bluff charges by male Sasquatch describe the beings having an erect penis and urinating while rushing toward the eyewitness. Not incidentally, male gorillas and other great apes have been noted to also be erect when bluff charging. Such posturing can be a sign of aggression (e.g., Short, n.d., p. 19) to assert dominance or dominion in the presence of a potential threat. If humans—and particularly males—urinate around trees or in the vicinity of Sasquatch as has been reported (e.g., Short, n.d., pp. 80–81), then said behavior may reasonably be interpreted as an act of aggression or attempt to establish dominance by these homins. Given that one of the prevailing claims for the existence of Sasquatch has been that reports of these homins support a great ape hypothesis, if people who report this rather specific behavior tied to bluff charges were fabricating their story, it would indeed be a creative and clever element for them to include, potentially increasing the perceived legitimacy of their narrative.

22. Reports of vocalizations (so-called *vocals* within the Bigfooting community) attributed to Sasquatch include them sounding like a woman being murdered (Roehl, 2022, May 2, 14:42–14:53).

23. While I have not heard of anyone confirming with a homin that the meaning of this behavior is meant to move interlopers out of the area, Carpenter's claim is a reasonable one given that this kind of behavior is observed elsewhere among hominoids and is interpreted the same.

24. The account of Kasandra Jacksen is one such encounter wherein pebbles were hurled at her back by an 8-foot-tall, hirsute biped who reeked of an awful smell. The incident took place at Pitt Lake, British Columbia while Jacksen and a male friend camped near the lake. Hammerson Peters summarizes the narrative and states that it was the first detailed Sasquatch encounter investigated by the BCSCC [British Columbia Scientific Cryptozoology Club], as noted in the files of Peters' friend, the late eminent cryptozoologist Gary Mangiacopra, whose archives Peters now possesses and has made available for free online (Peters, 2024, May 19).

25. Some of the most intriguing of the sign attributed to Sasquatch are the limb and tree twists, so called because they appear to be the result of a tremendous amount of torque being applied to wood, some of which is at least several inches thick, causing it to twist. For example, Chief Stickman attributed the twisting of a birch sapling of about 4 inches in diameter and 10 feet tall to Gilyuk, the cannibal Hairy Man of the Dene Nation. These structures are found in the absence of machinery that could have been responsible.

26. For more in-depth discussion of the PGF, I recommend Christopher Murphy's (2010) text, Coleman's (2003) text, and Jeffrey Meldrum's (2006) text.

27. This research is also discussed in the History Channel show *The Proof is Out There*, and specifically on episode 13 of season 2 (Gabriel, 2021, December 3), which presents a thoughtful and thorough episode on the following topics: a) research that Meldrum, Munns, and Tien (2022) conducted on the 1967 PGF, b) the 2021 Yowie thermal footage, and c) other relevant, potential evidence. For example, zoologist Floyd E. Hayes has shifted his opinion, instead conceding that the PGF might be genuine rather than fabricated after viewing some of the new analyses that are shared in the episode (Gabriel, 2021, December 3).

28. It is interesting to note that in both the PGF and the Freeman footage, the men had been casing the area where the incidents took place beforehand and had actually been looking for evidence in the form of footprints or a sighting when the encounter occurred. The same intention—to document evidence of a homin—led to what is perhaps the most well-known videographic evidence of a skunk ape, taken by Stacy Brown, Jr., and Stacy Brown, Sr., in 2012 (Blackburn, 2023, November 13).

29. Doug Hajicek has stated that no CGI was used in the footage, and that utilizing CGI would have been the only way that this footage could have been reasonably faked (Jevning, 2024, February 19). Moreover, the general appearance of the subject in the film could potentially be categorized within Coleman and Huyghe's (2006) taxonomy as an unknown pongid.

30. Author Levi Machovek (2022, p. 34) has even gone so far as to state that the Myakka Skunk Ape photos are the only visual evidence that rivals the quality of the PGF.

31. Some witnesses describe the conical shape as a "football head," presumably referring to the sagittal crest and/or sloping forehead that some of these beings sport. At just under an hour and 13 minutes into an episode of *Buckeye Bigfoot*, one witness says that the entity running toward him while he drove out of a hunting area "had a big ole' football head" (Warren, 2021, April 23).

Chapter 3

1. Cutchin notes that not all of the characteristics of Class B encounters can be classified as poltergeist-like, and employs a nuanced approach to his own hypothesis, proposing alternative explanations as well.

2. The late parapsychologist William G. "Bill"

Roll coined the term recurrent spontaneous psychokinesis (i.e., RSPK) to refer to the unintentional generation of observable physical effects that are displaced onto the environment via means other than traditional mechanical means (e.g., throwing a ball, knocking a glass over, etc.). Such effects may be the products of non-intentional psi (e.g., Hansen, 2001), or of extreme, repressed and/or suppressed negative emotions that are unable to be healthily expressed in the home or social environment.

3. With the lack of many confirmed visual sightings of Sasquatch actually twisting trees and branches, for example, the idea that the homin phenomenon overlaps with the poltergeist phenomenon leads to numerous interesting questions. One corollary of this insight is that at least a subset of the proposed evidence including tree and branch manipulation is the equivalent of spoon bending and other psychokinetic events within poltergeist cases, just on a much larger scale. Authors have posed some intriguing insights regarding this overlap—ideas which include Christopher Noël's (2023, p. 279) elucidating proposal that both humans and homins may manifest to varying degrees of tangibility in the three-dimensional reality that incarnate members of these groups occupy. Specifically, Noël hypothesizes that Sasquatch "are simply able to more readily manifest themselves after death than we are, to share time and space with their still-living kin and companions—and occasionally with us too" (Noël, 2023, February 16, 6:47–6:59). I find this position—which is stated both on his channel and in his 2023 book—to be quite intriguing, potentially parsimonious, and heuristically valuable regarding the ontological questions (e.g., the noted strangeness associated with reports) that have plagued and even divided much of the Bigfooting community. Indeed, it holds room for both the so-called paranormal theorists as well as the staunchest within the Bigfooting community who are committed to the solely flesh-and-blood hypothesis, and per its overlap with Cutchin's wildnisgeist, may at present be the most effective integrated hypothesis available that attempts to explain the Sasquatch phenomenon.

4. Psychologist Tony Jinks—academic, edge scientist and author, and field investigator—states that paraphysical is a term which applies to entities with characteristics that are "beyond physical" organisms (2019, p. 14).

5. The menehune may be, through some lenses, Little People, or perhaps what Coleman and Huyghe (2006, p. 29) refer to as Proto-Pygmies. This class of beings tends to not be reported above 5.5 feet tall.

6. Personas as well-known as Les Stroud of the popular show *Survivorman* have reported experiencing mindspeak (about 56 minutes into the episode), light orbs (about an hour and 12 minutes in), and more, and not knowing what to make of the event (Germer, 2019, February 3).

7. *Wétiko* is also known as *witiko*, *wendigo*, *windigo*, etc. (e.g., Forbes, 2011; Johnston, 1995; Peters, 2023; Short, 2024, p. 89).

8. I employ this term here to refer to the process by which a group's ways of being (*culturo*, culture) are eaten or consumed (*phagy*, to eat). In other words, it is an extreme form of appropriation wherein the culture ways of a host or substrate are taken in, metabolized, and extricated for the sole benefit of the consuming body; additionally, the substrate itself (which in this case, would be the Neanderthals themselves) is also fed upon (e.g., through physical and relational aggression) to the point where it is no longer able to maintain its integrity as it once did. Therefore, culturophagy may be argued to be a particularly virulent manifestation of the cannibal spirit.

9. Yurugu is particularly known for his impetuousness, as he climbed out of the placenta of Amma, the Creator, prematurely. Given that all beings were created with twin female and male souls, Yurugu—solely a male soul—was thereafter bound to be incomplete, and all of his strivings were also incomplete actions against harmony.

10. For example, part of the history and lore of *Gigantopithecus* is that Ralph von Koenigswald, the anthropologist associated with the discovery of this species, came across several molars attributed to this large specimen in an apothecary: touted as dragons teeth, they were being sold as medicine for their curative properties.

11. In other words, for a group under the rather regular potential threat of raids, genetic annihilation, abduction, or murder from another group of larger, stronger, faster beings, the love-hate relationship—coveting their power but fearing contact—may arise.

12. KJ Bear Medicine states that in addition to the entity being *Iimoitapi* (Hairy Man), another explanation of the incident was that the entity was a feral woman who had been expelled from the tribe previously and had stolen the baby.

13. Mindspeak is a term utilized within the Bigfooting community to refer to telepathic communication between Sasquatch and a human (e.g., Byron, 2024, March 25; Cobb & Sasser as cited by Arment, 2019, p. 89; Eichenberger, 2023; Noël, 2019). It can refer to clairvoyant (i.e., referring to visual stimuli, such as in Sophie's encounters; Noël, 2019, p. 99), clairaudient (i.e., referring to auditory stimuli, such as with *Survivorman* Les Stroud's experience; e.g., Noël, 2019, p. 72), and/or clairsentient (i.e., referring to felt stimuli or internal impression, such as in Michael Shepherd or Rich Germeau's experiences; e.g., Eichenberger, 2024, March 28; Noël, 2019, p. 31) reception of information without the aid of the conventional five senses. Clairsentience may be thought of as akin to an intuitive knowing (e.g., Connie Willis' experience of mindspeak; Noël, 2019, pp. 67–69). As Noël insightfully collates the works of eminent scholars such as Diane Hennacy, Rupert Sheldrake, Dean Radin, and David Bohm, drawing them into the homin phenomenon,

mindspeak may evince resonance with the kinds of fields that these authors discuss—or perhaps even the longbody alluded to elsewhere (Aanstoos, 1986; Porter, 2008; Roll, 1987). Generally speaking, reports of mindspeak tend toward neutral if not positive emotional tone and quality conveyed between homin and human (e.g., Richard Taylor/Hucklebridge's riveting experience with at Arla Williams' site in Oklahoma; Eichenberger, 2023; Noël, 2019), though there are reports of negative or even violent emotional tone as well (e.g., Roehl, 2023, October 27, 21:28–21:42).

Chapter 4

1. Cutchin (2025) provides an insightful summary of the many overlaps between the behavior and nature of the Predator and that of Sasquatch.

2. SunBôw has focused on Indigenous and traditional teachings and their relation to entities such as Sasquatch and the re-discovery of ancient wisdom (Bignell, 2023, October 19).

3. The two experiencers saw something that seemed to have cloaked, and which two Sasquatch kept away from the men as the latter were posted in oak trees on deer stands. However, the hunters were not sure quite what the entity was that had cloaked, and it may not have been a Sasquatch at all. With that said, there are enough Sasquatch encounter narratives involving perceived cloaking to warrant that there may well be some sort of basis to these reports beyond hoaxing or witness misperception.

4. Eyeglow has been reported in the annals of anthropology and biology since at least the 1920s. Humans spending significant time in the dark or living absent non-natural sources of light (i.e., not sun, moon, and stars) illustrate this remarkable feature rather well. For example, Singh and Zingg (1942, pp. 19–22) reflect on some extraordinary accounts of eyeglow of the colors of red and blue at the least, and state that this characteristic is found across races and in a variety of ecological conditions (i.e., among feral children, among adults who begin spending significant time in the dark, etc.). These reports appear to be genuine despite the fact that the tapetum lucidum (i.e., the membrane in the eye allowing for eyeshine in several primates such as the slow loris) is absent in the *Homo* genus and within the great apes and higher primates. Such examples overlap with Vendramini's (2009, p. 74) position on nocturnal vision in Neanderthals (although in his case, he posits a tapetum lucidum having convergently evolved in these beings due to its adaptive value in other nocturnal predators) and help to establish insightful precedents for accounts of homins bearing similar characteristics. For those interested in further information on the history of theorizing about this interesting and adaptively useful characteristic of the human eye, I would recommend looking into the extramission or emission theory of eyesight/vision, including literature on *scopaesthesia* (i.e., the sense of being stared at) by Rupert Sheldrake (e.g., Sheldrake, 2003; Sheldrake & Smart, 2023), Callum Cooper (2021), and other scholars. Indeed, Sheldrake and Smart (2023) have reiterated that data suggest that scopaesthesia seems to be most common when men, who tend to present more of a physical threat than do women, stare at a subject in public places. Such evidence suggests that the subject is being alerted to a potential threat—a matter that is directly relevant to the oft-reported occurrence of Sasquatch experiencers feeling uneasy and that they are being watched or stared at, particularly when the perceived gender of said homin is noticed.

5. As a point of clarity, some of those members of the Bigfooting community who subscribe to the flesh-and-blood hypothesis and think that the most likely scenario involves the homins being non-human great apes refer to themselves as "apers" (Lewis & Bartlett, 2025; Penford Media, 2024, April 16).

6. For anyone who has seen Vantablack, an array of carbon nanotubules that absorbs close to 100 percent of all visible light and which can be used as a coating, sensing the odd nature of the substance can require some getting used to. I would imagine that seeing a humanlike being who appears to be virtually coated in Vantablack would be an incident that is particularly unsettling, since per one set of epistemological frames, neither homins nor a nigh-perfectly black material should exist.

7. There are enough incidents and narratives from Indigenous and European America that involve people explicitly being warned to take caution when berry-picking or of encounters occurring while picking salmonberries, huckleberries, blueberries, blackberries, and the like to warrant more scrutiny (e.g., Paulides, 2017). Indeed, many Indigenous American narratives explicitly state that people have gone missing while berry-picking due to shape-shifting spirits who look like hairy bipeds or due to Hairy Man (e.g., Smyth, 2024, July 7).

8. The matter of breathing is another interesting aspect of the lore surrounding Sasquatch. Narratives wherein the witness is close enough to homins often report the sound of labored breathing as though the being has been running for a long distance.

9. Without further information, it is quite difficult if not actually impossible to determine what the process is that has led eyewitnesses to make these pronouncements. With that said, it is a helpful mental exercise to think about the mechanisms that may be at play in these reports.

10. This same experiencer was told later that night that there had been a large group of these Sasquatch-like homins who lived in the area and that their kind had lived alongside the Choctaw since time immemorial. It is important to note that, due to the Choctaw's forced removal from their ancestral lands in the eastern United

States and relocation to lands west of the Mississippi River, that if there is narrative truth behind this accounting, then the Choctaw were aware of homins both in their ancestral lands *and* in their newer home. Such an assertion gives further credence to the reports of homins being reported throughout the contiguous United States.

11. Mike does not elaborate on this point; however, my interpretation is that the word "stubs or something" refers to places along the trunk of the tree where he had pruned the branches, and that the Sasquatch was somehow imitating those pruned branches along the trunk of the tree. I would encourage the interested reader to watch the interview, as Sybilla Irwin's paintings are vibrant and illustrative attempts to capture Mike's experience.

12. However, veteran field investigator Steve Kulls states that he sought to determine whether any primates were escaped from zoos, for example, and was able to rule out any of the great apes as likely sources for the subject in the film (History, 2024, March 9).

13. As with the potential vocal production of so-called wood or tree knocks, one eyewitness in Alaska has stated that a homin "popping its teeth" sounds like rocks being struck together (Roehl, 2022, May 2, 7:52–8:48). Similar reports are discussed elsewhere by experiencers such as hunters (e.g., Byron, 2025, March 7, 57:00–1:00:07).

14. For example, co-founder of Project Zoobook, Amy Bue, states that some people have hypothesized that the sound is more like a "mouth pop" (Breedlove, 2025, April 14, 25:11–25:12).

15. I offer my thanks to guest Dana Beasley and her son Sam for bringing awareness to this audio recording (Byron, 2025, April 15).

16. While Blackburn notes that the Cowman narrative *may* be fictional, many elements of the story jibe with reports from elsewhere in the Sasquatch lore, such as the infamous Ruby Creek incident.

17. Dzonoqua is both a protectress and a cannibal giant, female embodiment of the guardian of the creative force, as well as an arbiter of taboo. She can be seen at the base of totem poles and is a very important figure within Indigenous American cultural systems.

18. Further, as Doug Hajicek has stated, there is sufficient evidence to be able to differentiate Sasquatch sounds from those that humans and other beings produce (King-Sharp, 2023, May 5).

19. Field investigator Barbara "Barb" Shupe has referred to a milder form of being zapped as being "sizzled" (Eichenberger, 2024, August 15, 12:12).

20. Prolonged as well as shorter-term effects are reported. About 20 minutes into her full interview for *A Flash of Beauty*, Sonya Zohar describes the physiological effects of being zapped during her encounter. She experienced the aftereffects for at least two weeks afterward (Eichenberger, 2024, January 1).

21. If you are interested in hearing what such a noise may sound like, I invite you to listen to an example in the audio recording played from 1:10:15–1:10:24 in the *Small Town Monsters* documentary titled "The Last Frontier" (Breedlove, 2023, December 31).

Chapter 5

1. It may surprise those who are less familiar with Sasquatch reports that when teeth are seen by the eyewitness, by and large, they do not tend to include descriptions of projecting canines. In fact, while there are definitely some exceptions (e.g., in Alaska; Breedlove, 2023, December 31), the opposite tends to be the case wherein homins are often said to have large, flat teeth without clearly noticeable incisors/eye teeth. Where scholars such as Alley (2018, p. 277) have noted that the great apes known to Western science do in fact tend to have large canines, the matter of homin ontology necessarily comes into further question.

2. Bear Chief relates that narrative as well during the same episode.

3. Newton (2005) aptly notes that "Mayan tribes-men knew [el sisemité] as Qetcux ("abductor")" (p. 428) and that the being seems to depict a tropical-type Bigfoot. The being is said to be "taller than the tallest man" (p. 428) and to have an appearance somewhere between that of a human and an ape.

4. It is a good thing that Dodds has captured this narrative because, at the time of the writing of this manuscript, the link to the Mausó (1999) source is no longer active.

5. It should be noted that the villagers in *The Mob Song* from said film willingly admit that their violent uprising and attempt to kill the Beast is driven by fear after Gaston goads them into invading the former's castle.

6. Due to the rather marked time difference between the encounter and the retelling, it should be noted that John Green (2004b), who interviewed Ostman about his experience, stated that in preparation for the interview, Ostman went about collecting everything that he could about that time in his life, and that he was only sure of the main elements of the story. Such a matter is important not just due to skeptical or debunking claims of the veracity of Ostman's account, but in that Ostman's statements about the validity of his own memory are in line with scholarship on memory which state that central details are typically more valid and reliable than are peripheral details (cf. Berntsen, 2002; Safer, Christianson, Autry, & Österlund, 1998). For people who have experienced a traumatic event and desire to flee, it is possible that essential information about the event will be retained with greater quality than less essential information. When it comes to this matter, Herlihy and colleagues state that the malleability of autobiographical memories can make those memories "broadly true" in their scope, even if they are not

"strictly accurate" in terms of the veracity of every single detail (2012, p. 671). Essentially, the gist of the event in question can be retained in memory even if the specifics are not.

7. For example, the red-haired *curupira* of the Guaraní of Brazil, who is said to sexually assault women and to kidnap children (Newton, 2005, p. 124), is generally known as having backwards facing feet. This feature may indicate the great stealth of entities such as curupira and the djinn, or the trouble that humans have capturing or following them.

8. Elsewhere (e.g., Porshnev, 2000, p. 16), lore persists that homins are essentially humans who are outcast by society due to any number of misdeeds or incongruities with civilized or otherwise healthy and well-adjusted folk.

9. As of the writing of this text, I have had no luck finding a newspaper article relating these events.

10. As stated previously, reports of threat of death and more communicated by mindspeak have been indicated by others as well (e.g., Roehl, 2023, October 27, 21:28–21:42). Additionally, according to Coy, the rest of Blackie's family treats him like an outcast and "like he's dangerous," and Fox had run Blackie out of the area for years (Totherow, 2020, November 9, 47:43–47:45). It is important to note that one might extrapolate from Coy's comments that Blackie had broken a taboo, at least as far as this family group was concerned, and was thereafter treated accordingly. Following our earlier considerations about Elder Brother and the cannibal spirit, Blackie has come to represent a potential that is to be feared by humans and, perhaps by homins as well. Further, Janice also reports having been disturbed to see Blackie masturbating occasionally when she was younger (Green & Coy, 2002, p. 158).

11. Unfortunately, Janice's daughter is not the only person who has reported being psychically assaulted in a similar fashion (Arnold & Agliolo, 2020, August 1; Roehl, 2023, October 27, 21:28–21:43). For example, Mark Barton describes being telepathically raped by several entities who had approached him while he was alone at a cabin in the woods one evening in 2020 (Arnold & Agliolo, 2020, August 1, 20:35–21:15). Part of the message that he received was that he was prey being hunted for sport. Understandably, recounting the event five months later was a challenging experience for him. Deeply traumatic experiences like those of the young girl in Tennessee and Mark's are the kind that can become embedded indelibly in individual and collective memory and can contribute to the pervasive death anxiety that is at times associated with homin encounters.

12. The many tales of homins stealing human food, let alone abducting humans, also illustrate the potentially transgressive tendencies among our hirsute neighbors. The flipside of this tension, wherein transgression is visited upon homins by humans, is an important matter. However, such consideration goes beyond the remit of the present volume.

13. Jason's description of the young Sasquatch who was so joyous and full of love is quite detailed given that the single encounter was long enough (i.e., at least seven to eight minutes) from quite close (i.e., about 30 feet away).

14. The apparent musculoskeletal structure of the subject that is discussed by Munns and Meldrum (2013) and is illustrated in Payan, Jr. (2022, February 14), for example, indicates that a hoax is exceedingly unlikely.

15. Artist RobRoy Menzies's depictions of the being are included on pages 24 and 25. In addition to Molly Hart Lebherz, editor of the 2024 publication of the *De Facto Sasquatch*, Menzies encouraged Short to include her rarely discussed encounters in the book. Thankfully, they (along with Menzies' depictions) are now preserved therein for posterity.

16. Forth (2022, p. 35) also notes that breasts capable of being slung over the shoulder is a feature attributed to homins around the world, and that it is also a characteristic at times noted in descriptions of humans such as Hottentots and Patagonians.

17. According to Cavalline's (2020) documentary, the entry for *The Creature* in the Catalog of Copyright Entries states that Jan Klement is a pseudonym for the book's publisher: John Tomikel (Third Series 1976—July–December; Library of Congress Copyright Office). Said information was uncovered by private investigator, author, and field investigator Steve Kulls (Cavalline, 2020) and was shared with me by the inimitable Sasquatch archivist Todd Prescott. When the book was initially published, Klement's background was shrouded in mystery. And while Klement's identity has been clarified, I posit that not only is the question of the authenticity of the book itself still unclear, but that even if it is a fabricated tale, the above account may at least indicate an interest among some humans in Sasquatch sexuality. Moreover, as Hansen (2001) has stated, proper identification of hoaxes can help to establish a more formal scientific paradigm within a discipline. With that said, due to the book's place within the lore of the Bigfooting community, I have decided to cite it to further illustrate the anti-structural character and ontological ambiguity of the homin phenomenon, as well as to indicate another case wherein Sasquatch sex is discussed explicitly.

18. Other witnesses report urinating on themselves as well (e.g., Eichenberger, 2023, December 20, 43:41; England, 2024, October 6, 13:23; Ramirez, 2024, June 26; Short, n.d., p. 181), as the fright of the incident induces release of control of one's bodily functions. Baranchok (2021, p. 135) notes that people can "get the piss scared out of us" or can be "scared shitless," illustrating the extent to which bodily functions can be compromised in the presence of these entities when fight-or-flight response is activated.

19. Some experiencers report arousal and urination going hand in hand during encounters, such as in the harrowing and tragic encounter that late experiencer David shares (Germer, 2022, July 1, 48:28–49:10). David recounts an encounter from over 40 years ago at the time (i.e., in 1981) from northern Louisiana. As the male homin stood in front of him began working himself up into a "bloodlust," he was "half-aroused" and was urinating on David's pants (48:38). Similar to Claire's encounter (Germer, 2019, July 31), for example, this detail seems oddly extraneous to add if people are merely misinterpreting their experiences or are fabricating them.

20. Narratives of homins bringing humans wood appear elsewhere in the literature and lore (e.g., Germer, 2018, September 8) as well.

21. Again, the idea that menstrual blood attracts the attention of Sasquatch is apparent in other narratives as well. Experiencer Heather Simpson notes that she perceives that the only reason that she was being followed by a male Sasquatch at a campsite in Montana was because she was on her monthly cycle (Warren, 2024, April 2).

22. At about 24 minutes into an interview, experiencer Dom elaborates on an encounter that he and his girlfriend at the time had in Mesa, Colorado sometime between 2009 and 2011. While having sex outside on the top of his truck one night, they started hearing heavy breathing right next to them. Dom states that he and his girlfriend speculated that the sex and menstruation may well have drawn in the attention of the Sasquatch (Byron, 2024, January 12). And reporting to *The Bigfoot Project* at about two hours and 17 minutes into an episode of the show, another experiencer simply referred to as "S" awoke around midnight to a large, male Sasquatch standing over her while she was camping with family in the Pisgah National Forest of North Carolina in late spring 2015. Her brother, father, and husband were sleeping around her, and S felt that the being had singled her out because she was "on her time of the month and the creature could smell it" (Smyth, 2022, December 23, 2:17:42–2:17:49), and experienced irrational fear of the being "carry[ing] [her] off into the woods, wrapped up like a wonton in [her] hammock" (Smyth, 2022, December 23, 2:17:32–2:17:36).

23. According to Thomas Sewid of Kwakwaka'wakw and Cree descent, Bukwas is "actually the keeper of the Ghost World—the small, bipedal, hair-covered creature about three or four feet high" that is honored during potlatches (Lynn, 2024, October 4, 14:25). Thus, Bukwas overlaps with but is separate from Dzonokwa and Sasquatch.

Chapter 6

1. I would encourage the inquiring reader to take a pause at this junction to allow that revelation to sink in. Sonya did not seem to be an otherwise irrational or illogical person, and her response to Jeremiah is evidence of the kind of deep and abiding drive that many people feel when it comes to the phenomenon.

2. Friending may also occur when experiencers only return to the site of the encounter if someone else goes with them. Additionally, animals have been shown to engage in friending behaviors, such as when deer being chased by Sasquatch run up to hunters and remain beside them.

3. While it goes beyond the remit of this text, the opposite may well have been the case too, with humans at times eradicating or coming close to wiping out homins. Indeed, despite some scholars suggesting that descendants of Neanderthals still exist, as Vendramini (2009) has posited, Neanderthals—our hairy bipedal predators—were eventually brought to their knees and eliminated by Cro-Magnons.

4. Relevant to our discussion, yet lying beyond the remit of the present text, Cutchin (2025, p. 76) states that retrocausality (à la Eric Wargo) may play a role in the paranormal, wherein trauma in the future may influence an entity encounter (e.g., with a homin) in the past.

5. Interestingly, there is a significant enough subset of literature regarding homins digging through trash cans, dumpsters, and garbage dumps in places that are as geographically disparate as Staten Island (i.e., "Trashsquatch"; Byron, 2024, July 8, 29:10) and Oregon (à la Stan Avery; Eichenberger, 2021).

6. Not incidentally, the very term "monstrous" derives from a Latin word meaning "to warn" (e.g., Giamatti & Asma, 2023, April 26, 8:21–8:30), which is a matter that we will return to in due course as concerns our central subject of interest.

7. It is important to note that food, animals, and shiny objects are precisely those items that have been reported as objects that have been "gifted" between humans and homins at so-called habituation sites in modern narratives.

8. Pfaller (2016) states that "Skanicum" as another variant of "skookum," stating that the term is the most prevalent form among the Indigenous people of the Pacific Northwest of North America for the name of the creature commonly known as Bigfoot or Sasquatch, and also lists "strong terror" and "evil genii" as other translations of the term (p. 10).

9. As I state elsewhere, fortunately, at least in terms of UFO experiencers and the contactee community, the master narrative seems to be changing at present in favor of a more accepting and open dialogue about non-pathologized or dismissive epistemologies to explain people's encounter narratives.

10. Throughout history, narratives of wildmen and wildwomen have been prevalent around the world, such as on the Eurasian landmass. Gregory Forth (2007), for example, discusses how themes and characterizations of wildmen varied both within and outside of European lore. Additionally, it should be noted that the entities mentioned

in Strain's (2008) text may not per se represent contemporary flesh-and-blood or even paranormal representations of Sasquatch, being variously "a man-eating cannibal, horrible monster, a thief, a trickster, a helper, and in a few stories, our creator" (Strain, 2008. p. 11). Indeed, experiencer Emerald Tucker of Aaniiih and Nakoda heritage says that after her encounter with "Silverback," she learned that "Bigfoot comes around for a purpose, you know. It could mean many things in a Native American culture, you know, good or bad. Or could be your helper" (Chief Bear & Upham, 2022, January 6, 14:18–14:27).

11. My colleague poignantly states the following: "I'm not sure why they [i.e., Sasquatch] can't be flesh-and-blood and have paranormal abilities: humans do" (Baranchok, 2024, March 11, 32:38–32:45). Indeed, others such as Ron Morehead (2024) have proffered similar thinking, which is both nuanced as well as accurate per the parapsychological literature.

Chapter 7

1. It is noteworthy that Levy's (2013) malignant egophrenia, which he ties to the Indigenous American formulation of the cannibal spirit, is suggested to arise as a daemonic force. Levy takes a good deal of inspiration from Jung.

2. Ani (2007, pp. 13–15) coined the term *utamawazo* to convey something akin to the thought structures that are borne out of a person's ideologies, worldviews, and larger cultural milieu.

Bibliography

Aanstoos, C. (Fall/Winter 1986). Psi and the phenomenology of the longbody. *Theta: The Journal of the Psychical Research Association, 13/14*(3/4), 49–51. https://docs.wixstatic.com/ugd/dd736b_11697bc18b054d7e871889f29e8971a4.pdf.

Aboultaif, E.W., & Tabar, P. (2019). National versus communal memory in Lebanon. *Nationalism and Ethnic Politics, 25*(1), 97–114. https://doi.org/10.1080/13537113.2019.1565183.

Abrahams, B. (director). (2017). *Love & saucers.* Curator Pictures.

Adams, W.W. (w/ D.R. Loy). (2023). *A wild and sacred call: Nature-psyche-spirit.* SUNY Press.

Allen, S. (2018, September). The science of awe [Executive summary]. *Greater Good Science Center.* https://ggsc.berkeley.edu/images/uploads/GGSC-JTF_White_Paper-Awe_FINAL.pdf.

Allen, T.D. (2008). Cheikh Anta Diop's Two Cradle Theory: Revisited. *Journal of Black Studies, 38*(6), 813–829. https://www.jstor.org/stable/40035025.

Alley, J.R. (2018). *Raincoast Sasquatch: The Bigfoot/Sasquatch records of southeast Alaska, coastal British Columbia & northwest Washington from Puget Sound to Yakutat.* Hancock House.

Alley, J.R. (2021). *Brushes with Bigfoot: Sasquatch behaviors reported in close encounters, Native and non-Native perspectives.* Muskeg Media.

Ambrose-Meyer Entertainment & Educational Channel. (2024, March 10). The mysteries of Bigfoot. In *Ambrose-Meyer Entertainment & Educational Channel.* YouTube. https://youtu.be/jLUttWSfuMM?si=7aCrCzAeL8Wv580g.

Ani, M. (2007). *Yurugu: An African-centered critique of European cultural thought and behavior.* Africa World Press.

Anne, M. (Host). (2023, May 28). Sunday special. In *Tactical Bigfoot Research.* YouTube. https://www.youtube.com/watch?v=r3Iiwi6aNcE.

Anne, M. (2024, April 25). "Terrain and Color (TAC): A comparison of subjects and the environment—A look at sighting reports using witness identified color definitions" [personal communication].

Arment, C. (2019). *The historical Bigfoot (Second Ed.).* Greenville, OH: Coachwhip Publications.

Arnold, K. (host), & Agliolo, D. (host). (2020, August 1). Mark Barton from "The Trail to Bigfoot" talks about his terrifying experience with a creature. In *Bigfoot Odyssey.* YouTube. https://www.youtube.com/live/yhohCWLJQIo?si=doF4i7wCQIHhsH8a.

Assmann, J. (2011). Communicative and cultural memory. In P. Meusburger, M. Hefferman, & E. Wunder. (Eds.), *Cultural memories: The geographical point of view* (pp. 15–28). Springer.

Assmann, J., & Czaplicka, J. (1995). Collective memory and cultural identity. *New German Critique,* (65), 125–133. http://www.jstor.org/stable/488538?origin=JSTOR-pdf.

Bader, C.D., Baker, J.O., & Mencken, F.C. (2017). Paranormal America: Ghost encounters, UFO sightings, Bigfoot hunts, and other curiosities in religion and culture. In *Paranormal America (Second edition).* New York University Press.

Bandura, A. (1999). A social cognitive theory of personality. In L. Pervin & O. John (Ed.), *Handbook of Personality (2nd edition)* (pp. 154–196). Guilford Publications. (Reprinted in D. Cervone & Y. Shoda [Eds.], The coherence of personality. Guilford Press.)

Barackman, C. (2024, December 12). A sighting in Skamania. In *North American Bigfoot Center.* YouTube. https://www.youtube.com/watch?v=iuX5F8E68kE&t=62s.

Barackman, C., & Fay, J. (Hosts). (2024, July 15). John Zada (No. 271) [Audio podcast episode]. In *Bigfoot & Beyond with Cliff & Bobo.* Audible. https://www.audible.com/podcast/Ep-271-John-Zada/B0D9GF8ZV5.

Barackman, C., & Fay, J. (Hosts). (2024, November 30). Bonus episode with Gregory Forth. In *Bigfoot & Beyond with Cliff & Bobo.* Spotify. https://open.spotify.com/episode/7goCbOPp7y3lgMeXO1MADv.

Baranchok, J.S. (2021). *Grasping Sasquatch: Prepping for scientific field research.* Hangar 1 Publishing.

Baranchok, J.S. (Host). (2023, December 11). BFRO—Encounter classification explained in detail (No. 13) [Video podcast episode]. In *Grasping Sasquatch.* YouTube. https://www.youtube.com/live/4_qf7Ua8aBE?si=0YDzWdHZlRHfNgfG.

Baranchok, J.S. (Host). (2023, December 18). Tree structures: An experimental design (No. 14) [Video podcast episode]. In *Grasping Sasquatch.*

YouTube. https://www.youtube.com/live/ParBJnKQLXY?si=VvoEcQuM9mjlfEzp.
Baranchok, J.S. (Host). (2024, March 11). "The Ketchum" Bigfoot DNA study-Controversies & questions (No. 26) [Video podcast episode]. In *Grasping Sasquatch*. YouTube. https://www.youtube.com/watch?v=xqvNckb2Bzw.
Barnett, D. L. (Host). (2024, April 21). Jeremiah Byron interview [Video podcast episode]. In Mythical Legends. YouTube. https://www.youtube.com/watch?v=Fx6-AtL0qho.
Bauer, H. (Fall 2022). On the fringe: Where science meets pseudoscience by Michael D. Gordin: Essay Review: Speaking of "pseudo-Science" entails scientism: The importance of not being earnest about science. *Journal of Scientific Exploration, 36*(3), 512–519. https://doi.org/10.31275/20222449.
Bauer, H.H. (2013). Cryptozoology and the trouble with "skeptics" and mainstream pundits. [Review of the book *Abominable science!: Origins of the Yeti, Nessie, and other famous cryptids*, by D. Loxton and D.R. Prothero]. *The Relict Hominoid Inquiry*. https://www.scientificexploration.org/docs/27/jse_27_4_EssayReviewBauerCryptozoology.pdf.
Baxter, L. (2021). *Abandoned: The history and horror of Port Chatham, Alaska*. Alasquatch Publishing.
Bayanov, D. (2012). Historical Evidence for the Existence of Relict Hominoids. *The Relict Hominoid Inquiry, 1*, 23–50. https://www.isu.edu/media/libraries/rhi/essays/Bayanov_rev.pdf.
Bayanov, D. (2014). *Russian hominology: The Bayanov papers-Fact & folklore*. Hancock House Publishers.
Bayanov, D. (2015). Normal science, revolutionary science: Notes on Bryan Sykes' *The Nature of the Beast*. *The Relict Hominoid Inquiry, 4*, 75–78. https://www.isu.edu/media/libraries/rhi/comments-amp-responses/Commentary-on-Sykes.pdf.
Bayanov, D. & Murphy, C.L. (2017). *The making of hominology: A science whose time has come*. Hancock House Publishers.
Bear Chief, C.L., & Upham, L. (Hosts). (2020, July 11). Meeting Blackfeet Bigfoot Medicine. In *Pikuni Bigfoot Storytelling Project*. YouTube. https://youtu.be/kXH-jomNuGs?si=Jq5jbVFPIG6ZnE7B.
Bear Chief, C.L., & Upham, L. (Hosts). (2022, January 6). Native woman encounters Bigfoot by Little Rocky Mountain range on the Fort Belknap Indian Rez. In *Pikuni Bigfoot Storytelling Project*. YouTube. https://www.youtube.com/watch?v=p4EYfweZHTw&t=2632s.
Bear Chief, C.L., & Upham, L. (Hosts). (2023, May 7). 3 scary encounters: Indigenous Sasquatch stories. In *Pikuni Bigfoot Storytelling Project*. YouTube. https://youtu.be/Bl3BQNTv9bc?si=PomenHxfQnKvCcoj.
Bear Chief, C.L., & Upham, L. (Hosts). (2023, May 28). Blackfeet wildland firefighter comes face-to-face with Bigfoot. In *Pikuni Bigfoot Storytelling Project*. YouTube. https://youtu.be/QDVAK7uOk8g?si=I0Y-BX29Bu4JN2B3.
Bear Chief, C.L., & Upham, L. (Hosts). (2024, September 20). Little sisters traumatizing brush with Sasquatch near home in remote mountains on Indian reservation. In *Pikuni Bigfoot Storytelling Project*. YouTube. https://www.youtube.com/watch?v=u1WRYG4HLg4.
Bear Chief, C.L., & Upham, L. (Hosts). (2025, February 1). Winnebago Sasquatch stories: The mystery of the White Beaver homestead. In *Pikuni Bigfoot Storytelling Project*. YouTube. https://www.youtube.com/watch?v=obvC_b8kDwk&t=260s.
Beck, F. (author), & Davenport, E. (illustrator). (1967). *I fought the Apemen of Mt. St. Helens*. Fred Beck.
Belz, M., & Fach, W. (2012). Theoretical reflections on counseling and therapy for individuals reporting ExE. In W.H. Kramer, E. Bauer, & G.H. Hovelmann (Eds.), *Perspectives of clinical parapsychology: An introductory reader* (pp. 168–189). Stichting Het Johan Borgman Fonds.
Bem, D., Tressoldi, P., Rabeyron, T., & Duggan, M. (2015). Feeling the future: A meta-analysis of 90 experiments on the anomalous anticipation of random future events. *F1000Research, 4*, 1–33. https://doi.org/10.12688%2Ff1000research.7177.2.
Bem, D.J. (2011). Feeling the future: experimental evidence for anomalous retroactive influences on cognition and affect. *Journal of Personality and Social Psychology, 100*(3), 407–425. https://doi.org/10.1037/a0021524.
Benchín, F. (2022). On Mystery: explorations on the experience of the numinous. *Journal of Analytical Psychology, 67*(1), 55–72. https://doi.org/10.1111/1468-5922.12776.
Berntsen, D. (2002). Tunnel memories for autobiographical events: Central details are remembered more frequently from shocking than from happy experiences. *Memory & Cognition, 30*(7), 1010–1020. https://doi.org/10.3758/bf03194319.
BFRO. (2002). 1994 Ohio—moaning howl. *BFRO*. https://www.bfro.net/avevid/mjm/ohrec.asp.
BFRO. (n.d.). The 'siege' at Honobia. *BFRO*. https://www.bfro.net/avevid/ouachita/siege-at-honobia.asp.
Bigfoot Encounters. (n.d.b.). *William Roe's sworn affidavit*. http://www.bigfootencounters.com/classics/roe.htm.
Bigfoot Tony (Host). (2017, July 26). The jumping Yeti from Russia video—Breakdown. In *Bigfoot Tony*. YouTube. https://www.youtube.com/watch?app=desktop&v=J-qqSusfE_Y.
Bindernagel, J.A. (1998). *North America's great ape: The sasquatch*. Beachcomber Books.
Bindernagel, J.A., & Hadj-Chikh, L. (2010). *The discovery of Sasquatch: Reconciling culture, history, and science in the discovery process*. Beachcomber Books.
Bindernagel, J.A., & Meldrum, J. (2012). Misunderstandings arising from treating the sasquatch as a subject of cryptozoology. *The Relict Hominoid Inquiry, 2*, 81–102. https://www.isu.edu/media/libraries/rhi/essays/BINDERNAGEL_final.pdf.
Bishop, G. (2016). *It defies language!: Essays on UFOs and other weirdness*. Excluded Middle Press.

Blackburn, L. (Host). (2022, September 13). Bigfoot attacks! [Audio podcast episode]. In *Blackburn's Monstro Bizarro Podcast*. Apple Podcasts. https://podcasts.apple.com/us/podcast/bigfoot-attacks/id1618958655?i=1000579361407.

Blackburn, L. (Host). (2023, November 3). Rise of the Skunk Apes (Part 1) [Audio podcast episode]. In *Blackburn's Monstro Bizarro Podcast*. Apple Podcasts. https://podcasts.apple.com/us/podcast/rise-of-the-skunk-apes-part-1/id1618958655?i=1000633617277.

Blackburn, L. (Host). (2023, November 13). Realm of the Skunk Apes (Part 2) [Audio podcast episode]. In *Blackburn's Monstro Bizarro Podcast*. Apple Podcasts. https://podcasts.apple.com/us/podcast/realm-of-the-skunk-apes-part-2/id1618958655?i=1000634675011.

Blackburn, L. (Host). (2024, October 3). Cowman of Copalis Beach [Audio podcast episode]. In *Blackburn's Monstro Bizarro Podcast*. YouTube. COWMAN of COPALIS BEACH - Monstro Bizarro Ep 19 with Lyle Blackburn—YouTube.

Block, C.M. (2020). *Researching the Paranormal: How to Find Reliable Information about Parapsychology, Ghosts, Astrology, Cryptozoology, Near-Death Experiences, and More*. Rowman & Littlefield Publishers.

Boulier, G.S. (2017). *Witnessing Bigfoot: Flesh and blood, Native American legend, or the devil himself?* Pine Winds Press.

Bowlby, J. (1988). *A secure base: Parent-child attachment and healthy human development*. Basic Books.

Boykin, A.W. (1986). The Triple Quandary and the Schooling of Afro-American Children. In: U. Neisser (Ed.), *The school achievement of minority children* (pp. 57–92). Erlbaum & Associates.

Boykin, A.W., Tyler, K., & Miller, O. (2005). In search of cultural themes and their expressiveness in the dynamics of classroom life. *Urban Education, 40*(5), 521–549. https://doi.org/10.1177/0042085905278179.

Bradley, M. (1973). *The cronos complex I: An enquiry into the temporal origins of human culture and psychology*. Nelson.

Bradley, M. (1991). *The iceman inheritance: Prehistoric sources of Western man's racism, sexism, and aggression*. Kayode Publications.

Brave Heart, M.Y. H., & Chase, J. (2011). Historical trauma among Indigenous peoples of the Americas: Concepts, research, and clinical considerations. *Journal of Psychoactive Drugs, 43*(4), 282–292. http://doi.10.1080/02791072.2011.628913.

Breedlove, S. (Director). (2015). *Minerva Monster*. Small Town Monsters.

Breedlove, S. (Director). (2019a). *Momo: The Missouri Monster*. Small Town Monsters.

Breedlove, S. (director). (2019b). *On the trail of Bigfoot: The legend*. Small Town Monsters.

Breedlove, S. (Director). (2023, September 24). On the trail of Bigfoot: The search—Full movie (Sasquatch evidence and encounters). In *Small Town Monsters*. YouTube. https://youtu.be/54kfvh9eGaA?si=FAN3DR395NPRCTlz.

Breedlove, S. (Director). (2023, December 31). The last frontier: On the trail of Bigfoot—Full movie (Alaskan Sasquatch evidence and encounters). In *Small Town Monsters*. YouTube. https://youtu.be/aWU1ZK5hpAs?si=d7dmr-bF6DkwDNjs.

Breedlove, S. (Director). (2024, March 17). The curse of Sasquatch (Bigfoot: The road to discovery). In *Small Town Monsters*. YouTube. https://www.youtube.com/watch?v=uG6OfbtVbE4.

Breedlove, S. (Director). (2024, June 2). Land of the missing: On the trail of Bigfoot—Full movie (Alaskan Sasquatch and missing people). In *Small Town Monsters*. YouTube. https://youtu.be/QHTMSsWOXok?si=BY1-kz6JzAmFzf8o.

Breedlove, S. (Director). (2024, August 25). They're hiding something!—Sasquatch unearthed: Buckeye Bigfoot (New cover-up evidence). In *Small Town Monsters*. YouTube. https://www.youtube.com/watch?v=UERw6Z2dbfE.

Breedlove, S. (Director). (2024, November 17). Police encounter the Adirondack Sasquatch: The Appalachian Bigfoot Files: (Sightings in New York). In *Small Town Monsters*. YouTube. https://youtu.be/BFc8V7VX4xs?si=d020UgeOJJnFfMnc.

Breedlove, S. (Director). (2024, November 28). The ancients: On the trail of Bigfoot—Full film (New evidence and encounters with Sasquatch). In *Small Town Monsters*. YouTube. https://youtu.be/0_qssglbSt4?si=haNfTOkxgLEKs7jC.

Breedlove, S. (Director). (2025, April 14). The roar behind the ridge—Heartland Sasquatch (vocalizations and audio evidence of Bigfoot). In *Small Town Monsters*. YouTube. https://www.youtube.com/watch?v=2MDX-wCg2ik.

Breedlove, S. (Director). (2025, April 16). The Hell-Town Sasquatch—Bigfoot Decoded (National park creature encounters and evidence). In *Small Town Monsters*. YouTube. https://www.youtube.com/watch?v=7L7Y12mKjMg&t=2541s.

Brewin, C.R., & Andrews, B. (2014). Why it is scientifically respectable to believe in repression: A response to Patihis, Ho, Tingen, Lilienfeld, and Loftus (2014). *Psychological Science, 25*(10), 1964–1966. https://www.jstor.org/stable/pdf/24543939.pdf?casa_token=5dMHtB_8dsMAAAAA:D-CVIHhD0gR0MAsGc_igwFBxWSyLXf7A-9VPjc4_JuMHJIaJDnN_zweZEgV8MSMYay-72wWmwZNd1FhLG879cs8f7K_4l1Mt8tt8O-gY-3mYcO_9uvmRYR0j.

Brewin, C.R., & Andrews, B. (2017). Creating memories for false autobiographical events in childhood: A systematic review. *Applied Cognitive Psychology, 31*, 2–23. https://doi.org/10.1002%2Facp.3220.

Brewster, D. (1970, August). Our last monster. *Seattle Magazine*, 29–33. http://www.bigfootencounters.com/articles/sasquatch2.htm.

Brightman, R. (2015). The return of the Windigo, again. *Semiotic Review, 2*, 1–15. https://www.semioticreview.com/ojs/index.php/sr/article/view/22/22.

Brightman, R.A. (1988). The windigo in the material world. *Ethnohistory*, 337–379. https://www.jstor.org/stable/482140.

Brink, K. (2021). *Hibagon: Japanese Bigfoot (2nd ed.).* [self-published].
Britannica. (n.d.). Hominidae. *Britannica.* https://www.britannica.com/animal/Hominidae.
British Cryptids. (2023, January 1). British cryptids: The woodwose of Cannock Chase. In *British Cryptids.* YouTube. https://youtu.be/loZwFNT8H_s?si=3L-wx1S4aL_AT5NH.
Brost, J. (Director). (2023). *Ci'tonga: Bigfoot, spirits, and faith.* Outkast Paranormal. https://www.youtube.com/watch?v=J0lkBb3CkNQ.
Brown, B., Luci, M., & Larson, C. (Hosts). (2024, March 3). This week in Bigfoot (No. 48) [Video podcast episode]. In *CARC Universal.* YouTube. https://youtu.be/GD8D4TgL4FM?si=IfpJJfjHOFShQclx.
Brown, S., Jr. (Host). (2012, December 1). The Brown footage. In *BigfootStacy.* YouTube. https://youtu.be/Q5WwoO5R5ig?si=SrbYwbLTSuczEKlK.
Brown, S. (Host), & Brown, J. (Host). Central Washington Bigfoot Encounters—New 2024 Sasquatch documentary—Spooky singing recorded. In *Salish Sasquatch.* YouTube. https://youtu.be/MMq0_nfzhP0?si=4GTFggeTkr_knlIR.
Brown, S. (Host), & Brown, J. (Host). (2025, March 4). Area X with Bob and Kathy Strain—Archaeologist's Bigfoot sighting—Giants, Cannibals & Monsters. In *Salish Sasquatch.* YouTube. https://www.youtube.com/watch?v=UHp_tovI96Q&t=696s.
Bruner, J.S. (1990). *Acts of meaning: Four lectures on mind and culture* (Vol. 3). Harvard University Press.
Buhs, J.B. (2009). *Bigfoot: The life and times of a legend.* University of Chicago Press.
Burns, J.W. (1929, April 1). Introducing B.C.'s hairy giants. *MacLean's Magazine* (pp. 9, 61–62). https://cryptozoologicalreferencelibrary.wordpress.com/wp-content/uploads/2020/06/burns-1929.pdf.
Burrow, N. (1924). Social images versus reality. *Journal of Abnormal Psychology & Social Psychology, 19*(3), 230–235. https://static1.squarespace.com/static/60ef8f3b562fab2367f4af5f/t/66c7827ff-f6ec67971ff06ae/1724351103326/Social+Images+versus+Reality+-+T.+Burrow.pdf.
Bynum, E.B. (1994). *The roots of transcendence.* Cosimo Press.
Bynum, E.B. (2012). *Dark light consciousness: Melanin, serpent power, and luminous matrix of reality.* Inner Traditions.
Byrne, P. (1976). *The search for Bigfoot: Monster, myth, or man?.* Pocket Books.
Byron, J. (Host). (2023, February 28). Clifford LaBrecque's bigfoot found: A conversation with David Bakara, owner of the Expedition Bigfoot Museum in Georgia (No. 230) [Audio podcast episode]. In *Bigfoot Society.* YouTube. https://youtu.be/bpUitI0ckt8?si=IGpdk5wcRRi54ka3.
Byron, J. (Host). (2023, August 28). A 4 year standoff with Sasquatch in Rainier, Oregon (No. 293) [Audio podcast episode]. In *Bigfoot Society.* YouTube. https://www.youtube.com/watch?v=z5v75Od-X38&t=595s.
Byron, J. (Host). (2023, September 26). Horrifying hairy man encounters of Alaska with Fred Roehl (No. 322) [Audio podcast episode]. In *Bigfoot Society.* YouTube. https://youtu.be/-NPJQgrwmo?si=wpzM4dk2G1-VHVGa.
Byron, J. (Host). (2023, October 22). "I wanted to scream, but fear gripped me…It was right there, watching me." (No. 343) [Audio podcast episode]. In *Bigfoot Society.* YouTube. https://www.youtube.com/watch?v=7VqcNLrB9iI&list=PLO0PqscYC6r3dvtydfs-091fVz2VGLwgu&index=107.
Byron, J. (Host). (2024, March 25). Something else lived on grandfather's farm in Tennessee! (No. 401) [Audio podcast episode]. In *Bigfoot Society.* YouTube. https://www.youtube.com/watch?v=B9IIhfF-Y6c.
Byron, J. (Host). (2024, May 10). The Bigfoot beast of Wallowa, Oregon (No. 428) [Audio podcast episode]. In *Bigfoot Society.* Audible. https://www.audible.com/es_US/podcast/The-Bigfoot-Beast-of-Wallowa-Oregon/B0D3R91YBJ.
Byron, J. (Host). (2024, July 8). Sasquatch siege of Staten Island! (No. 471) [Audio podcast episode]. In *Bigfoot Society.* YouTube. https://youtu.be/q-ETwDAoPUE?si=Kc2vatEeeGZrrR3D.
Byron, J. (Host). (2024, July 29). Horrifying Alaska Bigfoot encounters! (Encounter Archives) (No. 485) [Audio podcast episode]. In *Bigfoot Society.* YouTube. https://youtu.be/7xFB5UyGyAA?si=gZ_rdbLY6_u80g6z.
Byron, J. (Host). (2025, February 15). Nightmare on Blue Ridge!—Virginia (No. 681) [Audio podcast episode]. In *Bigfoot Society Podcast.* YouTube. https://www.youtube.com/watch?v=WKXN38lHq00&t=556s.
Byron, J. (Host). (2025, March 7). A hunter's experiences—Oregon (No. 701) [Audio podcast episode]. In *Bigfoot Society Podcast.* Apple Podcasts. https://podcasts.apple.com/us/podcast/a-hunters-experiences-oregon/id1453429066?i=1000698230622.
Byron, J. (Host). (2025, April 15). A mother, her autistic son…and the creature in the trees (No. 740) [Audio podcast episode]. In *Bigfoot Society Podcast.* YouTube. https://www.youtube.com/watch?v=S0UJadWV-mk.
Byron, J. (Host). (2025, April 22). The thing that screamed back: A Maryland Sasquatch story (No. 747) [Audio podcast episode]. In *Bigfoot Society Podcast.* YouTube. https://www.youtube.com/watch?v=7XMciN15M8k.
Byron, J. (Host). (2025, May 18). Sasquatch stands tall in Oregon—You won't believe what happened (No. 773) [Audio podcast episode]. In *Bigfoot Society Podcast.* YouTube. https://youtu.be/JSoWRSdU5D8?si=x_HqxWjDGnBUrGVq.
Cahill, S.P., & Pontoski, K. (2005). Post-traumatic stress disorder and acute stress disorder I: Their nature and assessment considerations. *Psychiatry (Edgmont), 2*(4), 14–25. https://www.ncbi.nlm.nih.gov/pmc/articles/PMC3004735/.
Cai, W., Tang, Y.L., Wu, S., & Li, H. (2017). Scale of

death anxiety (SDA): Development and validation. *Frontiers in Psychology, 8,* 1–11. https://doi.org/10.3389/fpsyg.2017.00858.
Campbell, J. (2008). *The hero with a thousand faces.* New World Library.
Cantrall, T. (2013). *Sasquatch: The search for a new man.* [self-published].
Canty, J.M. (2022). *Returning the self to nature: Undoing our collective narcissism and healing our planet.* Shambhala Publications.
Cardeña, E. (2015). The unbearable fear of psi: On scientific suppression in the 21st century. *Journal of Scientific Exploration, 29*(4), 601–620. https://www.researchgate.net/publication/287911609_The_Unbearable_Fear_of_Psi_On_Scientific_Censorship_in_the_21st_Century.
Cardeña, E. (2017). Anomalous experiences. *The Blackwell Companion to Consciousness,* 187–202.
Cardeña, E., Lynn, S.J., & Krippner, S. (2014). Introduction: Anomalous experiences in perspective. In E. Cardeña, S.J. Lynn, & S. Krippner (Eds.) *Varieties of Anomalous Experience: Examining the Scientific Evidence (Second Edition).* (pp. 3–20). American Psychological Association.
Carlson, C. (2005). *Weird Florida.* Sterling Publishing Co, Inc.
Carpenter, S. (2019). *The Nephilim among us (Updated).* [self-published].
Carpenter, S. (2022). The *Sasquatch Awareness Project.* [self-published].
Carpenter, T. (2024, April 15). Are the Sasquatch dangerous?—The Sasquatch Awareness Project. In *Scott Carpenter.* YouTube.
Carroll, K.K. (2018). Cheikh Anta Diop's 'Two cradle theory,' racism and the cultural realities of African descended people in America. In (Ed.) M.T. Tillotson, *Whispering out loud: Voices of Africana* (pp. 57–79). Africa World Press, Inc.
Cavalline, R. (2020). *Mountain Devil 2: The Search for Jan Klement.* MaddyGTV.
Chernipeski, J. (Host). (2024, January 3). Missing in the remote wilderness—Strange disappearances in our national parks. In *Mountain Beast Mysteries.* YouTube. https://www.youtube.com/watch?v=-3gOEgLIL5g.
Chesna's Footage Room. (2019, January 10). Bigfoot (1997) Henry Franzoni—Drumming for Bigfoot. In *Chesna's Footage Room.* YouTube. https://youtu.be/9VPdOq7x8uM?si=6q7h0aBRKHgtTbKw.
Christianson, S.A. (1989). Flashbulb memories: Special, but not so special. *Memory & Cognition, 17,* 435–443. https://doi.org/10.3758/bf03202615.
Clarke, A.C. (2013). *Profiles of the Future.* Hachette UK.
Coleman, B., & Frogner, E. (2011). *Ojibwa myths and legends.* Literary Licensing, LLC.
Coleman, L. (2006, December 27). Bigfoot tooth found?. In *Cryptomundo.* https://cryptomundo.com/cryptozoo-news/kybf-tooth/.
Coleman, L. (2008). A tale of two suits. *Cryptozoonews.* http://www.cryptozoonews.com/2-suits/.
Coleman, L. (2009). *Bigfoot!: The True Story of Apes in America.* Simon & Schuster.
Coleman, L., & Huyghe, P. (2006). *The field guide to Bigfoot and other mystery primates.* Anomalist Books.
Colyer, D.G., Higgins, A., Brown, B., Strain, K., Mayes, M.C., & McAndrews, B. (2015). *The Ouachita Project.* North American Wood Ape Conservancy. https://www.woodape.org/index.php/opmonograph/.
Cooper, C.E. (2021). Ecological approaches to scopaesthesia. *Australian Journal of Parapsychology, 21*(2), 164–182. http://nectar.northampton.ac.uk/16014/1/Cooper_Callum_AJP_2021_Ecological_Approaches_to_Scopaesthesia_Published.pdf.
Cooper, J.M. (January 1933). The Cree witiko psychosis. *Primitive Man,.6*(1), 20–24. https://doi.org/10.2307/3316222.
Cosper, R. (2018). Language in higher primates. *The Relict Hominoid Inquiry, 7,* 135–138. https://www.isu.edu/media/libraries/rhi/comments-amp-responses/Language_Cosper.pdf.
Croyle, W. (Producer). (2021). *Knievel's quest: Bigfoot.* Reality Entertainment.
Cundiff, V. (2021, September 27). There's a monster on the mountain! [No. 25]. In *My Bigfoot Sighting.* YouTube.
Cushman, P. (1996). *Constructing the self, constructing America: A cultural history of psychotherapy.* Addison-Wesley/Addison Wesley Longman.
Cutchin, J. (2016). *The brimstone deceit: An in-depth examination of supernatural scents, otherworldly odors, and monstrous miasmas.* Anomalist Books.
Cutchin, J. (2020). Wildnisgeist: Poltergeist of the woods?. *EdgeScience, 43,* 6–13. https://www.scientificexploration.org/docs/edgescience/edgescience-43.pdf.
Cutchin, J. (2022a). *Ecology of souls: A new mythology of death & the paranormal (Volume I).* Horse and Barrel Press.
Cutchin, J. (2022b). *Ecology of souls: A new mythology of death & the paranormal (Volume II).* Horse and Barrel Press.
Cutchin, J. (2025). *Fourth wall phantoms: Reflections on the paranormal, narrative, and fictions becoming fact.* Horse and Barrel Press.
Cutchin, J., & Renner, T. (2020a). *Where the footprints end: High strangeness and the bigfoot phenomenon (Volume 1: Folklore).* Dark Holler Arts.
Cutchin, J., & Renner, T. (2020b). *Where the footprints end: High strangeness and the bigfoot phenomenon (Volume 2: Evidence).* Dark Holler Arts.
Davidson, P.S.R, & Glisky, E.L. (2002). Is flashbulb memory a special instance of source memory? Evidence from older adults. *Memory, 10,* 99–111. https://doi.org/10.1080/09658210143000227.
Davidson, P.S.R., Cook, S.P., Glisky, E.L., Verfaellie, M., & Rapcsak, S.Z. (2005). Source memory in the real world: A neuropsychological study of flashbulb memory. *Journal of Clinical and Experimental Neuropsychology, 27*(7), 915–929. Retrieved from https://www.ncbi.nlm.nih.gov/pmc/articles/PMC2349094/.

Davis, A.K., Clifton, J.M., Weaver, E.G., Hurwitz, E.S., Johnson, M.W., & Griffiths, R.R. (2020). Survey of entity encounter experiences occasioned by inhaled N, N-dimethyltryptamine: Phenomenology, interpretation, and enduring effects. *Journal of Psychopharmacology, 34*(9), 1008–1020. https://doi.org/10.1177/0269881120916143.

Davis, M.K. (Host). (2024, February 7). Remove the film from under foot!. In *Greenwave2010fb*. YouTube. https://www.youtube.com/watch?v=wDTdsvHl_EM.

Dawson, W., Brewer, P.R., & Cuddy, L. (2024). Cryptid Communication: Media messages and public beliefs about cryptozoology. *International Journal of Communication, 18*, 470–491. https://ijoc.org/index.php/ijoc/article/view/21417/4444.

DeGrazier, M. (director). (2019). *Missing 411: The hunted*. NABS.

Deloria, V., Jr. (2022). Animals and the Sioux. In V. Deloria, Jr. (Ed.), *CG Jung and the Sioux traditions: Dreams, visions, nature, and the primitive* (pp. 115–131). Fulcrum Publishing.

Dendle, P. (2006). Cryptozoology in the medieval and modern worlds. *Folklore, 117*, 190–206. https://www.jstor.org/stable/30035486.

Dickey, C. (2021). *The Unidentified: Mythical Monsters, Alien Encounters, and Our Obsession with the Unexplained*. Penguin.

Dixon, P.W. (2004). The Hawaiian menehune in myth and paleontology. *Human Evolution, 19*(4), 287–292. https://link.springer.com/article/10.1007/BF02438866.

DMAX UK. (2025, February 4). RPG is struck with terrible headaches after possible Bigfoot encounter! | Expedition Bigfoot. In *DMAX UK*. YouTube. https://www.youtube.com/watch?v=VUL79QR3BZc.

Documentaries—Crash-Course Cryptozoology. (2023, October 9). Hibagon: Ape of Mount Hiba—Cryptozoology documentary 2023. In *Documentaries—Crash-Course Cryptozoology*. YouTube. https://www.youtube.com/watch?v=ZolohzW42Yo&t=29s.

Dodds, G.T. (2007). Monkey-spouse sees children murdered, escapes to freedom!: A worldwide gathering and comparative analysis of Camarena-Chevalier Type 714, II-IV tales. *ELO: Estudos de Literatura Oral* (13–14 (2007–2008)), 85–115. https://www.researchgate.net/publication/261832641_Monkey-spouse_sees_children_murdered_escapes_to_freedom_a_worldwide_gathering_and_comparative_analysis_of_Camarena-Chevalier_Type_714_II-IV_tales.

Dodds, G.T. (adapter), & Wessels, P. (annotator). (2011). *The missing link and other tales of apemen*. Black Coat Press.

Doubková, N., Preiss, M., & Sanders, E.M. (2024). Unpacking the concept of otherness: Philosophical and psychological perspectives. *Integrative Psychological and Behavioral Science*, 1–21. https://doi.org/10.1007/s12124-024-09820-4.

Eastburn, L. (Host). (2023, January 18). Bigfoot the language Part I. On *Linda Eastburn*. YouTube. https://www.youtube.com/watch?v=CiaMpSobIMA&t=1759s.

Eberhart, G.M. (2005). Mysterious creatures: Creating a cryptozoological encyclopedia. *Journal of Scientific Exploration, 19*, 103–113. https://www.scientificexploration.org/docs/19/jse_19_1_eberhart.pdf.

Eichenberger, B. (director). (2022). *A flash of beauty: Bigfoot revealed* [Film]. Resonance Productions. https://www.amazon.com/Flash-Beauty-Bigfoot-Revealed/dp/B09XVN6TMP.

Eichenberger, B. (director). (2023). *A flash of beauty: Paranormal Bigfoot* [Film]. Resonance Productions. https://www.amazon.com/Flash-Beauty-Paranormal-Bigfoot/dp/B0CP987WH1.

Eichenberger, B. (Host). (2023, December 17). A flash of beauty: Scott Nelson. In *A Flash of Beauty: Bigfoot Revealed*. YouTube. https://www.youtube.com/watch?v=-GjHq0ane7k.

Eichenberger, B. (Host). (2023, December 20). A flash of beauty: Mark Parker. In *A Flash of Beauty: Bigfoot Revealed*. YouTube. https://www.youtube.com/watch?v=L1g3mKGuiXI.

Eichenberger, B. (Host). (2023, December 25). A flash of beauty: Daryl Wilson. In *A Flash of Beauty: Bigfoot Revealed*. YouTube. https://youtu.be/Rvw8_WKnX70?si=MPaMNKodo9i8Hgc7.

Eichenberger, B. (Host). (2024, January 1). A flash of beauty: Sonya Zohar. In *A Flash of Beauty: Bigfoot Revealed*. YouTube. https://youtu.be/kz_SMaaThxc?si=XSOaHkq-7RvKYkT8.

Eichenberger, B. (Host). (2024, January 7). A flash of beauty: Brittany (Chad's wife—members only). In *A Flash of Beauty: Bigfoot Revealed*. YouTube.

Eichenberger, B. (Host). (2024, February 10). A flash of beauty: Mel Skahan. In *A Flash of Beauty: Bigfoot Revealed*. YouTube. https://www.youtube.com/watch?v=vGlLju364gI.

Eichenberger, B. (Host). (2024, February 14). A flash of beauty: Elaine Miles. In *A Flash of Beauty: Bigfoot Revealed*. YouTube. https://www.youtube.com/watch?v=3-15If94wdM&t=68s.

Eichenberger, B. (Host). (2024, February 19). A flash of beauty: Dr Michael Adamse. In *A Flash of Beauty: Bigfoot Revealed*. YouTube. https://youtu.be/1A54VqZDn4Q?si=Oqg8hufynNw_o36_.

Eichenberger, B. (Host). (2024, March 28). The experiencers: Michael Shepherd (Members only). In *A Flash of Beauty: Bigfoot Revealed*. YouTube. https://youtu.be/AeJPPEmiwe0?si=dy1ny_A80e4qOB9s.

Eichenberger, B. (Host). (2024, April 3). A flash of beauty: Meet Tobe Johnson. In *A Flash of Beauty: Bigfoot Revealed*. YouTube. https://youtu.be/lsHZoBIylRk?si=fQhlt3_ISjWr8eIQ.

Eichenberger, B. (Host). (2024, April 5). A flash of beauty: Bigfoot revealed is live from Metaline Falls!. In *A Flash of Beauty: Bigfoot Revealed*. YouTube. https://www.youtube.com/watch?v=Bsg49iAc4jg&t=171s.

Eichenberger, B. (Host). (2024, April 24). The experiencers: April Lynn. In *A Flash of Beauty: Bigfoot*

Revealed. YouTube. https://youtu.be/LrHj5AVJUBo?si=52-I0VkVOtS_MNa-.
Eichenberger, B. (Host). (2024, July 5). Paranormal Bigfoot: Arla Williams. in a Flash of Beauty: Bigfoot Revealed. YouTube. https://www.youtube.com/watch?v=CZGLkstAkUo&t=1424s.
Eichenberger, B. (Host). (2024, August 15). Paranormal Bigfoot: Barb Shupe. In *A Flash of Beauty: Bigfoot Revealed.* YouTube. https://youtu.be/GUs8JKBluDA?si=6hJYhT7G1kRjp-TT.
Eichenberger, B. (Host). (2024, October 25). A flash of beauty: Sonya. In *A Flash of Beauty: Bigfoot Revealed.* YouTube. https://youtu.be/ll8V8yemmHo?si=PyCKzS9zfQa7kIVS.
Eichenberger, B. (Host). (2024, November 14). The A Flash of Beauty Podcast: Constant contact/Ashlea Stinnett. In *A Flash of Beauty: Bigfoot Revealed.* YouTube. https://www.youtube.com/watch?v=g1C55XKh0KU&t=3932s.
England, C. (Host). (2024, October 6). Bow hunter in Tennessee has a chilling encounter in national forest. In *Base Camp Chris.* YouTube. https://youtu.be/0EINm38wvno?si=28Oi2SAbm9tE0ui9.
Esbjörn-Hargens, S. (2020, July). Our wild kosmos!: An exo studies exploration of the ontological status of non-human intelligences. *Exo Studies Institute, Research Paper* (1), 1–48. https://whatsupwithufos.com/wp-content/uploads/2020/06/Exo_Studies.pdf.
Esbjörn-Hargens, S. https://cihs.edu/research/center-for-anomalous-and-noetic-studies/.
Evans, A.M. (2024, January 3). Bigfoot encounters-A collection of Sasquatch appearances-Full documentary. In *Gravitas Documentaries.* YouTube. https://youtu.be/XBLmmyFEhvw?si=5E5yWRq6V-tbCwS2.
Fahrenbach, W.H. (1997–1998). Sasquatch: Size, scaling, and statistics. *Cryptozoology, 13,* 47–75. https://www.bfro.net/REF/THEORIES/WHF/FahrenbachArticle.htm.
Falconer, R., & Schwartz, R. (2023). *The others within us: Internal family systems, porous mind, and spirit possession.* Great Mystery Press.
Forbes, J.D. (2011). *Columbus and other cannibals: The Wétiko disease of exploitation, imperialism, and terrorism.* Seven Stories Press.
Fort, C. (2008). *The book of the damned: The collected works of Charles Fort.* Penguin.
Forth, G. (2007). Images of the Wildman inside and outside Europe. *Folklore, 118*(3), 261–281. https://www.jstor.org/stable/30035439.
Forth, G. (2022). *Between ape and human: An anthropologist on the trail of a hidden hominoid.* Simon & Schuster.
Forth, G. (2023). Comment on Investigating Homo floresiensis and the myth of the ebu gogo. *The Relict Hominoid Inquiry, 12,* 1–3. https://www.isu.edu/media/libraries/rhi/comments-amp-responses/Forth-Comment_final.pdf.
Foxon, F. (2024a). Bigfoot: If it's there, could it be a bear?. *Journal of Zoology,* 1–8. https://doi.org/10.1111/jzo.13148.
Foxon, F. (2024b). Heuvelmans the Heretic and Hidden Animals. *Interdisciplinary Science Reviews,* 0(0). 10.1177/03080188241233107.
Freeman, M.P. (2022). The end. In M.P. Freeman (Ed.), *Freeman Bigfoot Files* (pp. 271–274). Hangar 1 Publishing.
Freeman, P. (2022). *When I'm an old man.* [Audio file]. In M.P. Freeman (Ed.), *Freeman Bigfoot Files.* Hangar 1 Publishing.
Friedman, H.L., Radin, D., & Krippner, S. (2021). Parapsychology and transpersonal psychology in dialogue: Could these two movements be brought into better alignment? *International Journal of Transpersonal Studies, 40*(1), 123–135. https://doi.org/10.24972/ijts.2021.40.1.123.
Furek, M.W. (2024). *The lost tribes of Bigfoot.* Hangar 1 Publishing.
Fusch, E. (1992). *S'cweneyti and the Stick Indians of the Colvilles: The interaction of large bipedal hominids with American Indians.* Ed Fusch. http://www.bigfootencounters.com/biology/fusch.htm.
Gabriel, J. (director), Harris, T. (host). (2021, December 3). Bigfoot revealed. In *The Proof is Out There.* History Channel. https://youtu.be/s8Tbu3JfvK0?si=CouaE_bphC8O1cJ8.
Galán S., M.A., & Koren, S.A. (2024). Exploring the link between paranormal phenomena and plasma balls. *Journal of Scientific Exploration, 38*(4), 670–685. https://doi.org/10.31275/20243057.
Germer, W. (Host). (2018, September 8). I would not believe it if I didn't see it (No. 419) [Audio podcast episode]. In *Sasquatch Chronicles.* https://sasquatchchronicles.com/sc-ep419-i-would-not-believe-it-if-i-didn%E2%80%99t-see-it/.
Germer, W. (Host). (2018, September 28). Killing Sasquatch (No. 308) [Audio podcast episode]. In *Sasquatch Chronicles.* YouTube. https://www.youtube.com/watch?v=lBSJJ_aK0Hg.
Germer, W. (Host). (2019, February 3). Survivorman Les Stroud (No. 500) [Audio podcast episode]. In *Sasquatch Chronicles.* YouTube. https://www.youtube.com/watch?v=Gbx99oZNq6o&t=2821s.
Germer, W. (Host). (2019, July 31). I shouldn't be alive (No. 515) [Audio podcast episode]. In *Sasquatch Chronicles.* YouTube. https://www.youtube.com/watch?v=XJHoeIk4F04&t=2s.
Germer, W. (Host). (2020, September 8). It looked like a primitive man (No. 675) [Audio podcast episode]. In *Sasquatch Chronicles.* YouTube. https://www.youtube.com/watch?v=RJ4rovyf7EY&list=PL0sLO94JFopSeg_qZzDQAZPb2Mxkvq16e&index=119.
Germer, W. (Host). (2021, March 5a). It looked more human like (No. 708) [Audio podcast episode]. In *Sasquatch Chronicles.* YouTube. https://www.youtube.com/watch?v=pm-TTvwnqdk.
Germer, W. (Host). (2021, March 5b). SC EP: 709 The Mogollon Monster (No. 709) [Audio podcast episode]. In *Sasquatch Chronicles.* YouTube. https://www.youtube.com/watch?v=peUZQshLADw.
Germer, W. (Host). (2022, July 1). I thought I shot a man (No. 873) [Audio podcast episode]. In *Sasquatch Chronicles.* YouTube. https://www.youtube.com/watch?v=GYCoC9anZH0&t=2925s.

Germer, W. (Host). (2023, November 13). Season 1—Episode 3—These monsters chasing me (No. 715) [Audio podcast episode]. In *Sasquatch Chronicles.* YouTube. https://youtu.be/sD9P963clfE?si=0VK6NAwhUUde2lqV.

Germer, W. (Host). (2023, November 24). Season 4—Episode 10—Big game hunter shoots Sasquatch (No. 590) [Audio podcast episode]. In *Sasquatch Chronicles.* YouTube. https://youtu.be/50_b-CAslL0?si=jnKBicm90Cb70sIe.

Germer, W. (Host). (2023, December 15). I still have PTSD from this (No. 453) [Audio podcast episode]. In *Sasquatch Chronicles.* YouTube. https://www.youtube.com/watch?v=98NRzra9v5Q&t=1109s.

Germer, W. (Host). (2024, January 26). Seeing is believing (No. 842) [Audio podcast episode]. In *Sasquatch Chronicles.* YouTube. https://youtu.be/bpA-eCyJhV8?si=2VdyF_bXvirE2i1_.

Germer, W. (Host). (2024, May 8). Paralyzed with fear (No. 858) [Audio podcast episode]. In *Sasquatch Chronicles.* YouTube. https://youtu.be/yXK9EydUn1Q?si=6ZjrTmSalyVMDzMe.

Giamatti, P., & Asma, S. (Hosts). (2023, April 26). Talking monsters with Paul Giamatti & Stephen Asma (No. 4) [Audio podcast episode]. In *Chinwag Podcast.* YouTube. https://www.youtube.com/watch?v=ymRS-G4mzxk&t=1997s.

Gilgamesh. (J. Gardner & J. Maier, trans.). Vintage Books.

Glazier, J.W. (2023). Critical theory and exceptional experiences. In J.W. Glazier (Ed.), *Paranormal Ruptures: Critical Approaches to Exceptional Experiences* (pp. 1–20). Beyond the Fray Publishing.

Glickman, J. (1998). Toward a resolution of the Bigfoot phenomenon. [Research Report]. *North American Science Institute,* 1–43. https://www.semanticscholar.org/paper/Toward-a-Resolution-of-the-Bigfoot-Phenomenon-Glickman/900cbc7de26bc80f8c37ab14d9cbe8981763bd70.

Godfrey, L.S. (2016) *Monsters among us: An exploration of otherworldly Bigfoot, Wolfmen, Portals, Phantoms, and Odd Phenomena.* Tarcher-Perigee.

Gosselin, B., & Gosselin, S. (2018). *Abair Road: The true story.* [self-published].

Green, J. (2004a). Historical overview and basic facts involved in the Sasquatch or Bigfoot phenomenon. *Journal of Scientific Exploration, 18*(1), 37–51. https://www.scientificexploration.org/docs/18/jse_18_1_green.pdf.

Green, J. (2004b). *The best of Sasquatch/Bigfoot.* Hancock House.

Green, M.A., & Coy, J.C. (2001). 50 years with Bigfoot: Tennessee chronicles of co-existence [self-published].

Greenberg, J., & Arndt, J. (2012). Terror management theory. *Handbook of theories of social psychology, 1,* 398–415. https://psycnet.apa.org/doi/10.4135/9781446249215.n20.

Grobbelaar, D. (2020). The white lion as symbol of the archetype of the self and the cannibalization of the Self in canned hunting. *Jung Journal, 14*(2), 11–29. https://doi.org/10.1080/19342039.2020.1742550.

Grof, S. (2012). Revision and re-enchantment of psychology: Legacy of half a century of consciousness research. *Journal of Transpersonal Psychology, 44*(2), 137–163. https://galileocommission.org/wp-content/uploads/2019/03/RevisionAndReenchantment-of-Psychology.pdf.

Grof, S., & Grof, C. (1989). *Spiritual emergency: When personal transformation becomes a crisis.* Tarcher Putnam.

Gymlan, B. (Host). (2022, March 20). Unsettling Bigfoot activity in Georgia—Fan illustrated. In *Bob Gymlan.* YouTube. https://www.youtube.com/watch?v=6cjhx2dXFmI&t=907s.

Gymlan, B. (Host). (2022, October 23). Bigfoot News! The Mogollon Monster photo breakdown. In *Bob Gymlan.* YouTube. https://youtu.be/rdGzVK1U6u0?si=Lui-AnUBKQxdBLXv.

Gymlan, B. (Host). (2023, January 29). My favorite Bigfoot photo—with ASTOUNDING size comparison—the Beast of Seven Chutes. In *Bob Gymlan.* YouTube. https://www.youtube.com/watch?v=gxTJfONmBxw.

Gymlan, B. (Host). (2024, August 8). A chilling Sasquatch encounter while pulled over—the cop saw it!. In *Bob Gymlan.* YouTube. https://www.youtube.com/watch?v=b8pUF5moVes&t=1222s.

Hajicek, D. (Director). (2003). *Sasquatch: Legend meets science* [Film]. Whitewolf Entertainment.

Hajicek, D. (Director). (2004). Creature of Cumberland (Season 1, Episode 5). In *Mysterious Encounters.* https://youtu.be/93JNjdsRJxY?si=gnxE7xqdSQ2KnETk.

Hajicek, D. (2022). Expert footage analysis. In M.P. Freeman (Ed.), *The Freeman Bigfoot Files* (pp. 223–237). Hangar 1 Publishing.

Hajicek, D., & Hajicek, A. (Hosts). (2023, April 26). The Bigfoot purr revealed? Strange unknown sounds (No. 138). [Video podcast episode]. In *Untold Radio AM.* YouTube. https://www.youtube.com/watch?v=24LK_q-WDK4&t=2s.

Hajicek, D., & Hajicek, A. (Hosts). (2023, November 29). Strange Sasquatch communication with field investigator Jason Miller (No. 169). [Video podcast episode]. In *Untold Radio AM.* YouTube. https://www.youtube.com/watch?v=QQ2WNap25lg&t=3442s .

Hajicek, D., & Hajicek, A. (Hosts). (2023, December 20). The Ape Canyon mountain devil's mystery with Marc Myrsell (No. 172). [Video podcast episode]. In *Untold Radio AM.* YouTube. https://www.youtube.com/live/Ik5r3JJpuh4?si=XT3lwFiUtwnOKE6_.

Hajicek, D., & Hajicek, A. (Hosts). (2024, February 28). Life changing Bigfoot encounter with Alfred Santariga (No. 182) [Video podcast episode]. In *Untold Radio AM.* YouTube. https://www.youtube.com/watch?v=PuZio9jocSo&t=3251s.

Hajicek, D., & Hajicek, A. (Hosts). (2024, March 6). "Double" terrifying Bigfoot encounters (No. 183) [Video podcast episode]. In *Untold Radio*

AM. YouTube. https://www.youtube.com/watch?v=aAlyeTUw0Xs&t=4597s.

Hajicek, D., & Hajicek, A. (Hosts). (2024, March 14). "The stink" smelly Bigfoot encounters with Scott Angove, Marc DeWerth (No. 184) [Video podcast episode]. In *Untold Radio AM*. YouTube. https://www.youtube.com/watch?v=2OWH4Aq38-8&t=7371s.

Hajicek, D., & Hajicek, A. (Hosts). (2024, March 28). Monsters are very real with Steve Barcelo (No. 186) [Video podcast episode]. In *Untold Radio AM*. YouTube. https://www.youtube.com/live/exAlWA0IN3Q?si=xnCSLOJy1VegH1yN.

Hajicek, D., & Hajicek, A. (Hosts). (2024, April 24). Eastern Bigfoots by the numbers and facts with Steve Kulls (No. 190) [Video podcast episode]. In *Untold Radio AM*. YouTube. https://www.youtube.com/live/kUw0gkVGk3g?si=bTqLUP92-iRUYtho.

Hajicek, D., & Hajicek, A. (Hosts). (2024, July 17). Trauma—The Bigfoot witness experience with Rich Daniels (No. 202) [Video podcast episode]. In *Untold Radio AM*. YouTube. https://www.youtube.com/watch?v=EERvnuYoPzE&t=3055s.

Hajicek, D., & Perea, J., Jr. (Hosts). (2024, October 30). Ozark Bigfoot Research and Encounters with Mary Ann (No. 217) [Video podcast episode]. In *Untold Radio AM*. YouTube. https://www.youtube.com/live/edyFacfKB7k?si=6n09QRT59QWs3Xr_.

Halloran, T., & Halloran, D. (Hosts). (2024, June 24). Bigfoot population density with Dr. Esteban Sarmiento (No. 74) [Video podcast episode]. In *The Bigfoot Influencers*. YouTube. https://www.youtube.com/live/qU1xYzfhuPY?si=A8QolhTXYDwnX5xj.

Hanks, M., Waddell, D., & Smith, J. (Hosts). (2023, September 28). Matt Pruitt: The Phenomenal Sasquatch, Part Two (No. 50) [Audio podcast episode]. In *Sasquatch Tracks*. https://sasquatchtracks.com/2023/09/28/matt-pruitt-the-phenomenal-sasquatch-part-two-st-050/.

Hanks, M., Waddell, D., & Smith, J. (Hosts). (2025, April 13). Historical hominoids: Relicts from the past (No. 64) [Audio podcast episode]. In *Sasquatch Tracks*. https://sasquatchtracks.com/tag/relict-hominoids/.

Hansen, G.P. (2001). *The trickster and the paranormal*. Xlibris Corporation.

Haraway, D. (2008). When species meet: Introductions. In D. Haraway (Ed.) When *Species Meet* (pp. 3–42). Routledge.

Harguindey, S. (2000). Towards a quintessential approach to crisis and disease: The crossroads-crossfire-turning point-conflict theory (CCPC). *International Journal of Transpersonal Studies, 19*(1), 141–161. https://digitalcommons.ciis.edu/ijts-transpersonalstudies/vol19/iss1/17/.

Harold, J. (Host). (2024, February 9). What's the deal with Bigfoot? (No. 819) [Audio podcast episode]. In *The Paranormal Podcast*. https://jimharold.com/whats-the-deal-with-bigfoot-the-paranormal-podcast-819/.

Harrison, D. (Host). (2020, June 16). Yowie/Bigfoot sighting (Audio reports #160) in Sherbrooke Forest, Victoria. In *Yowiehunters Witness Reports*. YouTube. https://youtu.be/cG7pzLwlGiE?si=xtbsQatjD2Xoses1.

Harrison, D. (Host). (2020, July 27). Yowie/Bigfoot sighting (Audio Report #166) at Grassy Head, New South Wales. In *Yowiehunters Witness Reports*. YouTube. https://youtu.be/UVFiq2NXT4I?si=4J_Q5-3X2ZK1O0H7.

Harrison, D. (Host). (2021, March 27). Yowie/Bigfoot sighting (Audio Report #183) at Mount Hotham, Victoria. In *Yowiehunters Witness Reports*. YouTube. Yowie / Bigfoot Sighting (Audio Report #183) at Mount Hotham, Victoria.

Harrison, D. (Host). (2023, August 28). Yowie/Bigfoot sighting (Audio Report #197) at Birkdale, Queensland [Video episode]. In *Yowiehunters Witness Reports*. YouTube. https://youtu.be/nkm8zMTdYwQ?si=wZKg3_jn6ax5sUWN..

Haynes, R. (1980). The boggle threshold. *Encounter, August*, 92–96. https://www.unz.com/print/Encounter-1980aug-00092.

Healy, T., & Cropper, P. (2006). *The Yowie: In search of Australia's Bigfoot*. Anomalist Books.

Healy, T., & Cropper, P. (2023). *The Yowie file: Encounters with Australian Ape-men*. Fortean Publishing.

Hein, S. (2022). *Dark matter monsters: Cryptids, ball lightning, and the science of secret lifeforms*. Mount Baldy Press, Inc.

Henry, N., & Rodgers, L. (Hosts). (2023, September 27). Confessions from the Bigfoot Museum with David Bakara (No. 194) [Audio podcast episode]. In *Blurry Creatures*. https://www.blurrycreatures.com/listen/x36g5yzygjbxtrr-pha5w-27egr-hj69k-3kmx5-6fkxj-xjrxc-znhza-fh2z6-je32j-jfesb-eby55-t998t-45sbw-gkza8-a8wlf-78773-sxxjz.

Herlihy, J., Jobson, L., & Turner, S. (2012). Just tell us what happened to you: Autobiographical memory and seeking asylum. *Applied Cognitive Psychology, 26*(5), 661–676. https://psycnet.apa.org/doi/10.1002/acp.2852.

Heuvelmans, B. (1959). *On the track of unknown animals*. Bungay, Suffolk: Richard Clay and Company, Ltd.

Heuvelmans, B. (1983). How many animal species remain to be discovered? *Cryptozoology, 2*, 1–24.

Heuvelmans, B. (w/ Coleman, L., P. LeBlond, Trans.). (2016). *Neanderthal: The strange saga of the Minnesota Iceman*. Anomalist Books.

Heyman, S.R. (1977). Freud and the concept of inherited racial memories. *Psychoanalytic Review, 64*(3), 461–464. https://psycnet.apa.org/record/1978-30671-001.

Hill, S.A. (2017). *Scientifical Americans: The culture of amateur paranormal researchers*. McFarland.

Hillman, J. (2017). *The soul's code: In search of character and calling*. Ballantine Books.

Hilsmeyer, B. (producer). (2017). *Hairy Man: My life with Bigfoot-A Maine woman remembers*. Lincoln County Television.

History. (2021, May 26). MonsterQuest: Grassman stalks Ohio (Season 2, Episode 4)—Full episode. *History Channel*. YouTube. https://youtu.be/L6igCiiXW6Q?si=-eFNR1Gz_wr2uXzd.

History. (2024, March 9). The proof is out there: 5 mysterious Bigfoot encounters. In *History Channel*. YouTube. https://www.youtube.com/watch?v=rdneevYAwfc&list=PLO0PqscY-C6r01DlOKeFjeaCB0qWUvIjiv&index=88.

Horton, J. (Director). (2024, June 24). Bigfoot: King of the cryptids—must see Sasquatch documentary. In *J. Horton Films*. Prime Video. https://www.primevideo.com/detail/Bigfoot-King-of-Cryptids/0RXDSYQ4FFXPORTJLC9EA2EQAP.

Hoyland, G. (2018). *Yeti: An abominable history*. HarperCollins Publishers.

Huang, C.H. (2024, February 21). What's behind the evolution of Neanderthal portraits. *Sapiens*. https://www.sapiens.org/archaeology/neanderthal-art-paleolithic-archaeology/.

Hudson, T. (w/ Sheer, A.). (2020). *The Meadow Project: Explorations into the South's Skinwalker Ranch [narr. by Brian Jay, Audible]*. [self-published].

Hunter, J. (2021a). Deep weird: High strangeness, boggle thresholds and damned data in academic research on extraordinary experience. *Journal for the Study of Religious Experience, 7*(1), 5–18. https://www.academia.edu/48852176/Deep_Weird_High_Strangeness_Boggle_Thresholds_and_Damned_Data_in_Academic_Research_on_Extraordinary_Experience.

Hunter, J. (2021b). Mysterium horrendum. In B.R. Grafius & J.W. Morehead (Eds.), *Theology and Horror: Explorations of the Dark Religious Imagination* (pp. 41–54). Lexington Books/Fortress Academic.

Hurn, S. (2017). Introduction. In S. Hurn (Ed.), *Anthropology and cryptozoology: Exploring encounters with mysterious creatures (Multispecies Encounters)* (pp. 1–11). Routledge.

Hyman, I., Jr. (2000). The memory wars. In Neisser, U. & Hyman, I., Jr. (Eds.), *Memory observed: Remembering in Natural Contexts* (pp. 374–380). Macmillan.

Hynek, J.A. (1972). *The UFO experience: A scientific inquiry*. Henry Regnery Company.

Irwin, S. (Host). (2022, September 12). Face-to-face encounter in off-grid cabin in British Columbia Part 2: the encounter. In *Sketching Encounters*. YouTube. https://www.youtube.com/watch?v=8U4vsEctdgU&t=1141s.

Irwin, S. (Host). (2024, March 8). We were food… Fred Roehl shares his terrifying encounter that changed the way he views Sasquatch. In *Sketching Encounters*. YouTube. https://www.youtube.com/watch?v=8GVCqMWZ7KY.

Irwin, S. (Host). (2024, April 20). From a close encounter with a juvy Sasquatch, to "someone took possession of my son" in 24 hours!. In *Sketching Encounters*. YouTube. https://www.youtube.com/watch?v=YbDaP5Y8cmk.

Jackson, V.L. (Host). (2024, January 28). "What Legends are made of" Thom Cantrall Part 2 [Video podcast episode]. In *Muddy Creek Podcast: Wide Range of Strange*. YouTube. https://www.youtube.com/watch?v=DdKb3ftQq28&t=1156s.

Jackson, V.L. (Host). (2024, May 4). Georgia cryptid researcher, Tony Green [Video podcast episode]. In *Muddy Creek Podcast: Wide Range of Strange*. YouTube. https://www.youtube.com/live/5a1pLBAJJnY?si=Bf1Q1zaJ8VjXNT_Z.

Jacobi, J., & Jung, C. G. (2013). *Complex/archetype/symbol in the psychology of CG Jung*. Routledge.

Jacobs, C. (Host). (2024, May 30). Bigfoot stuff—Can the Sasquatch really shapeshift?. In *Chuck Jacobs—Arizona*. YouTube. https://www.youtube.com/watch?v=w08PN1ciS5g.

James, W. (1984). *Psychology: Briefer course*. The Library of America. (original work published 1890).

Jevning, W. (Host). (2024, February 19). Bigfoot! Monday review—Doug Hajicek (No. 35). In *Creek Devil* podcast. YouTube. https://www.youtube.com/watch?v=majNPE-rvu8.

Jinks, T. (2019). *Psychological perspectives on reality, consciousness and paranormal experience*. Palgrave MacMillan.

Johnson, T. (Host). (2021, January 24). Extended experiencers of Sasquatch—Rich Germeau & Sonya Zohar (No. 46). In *Owl Moon Lab*. YouTube. https://www.youtube.com/watch?app=desktop&v=Vdut10flH0A.

Johnson, T. (2023). *The Owl Moon Lab: A paranormal experiment*. Hangar 1 Publishing.

Johnson, T. (Host), Remensnyder, J. (Host), & Eichenberger, B. (Host). (2024, December 12). A flash of beauty live. In *A Flash of Beauty: Bigfoot Revealed*. YouTube. https://www.youtube.com/watch?v=5LuuyYU7jfg&t=1003s.

Johnston, B. (1995). *The Manitous: The supernatural world of the Ojibway*. HarperCollins.

Jones, B. (Host). (2023, January 16). Minnesota's Iceman with Terry Cullen [Video podcast episode]. In *Monday Morning Monsters*. YouTube. https://www.youtube.com/live/E3gC_Cgn8EM?si=PTRhtYcua-a4E4lJ.

Jones, B. (Host). (2024, May 6). An encounters traumatic effect with guest Rich Daniels (No. 54) [Video podcast episode]. In *Monsters on the Edge*. YouTube. https://www.youtube.com/watch?v=dvxBPtxO08g.

Jones, R.K. (2021). *The Appalachian Bigfoot*. Hangar 1 Publishing.

Jones, R.K. (2023). *Tracking the Stone Man: West Virginia's Bigfoot (2nd ed.)*. Beyond the Fray Publishing.

Jung, C.G. (1989). *Memories, dreams, reflections* (trans., Richard and Clara Winston, Revised Edition). Vintage Books.

Kaldy, A. (2020). *Track: Search for Australia's Bigfoot*. Gravitas Ventures. https://www.youtube.com/watch?v=U5ZiqEu1s2E.

Karnafel, R. (Host). (2023, December 15). In *Bigfoot Michigan Rob encounter story* [Video].

YouTube. https://youtu.be/Dwv6D-wlaFs?si=46i4tpdw_wdHaTJH.

Karnafel, R. (Host). (2023, May 6). Sasquatch manifests in front of couple—They follow tracks!. In *Bigfoot Michigan Rob.* YouTube. https://www.youtube.com/watch?app=desktop&v=VMsehYsGb6A.

Karnafel, R. (Host). (2024, November 8). Alaska's Fred Roehl ~ Surviving Sasquatch (No. 109) [Video podcast episode]. In *Brunch with Bigfoot Michigan Rob.* Spotify. https://open.spotify.com/episode/64XY4dlMTTg2rid3Fgkusi.

KayDee. (2024, August 18). The table" E1 Types of Bigfoot. In *Ancient Tracks: A Beast Inquiry.* YouTube. https://youtu.be/rTcMG5BsN_M?si=dYVwl2T2QQVhZoOV.

Kaye, J.B. (2021). Abject desires in the age of anger: Incels, femcels and the gender politics of unfuckability. In *Imagining" We" in the Age of" I"* (pp. 29–46). Routledge.

Kelleher, C.A., & Knapp, G. (2005). *Hunt for the skinwalker: Science confronts the unexplained at a remote ranch in Utah.* Paraview Pocket Books.

Keltner, D., & Haidt, J. (2003). Approaching awe, a moral, spiritual, and aesthetic emotion. *Cognition and Emotion, 17*(2), 297–314. https://doi-org.ciis.idm.oclc.org/10.1080/02699930302297.

King-Sharp, B. (Host). (2023, February 3). Baby Bigfoot caught on tape: The Freeman files (No. 225). In *Sasquatch Odyssey.* YouTube. https://youtu.be/20IrE6tvUNQ?si=hz75Yzrs1Tb6Ro6S.

King-Sharp, B. (Host). (2023, April 14). Bigfoot on the reservation: The Navajo Rangers X-Files! In *Weird Encounters (Untold Radio Network).* YouTube. https://youtu.be/1QVeB5MkUWM?si=aJRgWn5cBeRv3cxz.

King-Sharp, B. (Host). (2023, May 5). Sasquatch Legend Meets Science II: With Doug Hajicek (No. 208). In *Sasquatch Odyssey.* YouTube. https://www.youtube.com/watch?v=R67g5UNAWMI.

King-Sharp, B. (2024). *Bigfoot unleashed.* Hangar 1 Publishing.

King-Sharp, B. (Host). (2024, April 14). Almost taken by Bigfoot (No. 446) [Audio podcast episode]. In *Sasquatch Odyssey.* Apple Podcasts. https://podcasts.apple.com/jo/podcast/sasquatch-odyssey/id1552990311.

King-Sharp, B. (Host). (2024, May 5). Bush pilot Bigfoot Encounters Part Two (No. 455) [Audio podcast episode]. In *Sasquatch Odyssey.* Audible. https://www.audible.com/es_US/podcast/SO-EP-455-Bush-Pilot-Bigfoot-Encounters-Part-Two/B0D3CD6M1S.

King-Sharp, B. (Host). (2025, January 9). Bigfoot bait! (No. 556) [Audio podcast episode]. In *Sasquatch Odyssey.* Apple Podcasts. https://podcasts.apple.com/ca/podcast/so-ep-556-bigfoot-bait/id1552990311?i=1000683414583.

King-Sharp, B., & Barnett, D.L. (Hosts). (2024, April 1). Ranae Holland interview (No. 443) [Audio podcast episode]. In *Sasquatch Odyssey.* Audible. https://www.audible.com/es_US/podcast/SO-EP-443-Finding-Bigfoot-With-Ranae-Holland/B0D12LLL64.

King-Sharp, B., & Totherow, C.W. (Hosts). (2024, March 22). Bigfoot superhero (No. 38) [Audio podcast episode]. In *That Bigfoot Podcast.* Apple Podcasts. https://www.audible.com/es_US/podcast/TBP-EP-38-Bigfoot-Superhero/B0CYSLQ1QY.

Kirlin, R.L., & Hertel, L (1995). Estimates of pitch and vocal tract length from recorded vocalizations of purported bigfoot. In M. M. Halpin (Ed.), Manlike Monsters on Trial: Early Records and Modern Evidence (pp. 274–290). University of British Columbia Press.

Klement, J. (1975). *The creature: Personal experiences with Bigfoot (Fourth Print Edition).* Allegheny Press.

Klengel, T., Dias, B. & Ressler, K. (2016). Models of intergenerational and transgenerational transmission of risk for psychopathology in mice. *Neuropsychopharmacology, 41,* 219–231. https://doi.org/10.1038/npp.2015.249.

Klosin, A., Casas, E., Hidalgo-Carcedo, C., Vavouri, T., & Lehner, B. (2017). Transgenerational transmission of environmental information in C. elegans. *Science, 356*(6335), 320–323. https://science.sciencemag.org/content/356/6335/320.abstract.

Koffmann, M. (2014). Brief ecological description of the Caucasus relic hominoid (Almasty): Based on oral reports by local inhabitants and on field investigations [Article reprint]. In D. Bayanov (Ed.), *Russian hominology: The Bayanov papers-fact & folklore* (pp. 184–194). Hancock House.

Koffmann, M. (2015a). The almasty-yeti of the Caucasus [Article reprint]. *The Relict Hominoid Inquiry, 4,* 79–105. https://www.isu.edu/media/libraries/rhi/research-papers/Koffmann_1.pdf.

Koffmann, M. (2015b). The almasty of the Caucasus-Lifestyle of a hominoid [Article reprint]. *The Relict Hominoid Inquiry, 4,* 106–123. https://www.isu.edu/media/libraries/rhi/research-papers/Koffmann_2.pdf.

Kripal, J.J. (2019). *The flip: Epiphanies of mind and the future of knowledge.* Bellevue Literary Press.

Kronbauer, B. (2017, May 15). Sasquatch hunters—BC was awesome (No. 2). *Vancouver is Awesome.* https://www.vancouverisawesome.com/events-and-entertainment/we-need-to-work-together-to-tell-canadas-first-nations-stories-1933766.

Kruse, J. & Grover, J. (Hosts). (2019, December 11). Bigfoot DNA & research: Scott Carpenter. In *She-Squatchers Official.* YouTube. https://www.youtube.com/watch?v=30wxogRU3h8.

Kryder, R. (Hosts). (2024, September 10). Robert Kryder 2024-Bigfoot-Darkside presentation. In *KX Kryder Exploration.* YouTube. https://youtu.be/6XvgOz2iA0U?si=32BO4RpDaX-dpiG1.

Kübler, Ross, E. (1969). *On death and dying: What they dying have to teach doctors, nurses, clergy, and their own families.* Collier Books.

Kuhn, K.J. (2015). Relics from the «Lost Valley»: Discourses on the magic of masks. *The Ritual Year* (10), 203–212. https://www.zora.uzh.ch/id/eprint/111513/7/kuhn_rituals_magic_2015_relics.pdf.

Kuhn, T. (2012). *The structure of scientific revolutions (50th anniversary edition).* University of Chicago Press.

Lamana, L. (Host). (2023, October 12). The Solomon Island giants—Japanese encounter man-eaters. In *Wartime Stories.* YouTube. https://youtu.be/eTJOFkyE7L4?si=GRydc_iI3msQWmdx.

Lamana, L. (Host). (2024, March 18). The Choctaw war with Bigfoot. In *Wartime Stories.* YouTube. https://www.youtube.com/watch?v=hVC1Ia0VGjQ&t=499s.

Lamana, L. (Host). (2024, June 8). Military police officers mortified by Bigfoot encounters. In *Wartime Stories.* YouTube. https://www.youtube.com/watch?v=15G8-y9TUJU.

Lamana, L. (Host). (2024, November 22). These things can mimic other animals. In *Wartime Stories.* YouTube. https://youtu.be/lKbiTDXwpY0?si=etAm1XbDlBq8IDHJ.

Lancaster, A.H. (director), & Lancaster, B. (director). (2020). *Native Bigfoot.* Bilco Productions.

Lapseritis, K. (1998). *The psychic Sasquatch and their UFO connection.* Wild Flower Press.

LeGro, S. (Host). (2021, July 15). Sasquatch: Recluse of the Olympics (No. 300) [Audio podcast episode]. In *Into the Fray.* Apple Podcasts. https://podcasts.apple.com/ie/podcast/itf-300-sasquatch-recluse-of-the-olympics/id1042017993?i=1000528996404.

LeGro, S. (Host). (2024, May 16). Bigfoot of the Palisades (No. 448) [Audio podcast episode]. In *Into the Fray.* Apple Podcasts. https://podcasts.apple.com/nl/podcast/itf-448-bigfoot-of-the-palisades/id1042017993?i=1000655868840.

LeGro, S., & Hopf, G.M. (2019). *Beyond the Fray: Bigfoot.* Beyond the Fray Publishing.

Le Noël, E. (2001, Automne). Löchental: Le génocide helvétique des paléantropiens. *Hominologie & Cryptozoologie, 9.* https://garymangiacopraarchive.com/b3f5i1.

Levine, P.A. (2015). *Trauma and memory: Brain and body in a search for the living past.* North Atlantic Books.

Levy, E.P. (2005). The literary depiction of ontological shock. *The Midwest Quarterly, 46*(2), 107–122, 103. https://go.gale.com/ps/i.do?id=GALE%7CA129090502&sid=googleScholar&v=2.1&it=r&linkaccess=abs&issn=00263451&p=AONE&sw=w&userGroupName=anon%7E2056232a&aty=open-web-entry.

Levy, P. (2013). *Dispelling wetiko: Breaking the curse of evil.* North Atlantic Books.

Levy, P. (2021). *Wetiko: Healing the mind-virus that plagues our world.* Simon & Schuster.

Library of Congress Copyright Office. (n.d.). *Catalog of Copyright Entries (Third Series: 1976: July-December).*

Lipsitz, G. (1998). *The possessive investment in whiteness: How white people profit from identity politics.* Temple University Press.

Loeb, A. (2021). *Extraterrestrial: The first sign of intelligent life beyond earth.* Houghton Mifflin Harcourt.

Lomas, T. (2024). A history of scientific approaches to unidentified anomalous phenomena: Time to rethink their relegation to the paranormal and engage seriously?. *Journal of Scientific Exploration, 38*(1), 91–109. https://doi.org/10.31275/20243163.

Lomas, T., Case, B., & Masters, M.P. (2024). The cryptoterrestrial hypothesis: A case for scientific openness to a concealed earthly explanation for Unexplained Anomalous Phenomena. *Philosophy and Cosmology, 33,* 1–46. https://www.researchgate.net/publication/381405238_The_cryptoterrestrial_hypothesis_A_case_for_scientific_openness_to_a_concealed_earthly_explanation_for_Unidentified_Anomalous_Phenomena.

Lott, E. (1991). "The seeming counterfeit": Racial politics and early blackface minstrelsy. *American Quarterly, 43*(2), 223–254. https://doi.org/10.2307/2712925.

Loxton, D., & Prothero, D.R. (2013). *Abominable science!: Origins of the Yeti, Nessie, and other famous cryptids.* Columbia University Press.

Lyons, C.P. (1950). *The hairy giants of Laidlaw.* J.M. Dent & Sons.

Machovec, L. (2022). *The Sasquatch paradox: Scientific defiance to the recognition of relict hominoids.* Hangar 1 Publishing.

Mack, J.E. (1995). *Abduction: Human encounters with aliens (Revised edition).* Ballantine Books.

Maher, K. (2022, September 21). Some researchers are looking for Bigfoot-Just don't tell anyone. The *Wall Street Journal.* https://www.wsj.com/articles/some-researchers-are-looking-for-bigfoot-just-dont-tell-anyone-11663769929.

Margaryan, A., Sinding, M.H. S., Carøe, C., Yamshchikov, V., Burtsev, I., & Gilbert, M.T.P. (2021). The genomic origin of Zana of Abkhazia. *Advanced Genetics, 2*(2), 1–9. https://onlinelibrary.wiley.com/doi/epdf/10.1002/ggn2.10051.

Martin, R. (1999, September 30). Great Zulu shaman and elder Credo Mutwa…on alien abduction and reptilians: A rare, astonishing conversation. *Biblioteca Pleyades.* https://www.bibliotecapleyades.net/esp_credo_mutwa03.htm.

Martinez, G. (2017). *In the land of giants: Hunting monsters in the Hindu Kush* (D. Hahn, Trans.). Scribe Publications. (Original work published 2011).

Matthews, R. (2024). *Bigfoot: True-life encounters with the legendary Sasquatch.* Arcturus Publishing Limited.

Mayer, F.S., & Frantz, C.M. (2004). The connectedness to nature scale: A measure of individuals' feeling in community with nature. *Journal of environmental psychology, 24*(4), 503–515. https://doi.org/10.1016/j.jenvp.2004.10.001.

Mayes, M. (2022). *Valley of the apes: The search for sasquatch in Area X.* Anomalist Books.

Mazur, L.B. (2021). The epistemic imperialism of science. Reinvigorating early critiques of scientism. *Frontiers in Psychology, 11,* 1–12. https://doi.org/10.3389/fpsyg.2020.609823.

McDougall, S., III (2014). *Research methods in Africana Studies.* Peter Lang, Inc.

McGowen, T. (author), & Ambrus, V.G. (illustrator). (1981). *Encyclopedia of Legendary Creatures.* Checkerboard Press.

McGrath, A. (2022). *Beasts of the world (Vol. 1: Hairy Humanoids).* Hangar 1 Publishing.

McLuhan, R. (2024, March 29). Boggle threshold. *Psi Encyclopedia.* https://psi-encyclopedia.spr.ac.uk/articles/boggle-threshold#footnote1_5fqacl1.

MelBlanc222. (2016, December 17). Bigfoot 1994 Ohio Howls in (HD). In *Melblanc222.* YouTube. https://www.youtube.com/watch?v=l5UQ0uCj2XM.

Meldrum, J. (2006). *Sasquatch: Legend meets science.* Tom Doherty Associates, LLC.

Meldrum, J. (2016). Sasquatch & other wildmen: The search for relict hominoids. *Journal of Scientific Exploration, 30*(3), 355–373. https://journalofscientificexploration.org/index.php/jse/article/view/1090.

Meldrum, J. (2017). Paradigm shifts and the search for relict hominoids. *Capeia,* 1–7. https://beta.capeia.com/zoology/2017/12/15/paradigm-shifts-and-the-search-for-relict-hominoids.

Meldrum, J., & Guoxing, Z. (2012). Footprint evidence of the Chinese Yeren. *The Relict Hominoid Inquiry, 1,* 57–66. https://www.isu.edu/media/libraries/rhi/brief-communications/Footprint-Evidence-of-Chinese-Yeren.pdf.

Menakem, R. (2021). *My grandmother's hands: Racialized trauma and the pathway to mending our hearts and bodies.* Penguin UK.

Menzies, R.E., & Menzies, R.G. (2021). *Mortals: How fear of death shaped human society.* Allen & Unwin.

Mickes, L., Wilson, B.M., & Wixted, J.T. (2025). The cognitive science of eyewitness memory. *Trends in Cognitive Sciences,* 1–14. https://doi.org/10.1016/j.tics.2025.01.008.

Mitchell, D.S.B. (2022). Of color-confrontation and consumption: Black and Buddhist insights into racism. *The Arrow: A Journal of Wakeful Society, Culture, & Politics, 9*(2), 45–63. https://arrow-journal.org/between-amitabha-and-tubman-black-buddhist-thought/.

Mitchell, D.S.B. (2023). "What goes bump in the psyche": Relict hominoids and reality shifts as existential threats to Western culture. In J. Glazier (Ed.), *Paranormal Ruptures: Critical Approaches to Exceptional Experiences* (pp. 21–56). Beyond the Fray Publishing.

Moneymaker, M.J. (2024, April 9). More info about observable paranormal stuff connected with Bigfoots. In *BFRO (Bigfoot Field Researchers Organization)—est. 1995.* Facebook.

Moore, C., Jr. (w/ L. Blackburn). (2024). Southern Bigfoot: Examining cryptozoology's greatest mystery in the southern United States (Expanded Edition). [self-published].

Morehead, R. (2013). *Voices in the wilderness: A true story (2nd edition).* [self-published].

Morehead, R. (w/ D. Paulides). (2024). *Bigfoot unveiled: Scientific answers to Bigfoot mysteries.* [self-published].

Morris, D. (1994). *The human animal: A personal view of the human species.* BCA.

Moyano, D.B., & Leczano, R.A.G. (2020). Effects of infrasound on health: Looking for improvements in housing conditions. *International Journal of Occupational Safety and Ergonomics, 28*(2), 809–823. https://doi.org/10.1080/10803548.2020.1831787.

Mulligan, C.J., Quinn, E.B., Hamadmad, D., Dutton, C.L., Nevell, L., Binder, A.M., Panter-Brick, C., & Dajani, R. (2025). Epigenetic signatures of intergenerational exposure to violence in three generations of Syrian refugees. *Scientific Reports, 15*(1), 1–13. https://doi.org/10.1038/s41598-025-89818-z.

Munns, B., & Meldrum, J. (2013). Surface anatomy and subcutaneous adipose tissue features in the Patterson-Gimlin film hominid. *The Relict Hominoid Inquiry, 2,* 1–21. Munns—Meldrum-Final-draft.pdf.

Murphy, C.L. (2010). *Know the Sasquatch/Bigfoot: Astounding evidence of Sasquatch or Bigfoot in North America!* Hancock House.

Mussi, M. (2015). Europe: The outstanding universal value of a marginal area of the Palaeolithic world. In N. Sanz (Ed.), *Human Origin Sites and the World Heritage Convention in Eurasia (HEADS 4, Volume I)* (pp. 26–32). United Nations Educational, Scientific and Cultural Organization.

Mutwa, C. (1964). *Indaba, my children: African folktales.* Grove Press.

My Talk Show Heroes. (2016, May 4). Anna-Marie Goddard-"Bigfoot" Sighting. https://www.youtube.com/watch?v=nt6VPM6DhFQ.

Myers, J. (Host). (2024, April 17). Legend meets science: Where's the truth? (No. 58) [Video podcast episode]. In *Sasquatch Outpost Podcast.* YouTube. https://www.youtube.com/watch?v=LaDbf67R9EM.

Naish, D. (2014, September 17). Is cryptozoology good or bad for science? *Scientific American.* https://blogs.scientificamerican.com/tetrapod-zoology/is-cryptozoology-good-or-bad-for-science/.

Naish, D. (2016). *Hunting monsters: Cryptozoology and the reality behind the myths.* Arcturus Publishing.

Neely, T.J. (2020). *Revelations: The human-hominid connection.* [self-published].

Neisser, U., & Harsch, N. (1992). Phantom flashbulbs: False recollections of hearing the news about Challenger. In Winograd, E., & Neisser, U. (Eds.), *Affect and Accuracy in Recall* (pp. 9–31). Cambridge University Press.

Newkirk, G., & Newkirk, D. (Hosts). (2024, December 30). How Nutella finally captured Bigfoot [feat. Cliff Barackman] (No. 27) [Video podcast episode]. In *Haunted Objects Podcast.* https://www.youtube.com/watch?v=js7kMSV0NuE&t=2s.

Newton, M. (2005). *Encyclopedia of cryptozoology: A global guide to hidden animals and their pursuers.* McFarland

Nguyen, M.T. (2015). The hoodie as sign, screen, expectation, and force. *Signs: Journal of Women in Culture and Society, 40*(4), 791–816. https://doi.org/10.1086/680326.

Nickell, J. (2017 September/October). Bigfoot as big myth: Seven phases of mythmaking. *Skeptical Inquirer, 41*(5). https://skepticalinquirer.org/2017/09/bigfoot-as-big-myth-seven-phases-of-mythmaking/.

Nobles, W.W. (2006). *Seeking the sakhu: Foundational writings for an African psychology.* Third World Press.

Noël, C. (2009). *Impossible visits: The inside story of interactions with Sasquatch at habituation sites.* Xlibris Corp. [self-published]

Noël, C. (2019). *Mindspeak: Tapping into Sasquatch and science.* [self-published].

Noel, C. (2021). How to see a Sasquatch - Documentary. In *Impossible Visits.* YouTube. https://www.youtube.com/watch?v=DlpssL94Gso&t=5113s.

Noël, C. (2022). *Sasquatch and autism: Twelve parallels.* [self-published].

Noël, C. (2023). *There is no veil: At play in the vast here and now.* [self-published].

Noël, C. (Host). (2023, February 16). There is no veil, trailer 3: The Sasquatch connection. In *Impossible Visits.* YouTube. https://youtu.be/HtF3yg4mEzk?si=z2r0SSG5EvTQwVwl.

Nörenberg, H. (2017). The numinous, the ethical, and the body. Rudolf Otto's "The idea of the holy" revisited. *Open Theology, 3*(1), 546–564. https://doi.org/10.1515/opth-2017-0042.

Nunn, P.D., Kumar, R., Barrowman, H.M., Chambers, L., Fifita, L., Gegeo, D., ... & Waiwai, M. (2024). Traditional knowledge for climate resilience in the Pacific Islands. *Wiley Interdisciplinary Reviews: Climate Change,* 1–25. https://doi.org/10.1002/wcc.882.

Nunnelly, B. (n.d.). The Hebbardsville Hillbillies part 1. In *Kick Acts Magazine.* http://www.kick-acts.com/2010/01/04/the-hebbardsville-hillbillies-part-1-by-bart-nunnelly/.

Opit, G. (author), & Byrnes, P. (illustrator). (2009). *Australian cryptozoology: The Australian Yowie, New Guinea mermaid, big cats and other wildlife wonders.* Equilateral Enterprise.

Otto, R. (trans. J.W. Harvey). (1917). *The idea of the holy: An inquiry into the non-rational factor in the idea of the divine and its relation to the rational.* Oxford University Press. https://faculty.trinity.edu/mbrown/whatisreligion/PDF%20readings/Otto-Idea%20of%20the%20Holy.pdf.

Palacios, E. (Host). (2024, June 24). Brushy Creek Bigfoot eye witness—Expedition Brushy Creek. In *Media Palace.* YouTube. https://www.youtube.com/watch?v=nm6UlpI-kds&t=165s.

Palmer, G., & Braud, W. (2002). Exceptional human experiences, disclosure, and a more inclusive view of physical, psychological, and spiritual well-being. *Journal of Transpersonal Psychology, 34*(1), 29–59. https://www.atpweb.org/jtparchive/trps-34-02-01-029.pdf.

Palmer, G., & Hastings, A. (2013). Exploring the nature of exceptional human experiences. In H.L. Friedman & G. Hartelius (Eds.), *The Wiley Blackwell Handbook of Transpersonal Psychology* (pp. 333–352). Wiley Blackwell.

Paterson, M. (Host). (2023, March 28). Incredible encounter story with Michael Bleuler. In *Sasquatch Ontario.* YouTube. https://www.youtube.com/live/zB9N00fA0DQ?si=iteXrlsWQeSlYorc.

Patterson, G. (2020). *Beyond the Secret Elephants: Of mysterious relict hominoids and elusive legendary elephants.* Hangar 1 Publishing.

Patterson, R. (2018). *Do Abominable Snowmen of America really exist?.* Crypto Editions (Hancock House Publishers).

Paulides, D. (2009). *Tribal bigfoot.* Hancock House Publishers.

Payan, J., Jr. (Host). (2022, February 14). Patterson Gimlin Bigfoot new evidence!. In *Breaking Bigfoot.* YouTube. https://www.youtube.com/watch?v=CFkPzPdmHyY.

Petakov, A. (Director). (2024, March 10). The search for the Honey Island Swamp Monster: Bigfoot Beyond the Trail. In *Small Town Monsters.* YouTube. https://www.youtube.com/watch?v=EHUv-caRNo0&t=490s.

Petakov, A. (Director). (2025, March 2). Nightmare in the forest: encountering the Sasquatch (Bigfoot witness encounters). In *Small Town Monsters.* YouTube. https://www.youtube.com/watch?v=NX59Ms6r7M4.

Peters, H. (2023). *Mysteries of Canada (Volume IV).* [self-published].

Peters, H. (Host). (2024, April 14). Secrets from the Archive—Neanderthal genocide in the Swiss Alps (No. 3) [Video podcast episode]. In *Hammerson Peters.* YouTube. https://www.youtube.com/watch?v=XNW4tkBClhQ&t=266s.

Peters, H. (Host). (2024, May 19). The secret Sasquatch files (No. 1) [Video podcast episode]. In *Hammerson Peters.* YouTube. https://www.youtube.com/watch?v=24iT_d9j98U.

Peters, H. (Host). (2024, December 1). Wildman legends from Northern Canada [Compilation] [Video podcast episode]. In *Hammerson Peters.* YouTube. https://youtu.be/-PLt3OYWhc?si=ZupB4hXZn7jZze35.

Pierce, C.B. (1972). *The legend of Boggy Creek.* Howco.

Plutarch. (2003). *Moralia (Volume V).* Harvard University Press.

Pope, A. (2011). Pope, A. (2011). Modern materialism through the lens of Indo-Tibetan Buddhism. *International Journal of Transpersonal Studies,* 30(1-2), 171–177.. https://doi.org/10.24972/ijts.2011.30.1-2.171.

Porshnev, B. (2017). The struggle for troglodytes [Book section reprint]. *The Relict Hominoid Inquiry, 6,* 33–170.

Porshnev, B. (w/ Clark, C., L. Thomas, Trans.). (2000). *The Soviet Sasquatch.* CFZ Press.

Porter, T. (Sakokweniónkwas). (2008). *And Grandma said...Iroquois teachings as passed down through the oral tradition.* Xlibris Corporation.

Powell, T. (2015). *Edges of science.* Willamette City Press, LLC.

Powell, T. (2018). *The locals: A contemporary investigation of the Bigfoot/Sasquatch phenomenon.* Hancock House.

Powell, T. (2022). The final interview. In M. Freeman (Ed.), *The Freeman Bigfoot Files* (pp. 260–270). Hangar 1 Publishing.

Prescott, T. (Host). (2022, March 16). Minnesota Iceman Witness—Terry Cullen at the 1989 Sasquatch Evidence Symposium. In *The Sasquatch Archives.* YouTube. https://youtu.be/86zOfwuMPUY?si=DdiNw2qI5IC_0-Od.

Press, M. (2020, August 6). Mummies among us. *Aeon.* https://aeon.co/essays/when-we-lived-with-death-mummies-were-medicine-and-paint.

Prince-Hughes, D. (1997). *The archetype of the ape-man: The phenomenological archaeology of a relic hominid ancestor.* Dissertation.com.

Pruitt, M. (2023). The phenomenal Sasquatch: Seeking the natural origins of a cultural icon. [self-published].

Pyle, R.M. (2017). *Where Bigfoot walks: Crossing the dark divide* [Audible audiobook]. Catapult.

Quan-Baffour, K.P. (2012). Sankofa: 'Gazing Back' to Indigenous Knowledge and Skills for Socio-Economic Development of Ghana. *Studies of Tribes and Tribals, 10*(1), 1–5. http://krepublishers.com/02-Journals/T%20&%20T/T%20&%20T-10-0-000-12-Web/T%20&%20T-10-01-000-12-Abst-PDF/S-T&T-10-1-001-12-265-Quan-Baffour-K-P/S-T&T-10-1-001-12-265-Quan-Baffour-K-P-Tt.pdf.

Rabeyron, T. (2022). When the truth is out there: Counseling people who report anomalous experiences. *Frontiers in Psychology,* 5918, 1–18. https://doi.org/10.3389/fpsyg.2021.693707.

Radford, B. (2014). Bigfoot at 50: Evaluating a half-century of bigfoot evidence. In B. Farha (Ed.), *Pseudoscience and deception: Smoke and mirrors* (pp. 161–170). University Press of America.

Radford, B. (2024, January 19). Replication in skeptical investigation. *Center for Inquiry.* https://centerforinquiry.org/blog/experimental-replication-in-skeptical-investigation/.

Radford, B. (2024, January/February). Is Bigfoot dead?. *The Skeptical Inquirer,* 31–38. https://skepticalinquirer.org/2023/12/is-bigfoot-dead/.

Ramirez, M. (Host). (2024, June 26). Bigfoot encounter from Minnesota (the being was annoyed by our presence) [Video podcast episode]. In *Sasquatch Theory.* YouTube. https://www.youtube.com/watch?v=Lgjj7-zqWKs&t=2565s.

Randles, J. (2001). *Time storms: Amazing evidence for time warps, space rifts and time travel.* Judy Piatkus (Publishers) Limited.

Regal, B. (2011). *Searching for Sasquatch: Crackpots, eggheads, and cryptozoology.* Palgrave McMillan.

Reinhardt, C. (Host). (2024, January 8). Unseen Patterson Gimlin Footage? (No. 1) [Video podcast episode]. In *Discover Sasquatch.* YouTube. https://www.youtube.com/live/tGkyL-kooCU?si=BaNWBwWwr59umOwK.

Reinhardt, C. (Host). (2024, January 22). Wood boogers on Creepy Mountain/Discover Sasquatch Interviews with Mark Green (No. 3) [Video podcast episode]. In *Discover Sasquatch.* YouTube. https://www.youtube.com/live/1wcCD-HcQzc?si=SziNNXnvx2X4bYBE.

Reinhardt, C. (Host). (2024, March 18). Sasquatch and scripture: The link to the Fallen Ones (No. 10) [Video podcast episode]. In *Discover Sasquatch.* YouTube. https://www.youtube.com/watch?v=j5rX-46YolU.

Roberts, J.L. (2023). Uncanny technology, trauma, and world collapse in Ariel phenomenon. In J.W. Glazier (Ed.), *Paranormal ruptures: Critical approaches to exceptional experiences* (pp. 219–248). Beyond the Fray Publishing.

Roberts, T.B., & Winkelman, W.J. (2015). Psychedelic induced transpersonal experiences, therapies, and their implications for transpersonal psychology. In H.L. Friedman & G. Hartelius (Eds.), *The Wiley-Blackwell Handbook of Transpersonal Psychology* (pp. 459–479). Wiley Blackwell Publishing.

Roehl, F. (Host). (2022, May 2). No caribou today (No. 28) [Video podcast episode]. In *Subarctic Alaska Sasquatch.* YouTube. https://www.youtube.com/watch?v=Vbc2XfLlWKE&t=604s.

Roehl, F. (Host). (2022, May 5). Trappers nightmare (No. 30) [Video podcast episode]. In *Subarctic Alaska Sasquatch.* YouTube. https://youtu.be/2UtyRPv8KZY?si=wg5C2na525R7NMQI.

Roehl, F. (Host). (2022, May 16). Thomas and the Tongas Part 1 (No. 38) [Video podcast episode]. In *Subarctic Alaska Sasquatch.* YouTube. #38 THOMAS AND THE TONGAS PART1 - YouTube.

Roehl, F. (Host). (2023, February 8). Something wicked, this way comes (No. 129) [Video podcast episode]. In *Subarctic Alaska Sasquatch.* YouTube. https://www.youtube.com/watch?v=xpLvezS6z24.

Roehl, F. (Host). (2023, March 3). Ruby's Song (No, 130) [Video podcast episode]. In *Subarctic Alaska Sasquatch.* YouTube. https://www.youtube.com/watch?v=4ktJdNPljp4.

Roehl, F. (Host). (2023, March 20). Oilwell Rd Ninilchik Alaska (No. 135) [Video podcast episode]. In *Subarctic Alaska Sasquatch.* YouTube. https://youtu.be/xyaJRPb1sX0?si=o7Y2LAQSqvlHQnAI.

Roehl, F. (Host). (2023, October 27). More shots fired on the Yukon (No. 178) [Video podcast episode]. In *Subarctic Alaska Sasquatch.* YouTube. https://www.youtube.com/watch?v=EC-btUO0RnM.

Roehl, F. (Host). (2023, November 12). Tap tap tap (No. 182) [Video podcast episode]. In *Subarctic Alaska Sasquatch.* YouTube. https://youtu.be/8a—r_zanPY?si=fVH2FEKr3FBdFtdb.

Roehl, F. (Host). (2024, February 17). Village girls encounter circa 1981 (No. 207) [Video podcast episode]. In *Subarctic Alaska Sasquatch.* YouTube. https://www.youtube.com/watch?v=juVa6PIQgnY.

Roehl, F. (Host). (2024, May 8). It sounded like a demon + Alaska stuff intro (No. 229) [Video podcast episode]. In *Subarctic Alaska Sasquatch*. YouTube. https://www.youtube.com/watch?v=7HloKIbClnk.

Roehl, F. (Host). (2024, May 28). Biologist shares terrifying encounter (No. 233) [Video podcast episode]. In *Subarctic Alaska Sasquatch*. YouTube. https://www.youtube.com/watch?v=hbBBgMYUekM.

Roehl, F. (Host). (2024, October 3). High strangeness in remote Alaska (No. 256) [Video podcast episode]. In *Subarctic Alaska Sasquatch*. YouTube. (46) #256 HIGH STRANGENESS IN REMOTE ALASKA - YouTube.

Roehl, F. (Host). (2025, March 4). S E Alaska cannibal giants interview (No. 273) [Video podcast episode]. In *Subarctic Alaska Sasquatch*. YouTube. https://youtu.be/e2PI4kyBStA?si=JQJCRf_XCEUcUpvd.

Roll, W.G. (1987). Memory and the longbody. *Theta, 15*(1–4), 10–29. https://www.psychicalresearchfoundation.com/_files/ugd/dd736b_45dd0df2bd9449e0a84206233b1a268f.pdf.

Roosevelt, T. (1893). *Wilderness hunter* (Vol. 2). Putnam.

Runkle, M., & Marentette, T. (2025, March 6). Unravelling the Bigfoot mystery—Dr. Jeffrey Meldrum. In *The Runegade Podcast*. YouTube. https://www.youtube.com/watch?v=4EoarnbYtoQ&t=2s.

Safer, M.A., Christianson, S.Å., Autry, M.W., & Österlund, K. (1998). Tunnel memory for traumatic events. *Applied Cognitive Psychology: The Official Journal of the Society for Applied Research in Memory and Cognition, 12*(2), 99–117. https://psycnet.apa.org/doi/10.1002/(SICI)1099-0720(199804)12:2%3C99::AID-ACP509%3E3.0.CO;2-7.

Sagan, C. (1977). *Dragons of Eden: Speculations on the evolution of human intelligence*. Random House.

Sagan, C. (1979). *Broca's brain: Reflections on the romance of science*. Presidio Press.

Sagan, C. (1995). *The demon-haunted world: Science as a candle in the dark*. Random House.

Sagers, A. (Host). (2023, February 14). Bigfoot researcher Cliff Barackman on the state of Squatch! [Audio podcast episode]. In *Talking Strange: Paranormal Show [Den of Geek]*. YouTube.

Sagher, A.D., Butzer, B., & Wahbeh, H. (2019). The characteristics of exceptional human experiences. *Journal of Consciousness Studies, 26*(11–12), 203–237. https://psycnet.apa.org/record/2020-14361-009.

Sanderson, I.T. (2008). *Abominable snowmen, legend come to life: Bigfoot, Sasquatch, oh-mah, grassman, and skunk ape*. Createspace Independent Publishing Platform.

Sasquatch Confessions. (2022, August 6). St. Louis Co. Minnesota (Amazing Sasquatch Vocalizations). In *Sasquatch Confessions*. YouTube. https://www.youtube.com/watch?v=SCyK3fSZDks&list=PLO0PqscYC6r3LiPGjPmZczTNY58OZK78I&index=61.

Sasquatch Data Project. (2025, March 26). Beyond random chance: Multivariate analysis of Sasquatch witness reports with lunar, seasonal, and psychological data. [unpublished manuscript]. https://www.sasquatchdataproject.com/data-investigations.

Sass, L.A., & Woolfolk, R.L. (1988). Psychoanalysis and the hermeneutic turn: A critique of narrative truth and historical truth. *Journal of the American Psychoanalytic Association, 36*(2), 429–454. https://doi.org/10.1177/000306518803600208.

Schacter, D.L. (1996). *Searching for memory: The brain, the mind, and the past*. Basic Books.

Schacter, D.L. (2001). *The seven sins of memory: How the mind forgets and remembers*. Houghton Mifflin Company.

Schick, T., Jr., & Vaughn, L. (2014). *How to think about weird things: Critical thinking for a new age (7th edition)*. McGraw-Hill.

Schmolck, H., Buffalo, E.A., & Squire, L.R. (2000). Memory distortions develop over time: Recollections of the O.J. Simpson trial verdict after 15 and 32 months. *Psychological Science, 11*, 39–45. https://doi.org/10.1111/1467-9280.00212.

Shackley, M. (1982). The case for Neanderthal survival: Fact, fiction, or faction? *Antiquity, LVI*, 31–41. https://doi.org/10.1017/S0003598X00044549.

Shackley, M. (1983). *Still living?: Yeti, Sasquatch and the Neanderthal enigma*. Thames and Hudson.

Sheldrake, R. (2003). *The sense of being stared at: And other aspects of the extended mind*. Harmony.

Sheldrake, R., & Smart, P. (2023). Directional Scopaesthesia and Its Implications for Theories of Vision. *Journal of Scientific Exploration, 37*(3), 312–329. https://sheldrake.org/files/pdfs/papers/Scopaesthesia-and-Its-Implications-for-Theories-of-Vision.pdf.

Shermer, M. (2003) Show me the body. *Scientific American, 288*(5), 27. https://www.scientificamerican.com/article/show-me-the-body/.

Shiel, L.A. (2011). *Creature of controversy: Forbidden Bigfoot (Part One)*. Jacobsville Books.

Shiver. (2021, November 30). Bigfoot: The monster mystery that shocked the world. In *Shiver Paranormal Documentaries*. https://www.youtube.com/watch?v=Z5iyWtyLHNg&list=PLO0PqscYC6r01DlOKeFjeaCB0qWUvIjiv&index=20.

Short, B. (n.d.). *The De Facto Sasquatch*. [self-published].

Short, B. (2024). *The de facto Sasquatch: Cultural legacies and military encounters*. Hangar 1 Publishing.

Shute, C. (Host). (2024, February 19). Dr. Jeffrey Meldrum (Sasquatch: Legend Meets Science). In *Chuck Shute Podcast*. YouTube. https://youtu.be/Aw9U26Utabo?si=irAabHyiQwttU3s_.

Sinclair, B. (2024, March 1). Critical approaches to the paranormal: UFOs, AI, high strangeness, & Bigfoot with Dr. Jacob Glazier. In *Unravelling the Universe*. YouTube. https://youtu.be/zkMw3Gt7SEw?si=FDe1z_zjrVH4IqEf.

Singh, J.A.L., & Zingg, R.M. (1942). *Wolf-children and feral man*. Harper & Brothers Publishers.

https://archive.org/details/in.ernet.dli.2015.158185.
Slate, B.A., & Berry, A. (1976). *Bigfoot.* Bantam Books.
Smith, A.M. (1993). *Shoshone tales.* University of Utah Press.
Smith, D.L. (2007). *The most dangerous animal: Human nature and the origins of war.* St. Martin's Griffin.
Smyth, L. (Host). (2022, December 23). The best of the Bigfoot Project! [Video podcast episode]. In *The Bigfoot Project.* https://youtu.be/eaOmkwJzRLc?si=BCXwEyzL8HflpU9M.
Smyth, L. (Host). (2023, August 27). A collection of very strange encounters with Bigfoot [Video podcast episode]. In *The Bigfoot Project.* YouTube. https://youtu.be/k3307z7JmOA?si=hlI4zsLErvfqpAXC.
Smyth, L. (Host). (2023, October 1). 3 hour Bigfoot marathon December giveaway [Video podcast episode]. In *Bigfoot Case Files.* YouTube. https://www.youtube.com/watch?v=h1ZURr8Pyl8.
Smyth, L. (Host). (2023, October 18). The Bigfoot Project's most liked stories of 2023 [Video podcast episode]. In *The Bigfoot Project.* YouTube. https://youtu.be/2AyWP3-AAl0?si=3CaQnyd3SY03Sej_.
Smyth, L. (Host). (2023, December 30). Bigfoot saved my life [Video podcast episode]. In *Bigfoot Case Files.* YouTube. https://youtu.be/MqxM353BILI?si=-QRtG3Ez1wdr0Ivb.
Smyth, L. (Host). (2024, March 28). We shot a Bigfoot—no blood? [Video podcast episode]. In *The Bigfoot Project.* YouTube. https://youtu.be/fnIA-QshZLs?si=45aEVsOplGFY9oJB.
Smyth, L. (Host). (2024, March 31). Swamp Ape captured in Florida [Video podcast episode]. In *Bigfoot Case Files.* YouTube. https://youtu.be/v5BfgzEYNQs?si=-fxs2BLrLWh7bTUl.
Smyth, L. (Host). (2024, April 12). Bigfoot harasses families and attacks their dogs [Video podcast episode]. In *Bigfoot Case Files.* YouTube. https://www.youtube.com/watch?app=desktop&v=7JZOfujAymI.
Smyth, L. (Host). (2024, April 25). Facing something that isn't supposed to exist the human/hominid connection [Video podcast episode]. In *Bigfoot Case Files.* YouTube. https://youtu.be/NW2L2mgfrXk?si=rBFsFzIsAaxkzWzA.
Smyth, L. (Host). (2024, July 7). A gruesome find, girl never returns from berry picking. [Video podcast episode] In *Bigfoot Case Files.* YouTube. https://youtu.be/kv-tj1QC2Us?si=aoUH_n0-Wp7BljwH.
Society for Scientific Exploration. (2024, March 20). Panel on education in parapsychology [Video]. In *Society for Scientific Exploration.* YouTube. https://youtu.be/5bzDnF-Q0IQ?si=HlU9bSPDEDsProxx.
Sprague, R. (Host). (2024, April 4). Jeremiah Byron—The Bigfoot mystery [Video podcast episode]. In *Ryan Sprague.* YouTube. https://www.youtube.com/watch?v=8smEoRyPq2U.
Squatch Mafia. (Host). (2023, June 25). Bigfoot—Reflections FULL DOCUMENTARY Sasquatch, John Bindernagel, John Green. In *Squatch Mafia.* YouTube. https://youtu.be/qxRuLaQcxZE?si=v6R2jcrXNlJXaCRv.
Squatch Zone. (2016, August 15). Rhonda Morehead and her dad Ron Morehead talk Bigfoot!. YouTube. https://youtu.be/MbtO-vCCfyg?si=tSUjiXMwyVTc5Y3F.
Stollznow, K. (2014). *Language myths, mysteries and magic.* Springer.
Strain, K.M. (2008). *Giants, cannibals, & monsters: Bigfoot in Native culture.* Hancock House.
Strain, K.M. (2012). Mayak Datat: The Hairy Man pictographs. *The Relict Hominoid Inquiry, 1,* 1–12. https://www.isu.edu/media/libraries/rhi/research-papers/Mayak-Datat-Hairy-Man-Pictographs-1.pdf.
Strand, R.W. (2017). The forensic experiential trauma interview (FETI). *Arizona Coalition for Victim Services.* https://www.niwrc.org/sites/default/files/DV%20and%20LE%20Collection/FETI%20Information%20Sheet.pdf.
Strange Outdoors. (Host). (2017, November 25). The puzzling disappearance of Jared Negrete from Mount San Gorgonio [Video podcast episode]. In *Strange Outdoors.* https://www.strangeoutdoors.com/mysterious-stories-blog/2017/11/22/jared-negrete.
StrangeSpotting. (2023, January 8). The hidden truth revealed: Analyzing the Pennsylvania white Bigfoot sighting! [Video podcast episode]. In *StrangeSpotting.* YouTube. https://www.youtube.com/watch?v=BqPuQm-BOEU.
StrangeSpotting. (2023, July 15). Genoskwa is the terrifying man-eating stone giant of Iroquois legends behind the Missing 411 cases? [Video podcast episode]. In *StrangeSpotting.* YouTube. https://www.youtube.com/watch?v=A4vTcHNK2X0.
StrangeSpotting. (2024, March 2). Bigfoot mug shot follow-up Part 1 [Video podcast episode]. In *StrangeSpotting.* YouTube. https://youtu.be/gnQOVBYIuAY?si=iw0nKB92ZwPqD07G.
Strieber, A., & Strieber, W. (2016). *The communion letters.* Crossroad Press.
Strieber, W. (2016). *Communion: A true story.* Souvenir Press.
Strieber, W., & Kripal, J.J. (2016). *The super natural: A new vision of the unexplained.* Jeremy P. Tarcher-Penguin.
Stroud, L. (2020, December 10). Survivorman Bigfoot—Willow Creek (No. 5). In *Survivorman—Les Stroud.* YouTube. https://www.youtube.com/watch?v=_akddzGiPsU&list=PLdteC6yMLFpl_3hGoPWt1MklFJ2x7j-Bd&index=5.
Stroud, L. (2020, December 19). Survivorman Bigfoot—The hidden world (No. 9). In *Survivorman—Les Stroud.* YouTube. https://www.youtube.com/watch?v=Cz5Hj_1Dh24&t=640s.
Strozier, S. (2022). *Probable, possible, plausible: Explanatory guide to monsters and myth.* Dorrance Publishing.
Sullivan, D. (Host). (2023, December 17). Duke's encounters, dogman, giants, genoskwa, & gugwe

revealed! (No. 157). In *World Bigfoot Radio*. YouTube. https://www.youtube.com/watch?v=DyWbCDY8wbY.
Sykes, B. (2014). *The nature of the beast: The first scientific evidence on the survival of apemen into modern times*. Coronet Press.
Sykes, B. (2016). *Bigfoot, Yeti, and the last Neanderthal: A geneticist's search for modern apemen*. Disinformation Books.
Szilagyi, E. (Host). (2024, August 6). Greatest hits (No. 26) [Audio podcast episode]. In *uNcomfortable podcast*. Apple Podcasts. https://podcasts.apple.com/gb/podcast/ep170-greatest-hits-ep26-i-dont-know-what-it-was-but/id1553689988?i=1000664487285.
Szilagyi, E. (Host). (2025, April 18). Grasping Sasquatch with John Baranchok (No. 187) [Video podcast episode]. In *uNcomfortable podcast*. YouTube. https://www.youtube.com/watch?v=PnO4AgEDZ34.
Templer, D.I. (1970). The construction and validation of a death anxiety scale. *The Journal of General Psychology, 82*, 165–177. https://doi.org/10.1080/00221309.1970.9920634.
Terrell, B. (2024, May 26). A 2024 suburban Bigfoot documentary and investigation: The "White Witch" of Stinchcomb!. In *Red Dirt Cryptid Investigations*. YouTube. https://youtu.be/N1db2TuVo8M?si=mZBKSFzz53zKiwct.
Thompson, K. (1989). The UFO encounter experience as a crisis of transformation. In S. Grof & C. Grof (Ed.), *Spiritual emergency: When personal transformation becomes a crisis* (pp. 121–136). Tarcher.
Thomsen, D.K., & Brinkmann, S. (2009). An interviewer's guide to autobiographical memory: Ways to elicit concrete experiences and to avoid pitfalls in interpreting them. *Qualitative Research in Psychology, 6*(4), 294–312. https://doi.org/10.1080/14780880802396806.
Tian, I.Y., Munns, B., & Meldrum, J. (2022). Mathematically optimal restoration and stabilization of the Patterson-Gimlin film with computation feature detection. *The Relict Hominoid Inquiry, 11*, 263–287. https://www.isu.edu/media/libraries/rhi/research-papers/Tian-manuscript_revised.pdf.
Tillich, P. (2011). *Systematic Theology, Volume 3* (Vol. 3). University of Chicago Press.
Tompkins, S. (2021). The Bigfoot Mapping Project. *The Relict Hominoid Inquiry, 10*, 1–5. https://www.isu.edu/media/libraries/rhi/brief-communications/THE-BIGFOOT-MAPPING-PROJECT_final.pdf.
Tonnies, M. (2023). *The cryptoterrestrials: A meditation on indigenous humanoids and the aliens among us*. Anomalist Books.
Totherow, C.W. (Host). (2020, November 9). 50 years with Bigfoot, Janice Carter. Mannimal Research [No. 50]. In *Paranormal Odyssey*. YouTube. https://www.youtube.com/watch?v=ZliI121qsZQ.
Tréguer, P. (n.d.). The curious origin of 'the mind boggles.' *World Histories*. https://wordhistories.net/2018/06/05/mind-boggles-origin/.
Trey the Explainer. (2024, February 8). The Native Bigfoot. In *Trey the Explainer*. YouTube. https://www.youtube.com/watch?v=7zJhJsdoTYQ&t=1809s.
Truzzi, M. (1987). On pseudo-skepticism. *Zetetic Scholar*. http://www.anomalist.com/commentaries/pseudo.html.
Tulving, E. (1985). Memory and consciousness. *Canadian Psychology/Psychologie Canadienne, 26*(1), 1–12. https://psycnet.apa.org/doi/10.1037/h0080017.
U.S. Department of Veteran Affairs. (n.d.). *PTSD: National Center for PTSD*. https://www.ptsd.va.gov/professional/treat/essentials/dsm5_ptsd.asp#one.
Vallee, J.F. (2014). *Passport to Magonia: On UFOs, folklore, and parallel worlds*. Daily Grail Books.
Vallee, J.F., & Davis, E. (2005). *Incommensurability, orthodoxy, and the physics of high strangeness: A 6-layer model for anomalous phenomena*. 224–239. Porto: Edições Universidade Fernando Pessoa. https://bdigital.ufp.pt/bitstream/10284/781/1/223-239Cons-Ciencias.pdf.
Vaughn, M. (w/ J. Glazier). (2024). *My cosmic trigger: High strangeness in theory and practice*. Trine Day.
Vendramini, D. (2005). Noncoding DNA and the teem theory of inheritance, emotions and innate behaviour. *Medical Hypotheses, 64*(3), 512–519. https://doi.org/10.1016/j.mehy.2004.08.022.
Vendramini, D. (2009). *Them and us: How Neanderthal predation created modern humans*. Smashwords Edition.
Vendramini, D. (2022). *The second evolution: The secret role of emotion in evolution*. Arkangel.
Việt, T.H., Hải, T.H., & Meldrum, J. (2021). Research on wildmen in Vietnam. *The Relict Hominoid Inquiry, 10*, 6–28. https://www.isu.edu/media/libraries/rhi/research-papers/Viet-manuscript_final.pdf.
Wade, J. (2015). Transpersonal sexual experiences. In H.L. Friedman & G. Hartelius (Eds.), *The Wiley-Blackwell Handbook of Transpersonal Psychology* (pp. 382–400). Wiley Blackwell.
Wallace, D.R. (2003). *The Klamath Knot: Explorations of myth and evolution (20th anniversary ed.)*. University of California Press.
Wangyal, T. (1998). *The Tibetan yogas of dream and sleep*. Shambhala Publications.
Ward, C.N. (Host), & Radford, B. (Host). (2024, January 12). Requiem for Bigfoot (No. 218) [Audio podcast episode]. In *Squaring the Strange*. https://squaringthestrange.libsyn.com/episode-218-requiem-for-bigfoot.
Warren, N. (Host). (2021, April 23). Two hours of Bigfoot! Marathon #18—All are previously released encounters. In *Buckeye Bigfoot*. YouTube. https://youtu.be/RCJJJ81d-Ww?si=yDqYjjSrGC4JzgAo.
Warren, N. (Host). (2022, October 31). 2022 Halloween marathon—Let's get this party started!. In *Buckeye Bigfoot*. YouTube. https://youtu.be/_OX8elL5etw?si=IdSjvrvb-clMrWA6.

Warren, N. (Host). (2023, August 1). Choctaw family is visited again by a red Sasquatch their great-grandparents once helped. In *Buckeye Bigfoot*. YouTube. https://youtu.be/tZa5oW9N570?si=xjRzLi8bFzfSqRP4.

Warren, N. (Host). (2023, October 6). The lonely man's Sasquatch search. In *Buckeye Bigfoot*. YouTube. https://www.youtube.com/watch?app=desktop&v=yySBPgDprR0.

Warren, N. (Host). (2023, October 31). Bigfoot ultra marathon #22—Three hours of Bigfoot encounters. In *Buckeye Bigfoot*. YouTube. https://youtu.be/zyCPzgjmdA8?si=kslunj3fpKzdekX3.

Warren, N. (Host). (2023, November 17). Bigfoot ran them off their land!. In *Buckeye Bigfoot*. YouTube. https://youtu.be/Ixm9xg3ziM4?si=qQ5IazfsIgIVPI9v.

Warren, N. (Host). (2023, December 1). Sasquatch saves two bow hunters. In *Buckeye Bigfoot*. YouTube. https://youtu.be/iwq7vNmO_FU?si=1B0shtk628J_9qkO.

Warren, N. (Host). (2024, January 16). That Sasquatch waited for him to walk to the school bus. In *Buckeye Bigfoot*. YouTube. https://youtu.be/sNt3N3B106g?si=gcBOZq8QGJmz691e.

Warren, N. (Host). (2024, February 2). The Sasquatch was *too* interested in her—she could SEE IT!. In *Buckeye Bigfoot*. YouTube. https://www.youtube.com/watch?v=LYBMKmhb-68g&list=PLO0PqscYC6r01DlOKeFjeaCB0qWU-vIjiv&index=30.

Warren, N. (Host). (2024, February 13). Trapped in their car by Sasquatch. In *Buckeye Bigfoot*. YouTube. https://www.youtube.com/watch?v=V37A8YoK66k&t=294s.

Warren, N. (Host). (2024, March 8). He was innocent and trusted the Bigfoot family [Audio podcast episode]. In *Buckeye Bigfoot*. YouTube. https://www.youtube.com/watch?v=v6S_jrd1BpU&t=27s.

Warren, N. (Host). (2024, March 12). That Sasquatch FAFO'D—Don't Mess with Granny. Uncle Ezra's Pretty Shady, Too. In *Buckeye Bigfoot*. YouTube. https://www.youtube.com/watch?v=O19ppKTXPP0&t=848s.

Warren, N. (Host). (2024, April 2). The Sasquatch had her scent—and it was following her. In *Buckeye Bigfoot*. YouTube. https://youtu.be/jnUxq20RHcA?si=amZ3olpX-i9MoI35.

Warren, N. (Host). (2024, April 19). The adults didn't see it, but the little girl did. In *Buckeye Bigfoot*. YouTube. https://youtu.be/h-TWeobr_IE?si=FtLw_1w_HoAyFcVM.

Warren, N. (Host). (2024, April 30). They know they exist—But they aren't allowed to say it. In *Buckeye Bigfoot*. YouTube. https://youtu.be/BFXTSGECAag?si=1PDTSTv8Lf8Tsv2R.

Warren, N. (Host). (2024, May 11). His dad never saw the Squatch creeping up while he slept. In *Buckeye Bigfoot*. YouTube. https://youtu.be/4P7lTAlRdg4?si=x2pJvo9liXTriNaQ.

Warren, N. (Host). (2024, August 13). He was eye to eye with a Bigfoot. In *Buckeye Bigfoot*. YouTube. https://youtu.be/upzVHhOvkoc?si=B0VpQFYLnJEKckNG.

Washburn, M. (2024). *Recentering the self: A defense of the ego*. SUNY Press.

Watson, W.T. (2023). *The forest poltergeist: Class B encounters and the paranormal*. Beyond the Fray Publishing.

Webber, J. (2025, March 24). "Auras," the freeze response and how Sasquatch hides from thermal cameras (No. 27) [Video podcast episode]. YouTube. In *Idaho Bigfoot*. https://youtu.be/i3fJGio39Jk?si=fIOvYwL_Ha8ZkjZb.

Webley, S., & Zackariasson, P. (2023). From UFO to UAP, the ontology of belief structures: Why change now?. In J. Glazier (Ed.), *Paranormal Ruptures: Critical Approaches to Exceptional Experiences* (pp. 189–218). Beyond the Fray Publishing.

Weir, D. (Director). (2020). *Sasquatch among wildmen*. Enhanced Media, Occult Journeys.

Wells, J. (2014). *Bigfoot in Georgia: Legends, myths, and sightings*. Pine Winds Press.

Welsing, F.C. (2004). *The Isis papers: The keys to the colors*. Lushena Books.

White, M. (2025, February 28). 2022 Selkirk expedition A Pacific Northwest Bigfoot research documentary film. In *Grassman58*. YouTube. https://www.youtube.com/watch?v=ijKyz4tXxL4.

White, R.A. (1994). Exceptional human experience and the more we are: Exceptional Human Experience and identity. In *Academy of Religion and Psychical Research Proceedings Annual Conference*, 75(1), 1–13. https://www.ehe.org/display/ehe-pagea229.html?ID=70.

Whitley, S. (director). (2007). *Southern fried Bigfoot*. The Monkeyhouse.

Williams, A. (2010). *Enoch: A Bigfoot story*. CreateSpace Publishing.

Wixted, J.T., & Mickes, L. (2022). Eyewitness memory is reliable, but the criminal justice system is not. *Memory, 30*(1), 67–72. http://wixtedlab.ucsd.edu/publications/wixted2021/Wixted_Mickes_in_press.pdf.

Wixted, J.T., Mickes, L., & Fisher, R.P. (2018). Rethinking the reliability of eyewitness memory. *Perspectives on Psychological Science, 13*(3), 324–335. Retrieved from https://journals.sagepub.com/doi/pdf/10.1177/1745691617734878.

Wobogo, V. (1976). Diop's two cradle theory and the origin of white racism. *Black Books Bulletin, 4*(4), 20–29. https://bpb-us-w2.wpmucdn.com/u.osu.edu/dist/a/1573/files/2015/01/Diops-Two-Cradle-Theory-and-the-Origin-of-White-Racism-1ej9e7o.pdf.

Wrangham, R., & Peterson, D. (1996). *Demonic males: Apes and the origins of human violence*. Mariner Books.

Yalom, I.D. (2011). *Staring at the sun: Being at peace with your own mortality*. Hachette UK.

Yowiehunters Witness Reports. (2021, October 27). Yowie footage revisited—A closer look at the AYR footage obtained in April of 2021. In *Yowiehunters Witness Reports*. YouTube. https://youtu.be/-g15ky_dm0o?si=jQbQeExD1kHtXWkj.

Zada, J. (2019). *In the valleys of the noble beyond: In search of the Sasquatch.* First Grove Atlantic.
Zellner, D. (director), & Zellner, N. (director). (2024). *Sasquatch Sunset.* Square Peg.
Zhang, Y., & Harrison, T. (2017). Gigantopithecus blacki: A giant ape from the Pleistocene of Asia revisited. *American Journal of Physical Anthropology, 162,* 153–177. https://doi.org/10.1002/ajpa.23150.

Index